The Merge Hypothesis

The Merge Hypothesis is the central empirical theoretical contribution of the Minimalist Program (MP) to syntactic theory. This book offers an accessible overview of the MP, debunking common misunderstandings about its aims and goals, and demonstrating the profound insights it has made. Hornstein shows how the Merge Hypothesis can be extended to cover the generalizations discovered in the past sixty years of Generative research, culminating in GB theory. He introduces the Fundamental Principle of Grammar, which advocates including labels as part of the Merge operation and centering the notion of the constituent as the key domain of syntactic commerce. The early chapters identify the goals of the MP, how they arose from earlier descriptive and explanatory successes of the mentalist tradition within Generative Grammar, and how to develop them in future work to expand its descriptive and explanatory range. It is essential reading for anyone interested in contemporary syntactic theory.

NORBERT HORNSTEIN is Professor Emeritus in Linguistics at the University of Maryland, College Park. He has written several books on Minimalist Syntax, including *A Theory of Syntax* (2008), *Move!* (2001) and *Understanding Minimalism* (2005, with Nunes and Grohmann).

The Merge Hypothesis
A Theory of Aspects of Syntax

Norbert Hornstein
University of Maryland at College Park

CAMBRIDGE
UNIVERSITY PRESS

CAMBRIDGE
UNIVERSITY PRESS

Shaftesbury Road, Cambridge CB2 8EA, United Kingdom

One Liberty Plaza, 20th Floor, New York, NY 10006, USA

477 Williamstown Road, Port Melbourne, VIC 3207, Australia

314–321, 3rd Floor, Plot 3, Splendor Forum, Jasola District Centre, New Delhi – 110025, India

103 Penang Road, #05–06/07, Visioncrest Commercial, Singapore 238467

Cambridge University Press is part of Cambridge University Press & Assessment, a department of the University of Cambridge.

We share the University's mission to contribute to society through the pursuit of education, learning and research at the highest international levels of excellence.

www.cambridge.org
Information on this title: www.cambridge.org/9781009415743

DOI: 10.1017/9781009415750

© Norbert Hornstein 2024

This publication is in copyright. Subject to statutory exception and to the provisions of relevant collective licensing agreements, no reproduction of any part may take place without the written permission of Cambridge University Press & Assessment.

First published 2024

A catalogue record for this publication is available from the British Library

A Cataloging-in-Publication data record for this book is available from the Library of Congress.

ISBN 978-1-009-41574-3 Hardback
ISBN 978-1-009-41577-4 Paperback

Cambridge University Press & Assessment has no responsibility for the persistence or accuracy of URLs for external or third-party internet websites referred to in this publication and does not guarantee that any content on such websites is, or will remain, accurate or appropriate.

Contents

Preface	vii
List of Abbreviations	xi
Introduction	1
1 A Whig History of Generative Grammar	13
2 Tools and Particulars	47
3 Adding Labels	75
4 Construal and the Extended Merge Hypothesis (1): A-Chain Dependencies	101
5 Construal and the Extended Merge Hypothesis (2): A'-Chain Dependencies	127
6 A Partial Wrap-Up and Segue	167
7 Labels	184
8 Odds and Ends	207
9 Conclusion	230
Bibliography	234
Index	240

Preface

Research monographs are not detective stories or magic tricks. Nothing is gained by coyly hinting at one's main points and slowly sneaking up on them after various twists, turns and mis-directions. Without doubt such maneuvers enhance magic tricks and Scandinavian noir detective novels, but setting things up so that the rabbit pulled from your hat generates delight comes at the high cost of making the reader work harder than s/he should to receive what is often a meager reward. Better to state the conclusions upfront so that the reader can more easily follow the argument's thread, and more importantly, so that the reader can more efficiently decide whether the destination is worth the bother at all. With this in mind, let me tell you the main point for which this book argues.

The proposal is the following: I argue for an extended version of the Merge Hypothesis that I dub the Extended Merge Hypothesis (EMH). It incorporates as an axiom a principle I modestly dub the "Fundamental Principle of Grammar" (FPG). The EMH adopts a generic conception of Merge and, importantly, incorporates a linguistically bespoke conception of labels. The EMH plus the FPG deliver a conception of the faculty of language (FL) that outputs grammars with many of the properties Generativists have discovered to be characteristic of grammars we find in natural language. That's the central claim. Here is a little elaboration.

I first outline and show the virtues of the EMH. The EMH showcases a particular conception of Merge and makes it the primary (actually, for my money, the sole) grammatical operation. The central conjecture is that all grammatical dependencies are licensed under Merge. So, for example, if α and β are in a theta dependency as α theta marks β then for α to do its business requires that α and β merge. Same thing for α controlling β or α binding β or α case marking β or α checking features of β or ... . You get the point, right? The EMH insists that *all* grammatical commerce be conducted under Merge. There is no other way to grammatically couple two syntactic expressions in order to establish a grammatical dependency. I dub this requirement the Fundamental Principle of Grammar. The FPG considerably extends the reach of Merge. Contemporary Minimalism is comfortable analyzing structure building and movement as instances of Merge. The FPG extends Merge's purview to all other grammatical dependencies, most especially construal relations. So, just as θ-marking is discharged under Merge and *Wh*-movement is a product of Merge, so too are control, binding, case and every other grammatical dependency.

That is the core idea. For the proposal to go from slogan to content requires specifying the Merge operation and then demonstrating how this conception of Merge (guided by the FPG) applies so as to derive the properties of grammar that Generativists have discovered over the last sixty years of inquiry. The book doesn't entirely succeed in deriving *all* these properties, but it gets quite far, or so I will argue.

Two important details to fix ideas. First, the FPG requires a classical conception of Merge, one where the operation combines two expressions *and* labels the result. In other words, Merge is here understood as syntactically generating classical constituents. In this specific sense, then, the proposal offered below treats the classical constituent as the fundamental syntactic object and the operation that forms constituents (i.e. Merge) as the fundamental syntactic operation. This is not how many currently understand Merge, but it is required, as we shall see, to operationalize the FPG.

Second, EMH adopts a *very strong* conception of Merge's role in grammar. If EMH is even roughly correct, the modular complexity of standard Generative models of the Principles and Parameters variety is merely apparent. In fact, if this is on the right track, there is no internal modularity as *all* dependencies are surface realizations of a single generative procedure, Merge. Part of this should not surprise a thoroughly modern Minimalist. Most well-educated syntacticians are now ready to accept that phrase structure building and movement are flip sides of the same Mergish coin, the former the result of E-merging two expressions, the latter the product of I-merging two ('E' and 'I' acting as useful mnemonics rather than signaling ontological difference). The 'E' that the EMH prefixes to 'MH' signals that the project of unification extends beyond phrase structure rules and movement transformations to include every grammatical dependency. "Extended" indeed!

This is the core of the book. However, it is not all. I add some dessert at the end to round off the main meal. At the end I return to the combine+label conception of Merge adopted to do the heavy lifting for the EMH and ask the quintessentially minimalist question: Which part of the operation is linguistically bespoke and which part cognitively/computationally general? I will suggest that labels are linguistically special in the sense that the labeling operation is responsible for giving us the unbounded hierarchical recursive structures characteristic of natural language grammars. More to the point: If we add labels to the soup of a-linguistic cognitive operations, a soup that includes a simple combination operation, and insist that grammatical dependencies all be subject to the FPG, then out pop grammars like those we find in natural language. In fact, once we add labels we create sets whose hierarchically structured members can be recursively generated.

So that's the main claim of what follows: The EMH incorporating the FPG based on a generic conception of Merge incorporating a linguistically bespoke conception of labels suffices to deliver natural language grammars with very many of the properties Generativists have discovered to be characteristics of those we find in natural language.

Before proceeding, a few thanks are in order. My field work mainly consists in having lunch with friends and talking over stuff I and/or they are thinking of. So, first off, I would like to thank my consultants Elan Dresher, Bill Idsardi and Paul Pietroski for endless discussions on the topics covered below and for their reading and commenting on earlier drafts. Without them as sounding boards, sources of inspiration, and general critical kibbitzing, none of this would have seen the light of day. Now you know who to blame.

Second, the line of inquiry that ends here started with a question posed by Roz Thornton about why Government Binding (GB) theory doesn't allow movement into θ-positions. Much to my surprise, I was unable to find many even halfway decent reasons for adopting this central feature of GB (and indeed, earlier (and many current) theories of grammar). Thinking through the consequences of Roz's question led me to what is outlined below after a couple of decades of rumination.

My third intellectual debt is to Noam Chomsky (as the subtitle of the book should make clear). I am quite sure that he would not endorse the final product. However, I would not have gotten to the end of *my* intellectual road without having read and thought a lot about his.

My fourth debt is actually less a debt than an outright theft. Principles very like the FPG (if not identical) were proposed by at least two earlier authors, Sam Epstein (1999) and John Collins (2007). Let me make my confession stronger still; the idea pursued here as the Extended Merge Hypothesis was first conceived by Epstein, and a version thereof has been developed in collaboration with Kitahara and Seely (see Epstein 1999, Epstein et al. 2015, 2022).[1] The only words I can offer in mitigation of my crime is that I was not consciously aware of my malfeasance. I had not read Collins' paper when I first developed the FPG. I had read Epstein's (indeed, it appears in a volume I co-edited with him) but clearly did not understand its importance. Both of these are hanging offenses and I offer my neck (and my apologies) in penance.

---

[1] I thank reviewer #4 for making this crystal clear to me on every other page of the generous review. I really am grateful.

While confessing to the unpardonable let me add that Epstein's (1999) discussion can be anachronistically understood as tying (his version of) the FPG to the strong minimalist thesis in the way that I do below. That his paper does so made me very happy, for if Sam had already scoped out a version of the FPG and urged its centrality to the Minimalist Program then I could be much more confident in my decision to do the same. Shoulders and giants and all that. At any rate, if you like the work the FPG does here in the context of the EMH, know that Sam and John got there first.

I have yet more intellectual debts. I have worked with many very talented collaborators on previous projects related to this one. Let me especially thank Cedric Boeckx, Kleanthes Grohmann, Jairo Nunes, Paul Pietroski and Masha Polinsky. As the reader will see below, this work, as well as the non-collaborative research of the aforementioned, has greatly influenced the final product presented here.

Three more thank-yous before delving in. There were four reviewers who made useful comments buried in sufficient praise. I thank all four, including the notorious reviewer #2. Thanks as well to the team at Cambridge University Press, who considerably reduced the bother of getting an eager but disheveled manuscript gussied up enough to get to the printer. In particular, thanks to Helen Barton and Isabel Collins for all their help, and a very special thanks to Sue Browning (who, I am sure, is a senior member of the copy-editing Olympus), who edited the prose provided and allowed me to say more clearly what I wanted to say. Last, I would also like to thank Maša Bešlin for very useful comments, constructing the index, and helping with final editorial processes.

Abbreviations

AP	articulatory–phonetic (interface)
BC	backwards control
CI	conceptual–intentional (interface)
CTM	Copy Theory of Movement
DoI	Duality of Interpretation
EC	Extension Condition
ECP	Empty Category Principle
EMH	Extended Merge Hypothesis
FL	faculty of language
FPG	Fundamental Principle of Grammar
G	grammar
GB	Government Binding (theory)
IC	Inclusiveness Condition
LAD	language acquisition device
LC	linguistic creativity
LDA	long-distance anaphor
LF	logical form
LFL	linguistic flexibility
LH	Labeling Hypothesis
LI	lexical insertion
MH	Merge Hypothesis
MoM	Merge over Move
MP	Minimalist Program
NTC	No Tampering Condition
OC	obligatory control
PF	phonological form
PLD	primary linguistic data
PM	phrase marker
PS	phrase structure

RP	resumptive pronoun
SCO	strong crossover
T-rules	transformation rules
UG	Universal Grammar
WCO	weak crossover

Introduction

This book is entitled *The Merge Hypothesis: A Theory of Aspects of Syntax*. The educated reader (all of you) has no doubt picked up the homage to Chomsky (1965). Please excuse the self-aggrandizement. Truth be told, I could have also called the book *Minimalism: Footnotes to GB*, though I am not sure the Cambridge University Press marketing department would have approved. Nonetheless, the second title would have tickled my fancy in two different ways. How so?

First, it would have honored the tradition I was raised in, a tradition in which footnotes and marginalia are the locus of intellectual excitement. Nobody who has reveled in Chomsky's footnotes can be immune to their charms. Chomsky came by this literary form honestly. And it has served him well. It is where he lets his imagination roam most freely.

Second, the title would emphasize a main (negative) theme in what follows. It is that much (most) research that flies under the minimalist flag has misconstrued the explanatory goal of the Minimalist Program. Worse, this misunderstanding has been at the root of much of the skepticism concerning the success of the program and has also fertilized much of the negativity concerning the vitality of the larger Generative Grammar enterprise of which Minimalism is the most recent stage. It is not hard to find obituaries that insist that the Generative Program in linguistics is both (whew!) finally dead and deservedly buried. Often a paragraph therein is dedicated to the minimalist phase that, it is often claimed, demonstrates the sterility of the whole Generative approach, the implicit argument being that Minimalism is the self-evident reductio of the Generative absurdum.

All of this is bunk. But it is bunk that rests on a (possibly[1]) honest mistake about the goals that the Minimalist Program has set for itself. I intend to show that once these ambitions are clarified, these harsh conclusions prove groundless.

---

[1] I don't exactly believe this. Much (to most) of the "death of Generative Grammar" literature is advanced by those that know little about *any* of it. A lot of it is done in bad faith without even a thin sprinkling of interpretive charity. So, the one way of reading the bracketed modal above is indicating logical (rather than real) possibility. That said, I also believe that there is

Or, to put this point another way, this book has a simple positive message. It is going to argue that the research program of modern Generative Grammar has been a resounding success. More particularly, it argues that the most current stage of this more general enterprise, the Minimalist Program (MP), has provided profound insights into the structure of the faculty of language (FL). This conclusion will strike many as obtuse. The word on the street (at least many words on many streets close to my ears) is that the MP, despite a few additions to the technical armamentarium of grammatical research (e.g. Probe-Goal/Agree technology), has been at best overhyped, and at worst a failure. Many, both within and without the Generative community of scholars, look at MP and see a program unmoored from data and overegged with theoretical pretension. They often take the perceived airiness of MP to be the *reductio* that suffices to discredit the whole Generative enterprise. This book argues that they are wrong, very wrong, dead wrong. What follows argues for two broad conclusions: (i) that MP is the logical next step within the very successful Generative research program and (ii) that MP has considerably pushed forward our understanding of the fine structure of FL. Furthermore, like any good program, MP has encouraged novel explanations, pointed to new research questions, led to the discovery of new data, led to the postulation of new kinds of grammatical dependencies and has offered up a diverse group of interesting new anomalies and puzzles worthy of solution. In other words, MP has all the (Lakatosian) marks of a lively, healthy, and robust research program. Or so this book argues.

The book is organized as follows.

First, it identifies and briefly describes the central questions of Generative research.[2] It then reviews some high points of *theory* within the Generative Program. This is important, for whereas programs are fecund or sterile, their products (namely theories/hypotheses) are intended to be truth evaluable. Indeed, the only useful measure of the fecundity of a research program is the verisimilitude of the theories that its perspective and central questions generate

---

sufficient conceptual confusion to engender skepticism even in the absence of bad faith. The discussion that follows is mostly directed to the latter group (a group for whom argument will matter (remember the useful adage: "You cannot argue someone out of a position that they were not argued into")), though I cannot say that I regret the joyous potshots I aim at the former. You know who you are.

[2] More accurately, the Chomsky program in Generative Grammar. The technology that Generative Grammar spawned is now widely adopted and not all the work that uses it aims to answer the questions that the technology was first deployed to address. This is fine. One of the great things about successful programs is that they overrun their banks and fertilize domains of inquiry that are (even many steps) removed from the questions and problems that initially motivated them. As I said, this is fine. What is not fine is confusing the technology with the questions of interest. That is why I identify the topic of discussion in what follows as grounded in the version of Generative inquiry that Chomsky has done so much to motivate and advance. If asked, I would say that this book should be understood as a long footnote to this work.

and nurse. Using this standard, the Generative research program has been an unbelievable triumph, identifying as it has many non-obvious, non-trivial, empirically substantiated features of FL. From where I sit, many critics of the Generative program appear to be ignorant of these successes. They seem to know (next to) nothing of the theories of grammar Generativists have developed, how these theories naturally build on one another or what facts speak on their behalf. Sadly, there will not be room to do justice to this rich history of discovery here. But it will be important to review some illustrative high points as they become *explananda* at subsequent stages of Generative inquiry. Government Binding (GB) theory will be of particular interest. Viewed correctly (i.e. from the perspective elaborated here), the goal of MP is to *explain* the GB principles and generalizations developed from the mid-1970s to the mid-1990s.[3]

Let me reiterate this point as it will be a major theme in what follows. Progressive research programs build on the results of earlier theories that the program generates. In particular, the axioms of the earlier period become the targets for explanation for later theories. These (earlier) axioms are explained by being *derived* from simpler more natural (i.e. deeper) novel axioms. Derivation from "better" starting points is what explanation is all about. The biggest item on any theoretical research agenda is providing reasonable ways of fleshing out notions like "simpler" and "more natural." What this book argues is that MP has provided reasonable explications of these notions (no mean feat, I might add) and has gone a long way towards showing how the axioms of prior theory (what I will refer to as GB's "laws of grammar") can be derived in an insightful and principled way from these simpler more natural starting points. If this is correct (and it is, it really is) then MP, the most recent continuation of the Generative enterprise, is a raging success and should be recognized as such. Or, to put the same point more belligerently, many of MP's skeptics have failed to appreciate the *point* of the Minimalist Program and have been disappointed because MP has addressed its own questions rather than ones that (usually hostile) critics think it should have tackled.

Nor has this critical failure been because critics have demonstrated that these MP questions are ill-conceived. No, criticisms of MP have generally failed to understand the problem that Minimalism has set for itself and thus they fail to take the program on its own terms. As a result, the criticisms leveled against MP denigrate it not for failing to pose interesting questions (indeed, I will show that MP's questions are very good ones) or failing to

---

[3] Yes, I know that this is anachronistic. *Lectures on Government and Binding* (LGB) after all was not published till 1981. However, LGB is the mature statement of a line of investigation starting with Chomsky (1973). I will list the principles and generalizations of interest in Chapter 1.

answer the questions the program takes up but for failing to answer questions at right angles to the program (and, hence, irrelevant to it). Let me clearly stipulate that there are many, many, many questions that MP does ***not*** address. And this has zero significance when it comes to evaluating the success of the program. So, if the aim is to evaluate how far MP has come (and that is a prime ambition of this book) then it is going to be very important to get the questions that MP poses clearly in focus, for it is success in answering *these* questions that we are (or should be) interested in evaluating.

Before getting the MP problem straight, I want to rant a little (or maybe I should say "a little more"). I believe that the "misinterpretation" of MP's goals is not due only to inattention or malice (though, to be sure there is some (much?) of both). Rather, it is rooted in an endemic fissure in the practice of Generative Grammar, one that was (prior to MP) relatively innocuous, easily managed and therefore benign but that the Minimalist project has widened and deepened. The fissure separates the philologically inclined (whose main interest lies in the (surface/observable) properties of languages) and the cognitively/biologically inclined (who, following Chomsky's formulation of the Generative agenda, understand the object of study to be the mental capacities that underlie linguistic facility). I have previously called these different Generative investigative strands l*a*nguistics vs l*i*nguistics (the 'a' signaling a focus on language, the 'i' highlighting the interest on I-language).[4] This distinction is intended to be clarificatory rather than invidious. Both forms of investigation have their charms. I, however, am interested in the Chomsky version (i.e. the one that focuses on I-language) and wish to defend its integrity against l*a*nguistic methodological precepts. To my mind, the idea that l*i*nguistic investigations must honor l*a*nguistic goals and standards lies behind much of the mooted disappointment with MP.

Second, the chapters that follow illustrate how MP is the natural extension of earlier Generative results, most particularly, those of GB-style theories developed from about the mid-1970s to the mid-1990s. I argue that MP begins the theoretical job of *explaining* the principles of grammar (i.e. universals of FL) that GB discovered. To put this crudely, MP builds on the results of this earlier GB research and MP's insights cannot be appreciated unless projected against a GB screen. MP aims to understand *why* FL has the kinds of properties Generative research (especially the GB variety) identified. In other words, the fundamental MP question is *why does FL have the properties that Generative/GB research over the last sixty years has discovered it to have?* Please note that

---

[4] This nomenclature is not original with me, sadly. I heard someone else use it but I cannot remember who or where. So thanks to the originator and sorry for the memory gap.

this question *presupposes* that FL does indeed have these properties, and, in this sense, MP builds on the (perceived) success of this earlier inquiry. Thus, MP takes earlier Generative inquiry to have discovered key features of FL (i.e. MP assumes that GB is (more or less) empirically accurate), but rather than taking these to be fundamental features of FL, MP assumes that they are in need of deeper grounding. Thus, MP builds on the accumulated insights of earlier inquiry (as all decent science does). *How* it does so is the main technical theme of the book.[5]

It is worth noting that *if* a minimalist theory of grammar can derive the principles of Universal Grammar (UG) as articulated in GB it is *then* possible to answer two questions regarding FL that are in apparent tension. The first question is the one that the GB theory of FL specifically addresses and that Chomsky has dubbed "Plato's Problem." Plato's Problem is how it is possible to acquire one's native grammar despite the poverty of the linguistic input used to build that grammar. The GB answer to Plato's Problem rests on a rich, linguistically bespoke theory of Universal Grammar, the principles of which describe the fine structure of FL. The idea is that a rich FL compensates for the poverty of the linguistic stimulus the language acquisition device (LAD, aka the child) has access to in building its particular grammar (G). The richer the FL, the less the LAD needs to be guided in its grammatical choices by the data available to it.

Conceptually, this is the right kind of answer to Plato's Problem in the domain of language. The problem is that this answer raises an equally serious question: How did this richly structured linguistically dedicated FL arise in humans to begin with? We can call this "Darwin's Problem," as it involves the evolvability of FL. The problem is that the richer and more linguistically special the FL, the wider the distance between the cognitive wherewithal of our ancestors (who, by assumption, were not linguistically adept like we are) and our cognitive economy (which, again by assumption, includes FL). And the wider the distance between our minds/brains and those of our ancestors, the harder is the problem of explaining how the linguistically richer human mind arose from the linguistically poorer primate ancestor mind. Darwin's Problem strongly prefers a modest FL while Plato's Problem strongly favors a richer one. They thus pull in opposite directions, the tension between them setting the scene for a minimalist resolution. Here is the basic idea.

---

[5] Observe one important consequence of this perspective on MP: The theories it generates *presuppose* that earlier GB results are essentially correct. As such, MP accounts are not direct competitors of earlier GB accounts given that they take them to be roughly accurate. 'Accurate,' however, does not mean 'fundamental.' MP proposes that we understand GB results as largely correct (i.e. good but imperfect) empirical boundary conditions on a more basic theory that has them as consequences.

Minimalism is the conjecture that it is possible to sail comfortably between the Scylla of Plato and the Charybdis of Darwin. How so? By deriving the fundamentals of GB theory within a framework of minimalist assumptions. The program is to simplify the GB picture of FL so that the remaining principles are either cognitively/computationally general or they are bespoke but very few in number (in the best case just one!) and very simple (in a way to be determined). The idea is that simple principles could arise through adventitious mutation. And if there is really only *one* difference between a linguistically capable mind and one that is not, and if this difference is "simple," and if this principle in combination with other cognitively/computationally general (i.e. non-linguistically specific) principles yields the laws of grammar as articulated by GB, then we can solve both Plato's Problem and Darwin's Problem. In other words, the simpler, more elegant, and more basic assumptions that can *explain* why FL has GB properties can also serve to explain how our FL with its useful "learnability" features could have arisen in the species. In other words, once we ask about FL's evolvability and we take GB as giving a reasonable (but not fundamental) description of FL, and we take these principles to be the explananda of an adequate minimalist theory, we are addressing the question of how to resolve the Plato/Darwin conceptual tension noted above.

Or, saying this another way: just as GB took FL's role in learnability to be a boundary condition on any theory of FL, MP takes evolvability of a GBish FL to be a boundary condition on an adequate FL. Simple and elegant are not *just* methodologically important features of the right FL (though they are this as well), they are also empirically required to solve Darwin's Problem.[6]

Third, the book identifies some MP novelties. Fecund research programs generate theories that manage to balance three demands: they save the results of the past, they discover "novel" data and mechanisms, and they point to new research questions. I have already mentioned that one goal (maybe the

---

[6] This is not to deny that quite often the methodological strictures regarding simplicity can also be interpreted in terms of evolvability, and vice versa. For example, many of Chomsky's (1993) arguments against theory-internal constructs like D-structure and S-structure can also be interpreted as removing linguistically bespoke structure from FL and thus making it less cognitively peculiar (and thus advancing efforts to explain its evolvability). Similarly for a host of grammar-internal formatives like traces, PRO, and, in my view, reflexives, bound pronouns and R-expressions. There are good methodological reasons for not taking these constructs as theoretically basic. Interestingly, evolvability considerations support these same conclusions. That said, the notions, I believe, need not always pull in the same direction, at least as a matter of emphasis. Simplicity relevant to Darwin's Problem peeks at the cognitive/computational capacities of our non-linguistic ancestors and asks what we must add *to them* to get FL. This notion need not track more generic methodological conceptions. I return to this issue in Chapter 7 in discussing labels.

key achievement to date) of MP has been to provide more principled foundations for earlier Generative results (i.e. to *explain* what earlier Generative Grammar described). And, let me repeat, doing this, *if it can be done*, is a big f***in' deal (to paraphrase Joe Biden). However, a second mark of a program's fecundity is that it does not leave earlier results entirely untouched (recall, GB's principles are not fundamental, though they are roughly correct). A decent MP account conserves much of what preceded, but it also changes it, rejecting some central premises, making novel "predictions," solving old puzzles, providing principled accounts for previous stipulated description, and so on. This book will identify and lovingly tease out some of the ways that MP has improved the explanatory depth of earlier accounts, for it is in terms of these novelties that theories are compared, evaluated and judged.

In particular, the theoretical unification that lies at the heart of the MP project, if rigorously deployed, leads to a picture of UG and FL radically different from the modular view of FL that is a central feature of GB. More pointedly, the Extended Merge Hypothesis (EMH) implies that FL has *no* internal modules and *that all grammatical relations are Merge-mediated relations* (please observe: **this idea is NOT original to me. To my knowledge, Sam Epstein thought it up first in his** Epstein (1999), **and** Collins (2007) **endorsed it as well**).[7] It thus implies that the articulated modular distinctions embedded in the GB model of FL/UG are actually a mirage. More specifically, if all dependencies are Merge dependencies, then the differences GB identifies between phrase/structure building, movement, construal, control, theta assignment, case assignment and the like are *all reflections of the very same unique generative procedure*. Thus, if the EMH is correct, the formal differences that GB identifies are merely apparent. Of course, this is a big claim, and it will only be partially redeemed here. Still, the hope is that it will be redeemed *enough* to serve as a useful working hypothesis going forward and will suffice to motivate ambitious grad students to solve the remaining reservoir of problems (and discover new ones to be solved). That's the way programs function. Problems *always* remain, and some (elevated to the status of anomalies) hang around for quite a while. Their function is to tantalize, not to discourage.

In service of this, the book (following Epstein (1999) and Collins (2007)) identifies a particular "axiom" and makes it the central feature of the Extended

---

[7] Hereon in, whenever I mention the Extended Merge Hypothesis (EMH) or the Fundamental Principle of Grammar (FPG) (and I will mention both a great deal) I want the reader to hear in his/her mind's ear my insistent voice plangently intoning that the ideas are not original with me. See the Preface for further admission that I am following Epstein's lead in putting these ideas at the center of Minimalist theory.

Merge Hypothesis. I dub this axiom the Fundamental Principle of Grammar (FPG).[8] Here it is:[9]

(1)   **The Fundamental Principle of Grammar (FPG):** α and β can be grammatically related (G-related) only if α and β have merged.

The FPG states that *if* there exists a G relation between any two elements in a phrase marker, then at some point in the derivation of the phrase marker containing them these elements must have formed a unit/constituent. So, if α theta marks β then at some point in the derivation α and β formed a unit/constituent. If α case marks β then at some point in the derivation α and β were a unit/constituent. If α antecedes β then … . Well, you get the point.[10]

Here's one thing I really like about the FPG: It places *constituency* at the very center of FL's organizing principles. As anyone who has taken an introductory

---

[8] I was tempted, following the lead of biologists, to refer to it as the Central Dogma of Grammar (CDG). It was hard to choose between the two names, though in some earlier talks I settled on the more modest "Fundamental Principle of Grammar," which I will stick to. But the more brash "Central Dogma of Grammar" has some charms. First, it is useful to identify fundamental axioms and emphasize their axiomatic character. The tongue-in-cheek replacement of "Fundamental Principle of Grammar" with the "Central Dogma of Grammar" would serve to do this nicely (and it may even irritate some thin-skinned party-poopers on the way (one can only hope)). Second, it would emphasize the regulative function of the principle. I hope that the FPG/Central Dogma functions as a boundary condition on MP theory going forward. At the least, in what follows it cleanly encapsulates the empirical oomph of the Extended Merge Hypothesis by strongly restricting the *kinds* of grammatical operations and dependencies FL can license. It really is amazing how sparse the theoretical options are if the Fundamental Principle/Central Dogma is reverenced.

[9] As already noted, the FPG is not original with me. I always like being in a large crowd when suggesting something that looks too good to be true. The earliest published precursor to the EMH seems to be in Epstein (1999: 321–22, (2)), where he proposes the following: (i) Syntactic relations are established between syntactic categories X and Y iff X and Y are transformationally concatenated by Merge or Move during the derivation, and (ii) The fundamental structure-building operation is "Concatenate X and Y thereby forming Z." This comes very close, when his technology is translated into modern Merge terms, to the FPG. A related yet earlier version of this that argues for a convergence of Merge with Categorial Grammar can be found in Berwick and Epstein (1995). In addition to Epstein (1999), Collins (2007: 838) deploys a principle virtually identical to the FPG: "*The Merge Assumption*: Every syntactic relation is a function of a binary combinatorial operation."

Given its august origins, it is clear that something like the FPG *must* be correct. At times, arguments from authority are clearly dispositive. As any impartial reader will admit, this is clearly one of those times. For the record, as one reviewer missed this, this last paragraph is not an argument but a way of admitting (i) that I like the FPG a lot and (ii) that I again reiterate that Epstein and Collins proposed it first.

[10] If one makes the further assumption that every grammatical dependency is expressed as a form of checking some grammatical feature, then we can strengthen the FPG into a biconditional incorporating the principle of Greed. I don't do this here, however. Why not? Because it is not clear what a grammatical feature is. The earliest MP attempts to understand features as morphologically expressed elements did not succeed that well empirically. And there are no other really good suggestions on offer that don't trivialize the notion so that it means nothing more than that some grammatical operation took place.

linguistic course knows, one of the great discoveries ever is the fact that natural language expressions are assemblages of constituents that themselves can contain further constituents. Constituency begets hierarchy.[11] The EMH rests on the premise that what makes language special is the fact that it allows for unboundedly complex hierarchically ordered *constituents*. The FPG recognizes the centrality of the (immediate) constituent and raises its importance another notch by making it the locale/domain for *all* G-dependencies. To say as the FPG does that all G-dependencies are Merge mediated is just to say that all grammatical commerce takes place among constituents (hierarchically organized (labeled) objects).[12]

In what follows, the FPG will play the role of a theoretical "forcing mechanism," meaning an assumption held rigorously constant to open up avenues for theoretical exploration. Where the FPG points I will follow. The EMH is a theory that emerges from the FPG forcing mechanism. Of course, if the EMH proves to be attractive, then the FPG has the right to claim pride of place as a foundational axiom. But, whether you rush to embrace this conclusion or not, in my opinion, the fecundity of the FPG as a forcing mechanism is sufficient reason for taking it seriously, at least for one book-length investigation.

A momentary segue: I should add a warning here to prevent some of my more Minimalistically up-to-date readers from hyperventilating. I am going to *initially* adopt a very traditional conception of constituency and, consequently, a less contemporary conception of Merge. In particular, I will *initially* assume that constituents are categorized units like NPs, VPs, TPs (etc.) and that Merge both puts expressions together *and* labels the resulting combination. This is *not* the contemporary way that (some) syntacticians understand Merge. Some limit the operation to forming units[13] from (pairs of) syntactic objects and treat labels as not visible to the syntax per se but as the products of a labeling algorithm that is part of the Transfer operation that maps syntactic objects to the interfaces (particularly the conceptual–intentional (CI)). The main idea seems to be that labels are not required "in the syntax" but are only necessary for "semantic" interpretation. As the reader will discover in Chapter 7, I don't buy this. I think that labeling is a syntactic operation (i.e. I doubt that labels can be motivated as formal prerequisites of CI interface legibility) and I will argue that the EMH *requires* labeling for its successful operationalization. However,

---

[11] In Chapter 7, I argue that it really does *beget* it. In particular, labeled units when merged inevitably yield further hierarchically organized constituents. Also, as argued in Chapter 3, given the standard No Tampering Conditions associated with Merge, we must assume that merged units are labeled to operationalize the FPG. This, thereby, gives some theoretical grounding to the standard idea that constituents (i.e. categorized complex units) are the basic units of linguistic computation.

[12] Again, this is very close to the First Law in Epstein (1999).

[13] Akin to sets, but see discussion in Chapter 2 where we will see that the set assumption is more convenience than fact.

I sympathize with the minimalist sentiment that (I believe) lies behind banishing labeling from the syntax. In the best of all possible minimalist worlds there is at most *one* linguistically bespoke feature of FL. I will suggest that labeling is the true secret ingredient. See the sixth listed point below for some preview.

To return to the FPG, I have yet higher ambitions for it. I intend it to make flesh two related ideas: (i) that the fundamental (indeed, the only *specifically* grammatical) operation of the grammar is the operation which forms constituents, and (ii) that the emergence of the constituent as a central element of FL is what underlies the rise of grammatical competence in humans. The earliest minimalist conception of Merge had this property. The Merge Hypothesis (sans the "Extended" part) is the idea that Merge is the cognitively special something that underlies human grammatical competence. This idea refracted through the FPG states that once one adds Merge (the operation that builds constituency) to the biological cognitive mix, out drops something with more or less the properties of the human FL as described more or less accurately by GB. So, why do humans have a GB kind of FL? Because FL contains an operation like Merge that it uses to mediate all G-dependencies, that's why. In what follows we will have a lot more to say about both Merge and the FPG and how they combine to derive many (most?) of the principles of FL/UG that Generativists have discovered over the last sixty years. This will, in fact, constitute the substantive empirical/theoretical core of what follows.

Fourth, the book adopts a particular method. It argues that a central feature of MP is to distinguish those features of FL that are linguistically parochial from those that are, plausibly, cognitively and/or computationally generic. Indeed, one goal of MP is to distinguish those features of FL that are *linguistically* bespoke (specifically *grammatical* operations and principles) from those that FL deploys but are *not* linguistically special. The EMH makes the claim that Merge *alone* (understood as the operation that generates constituents and that mediates all grammatical dependencies as per the FPG) is linguistically (or, more exactly, syntactically) special within FL.[14] All other operations and principles are, in principle, reflections of more general features of cognition/computation.[15]

In order to flesh out the EMH and its consequences, what follows will proceed piecemeal through the GB properties to be explained and identify the particular assumptions EMH requires to derive them. So, for example, some properties will follow from those of the combinatorics of the Merge operation

---

[14] To be more precise, Chapter 7 argues that labeling is the unique syntactically special operation. The combination part of the Merge operation is not uniquely linguistic.

[15] Note the weasel word 'reflection.' I would love to be able to actually reduce/unify the non-Merge assumptions to other clearly identified cognitive/computational operations and principles. Alas, I will largely not be able to do this. What I will do, I hope, is provide reasons for thinking that this is a rational hope, for at least some of these. See Chapter 8 for more discussion.

itself. Others require adverting to the labeling properties of Merge, and still others to the locality conditions grammars respect or idiosyncratic features that particular constructions impose. The goal here is to slowly expand the reach of the EMH by adding in these ancillary assumptions bit by bit so that it is possible to identify which assumptions drive which conclusions. This should allow for a better appreciation of how successful the particular MP theory developed here is and should allow for a clearer evaluation of the degree to which the success is a reflection of core MP conceptions and how much is just fudge. Chapter 6 reviews the results from Chapters 2–5 in a more concise easy-to-use format.

Fifth, as the aim is to demonstrate how rich MP has been, we will stop to smell some of the many beautiful flowers it has nursed. Here's what I mean. As noted, one evaluates a program by the theories it generates, and one evaluates and compares theories in terms of their explanatory depth, novel consequences and newly discovered phenomena. MP has some of all three. It explains where earlier theory stipulated. But it also "predicts" dependencies that are entirely novel, *some of which appear to be empirically grounded*. Of course, I will focus on these as they constitute explanations original with MP. It also supports novel kinds of operations and dependencies (or at least some versions of MP do) and I will highlight these as well. As I noted, a theory that aims to take earlier theoretical insights as the targets of explanation (as its *explananda*) will necessarily recapitulate the empirical insights of these accounts. In this sense, the new theory, even if offering greater explanatory oomph, will nonetheless cover much of the same empirical ground. *And this is both a good thing and a very important thing to do*. However, we want more (in fact, this is the scientist's general existential condition, s/he always wants *more*). We want new "predictions" and new phenomena. Well, MP has some of these and we will discuss them as well.

Sixth and last, at the very end, I argue for a substantive thesis, call it the "Labeling Hypothesis" (LH). LH holds that Merge should be divvied up and the labeling piece distinguished from the "putting-together" combination part. This is now standard practice. What is somewhat novel here is that LH takes the former to be linguistically special and the latter to be cognitively generic. LH proposes that LH coupled with a generic Merge-like operation yields grammars (G) that generate the unbounded hierarchical structures characteristic of natural language (known to Generative linguists as the Basic Property) and that obey the laws of grammar that GB identified. As argued in Chapter 7, LH identifies the core feature of FL to consist in the specification of equivalence classes of expressions with lexical atoms as moduli. This reflects the traditional notion of constituency. Classically, constituents are not simply generic units, they are units with names, units that fall into a finite number of specially identified groups (e.g. *Noun* phrase and *verb* phrases and *preposition* phrases, etc.). LH can be understood to be very sympathetic to this classical conception of constituency (and in this it differs from most contemporary theories of Merge).[16] If LH sounds obscure to you, dear reader, hopefully it will not be by the end of the book. My basic claim is that adding the label operation to more general cognitive operations begets the central properties of FL that GB identifies. In fact, when labels are added to a generic combination operation they *allow for* a recursive definition of the domain of linguistic objects, and labeling does this by closing the combination operation in the domain of the lexical atoms. That will be the claim. If it sounds obscure and over the top, don't worry. I will elaborate and hopefully satisfy.

However, for most of the book, the role of the Labeling Hypothesis is backgrounded. If you don't like it, well much of the Merge Hypothesis remains. The choice between treating recursive Merge as the special sauce or labeling as the linguistically bespoke addition to FL is (of course) interesting, but, in an important sense, secondary. If you have bought everything except the Labeling Hypothesis, you will be well convinced that the Minimalist Program has been a raging success.

Chapter 8 gingerly treats some further general consequences assuming that the EMH is more or less correct. I take up several topics briefly: (i) the non-modular nature of FL and its radical non-constructionist mien, (ii) the EMH and the non-linguistic source for locality conditions that regulate grammatical operations, (iii) the incompatibility of the Empty Category Principle with any version of the Merge Hypothesis, and (iv) the Y-model of derivations and the (E)MH. I don't get into these topics in great detail and much of the discussion is inadequate. However, if the (E)MH is roughly correct then here are places where an MP Merge-based conception of FL differs dramatically from the prior GB version. For this reason it is worth outlining just how different.

That's the book. The rest are details. Time to get to them.

---

[16] See Hunter (2021).

1 A Whig History of Generative Grammar

1.0 Introduction

Fish swim, birds fly, people speak. For the first two, the standard wisdom is that fish and birds do what they do *partly* in virtue of being biologically built to do what they do. Mentalist conceptions of linguistics apply similar reasoning to humans and their linguistic behavior. So situated, the goal of linguistics is to describe and explain the mental/brain properties that allow for human linguistic facility. More specifically, just as ornithologists take it for granted that many features of birds are biologically dedicated to efficiently supporting flight, and ichthyologists assume that fish come with many properties to optimize swimming, linguists (of the mentalist variety) propose that humans come with a faculty of language (FL) endowed with linguistically bespoke properties which *partly* ground the linguistic competence characteristic of humans.

We even know a little about the fine structure of FL due to sixty-five years of research by Generative grammarians. We know, for example, two very general things. First, that part of linguistic competence consists in having acquired a Grammar (G) able to recursively generate an unbounded number of distinct hierarchically organized structures that pair an articulation with a meaning (i.e. $<\pi,\lambda>$ pairs). Second, we also know that any (non-pathological) child can acquire the G of any language and that the course of acquisition of that G is more or less the same across all acquirers and all Gs. This does *not* mean that there are no individual differences. Rather, the targets of acquisition and the time course of their acquisition is largely unaffected by anything other than placement in the appropriate speech community. Put any kid in any English/Swahili/Basque/... speaking environment and the child will acquire facility in English/Swahili/Basque/... in more or less the same way in more or less the same time. And acquiring facility *means* (at least) being able to pair an articulation π with a meaning λ over an *unbounded* domain of linguistic objects.

The "unbounded" part above directly implicates the existence of an acquired G; for the *only* way for a finite entity (the brain) to display an unbounded capacity like the one we find manifest in linguistic behavior (which we know involves dealing with unboundedly many different discrete hierarchically organized objects) is as the expression of a finitely specifiable generative procedure that takes its prior computed outputs as subsequent inputs for further computation. In other words, the unbounded nature of human linguistic facility implicates the existence of Gs (i.e. recursive rule systems) that generate an infinity (i.e. unbounded number) of distinct hierarchically organized objects from a finite specifiable set of atoms, by combining these atoms together into larger structures that can themselves be further combined into yet larger structures. All of this we know, and we have known it for quite a while, and it should be neither controversial nor tendentious.

What is (rightly) debated and still under active investigation is the exact specification of the recursive procedures found in human Gs. To say that human Gs are recursive leaves open the question of what the relevant generative procedures look like. And this is a very, very, very BIG question. There are an infinite number of possible recursive functions, only a very, very, ... very small number of which (maybe just one really!) are attested in natural language grammars. Therefore, not surprisingly, generative research over the last sixty-five years has explored many options and has changed its collective mind repeatedly about the nature of the procedures that FL makes available to generate linguistic structures and establish linguistic dependencies. In what follows, I outline how the mentalist Generativist project has investigated the fine structure of FL and Universal Grammar (UG).[1] The goal is to appreciate the logic of this roughly seventy-year project and identify how the Minimalist Program (MP) conceptually fits into that project. Here goes.

1.1 Some Salient Facts, Some Obvious Consequences, and the Questions They Raise

The Generative Program began with a focus on two salient facts. The first is that native speakers of a (human) language are *linguistically creative* in the sense that they are capable of producing and understanding an unbounded number of qualitatively different discrete kinds of linguistic expressions (e.g. phrases and sentences).[2] The second salient fact, let's call it *linguistic*

---

[1] From now on, when I use the term 'Generative Program' I mean the mentalist (Chomskyan) version.
[2] In the immortal words of Noam Chomsky: "a mature native speaker can produce a new sentence on the appropriate occasion, and other speakers can understand it immediately, though it is equally new to them" (Chomsky 1964: 7). Importantly, these linguistic forms are discretely different, with very different contents over an effectively unbounded domain.

One further important point. 'Creativity' has been used in two very different ways in the Generative literature. The first, focused on here, deals with finitely specifying the unbounded number of well-formed structures that a native speaker can use and understand. The second, largely ignored in what follows, adverts to an observation that Chomsky highlights in his more philosophical work; namely, that language use is creative in the sense of not being

1.1 Facts, Consequences and Questions

flexibility, is that *any* human child can acquire *any* human language if placed in the appropriate speech community. Further, so far as we can tell, the capacity to acquire competence in a specific language L is more or less uniform in the species in that the end state attained (linguistic competence) is (more or less) the same and its course of development is (roughly) uniform regardless of the child and regardless of the language.[3]

These two facts are not subtle. Nobody will win a fancy prize for doing clever and laborious experiments to discover their existence. However, until Chomsky noted them over sixty years ago, they were little noticed, and few bothered to ask how either was possible. A central ambition of the Generative Program has been to address how these two facts could be true. What allows humans to be linguistically creative and linguistically flexible? More specifically, what kinds of minds could support these two related yet different kinds of capacities?

The Generative answer to this pair of questions is now relatively well known. Here is a snapshot version.

Linguistic creativity (LC) is explained by assuming that native speakers of a human language L have a particular kind of knowledge of L. What kind? Native speakers have acquired a grammar (G) (aka, a generative procedure) that recursively specifies an open-ended number of meaning–sound pairs for that language. In other words, linguistic creativity in L (LC_L) rests (at least in part) on having a G of L (G_L). The fact that G_L is recursive explains LC's open-ended nature, in that creatures endowed with G_Ls will have knowledge of an unbounded number of linguistic objects. That's what recursive systems do. They *finitely* specify a capacity that extends over an *unbounded* (i.e. infinite) domain. LC reflects the fact that native speakers have internalized such a recursive system, and this recursively specified G is what (at least in part) endows native speakers with the power to produce endlessly many novel sentences/

---

stimulus bound. Here 'creativity' points to the fact that humans (generally) use language in ways appropriate to a context even though there is no sense in which the context "causes" their linguistic behavior (though, to use Cartesian terminology, it may "incline" them in certain ways – what the difference is between "causing" and "inclining" is a topic I will studiously avoid). This use of the term 'creative' points to very deep Cartesian issues concerning the distinctive nature of mental vs physical substance that lay at the heart of the Cartesian dualist project (and that twenty-first-century intellectuals have very little sympathy with today). At any rate, what is critical here is that the Generative Program has absolutely nothing of interest to say about this second sense of 'creativity.' Indeed, so far as I can tell, *nobody* has anything interesting to say about it. For a review of this issue in a psychological setting, the reader can do no better than reread Chomsky's wonderful review of Skinner's *Verbal Behavior* (1967). For what follows, however, the reader should simply assume that nothing we say here bears on the deep Cartesian issues alluded to.

[3] Note the qualifiers 'more or less' and 'roughly.' Of course children differ, but the milestones along the acquisition path and the end state attained are very similar and seem to be largely independent of the target language being acquired. See Brown (1973) and Slobin (1986) for discussion.

phrases and allows them to understand such novelties upon hearing them. So, to the question: how is it that competent native speakers can be linguistically creative?, we have the answer: in virtue of having internalized a G_L, a recursive generative procedure, that specifies the (unboundedly many) objects of L for their particular native language L. So LC is (in part) explained in terms of internalized G_Ls.[4]

And what of linguistic flexibility (LFL), the capacity humans have to acquire any G_L under the right input conditions? The possibility of LFL follows if humans come equipped with a faculty of language (FL) with the power to yield grammars when fed the (linguistically) relevant data. In the simple case, such data will be bits of language L produced/uttered by proficient native speakers of L based on the G_Ls that they as proficient native speakers have internalized.[5] So, LFL follows if humans are endemically endowed with FLs that can map the bits of a language L a child is exposed to (and takes in) (aka, "primary linguistic data of L" (PLD_L)) onto a grammar of L (G_L). Or pictorially:

(1) $PLD_L \rightarrow FL \rightarrow G_L$

In other words, FL is a function that takes PLD_L and maps it onto a G_L (i.e. $FL(PLD_L) = G_L$). From the perspective of the Generative Program so construed, G and FL are empirical hypotheses about how two facts (i.e. LC and LFL) are possible. From this perspective, the program identifies the focus of inquiry to be G_Ls (specific generative procedures internalized by native speakers of particular Ls) and FL (the recipe that allows humans to acquire G_Ls when appropriately linguistically placed).

That G_Ls exist in native speakers and *that* FL exists as a human biological endowment are **NOT** exciting claims. They are close to the conceptual minimum required to accommodate our two very salient facts, LC and LFL.

---

[4] Let me emphasize, recursively specifying the well-formed objects of L via a G_L is a necessary but not sufficient step in explaining the fullness of linguistic creativity. Gs are not parsers and Gs are not producers (which have in addition, for example, memory structures (i.e. a "tape" or "stack"), write-to and read-from procedures, among other things, as well as a specification of the relevant G rules specified in the machine table), though they are a necessary part of both (see Berwick and Weinberg (1984) for elaboration). This noted, the Generative Program has focused on (i) specifying the generative procedures that Gs contain and (ii) explaining why particular Gs contain these and not others.

[5] But this really is the simple case. It appears that humans can create Gs from much thinner linguistic input if the emergence of creoles from pidgins is any indication. And from rather confusing input: as the linguistic products of many Gs (say in multilingual settings) allow for the simultaneous emergence of multiple relatively neatly segregated Gs rather than a single G farrago of the different inputs. The generative program has largely restricted attention to the simple case, assuming that explicating how it might arise is challenging enough, and assuming that the complex cases will build on mechanisms identified in the simple one. For discussion and references, see Bickerton (1984) and accompanying critical notes.

That something like these two cognitive (and ultimately biological) objects exist is really a no-brainer. After all, to say that a native speaker has internalized a G_L is to acknowledge that s/he has an unbounded capacity to use and understand L. And to say that someone has an FL is just to say that s/he has a second-order capacity to acquire the first-order capacity specified by a G_L. But given that native speakers *are* quite obviously linguistically creative and given that humans *are* quite obviously capable of acquiring any G_L if exposed to PLD_L, the supposition that G_Ls and FLs "exist" and are legitimate objects of inquiry must be correct. The inferential leaps from LC to G_Ls and from LFL to FL are very, very short.

The hard empirical question, then, is not *whether* these objects exist, but *what they look like* in detail. In other words, the hard part of the Generative Program is specifying what G_Ls look like (i.e. what *kinds* of recursive generative procedures they embody) and what the fine structure of FL is (i.e. what principles it must embody to allow for the acquisition of G_Ls for arbitrary Ls).

Given this framing, an important subsidiary question of interest is the degree to which the structures of G_Ls and the fine structure of FL are linguistically bespoke or cognitively and/or computationally generic. In other words, a central sub-project of the program will be to determine to what extent (if any) our first- and second-order linguistic facilities require a mental apparatus specifically tuned to the properties of language and to what extent the capacities manifested in linguistic behavior reflect our combined cognitive and computational powers more generally.

In case you haven't noticed, this last question is quite definitely an empirical one. To date, the Generative answer has been that linguistic proficiency *does* require specifically linguistic cognition. The minimalist codicil to this general conclusion has been that it only requires a dollop of such, rather than a large heaping shovelful. We will return to this issue anon, but for now, let's take a quick trip through the history of Generative Grammar so that we can appreciate how Minimalism, the latest step in the Generative Program, fits into the entire Generative Grammar project.[6]

---

[6] This chapter is titled "A Whig History of Generative Grammar." According to *Wikipedia*, a Whig history is "a form of historiography that presents the past as an inevitable progression towards ever greater ... enlightenment culminating in modern forms." In other words, it is not "real" history. Rather it is what my good and great friend Elan Dresher has described as "history we can use." Philosophers label such accounts "rational reconstructions." What makes Whig histories useful is that they adopt the charming conceit that actual intellectual development tracks the logic of the ideas involved. History is then a movement from good ideas to even better ones, with historical progression tracking intellectual improvement. This, we know, is not true of real intellectual history. Real history is much bumpier and haphazard. Whig history, then, is not so much a description of what actually happened but of what *should have* happened. And that is precisely what makes it useful, for it exposes the intellectual linkages among the evolving successful ideas.

1.2 The First Two Stages of the Generative Program

Again, let's start with the two big facts (i.e. LC and LFL) and ask how to rationally investigate them. Recall that addressing LC requires saying something about the G_Ls that a native speaker of L has acquired, in particular a specification of the generative procedures that it embodies (i.e. the particular rules of grammar that characterize a native speaker's (unbounded) knowledge of/sense of the language L). And addressing LFL requires specifying the fine structure of FL that allows humans to become native speakers of a particular L, which means specifying how a person uses PLD_L to acquire their G_L.[7]

This description of the research problem immediately suggests a rational order of inquiry. To address LFL questions requires having some G_L specimens. After all, the LFL question is how humans acquire *grammars*, and unless we have some idea of what kinds of grammars humans actually acquire, it will be well-nigh impossible to investigate how humans do what they/we do.[8] So, as a practical matter, the first step in the Generative Program will be to find some plausible candidate rules of grammar embodied in particular G_Ls. Not surprisingly, this kind of investigation indeed characterizes a good deal of the first stages of Generative inquiry.

So, the first question on the research agenda should have been (and was): What properties (rules, generative procedures, principles) characterize individual Gs? More particularly, what kinds of recursive rules do G_Ls incorporate?

We know part of the answer to this last question because of another obvious fact about natural languages: The kinds of linguistic objects that Gs relate are meaning–sound pairings. For example, among the things a native speaker of English knows is that *Dogs chase cats* does not mean the same thing as *Cats chase dogs* while *Cats are chased by dogs* does. There are an unbounded number of such systematic facts that a competent native speaker of a given natural language knows.

---

[7] Note that this is an *idealization* of the problem. Nobody actually believes that native speakers have unique Gs. For example, it is widely recognized that native speakers have different "registers" (i.e. Gs) that they switch between. However, idealizing to the situation where a person's competence is restricted to a single G and where the relevant PLD used is uniform and unsullied still leaves a *very* hard acquisition problem. Moreover, there is little reason to think that solving this simplified problem will involve different mechanisms than solving the more realistic one, in the sense that we will have to adopt entirely different generative procedures or FL principles when we weaken this idealization. The more realistic case, in other words, should involve the same kinds of rules and principles *and then some*, rather than completely different kinds of rules and principles than are useful in the idealized case. For those that like analogies to physics (a "real" science), think *frictionless* inclined planes.
[8] The 'they' is a nod to Chomsky's rational Martian scientist (the equivalent in Chomsky's world to Fodor's grandmother in his).

1.2 First Two Stages of the Generative Program

Thus we know two important things about any G_L: (i) it involves recursive rules and (ii) it produces meaning–sound pairings.

The first fact suggests that linguistic competence consists (in part) in mastery of a system of rules that specifies the natural language mastered. Why a rule system? Because that is the only way to finitely specify an effectively infinite capacity. We cannot just list the objects in the domain of a native speaker's competence and treat the capacity as akin to looking things up on a giant list because, given LC, the list would have to go on forever. The capacity can only be specified in terms of a finite procedure that describes (i.e. generates) it. Thus, we conclude that linguistic mastery of a language L consists (in part) in acquiring a set of rules (i.e. a G_L) that generate the kinds of linguistic objects that a native speaker of L is competent with.

The second fact tells us something more about these G_Ls. They must specify pairings of meanings with sounds. Thus the rule systems that native speakers have mastered are rules that generate objects with two distinctive properties. G_Ls consist of generative procedures that tie a specific meaning profile together with a specific sound profile,[9] and they do this over an effectively infinite domain. So G_Ls are functions whose range is meaning–sound pairs, viz. an infinite number of objects like this: <m,s>. What's the domain? Some finite set of "atoms" that can combine again and again to yield more and more complex <m,s> pairs. Let's call these atoms "morphemes."

Putting this all together, we know from the basic facts and some very elementary reasoning that native speakers master G_Ls (recursive procedures) that map morphemes into an unbounded range of <m,s>s. **THIS. WE. KNOW.** What we don't know is what the specific rules that Gs contain look like (or, for that matter, what the 'm's and 's's look like). And that brings us to our first research question: *describe specific rules characteristic of natural language Gs and specify their variety and interactions.* The earliest Generative research aimed to provide some candidate rules of specific grammars and show how their interactions would mirror some of the complexities that native speakers' competence displays. In other words, the first order of business in Generative research involved producing detailed model grammars of the kinds of rules that particular G_Ls have and how these rules interact. Many different rules were investigated: movement rules, deletion rules, phrase structure rules and binding rules, to name four. And their complex modes of interaction were limned. Consider some details.

---

[9] Typically, a "sound" profile involves vocal tracts and auditory perception. However, this is not required, as the existence of signed languages indicates. Here the articulators are manual and facial and the perceptual system is visual.

1.3 Step 1: Some Possible Rules of G_Ls

Recall that one of the central facts about natural languages is that they contain a practically infinite number of objects that pair a meaning with a sound.[10] They also contain dependencies defined over the structures of these objects. In early theories of Generative Grammar, phrase structure (PS) rules recursively specified the infinite class of well-formed "base" structures in a given G. Lexical insertion (LI) rules specified the class of admissible local dependencies in a given G, and transformational (T) rules specified the class of non-local dependencies in a given G.[11] Let's consider each in turn.

PS-rules are recursive and their successive application creates bigger and bigger hierarchically organized structures on which LI- and T-rules operate to generate other structures and dependencies.[12] (2) provides some candidate PS-rules (the '(...)' indicates optional expansion):

(2)   a. $S \to NP$ aux VP
        b. $VP \to V\,(NP)\,(PP)$
        c. $NP \to (det)\,N\,(PP)\,(S)$
        d. $PP \to P\,NP$

These four rules suffice to generate an unbounded number of hierarchically structured objects. Thus, a sentence like *John kissed Mary* has the structure in (3) generated using rules (2a,b,c).

(3) $[_S\,[_{NP}\,N]\,\text{aux}\,[_{VP}\,V\,[_{NP}\,N]]]$

LI-rules like those in (4) insert terminals into these structures, yielding the structured phrase marker (PM) in (5):

---

[10] Linguists have known for quite a while that these objects have a hierarchical as well as a linear structure. I put this aside for now.

[11] The earliest Generative grammars' PS-rules characterized the class of "kernel" sentences. These were very simple and involved no embedding. The action in these theories was with two kinds of transformations, one that combined two kernels and one that changed the structure of a given input. I am abstracting from most of these complexities here. Remember what you are getting here is a *Whig* history, not the real thing.

[12] Strictly speaking, until the Minimalist Program period, Generativists took the string to be the basic ontological unit. The rules in (2) were defined in terms of strings and sets of sets (of sets ...) of strings. Recursive rules did not output hierarchical objects (i.e. derived phrase markers) but specified recursive generation paths (i.e. derivation trees), though this is how linguists thought of things. I abstract from these issues here, important though they are, especially in light of the fact that one of the interesting features of Minimalism has been the rejection of strings as the fundamental ontological grammatical unit. What I mean by this is that phrases and transformations in early Generative theories are objects defined in terms of strings, not themselves basic units. Minimalism fundamentally reverses this metaphysics. Merge treats sets (or, more accurately, constituents) as the fundamental units of analysis, with phrases and movement (transformational) dependencies as ontologically fundamental. In the standard minimalist versions, strings are secondary objects with little grammatical potency. This is a very big change in perspective, and I will ignore it in the discussion of the Whig history that follows.

1.3 Some Possible Rules of G_Ls

(4) a. N → John, Mary ...
     b. V → kiss, ...
     c. aux → past

(5) [$_S$ [$_{NP}$ [$_N$ John]] [$_{aux}$ past] [$_{VP}$ [$_V$ kiss] [$_{NP}$ [$_N$ Mary]]]][13]

PMs like (5) also reflect local inter-lexical dependencies. Note that replacing *kiss* with *arrive* yields an unacceptable sentence: **John arrived Mary*. The PS-rules can generate the relevant structure (i.e. (3)), but the LI-rules cannot insert *arrive* in the *V* position of (3) because *arrive* is not lexically marked as transitive. In other words, *NP^kiss^NP* is a fine local dependency, but *NP^arrive^NP* is not.

Given structures like (5), T-rules can apply to rearrange them, thereby coding for a variety of non-local dependencies.[14] What kind of dependencies? The unit of transformational analysis in early Generativism is the construction. Some examples include: Passive, *Wh*-questions, Polar questions, Raising, Equi-NP Deletion (aka control), Super Equi, Topicalization, Clefting, Dative Shift (aka Double Object Constructions), Particle Shift, *There* constructions (aka Existential Constructions), Reflexivization, Pronominalization, Extraposition, among others. Though these rules fall into some natural formal classes (see below), they also contain a great deal of construction-specific information, reflecting construction-specific morphological peccadillos and restrictions. Here's an illustration.

Consider the Passive rule in (6). 'X'/'Y' in (6) are variables. The rule says that if you can factor a string into the parts on the left of the arrow (viz. the structural description) you can change the structure to the one on the right of the arrow (the structural change). Applied to (5/7a), this yields the derived phrase marker (7b).

(6) X - NP$_1$ - AUX - V - NP$_2$ - Y → X - NP$_2$ - be+en - V - by NP$_1$ - Y

(7) a. X- [$_{NP}$ John] [$_{aux}$ past] [$_V$ kiss] [$_{NP}$ Mary]-Y
     b. X- [$_{NP}$ Mary] [$_{aux}$ past] be+en [$_V$ kiss] by [$_{NP}$ John]-Y

Note that the rule codes the fact that what was once the object of *kiss* is now a derived subject. Despite this change in position, *Mary* is still understood as

---

[13] What does (5) code? It makes explicit the grammatical 'is-a' relation. For example, it "says" that *John-past-kiss-Mary* is an S. It also "says" that that *Kiss-Mary* is a VP and that *Mary, John* are each an NP. The possible factoring of strings according to the is-a relation allows for the specification of rules that change a string that has one factorization (aka, structural description) into another via a rule. This is illustrated in (6) and (7).

[14] In the earliest Generative theories, recursion was also the province of the transformational component, with PS-rules playing the far more modest role of specifying the kernel sentences. However, from *Aspects* (Chomsky 1965) onward, the PS-rules become the recursive engine of the grammar. Transformations do not generally create "bigger" objects. Rather, they specify licit grammatical dependencies within PS-created structures.

the kissee. Similarly, *John*, the former subject of (5) and the kisser, is now the object of the preposition *by*, and still the kisser. Thus, the passive rule in (6) codes the fact that *Mary was kissed by John* and *John kissed Mary* have a common thematic structure as both have a derivation which starts from the same underlying PM in (5). In effect, this proposal tracks the non-local dependency between *Mary* and *kiss* in *Mary was kissed by John* by proposing that the input to this sentence involves a PM where *kiss* and *Mary* are locally proximate (as in (5)).

The research focus in this first phase of grammatical investigation was on carefully describing the detailed features of a variety of different constructions, rather than on factoring out their common features.[15] Observe that (7b) introduces new morphemes into the PM (e.g. *be+en, by*), in addition to rearranging the nominal expressions. T-rules did quite a bit of this, as we shall see below. What's important to note for current purposes is the division of labor between PS-, LI- and T-rules. The first generates unboundedly many hierarchical structures, the second "chooses" the right ones for the lexical elements involved (and locally codes their "thematic" properties) and the last rearranges them to produce novel surface forms that retain the "thematic" relations specified in the inputs to the T-rules, even when the relata are no longer in their original proximate positions.[16] So, for example, in (7b) *Mary* is still understood as the kissee despite no longer being adjacent to the verb *kiss*.

T-rules, despite their individual idiosyncrasies, fall into a few identifiable formal families. For example, control constructions are generated by a T-rule (Equi-NP Deletion) that deletes part of the input structure. Sluicing constructions also delete material but, in contrast to Equi-NP Deletion, they do not require a PM-internal grammatical trigger (aka antecedent) to do so. Movement rules (like Passive in (6) or Raising) rearrange elements in a PM. And T-rules that generate Reflexive and Bound Pronoun constructions neither move nor delete elements but replace the lower of two identical lexical NPs with morphologically appropriate formatives (as we will illustrate presently).

In sum, the first epoch of Generative inquiry provided a budget of *actual examples* of the kinds of rules that Gs contain (i.e. PS, LI and T) and the kinds of properties these rules had to have to be capable of specifying the kinds of recursion and the kinds of dependencies characteristically found within natural languages. In other words, early Generative work developed a compendium of examples of *actual* G rules *in a variety of languages*.

---

[15] This is not quite right, of course. One of the glories of early Generative research is Ross's discovery of islands, and many different constructions obeyed them.

[16] Thematic is in scare quotes because the term is anachronistic. It was not used in the earliest papers, though the later term correctly describes what Deep Structures were intended to represent.

1.3 Some Possible Rules of G_Ls

Nor was this all. Early Generative Grammar also provided models for how these different rules interact. Recall that one of the key features of natural languages is that they include effectively unbounded hierarchically organized objects. This means that the rules talk to one another and apply to one another's outputs to produce an endless series of complex structures and dependencies. Early Generative research started exploring how G rules could interact and it was quickly discovered how complex and subtle G interactions could be. For example, in the Standard Theory, rules apply cyclically (from smaller domains to larger domains that contain these smaller domains) and in a certain fixed order (e.g. PS-rules applying before T-rules). Sometimes the order of rule application is intrinsic (follows from the nature of the rules involved) and sometimes not. Sometimes the application of a rule creates the structural conditions for the application of another (feeding), sometimes it destroys the structures (bleeding) thereby preventing a possible operation from applying. These rule systems could be very complex, and these initial investigations gave linguists a first serious taste of what a sophisticated capacity natural language competence was.

It is worth going through an example to get a feel for this complexity. For illustration, consider some binding data and the rules of Reflexivization and Pronominalization, and their interactions with PS-rules and T-rules like Raising.

Lees and Klima (L&K) (1963) offered the following two rules to account for an interesting array of binding data in English (see data in (10)–(13)).[17] These rules must apply when they can and are (extrinsically) ordered so that (8) applies before (9).

(8)   Reflexivization:
        $X - NP_1 - Y - NP_2 - Z \rightarrow X - NP_1 - Y - \text{pronoun+self} - Z$
        (where $NP_1 = NP_2$, pronoun has the phi-features of NP_2, and NP_1/NP_2 are in the same simplex sentence)

(9)   Pronominalization:
        $X - NP_1 - Y - NP_2 - Z \rightarrow X - NP_1 - Y - \text{pronoun} - Z$
        (where $NP_1 = NP_2$ and pronoun has the phi-features of NP_2)

As is evident, the two rules are formally very similar. Both apply to identical NPs in a phrase marker and morphologically convert one to a reflexive or to a pronoun. (8), however, only applies to nominals in the same simplex clause (i.e. to "clause-mates"), while (9) is not similarly restricted. As (8) obligatorily applies

---

[17] Chomsky's (1975 (1956)) *Logical Structure of Linguistic Theory* (LSLT) was a very elaborate investigation of an English G. The Lees and Klima (1963) rules for pronouns and reflexives discussed here have direct antecedents in LSLT. However, the specific rules discussed above as illustrations here are those offered in Lees and Klima (1963).

before (9), Reflexivization will bleed the environment for the application of Pronominalization by changing NP_2 to a reflexive (thereby rendering the two NPs no longer "identical"). A consequence of this ordering is that Reflexivization and Pronominalization rules apply in distinct domains. In English, this means that Reflexives and (bound) pronouns must be in complementary distribution.[18]

An illustration should make things clear. Consider the derivation of (10a) (where *himself/him* are understood as anaphorically dependent on $John_1$). It has the underlying form (10b). We can factor (10b) as in (10c) as per the Reflexivization rule (8). This results in converting (10c) to (10d) with the surface output (10e) carrying a reflexive interpretation. Note that the Reflexivization derivation codes the fact that *John* is both washer and washee, as well as that *John* non-locally relates to *himself*.

(10)   a. $John_1$ washed himself/*him
          b. John washed John
          c. X-John-Y-John-Z
          d. X-John-Y-him+self-Z
          e. John washed himself

What blocks *John likes him* with a similar anaphoric reading (i.e. where *John* is co-valued with *him*)? To derive this structure Pronominalization must apply to (10c). However, it cannot, as (8) is ordered before (9) and both rules are obligatory (i.e. they must apply when they can apply). But once (8) applies, we get (10d), which no longer has a structural description amenable to (9). Thus, the application of (8) bleeds the grammatical context for the application of (9) and *John likes him* with a bound reading of the pronoun cannot be derived (i.e. there is no licit grammatical relation between *John* and *him*).

This changes in (11). Reflexivization cannot apply to (11c) as the two *John*s are in different clauses. As (8) cannot apply, (9) can (indeed, must) as it is not similarly restricted to apply to clause-mates. In sum, the inability to apply (8) allows (and demands) the application of (9). Thus does the L&K theory derive the complementary distribution of reflexives and bound pronouns.

(11)   a. John believes that Mary washed *himself/him
          b. John believes that Mary washed John
          c. X-John-Y-John
          d. X-John-Y-him
          e. John believes that Mary washed him

There is one other feature of note: The binding rules in (8) and (9) also effectively derive a class of (what are now commonly called) Principle C effects,

---

[18] Cross-linguistic work on binding has shown the complementary distribution of reflexives and bound pronouns to be robust across natural languages, and so deriving the complementarity has become a boundary condition on the empirical adequacy of binding theories.

1.3 Some Possible Rules of G_Ls

given the background assumption that reflexives and pronouns morphologically obscure an underlying expression which is identical to the antecedent. Thus, the two rules prevent the derivation of structures like (12) in which the bound reflexive/pronoun c-commands its antecedent.[19]

(12)   a. *Himself$_1$ kissed Bill$_1$
         b. *He$_1$ thinks that John$_1$ is tall

It should be noted that deriving Principle C effects in this way is not particularly deep. The rules derive the effect by stipulating that it should be the higher (actually, leftmost) of two identical NPs that is retained in the structural change of the relevant transformation while the lower (rightmost) one is replaced by a reflexive/pronoun.[20]

The L&K theory can also explain the data in (13) and (16) in the context of a G with a rule like Raising to Object in (14), which, let's assume, obligatorily applies before (8)/(9).

(13)   a. *John$_1$ believes him/he-self$_1$ is intelligent
         b. John$_1$ believes he$_1$ is intelligent

(14)   Raising to Object:
         X - V - C - NP - Y → X - V - NP - C - Y
         (where C, the complementizer, is phonetically null and non-finite)[21]

(14) cannot apply to raise the finite embedded subject in (15) to the matrix clause, as the null complementizer C of the embedded clause is finite. This prevents (8) from applying to derive (13a), as (8) is restricted to NPs that are clause-mates. But, as failure to apply (8) requires the application of (9), the mini-grammar depicted here leads to the derivation of (13b) from (15).

(15)   John$_1$ believes C John$_1$ is intelligent

Analogously, (8), (9) and (14) also explain the facts in (15), if (14) is obligatory and must apply when it can.[22]

---

[19] α c-commands β iff every branching category that dominates α dominates β.

[20] Depending on how "identical" is understood, the L&K theory also prevents the derivation of sentences like *John kissed John* where the two *John*s are understood as referring to the same individual. How exactly to understand the identity requirement was a vexed issue that was partly responsible for the replacement of the L&K theory. One particularly acute problem was how to derive sentences like *Everyone kissed himself*. It clearly does not mean anything like 'everyone kissed everyone.' What then is its underlying form so that (8) could apply to it? This was never satisfactorily cleared up and led to revised approaches to binding, as we shall see.

[21] This is not how the original raising to object rule was stated, but it's close enough. Note too, that saying that C is finite means that it selects for a finite T. In English, for example, *that* is finite and *for* is non-finite. We are here assuming that there is a phonetically null version of each of these Cs.

[22] I leave the relevant derivations as an exercise.

(16) a. John$_1$ believes himself$_1$ to be intelligent
b. *John$_1$ believes him$_1$ to be intelligent

The L&K analysis can be expanded further to handle yet more data when combined with other rules of G. And this is exactly the point: to investigate the kinds of rules Gs contain by seeing how their interactions derive non-trivial linguistic data sets. This allows us to explore what kinds of rules exist (by proposing some and seeing how they work) and what kinds of interactions rules can have (they can feed and bleed one another, they are ordered, obligatory, etc.).

The L&K analysis above illustrates two important features of these early proposals. First, it (in combination with other rules) compactly summarizes a (practically infinite) set of binding "effects," patterns of data concerning the relation of anaphoric expressions to their antecedents in a range of phrasal configurations. It doesn't outline *all* the data that we now take to be relevant to binding theory (e.g. it does not address the contrast in *John$_1$'s mother likes him/*himself$_1$*), but many of the data points discussed by L&K have become part of the canonical data set that any theory of binding is responsible for. Thus, the complementary distribution of reflexives and (bound) pronouns in these sentential configurations is now a canonical fact that every subsequent theory of binding has aimed to explain. So too the locality (viz. the clause-mate condition) required between antecedent and anaphor for successful reflexivization, the anti-locality requirement on licit bound pronouns (i.e. bound pronouns and their antecedents *cannot* be clause-mates) and the prohibition against anaphors c-commanding the antecedents of which they are anaphoric dependents.

The *variety* of data L&K identifies is also noteworthy. From very early on, the Generative Program understood that both positive and negative data are relevant for understanding how FL and Gs are structured. Positive data is another name for the "good" cases (examples like (10e) and (11e)), where an anaphoric dependency is licensed. Negative data are the * cases (examples like (12a) and (16b)) where the relevant dependency is illicit. Grammars, in short, not only specify what *can* be done, they also specify what *cannot* be done. Generativists have discovered that negative data often reveals more about the structure of FL and a particular G than positive data does.[23]

Second, L&K provides a *theory* of these effects in the two rules (8) and (9). As we shall see, this theory was *not* retained in later versions of Generative Grammar.[24] The L&K account relies on machinery (obligatory rule application,

---

[23] The focus on negative data has also been part of the logic of the Poverty of Stimulus (POS) argument (aka Plato's problem). Data that is absent is hard to track without some specification of what absences to look for (i.e. some specifications *not provided by the data itself* of where to look). More important still to the logic of the POS is the impoverished nature of the PLD available to the child. We return to this at the end of the next section.

[24] Though I am personally rather fond of the L&K theory and have argued that we should return to a modern version of it. For some relevant discussion which I don't currently entirely endorse, see Hornstein (2008).

bleeding and feeding relations among rules, rule ordering, Raising to Object, etc.) that was replaced in later theory by different kinds of rules with different kinds of properties. The L&K rules themselves are also very complex (e.g. they are extrinsically ordered). Later approaches to binding attempt to isolate the relevant factors and generalize them to other kinds of rules. We return to this anon.

One more terminological point: In what follows, it is useful to distinguish between "effects" and "theory." As Generative theories changed over the years, discovered effects (e.g. that Reflexivization and Pronominalization are in complementary distribution, that *Wh*-movement out of islands is illicit, that PRO appears in non-finite subject positions, etc.) have been largely retained, though the theories developed to explain these effects have often changed significantly.[25] For example, as we will see below, the L&K theory was replaced by Principles A, B and C of the binding theory, yet a central binding effect (viz. the complementarity between Reflexivization and Pronominalization) was retained. This is similar to what we observe in the mature sciences (think ideal gas laws with respect to thermodynamics and later statistical mechanics). What is *clearly* cumulative in the history of Generative Grammar is the conservation of discovered effects. Theory changes, and deepens. Some theoretical approaches are discarded, some refashioned and some resuscitated after having been abandoned. Effects, however, are largely conserved and a standard boundary condition of theoretical admissibility in later theory is that the new theory with its novel assumptions explain the effects that the older replaced theory explained.

I should also add that for large stretches of theoretical time, basic theory has also been conserved (e.g. some version of the cycle has been with us since almost the inception of the Generative Program). However, the cumulative nature of Generative research is most evident in the preservation of the various discovered effects. In Section 1.6, I list a number of these. It is an impressive group. But first, let's take a look at how establishing a set of plausible G rules sets the stage for addressing the second Generative question concerning linguistic flexibility.

1.4   Step 2: Categorizing, Simplifying and Unifying the Rules

As noted, the first stage of Generative research yields a bunch of rules describing a bunch of linguistic constructions in addition to providing early models of how the different kinds of rules might interact to generate an unbounded number of <m,s>s within a given natural language L. Here we look at how this prepared the way for research focusing on the second question concerning the

---

[25] Though, like all theory, earlier ideas are recycled with some reinterpretation. See below for illustration.

nature of linguistic flexibility (LFL): *what must FL look like given that it can produce G_ls with these kinds of rules and these kinds of interactions?* At the risk of stating the obvious (not a risk I worry much about), observe that asking this question only makes *practical* sense once we have serious candidate G_Ls, language-specific generative procedures. For the LFL question to be fecund *presupposes* that we have identified *some* G_L rules with the right properties, for it is G_L rules *like these* that we want FL to target. Given this, it is not surprising that LFL issues awaited (partial) answers to the conceptually prior LC question.

Investigations into FL moved along two tracks: (i) cross-linguistic investigations of G_Ls different from English to see to what degree the G_Ls proposed for English carry over to those of other natural languages and (ii) simplification and unification of G_Ls so as to make them more natural "fits" for FL. The second Generative epoch stretches from roughly the mid-1970s to the early 1990s. Within the Chomsky mentalist version of the Generative Grammar Program, the classical example of this kind of work is *Lectures on Government and Binding* (LGB; Chomsky (1981)). Our question in this section is: What did LGB accomplish and how did it do this?

LGB was a mature statement of the work that began with Chomsky's (1973) *Conditions on transformations*. This work aimed to simplify the rules that G_Ls contain by distilling out those features of particular G rules that could be attributed to FL more generally. The distilled features were attributed to FL as design features and were dubbed "Universal Grammar" (UG). The basic GB research strategy was to simplify particular G_Ls by articulating the innate UG principles of FL. Part of this consisted in categorizing the possible rules a G_L could contain. Part involved postulating novel theoretical entities (e.g. traces) which served two functions: (i) they allowed the T-rules to be greatly simplified and (ii) they allowed for a partial unification of two, heretofore distinct, parts of the grammar, namely binding and movement.

Articulating FL in this UGish way also had a natural acquisition interpretation relevant to addressing the fact of linguistic flexibility: in learning a particular G_L, the language acquisition device (LAD, aka the child) need "abstract"/"induce" only simple rules from the data, with the more recondite forms of knowledge attained by the child (that earlier theory had coded as part of a rule's structural description) now being traced to built-in (i.e. innate) structural features of FL (aka the principles of UG). As UG principles are innate, they need not be acquired and so are not hostage to the details of the PLD. That's the logic, and the program was to simplify language-specific rules by offloading many of their most intricate features to endemic properties of FL as embodied in principles of UG.

As noted, rule simplification has an appealing consequence for acquisition. As language-specific rules can (and do) vary, they must be learned. Thus,

1.4 Categorizing, Simplifying and Unifying Rules

simplifying them makes them easier to acquire, while enriching UG allows this simplification to occur without (it is hoped) undue empirical loss. That was the logic. Here are some illustrations.

LGB postulated a modular structure for natural language Gs with the following components and derivational flow.

(17) The LGB Grammar
  A Rule Types/Modules
   1. Base rules:
      a. X'-Theory
      b. Theta theory
   2. Movement rules (A and A')
      a. Subjacency theory
      b. Empty Category Principle (ECP)
   3. Case rules
   4. Binding rules:
      a. Principle A, anaphors
      b. Principle B, pronominals
      c. Principle C, R-expressions
   5. Control rules
  B. The Derivational Y-Model:

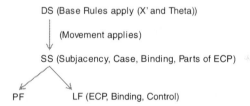

The general organization of the grammar, the 'Y'-model (17/B), specifies how/where in the derivation these various rules/conditions apply. The Base Rules (17/1) generate X'-structured objects (17/1a) that syntactically reflect "pure GF-θ" (17/1b) (viz. that all and only thematic positions are filled; so logical subjects and logical objects are, at DS, grammatical subjects and grammatical objects), creating phrase markers analogous to (but not exactly the same as) Deep Structures in the Standard (i.e. *Aspects*) theory. Targets of movement operations are positions generated by the X'-rules in the base which lexical insertion (LI) rules have not lexically filled.[26] The output of the base component (the combination of X'-rules and LI-rules) is input to the T-component,

---

[26] X'-theory eliminates PS-rules and substitutes the idea that syntactic structure is projected (according to the X' schema) from heads coded with the relevant subcategory and selection information. Prior theories of the base were redundant in that subcategorization restrictions were coded twice, once in the PS-rules and then again in the lexical insertion filters. X'-theory eliminates this redundancy.

the part of the grammar that includes movement operations (and that extends the derivation from DS to SS). At SS, various relations are licensed (case, binding, some ECP trace licensing conditions). Derivations then split, with the grammatical structure relevant to sound interpretation (the phonological form (PF)) separated from that required for meaning interpretation. The latter is then mapped via (possible additional) abstract movement rules (rules that have no overt phonetic realization) to logical form (LF), which is the phrase marker that codes the grammatical information relevant to meaning interpretation.[27]

Let's consider some of the key theoretical and conceptual innovations in the GB model.

Movement rules are entirely reconceptualized in LGB in two important ways. First, they are radically simplified. The simplification involves stripping movement of its constructional specificities (abstracting away from what was moved (e.g. a Topic, or a *Wh*-morpheme or a Focused element)) and distilling out the fundamental movement operation (dubbed "Move α"). The rule Move α can move any expression anywhere, subject to one restriction: all G rules, including Move α, are structure preserving in the sense that all the constituency present in the input to the rule is preserved/conserved in the output of the rule.[28]

In concrete terms, this preservation/conservation assumption motivates the second key innovation in LGB: Trace theory. Trace theory has two important *theoretical* consequences: (i) it is a necessary ingredient in the simplification of movement rules to Move α and (ii) it serves to unify movement and binding theory.

So, simplification, unification and conservation are all pressed into service in developing the GB theory of FL. Let's consider how unifying and simplifying earlier Standard Theory accounts of G operations gets us to a GB-like theory.

First the process of simplification: LGB replaces complex construction-based rules like Passive, which in the Standard Theory look something like (18), with the simple rule of "Move NP," this being an instance of Move α with $\alpha = NP$.

(18) $X - NP_1 - Y - V - NP_2 - Z \rightarrow X - NP_2 - be+en - V - by\ NP_1$
         (where NP_1 and NP_2 are clause-mates)

Move NP is simpler in three ways. First, (18) involves the movement of two NPs (note: the structural change on the right of the arrow differs from the

---

[27] A friend tells me that this paragraph is heavy lifting for the uninitiated. There are excellent texts that go into the details of how the model works. My preferred text is Haegeman (1991) and I recommend it for anyone wishing to get into the glorious details. Luckily, knowing these is unnecessary for understanding the main points of what follows.

[28] Up to adjunction, which can create some new structure. The exact nature of adjunction was and remains a thorny theoretical problem. I will ignore it here.

1.4 Categorizing, Simplifying and Unifying Rules

structural description on the left in that NP_2 has moved to near the front of the string from post-verbal position and NP_1 has moved from the left edge to the right and now forms part of a *by*-phrase). Passivization, when analyzed in Move α terms (aka Move NP when α = NP), involves two applications of the simpler rule rather than one application of the complex one. Second, (18) not only moves NPs around, but it also inserts passive morphology (*be* + *en*) as well as a *by*-phrase. Third, in contrast to (18), an application of Move α (where α=NP) allows any NP to move anywhere. Thus, the Move α analysis of Passive *factors out* the NP movements from the other features of the passive rule. This effectively eliminates the construction-based conception of rules characteristic of the earlier Standard Theory and replaces it with a far more abstract conception of a G rule; it effectively treats earlier construction-based rules as interactions and combinations of simpler ones.

These simplifications, though theoretically desirable, create empirical problems. How? Rules like Move NP left to themselves wildly overgenerate, deriving all sorts of ungrammatical structures (as we illustrate below).[29] GB addresses this problem in a theoretically novel way. It eliminates the empirically undesirable consequences by *enriching* UG. In particular, GB theory targets two related dimensions: it *simplifies* the rules of G_L while *enriching* the structure of FL/UG. Let's consider this in more detail.

Move α is the simplest possible kind of movement rule. It says something like "move anything anywhere." Languages differ in what values they allow α to assume, thus allowing for a natural locus of cross-linguistic variation. So, for example, English moves *Wh* words to the front of the clause to form interrogatives. Chinese doesn't. In English α can be *Wh*, in Chinese it cannot be. Or Romance languages move verbs to tense, while English doesn't. Thus in Romance α can be V, while in English it can't. And so on. Again, while so simplifying the rules has some appeal, the trick is to simplify without incurring the empirical costs of overgeneration. GB achieves this (in part) via Trace Theory, which is itself a consequence of the Projection Principle, a more general conservation principle that bars derivations from *losing* syntactic information. Here's the story.

---

[29] One mark of an ungrammatical structure is that the sentences that coincide with these structures are judged unacceptable. However, '(un)grammatical' is a predicate of syntactic structures (and it therefore carries theoretical content) while '(un)acceptable' is a descriptive predicate applied to data. These two terms are often used interchangeably, which can result in quite a bit of unnecessary confusion. Speakers don't have judgments concerning grammaticality, though they are expert concerning acceptability. What Chomsky discovered is that acceptability judgments by native speakers can be used to investigate the grammaticality of linguistic structures. But – and this is important – there are various sources for unacceptability besides ungrammaticality and the two notions need not swing together, though they often do (which is why querying for acceptability is an excellent source of data concerning grammaticality).

In the GB framework, Trace Theory implements the general computational principle that derivations be monotonic. For example, if a verb has a transitive syntax in the base, then it must retain this transitive syntax throughout the derivation. Or, put another way, if some NP is an object of a V at some level of representation, the information that it was must be preserved at every subsequent level of representation. In a word, information can be created but not destroyed; that is, G rules are structurally monotonic in the sense that the structure that is input to a rule is preserved in the structure that is output from that rule. Within GB, the name of this general computational principle is the *Projection Principle*, and the way it is formally implemented is via Trace Theory.

This monotonicity condition is a novelty. Operations within the prior Standard model are not monotonic. To illustrate, take the simple case of Raising to Subject, which can be schematized along the lines of (19):[30]

(19) X - T(ense)1 - Y - NP - T(ense)2 - Z → X - NP - T1 - Y - T2 - Z
(T2='to')

This rule can apply in a configuration like (20a) to derive a structure like (20b):[31]

(20) a. [$_{TP}$ [$_T$ present] [$_{VP}$ seem [$_{TP}$ John [$_T$ to] [$_{VP}$ like Mary]]]]
      b. [$_{TP}$ John [$_T$ present] [$_{VP}$ seem [$_{TP}$ [$_T$ to] [$_{VP}$ like Mary]]]]

Note that the information that *John* had been the subject of the embedded clause prior to the application of (19) is lost, as the embedded TP in (20b) no longer has a subject like it does in (20a).

As noted, Trace Theory is a way of implementing the Projection Principle. How exactly? Movement rules in GB are *defined* as operations that leave traces in positions from which movement occurs. Given Trace Theory, the representation of (20a) after Raising has applied is (21):

(21) [$_{TP}$ John$_1$ [$_T$ present] [$_{VP}$ seem [$_{TP}$ t$_1$ [$_T$ to] [$_{VP}$ like Mary]]]]

Here t_1 is a trace of the moved *John*, the co-indexing coding the fact that *John* was once in the position occupied by its trace. As should be clear, via traces, movement now preserves prior syntactic structure (the subject position in (20a) is retained in (21)). As noted, this kind of information-preserving

---

[30] Ditto with Passive. The Passive rule (18) syntactically detransitivizes a transitive verb, viz. the V in the structural output of the rule no longer has a direct object, though it did have one in deep structure. We leave the details as an exercise for those inclined to build up their syntactic muscles.

[31] More exactly, (20a) informs us that we can factor the string *present-seem-John-to-like-Mary* as X - T - Y - NP - T - Z (note X, Y, Z are null in this case) and so change it to a string that will have the structure in (20b) and so the factorization displayed on the right side of the arrow in (19).

1.4 Categorizing, Simplifying and Unifying Rules

principle (i.e. that grammatical operations cannot destroy structure) becomes a staple of all later theory.[32]

Trace Theory is GB's first step towards simplifying G rules. The second bolder step is to propose that traces require licensing, and the third boldest step is to execute this by using traces to unify binding and movement. Specifically, binding theory expands to include the relation between a moved α and its trace. Executing this unification, given other standard assumptions (particularly that D-structure represents pure GF-θ) requires rethinking binding and replacing construction-specific rules like Reflexivization in favor of a more abstract way of coding the anaphoric dependency. Again, let's illustrate.

Say we treat Raising as just an instance of Move α, then we need a way of preventing the derivation of unacceptable sentences like (22a) from sentences with the underlying structure in (22b).

(22) a. *John seems likes Mary
b. [$_{TP}$ [$_T$ present] [$_{VP}$ seem [$_{TP}$ John [$_T$ present] [$_{VP}$ like Mary]]]]

Now, given a rule like (19), this derivation is impossible. Note that the embedded T is not *to* but *present*. Thus, (19) cannot apply to (22b) as its structural description is not met (i.e. the structural description of (19) codes its inapplicability to (22b) thus preventing the derivation of (22a)).[33] But, if we radically simplify movement rules to "move anything anywhere" (i.e. Move α), the restriction coded in (19) is not available and overgeneration problems (e.g. examples like (22a)) emerge.

To recap, given a rule that simply says "Move NP," there is nothing preventing the rule from applying to (22b) and moving *John* to the higher subject position. The unification of movement and binding via Trace Theory serves to prevent such overgeneration. How? By treating the relation between a trace and its antecedent as syntactically identical to that between an antecedent and a reflexive anaphor. Specifically, if the trace in (23a) is a kind of "reflexive" then the derived structure is illicit as the trace left by movement is not bound. In effect, (23a) is blocked in basically the same way that (23b) is.

(23) a. [$_{TP}$ John$_1$ [$_T$ present] [$_{VP}$ seem [$_{TP}$ t$_1$ [$_T$ Present] [$_{VP}$ like Mary]]]]
b. [$_{TP}$ John$_1$ [$_T$ present] [$_{VP}$ believe [$_{TP}$ he-self/him-self$_1$ [$_T$ Present] [$_{VP}$ like Mary]]]]

Let's pause and revel (maybe even wallow!) in the logic on display here: If derivations are monotonic (i.e. obey the Projection Principle) then when move NP (i.e. Move α, with α=NP) applies it leaves a trace in the moved-from

---

[32] Indeed, the principle gets strengthened in one important way. Traces make way for copies, so that an occurrence of a moved expression replaces earlier traces. See Chapter 2 for discussion.
[33] Actually, the structure underlying (22a), but you get the point.

position thereby preserving the syntactic structure. Further, if the relation between a moved α and its trace is the same as an anaphor to its antecedent, then the licensing principles that regulate the latter must regulate the former.[34] So, *simplifying* derivations by making them monotonic and *unifying* movement and binding allows for the radical *simplification* of movement rules (i.e. to a Move α format) without *any empirical costs*. In other words, simplifying derivations, unifying the modules of the grammar (always a theoretical virtue if possible) serves to advance the simplification of its rules.[35] The GB virtues of simplification and unification are retained as regulative ideals in contemporary Minimalist thinking.

That's the basic idea. However, we need to consider a few more details, as reducing (23a) to a binding violation requires reframing the theory of binding. More specifically, it requires that we abstract away from the specifics of the binding constructions and concentrate on the nature of the relations they specify. Here's what I mean.

The Lees–Klima rule of Reflexivization contrasts with rules like Raising in that the former turns the lower "dependent" into a reflexive while the latter deletes it. Moreover, whereas Reflexivization is a rule that applies exclusively to clause-mates, Raising only applies between clauses. Lastly, whereas Reflexivization is an operation that applies between two identical lexical items (viz. two items introduced by lexical insertion in Deep Structure), Raising does not (in contrast to Equi, for example).[36] From the perspective of the Standard Theory, then, Raising and Reflexivization could not look more different and unifying them would appear unreasonable. The GB theory, in contrast, by applying quite generally to *all* nominal expressions, highlights the relevant *dependencies* that they can enter into (and that differentiate them) and does not get distracted by other (irrelevant) features of the constructions (like their differing morphology or even their formal etiology).

---

[34] Well, more specifically, the unification is possible if we reanalyze reflexivization as Principle A, as we do below. Pardon the imprecision.

[35] There was another interesting theoretical consequence of this rule simplification. Consider a sentence like (i):
 (i) John was believed (by Fred) to be intelligent.
Within the Standard Theory such a sentence raised a curious question: is (i) derived by Raising *John* or by Passivizing the sequence *(Fred) believed John* (which is part of the structure underlying (i))? Note that *John* is an embedded subject and so it has raised. But the predicate over which it has moved is passivized so it has also been passivized. So which is it? Given the replacement of construction-specific rules by Move α, the question disappears. Both Passivization and Raising are instances of Move α and so the problem of deciding disappears. This is a purely theoretical virtue of recasting the issues in GB terms. It answers a why-question by showing that correctly framed it is ill-posed. A confession: I *love* these kinds of explanations!

[36] Equi-NP Deletion (aka Equi) is the rule that underlies the derivation of sentences like (i), where the matrix subject is understood as determining that value of the embedded subject:
 (i) John tried to win (=John tried so that John wins)

1.4 Categorizing, Simplifying and Unifying Rules

Let me state this another way. The construction specificity of the rules in the Standard Theory has the consequence that most rules look formally different from one another. Thus, unifying Reflexivization and Equi or Equi and Movement does not seem particularly plausible when one considers the formal features of the rules. Only Trace Theory and the abstractions it introduces makes the potential similarities between these various constructions readily visible.

In particular, GB unifies movement and binding via Trace Theory by recasting the rule of Reflexivization. Recasting Reflexivization constructions as Principle A effects allows FL to treat the *relation* between the nominal that has moved and the trace left by this movement and the *relation* between the reflexive and the nominal that serves as its antecedent as the same relation. The GB accomplishes this by treating A-traces and reflexives as morphemes of the same kind, subject to the same licensing condition. Thus, critically, this unification requires moving from binding rules like Reflexivization to licensing conditions like Principle A. Let's consider how.

GB binding theory (BT) divides all nominal (overt) expressions into three categories and associates each with a licensing condition. The three are (i) anaphors (e.g. reflexives, reciprocals, PRO), (ii) pronominals (e.g. pronouns, PRO, pro) and (iii) R-expressions (everything else). BT regulates the interpretation and distribution of these expressions. It includes three conditions, Principles A, B and C, and a specification of the relevant domains and licit dependencies:

(24) GB Binding Principles:
 A. An anaphor must be bound in its minimal domain
 B. A pronoun must be free in its minimal domain
 C. An R-expression must be free

(25) α is the minimal domain for β if α is the smallest clause (TP) with a subject distinct from β.[37]

(26) An expression α is bound by β iff β c-commands α, and β and α are co-indexed.

These three principles together capture all the data we noted in (4)–(10). Let's see how. The relevant examples are recapitulated in (27). (27a,b,e,f) illustrate that bound reflexives and pronouns are in complementary distribution. (27c,d) illustrate that R-expressions cannot be bound at all.

(27) a. John$_1$ likes himself/*him$_1$
 b. John$_1$ believes Mary likes *himself/him$_1$

---

[37] Things can be (and are) more complex than this. What counts as a clause might differ (TP or CP) and one can extend BT to nominal domains as well with an extension of the notion "subject." We will put these complications aside here and assume that clause means TP.

        c. *I expect himself$_i$ to like John$_i$
        d. *He$_i$ expects me to like John$_i$
        e. John$_i$ believes *himself/he$_i$ is intelligent
        f. John$_i$ believes himself/*he to be intelligent

How does BT account for these data? Reflexives are categorized as anaphors and so subject to Principle A. Thus, reflexives must be bound in their minimal domains. Pronouns are pronominals subject to Principle B. Thus, a pronoun *cannot* be bound in its minimal domain. Thus given BT, pronouns and reflexives must be in complementary distribution.[38] This accounts for the data in the mono-clausal (27a) and the bi-clausal data in (27b). It also accounts for the data in (27f). The structure is provided in (28):

(28)   [$_{TP1}$ John Present [$_{VP}$ believe [$_{TP2}$ himself/he to be intelligent]]]

The minimal domain for *himself/he* is the matrix TP1. Why? Because of (25), which requires that the minimal domain for α must have a subject distinct from α. But *himself/he* is the subject of TP2. The first TP with a distinct subject is the matrix TP1 and this becomes its binding domain. In TP1 the anaphor must be bound and the pronoun must be free. This accounts for the data in (27f).

(27e) requires some complications. Note that we once again witness the complementary distribution of the bound reflexives and pronouns. The minimal domain should then be the embedded clause if BT is to explain these data. Unfortunately, (25) does not yield this. This problem received various analyses within GB, none of which proved entirely satisfactory. The first proposal was to complicate the notion 'subject' by extending it to include the finite marker (which has nominal *phi*/φ (i.e. person, number, gender) features).[39] This allows the finite T to be a subject for *himself/he* and their complementary distribution follows given the contrary requirements that A and B impose on anaphors and pronominals.[40]

Principle C excludes (27c,d), as in both cases *he/himself* binds *John*. (27c) also violates Principle A.

---

[38] Recall: This fact was also accounted for by the Lees–Klima theory surveyed in Section 1.1, albeit in a very different way. Effects constant, theories different. Just what we want.

[39] This effectively analogizes agreement markers to pronominals. Pronouns are also just bundles of person, number and gender features. Later approaches to binding were able to eliminate this assumption. See note 41.

[40] A later proposal (see Chomsky 1986a) suggested a more radical approach. Chomsky, following a proposal by Lebeaux, assumed that to be bound, reflexives must (covertly) adjoin to a position proximate to the antecedent (in this case matrix T, akin to what Romance reflexives do overtly). Such a movement is (plausibly) an ECP violation. Observe, that accommodating the data in this way effectively points to reducing binding to conditions on movement rather than movement to conditions on binding (see Hornstein (2008) for an elaboration of this idea, which, to be fair, has not received the traction Hornstein had hoped it would).

For what it is worth, neither the fix in the text nor the one in this note is without additional problems, but both serve for current purposes, which is to derive the contrast in (27e).

1.4 Categorizing, Simplifying and Unifying Rules

In sum, BT accounts for the same binding effects the earlier L&K theory does, though in a very different way. It divides the class of nominal expressions into three groups, abstracts out the notion of a binding domain, and provides universal licensing conditions relevant to each.[41] As with the GB movement theory, most of the BT is plausibly part of the native ("universal") structure of FL and hence need not be acquired on the basis of PLD. What the learner needs to determine (i.e. acquire) is what group a particular nominal expression falls into. Is *each other* an anaphor, pronominal or R-expression? Once this is determined, where it can appear and what its antecedents can be follow from the innate architecture of FL. Thus, BT radically *simplifies* FL by distinguishing what binding applies to from what binding is, and this has a natural interpretation in terms of acquisition: knowledge of what belongs in which category must be acquired, while knowledge of what the relevant categories are and how something in a given category behaves is part of FL and hence innate.[42]

With this as background, let's return to how GB allows for the unification of binding and movement via Trace Theory. Recall that BT divides *all nominal expressions* into three groups. Traces are nominal expressions (viz. $[_{NP}\ e]_i$) and so it is reasonable to suppose that they too are subject to BT. Moreover, as traces determine the θ-roles of their antecedents, they *must* be related to them for semantic reasons. This would be guaranteed were traces treated like anaphors falling under Principle A. This suffices to assimilate (23a) to (23b) and so it closes the explanatory circle.[43]

So, by generalizing binding considerations to *all* nominal expressions, and by recasting the binding theory so as to showcase binding domains and binding dependencies, GB makes it natural to unify movement and binding by categorizing traces as anaphoric nominal expressions (a categorization that would be part of FL, hence innate and so in no need of learning). So, simplifying derivations with the Projection Principle leads to Trace Theory, which in turn allows

---

[41] It is worth noting that the GB version of the binding theory requires no extrinsic ordering (i.e. stipulative ordering) of the operations that license reflexives and those that license pronouns. One can "apply" A and B in any order with the same results, in contrast to (8) and (9). As stipulation is never theoretically welcome, its elimination in the repackaging of the BT is a theoretical step forward.

[42] Chomsky has often noted that GB eliminates constructions as fundamental units of analysis. He is, once again, entirely correct. Note that both the simplification of movement and binding and their unification builds on distinguishing the relation itself (e.g. A-binding, *Wh*-movement) from the relata involved in the relation (a reflexive anaphor and its DP antecedent, a WH DP and the trace left behind). This is what frees GB operations from the constructional specificity of earlier Standard Theory rules and which allows for the unification of movement and binding central to the LGB theory. Thus, the elimination of constructions as fundamental units of analysis is key to GB's theoretical success.

[43] It was reasonably assumed that FL/UG categorized the various flavors of empty categories. Hence which category A-traces (under BT-A) or *Wh*-traces (under BT-C) fell into did not have to be learned as their categorization is given innately.

for the unification of movement and binding, which in turn leads to a radical simplification of movement transformations, all without any apparent diminution of empirical coverage.

Let me add one more point concerning linguistic flexibility: recall that one of the big questions concerning language concerns its acquisition by kids on the basis of relatively simple input. The GB story laid the foundations for an answer: The rules were easy to learn because where languages vary the differences are easy to acquire on the basis of simple PLD (e.g. is α = NP or V or *Wh* or …). GB factors out the *intricacies* of the Standard Theory rules (e.g. ordering statements and clause-mate conditions) and makes them intrinsic features of FL; hence a child can know them without having to acquire them via PLD. Thus, not only does GB radically simplify and unify the operations in the Standard Theory, a major theoretical accomplishment in itself, it also provides a model for successfully addressing what has been called "Plato's Problem": How does knowledge of Gs arise in native speakers despite the relative paucity of data available in the PLD to fix their properties? In other words, how can kids acquire Gs despite the impoverished nature of the PLD?

Let's end this section. We have illustrated how GB, building on earlier research (and conserving its discovered effects), constructed a more principled theory of FL. Though we looked carefully at binding and movement, the logic outlined above was applied much more broadly. Thus, phrase structure was simplified in terms of X'-theory (pointing towards the elimination of PS-rules altogether in contemporary theory) and island effects were unified under the theory of Subjacency. The latter echoed the discussion above in that it consolidated the view that T-rules are very simple and not construction centered. Rather constructions are complexes of interacting simple basic operations. The upshot is a rich and articulated theory that describes the fixed structure of FL in terms of innate principles of UG. In addition, the very success of GB theory opens a *further* important question for investigation. Just as research in the Standard Theory paves the way for a fruitful consideration of linguistic universals and "Plato's Problem," the success of GB allows for a consideration of "Darwin's Problem": How could something like FL have arisen in the species so rapidly and remained so unchanged since its inception? We turn to this in the next chapters, but first, as promised, a (by no means exhaustive) list of effects that sixty years of Generative Grammar research has unearthed.

1.5 Some Effects Generative Grammar Has Discovered over the Last Sixty Years

Here is a partial list of some of the effects that are still being widely investigated (both theoretically and empirically) within Generative research. Some of these effects can be considered analogous to "laws of grammatical structure"

1.5 Some Effects Generative Grammar Has Discovered

which serve as probes into the inner workings of FL. As in the case of L&K's binding proposal, the effects comprise both negative and positive data and they have served as explanatory targets (and benchmarks) for theories of FL.

These effects also illustrate another distinguishing mark of an emerging science. In the successful sciences, most of the data is carefully constructed, not casually observed. In this sense, it is not "natural" at all, but factitious. The effects enumerated here are similar. They are not thick on the conversational ground. Many of these effects concentrate on what *cannot* exist (i.e. negative data). Many are only visible in comparatively complex linguistic structures and so are only rarely attested in natural speech or PLD (if at all). Violations of the binding conditions such as *John believes himself is intelligent* are never attested outside of technical papers in Generative syntax. Thus, in Generative research (as in much of physics, chemistry, biology, etc.) much of the core data used to probe FL is constructed, rather than natural.[44] To repeat, this is a hallmark of modes of investigation that have made the leap from naturalistic observation to scientific explanation. The kinds of data that drive Generative work are of this constructed kind.[45]

Here, then, is a *partial* list of some of the more important effects that Generative Grammar has discovered.[46]

(29) A partial list of empirically discovered laws of grammar
   1. Island effects
      a. Weak island effects
      b. Strong island effects
   2. Crossover effects
   3. Control vs Raising effects
   4. Minimal distance effects in control configurations
   5. Binding effects (A-effects-B-effects)
   6. Cyclicity effects
   7. Principle C-effects: an anaphoric element cannot c-command its antecedent
   8. CED (condition on extraction domain) effects
      a. Subject condition effects
      b. Adjunct condition effects
   9. Fixed subject effects
   10. Unaccusativity effects
   11. Connectedness effects
   12. Obligatory control vs non-obligatory control effects
   13. The subject orientation of long-distance anaphors

---

[44] See Cartwright (1999) for discussion of this in the context of the "real" sciences.
[45] Constructed data are generally more robust than naturalistic data, as Cartwright (1999) observes. Furthermore, it allows for investigations to be more systematic by allowing researchers to put their own questions to nature and make it answer these rather than simply waiting until nature voluntarily gives up its secrets.
[46] For a similar annotated list, see D'Alessandro (2019).

14. Case effects
15. Theta Criterion effects (Principle of Full Interpretation)
16. NPI (negative polarity item) licensing effects
17. Phrasal headedness effects
18. Clause-mate effects
19. Expletive-associate locality effects
20. Parasitic gap effects
21. Pro-drop effects
22. ECP (Empty Category Principle) effects
23. Weakest crossover effects
24. Coordinate structure constraint
    a. ATB (across-the-board) effects
25. Ellipsis effects
26. A-movement/scrambling obviating WCO (weak crossover) effects
27. Intervention/minimality effects
28. Constituency effects
29. Scope reconstruction effects
30. Lexical integrity effects
31. Psych verb effects
32. Double object construction effects
33. Predicate-internal subject effects

As in the case of the L&K binding proposal outlined above, just describing these effects involves postulating abstract rules that derive natural language expressions and abstract structures that describe them. Thus, each effect comes together with sets of positive and negative examples and rules/restrictions that describe these data. As in any scientific domain, simply describing the effects already requires quite a bit of theoretical apparatus (e.g. what's an island, what's a deletion rule, what's the difference between A- and A'-movement, what's case, what's a clause, etc.). And, as is true elsewhere, the discovery of such effects sets the stage for the next stage of inquiry: explaining why we find these particular effects and seeing what these explanations can tell us about the structure of FL.

1.6 The Minimalist Program and a Novel Research Question

Where are we? Here is a quick recap.

First on the agenda was the problem of linguistic creativity, the fact that native speakers of a given language L have the capacity to understand an unbounded number of different expressions of L. This fact raised the obvious question: How is this possible? The answer: This capacity supervenes on having an internalized finitely specified G that recursively characterizes the linguistic objects of L. So, (part of) the explanation for the fact that native speakers are linguistically creative in their language L is to give a recursive characterization of what constitutes a possible object of L and treat this recursive specification as part of a native speaker's mental make-up.

1.6 The MP and a Novel Research Question

More specifically, we reviewed how the first period of syntactic research investigated how grammars might be structured so that they could generate an unbounded number of distinct hierarchically organized objects. The research strategy was to propose specific Gs for given Ls whose interacting rules yielded interesting empirical coverage, generating both a fair number of acceptable sentences and *not* generating an interesting number of unacceptable sentences. In the process, Generativists discovered an impressive number of effects that served as higher-level targets of explanation for subsequent theory. To say the same thing a little more pompously, early Generative Grammar discovered a bunch of "effects" which catalogued deep-seated generalizations characteristic of the products of human Gs. These effects sometimes fell together as "laws of grammar" taken to reflect the built-in design features of FL. More simply, these effects are plausible reflections of the properties of FL and so can be used to explore the structure of FL.

Or to say this slightly differently, the success in adumbrating properties of particular Gs led to a second further stage of research that built on this success, and which targeted a related, yet different, question: How must humans be built so that they can acquire Gs with the properties we discovered Gs to have? The project, in effect, comes down to specifying the class of possible human Gs.

Importantly, the project of adumbrating the range of possible Gs becomes fruitful once we have a budget of empirically plausible properties of actual Gs! Without some decent examples of actual Gs with their identified properties, it makes little sense to ask how to delimit such Gs. To say this another way, we need to *empirically* bound the domain of inquiry to make it tractable (and worth investigating), and this is why investigating the properties of FL (properties that will serve to limit the range of possible Gs) only becomes a fertile pursuit once Generativists have identified some features of actual Gs to serve as targets of explanation.

So, we have some empirically plausible features of Gs and we want a theory of FL (or UG) to explain why we find Gs with these properties and not others. Plato's Problem served as an additional boundary condition on this line of inquiry into FL/UG. Plato's Problem is the observation that what native speakers know about their languages far exceeds what they could have learned about it by examining the PLD available to them in the course of their G acquisition. Conceptually, addressing Plato's Problem in the context of a budget of identified G effects suggested a two-pronged attack: first, radical simplification of the rules that Gs contain, and second, enrichment of what FL/UG brings to the task of G acquisition. Eliminating the complexity built into *Aspects*-style rules and factoring out some simple very general operations like Move α made the language-particular rules that children acquired *easier* to acquire. This simplification, however, threatened generative chaos by allowing for massive overgeneration of ungrammatical structures. The theoretical task was to prevent this. This was accomplished by enriching the innate structure of FL/UG in principled ways. The key theoretical innovation was Trace Theory motivated by the idea that derivations are information preserving (monotonic). Traces simplified derivations by making them structure preserving, and this further allowed for the unification of movement and binding. These theoretical moves together addressed the overgeneration problem.[47]

This line of inquiry coalesced around a "standard" model of FL/UG (i.e. GB). In particular, GB provided a substantive model of FL/UG and thereby set the stage for contemporary minimalist investigations. More specifically, just as the success of early Generative inquiry into language-particular Gs allowed us to fruitfully address the question why we have *these* Gs and not others (answer: because we have a GBish FL/UG), adumbrating an empirically substantive conception of FL/UG now allows Generativists to ask the next obvious question: Why does FL/UG have *these* GBish properties and not others? Moreover, just as asking the question concerning the limits on human Gs would have been premature (and so idle) without first discovering some of the empirical features of actual Gs, so too investigating why we have the FL/UG we actually have (rather than another with other possible organizing principles) would have been premature without first having some reasonable empirically grounded theory of FL/UG like the one GB delivered.[48]

---

[47] A remark for the cognoscenti: The prettiest possible theory, one that Chomsky advanced in early GB, failed to hold empirically. The first idea was, effectively, to treat *all* traces as anaphoric. Though this worked very well for A-traces, it proved inadequate for A'-traces, which seemed to function more like R-expressions than anaphors (or at least the "argument" A'-traces did). A virtue of assimilating A'-traces to R-expressions is that it led to an explanation of strong crossover effects in terms of Principle C. Unfortunately, it failed to explain a range of subject–object and argument–adjunct asymmetries that crystalized as the ECP. These ECP effects led to a whole new set of binding-like conditions (so-called "antecedent government") that did not fit particularly comfortably with other parts of the theory. Indeed, the bulk of GB theory in the last part of the second epoch consisted in investigations of the ECP and various ways of trying to explain the subject–object and argument–adjunct effects. Three important ideas came from this work. First, that the domains relevant for ECP effects are largely identical to those relevant for subjacency effects. Second, that ECP effects really do come in two flavors, with the subject–object cases being quite different from the argument–adjunct cases. Third, relativized minimality. This was an important idea due to Rizzi (1990b), and one that fit very well with later minimalist conceptions. This said, ECP effects, especially the argument–adjunct asymmetries, have proven theoretically refractory and still remain puzzling, especially in the context of minimalist theory. Importantly, recent empirical work (see Lu et al. 2020) suggests that perhaps the argument–adjunct asymmetry does not exist, which would explain its refractory theoretical obstinacy. I discuss this further in Chapter 8.

[48] I am focusing on GB here because that is the theory whose basic properties the Minimalist Program (as I understand it) has tried to explain. However, there were many (putative) alternative conceptions of FL/UG developed in the period from the mid-1970s to the mid-1990s. In my opinion, these were far less different from GB than generally advertised (there is, after all, a premium gained by claiming novelty). However, the kind of argument outlined in the chapters that follow can be pursued using any of these conceptions of FL/UG, though, no doubt, the details will differ.

1.6 The MP and a Novel Research Question

I want to emphasize, re-emphasize and re-re-emphasize this point before getting into some details in the following chapters. I have often heard the claim that Minimalism offers nothing new to the Generative enterprise, methodologically speaking. I agree with part of this. Generative Grammar has always prized explanation, and so the hallmarks of explanation (i.e. deriving the properties one wants explained from simple, elegant, theories that derive them) have also always been valued. To wit: We *explain* the basic features of a given native speaker's linguistic productivity in L by showing how they result from a G_L that generates the unboundedly many different hierarchical <m,s>s characteristic of that L (or more exactly, that coincides with a native speaker's "sense" of L) and does not generate any pairs inconsistent with a native speaker's competence in L. Similarly, we *explain* why we find the G_Ls that are empirically attested by showing that our theory of FL/UG (e.g. GB) derives G_Ls with these properties and does not derive any without them. In both cases we prize simple elegant theories over more complex inelegant ones for the reasons that scientific inquiry has always prized the former over the latter. In the first two periods of Generative Grammar, the methodology remained constant, *even as the questions addressed changed*.

So too as regards the current minimalist stage of Generative inquiry. We still want simple, elegant theories, but now their derivational target is (roughly) GB and the laws of grammar (and concomitant effects) it adumbrates. These are what minimalist theories aim to explain. Or, to be more precise, we now want theories that derive the theoretical principles of GB and/or the associated effects that these GB principles aimed to explain. Note, we have the same methodological standards as ever (simplicity, elegance, naturalness), *but we are now entertaining a different explanandum*. Moreover, as we have noted above, targeting the principles of GB and its associated laws of grammar for explanation only really makes sense if we take GB to be reasonably well grounded, both empirically and theoretically.

Let me put this point more broadly: There is a reason Minimalism was a brainchild of the mid-1990s. **It took that long to make it a substantive project.** Minimalism awaited a plausible theory of FL/UG, which in turn awaited plausible Gs of particular Ls. And all of that took about forty years to develop. By the mid-1990s Generative Grammar had an empirically viable (though not perfect) theory of FL/UG (i.e. GB) and so it made sense to investigate its properties and ask why they are the way they are.

So, is Minimalism just the same old, same old or something new? And by now I hope you know the right answer: YES! It is both nothing new and something very different. That is what makes the Minimalist Program (MP) interesting.

1.7 The Minimalist Program: Explaining the Properties of GB

How should one go about explaining why FL/UG has the properties it does? By deriving them from simpler, more natural, more economical assumptions. And this entails assuming that whatever GB's merits, it is not the *fundamental* theory of FL. Standard methodological considerations lend credence to this last assumption. GB is simply too complex to be fundamental. And also too linguistically sui generic. Here's what I mean.

For Generativists, FL is a *human*-specific cognitive capacity. This entails that the human-specific linguistic capacity evolved from pre-human ancestors that were not linguistically proficient (at least not the way we are). In other words, FL, the capacity to acquire and deploy Gs, is cognitively novel in humans. In this evolutionary context, GB is a problematic account of FL's basic properties precisely because it is too "complex" and too linguistically specific. In particular, the more FL's properties are linguistically bespoke (rather than cognitively and computationally generic), and the more complex the internal organization of FL, the harder it is to explain how it arose from non-linguistic minds (i.e. minds bereft of FLs). Put more positively, the simpler the structure of FL, and the less linguistically specific its operations and principles, the easier it should be to explain how they could have arisen from a-linguistic minds. And this line of thought has an immediate consequence and suggests a concrete research program. The consequence is that though GB might be a good description of FL, it cannot be the *fundamental* theory of FL. The fundamental theory *must* be simpler and less linguistically specific. The program is to develop such a simpler theory that has (roughly) GB and its properties as limit consequences. Let's flesh these general points out bit.

Within GB, FL is both very complex and the proposed innate principles and operations are very linguistically specific. The complexity is manifest both in the overall modular architecture of the basic GB theory and in the specific principles and operations characteristic of each module. (30) and (31) reiterate the basic structure of the theory.

(30) a. X'-theory of phrase structure
      b. Case
      c. Theta
      d. Movement
          i. Subjacency
          ii. ECP
      e. Construal
          i. Binding
          ii. Control

1.7 The MP: Explaining the Properties of GB

(31)

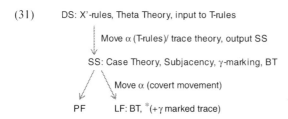

Though some critical relations crosscut (many of) the various modules (e.g. government), the modules each have their own special features. For example, X'-theory traffics in notions like specifier, complement, head, maximal projection, adjunct and bar-level. Case theory also singles out heads but distinguishes between those that are case assigning and those that require case. There is also a case filter, case features and case assigning configurations (government). Theta theory also uses government but for the assignment of θ-roles, which are assigned in D-structure by heads and are regulated by the Theta Criterion, a condition that requires every argument to get one and at most one θ-role. Movement exploits another set of concepts and primitives: bounding node/barrier, escape hatch, subjacency principle, antecedent government, head government, γ-marking, γ-checking and more. Last, the construal rules come in four different types: one for PRO, one for local anaphors like reflexives and reciprocals, one for pronouns and one for all the other kinds of DPs, dubbed R-expressions. There is also a specific licensing domain for anaphors and pronouns, indexing procedures for the specification of syntactic antecedence relations and hierarchical requirements (c-command) between an antecedent and its anaphoric dependent. Furthermore, all of these conditions are extrinsically ordered to apply at various derivational levels specified in the Y-model.[49]

If the information outlined in (30) and (31) is on the right track, then FL is richly structured with very domain-specific (viz. linguistically tuned) information. And though such linguistic specificity is a positive with regard to addressing Plato's Problem, it raises difficulties when trying to address Darwin's Problem. Indeed, the logic of the two problems has them largely pulling in opposite directions. A rich linguistically specific FL plausibly eases the child's task by restricting what the child needs to use the PLD to acquire. However, the more cognitively *sui generis* FL is, the more complicated the evolutionary path to FL. Thus, from the perspective of Darwin's Problem, we want the operations

---

[49] By 'extrinsically' we mean that the exact point in the derivation at which the conditions apply is empirically motivated but theoretically stipulated.

and principles of FL to be cognitively (or computationally) general and very simple. It is this tension that the Minimalist Program aims to resolve.

The tension is exacerbated when the evolutionary timeline is considered. The consensus opinion is that humans became linguistically capable about 100,000 years ago and that the capacity that evolved has remained effectively unchanged ever since.[50] Thus, whatever the addition to a-linguistic minds that made them "language ready," it must have been relatively minor (the addition of at most one or two linguistically bespoke operations/principles). Or, putting this another way, our FL is what you get when you wed (at most) one (or two) linguistically specific features with a cognitively a-linguistic generic brain.

Navigating the narrows between Plato's Problem and Darwin's Problem suggests a twofold strategy: (i) Simplify GB by unifying the various FL-internal modules and (ii) Show that this simplified FL can be distilled into largely general cognitive/computational parts plus (at most) one linguistically specific one.[51]

Before proceeding, please note yet again *that GB is the target of explanation*. In other words, the Minimalist Program takes GB to be a good approximate model of FL's fine structure. It is not fundamental, but it is still very good, in that Minimalism assumes that GB has largely correctly identified (and described) phenomena (laws) that directly reflect the innate structure of FL. If MP is realizable, then FL is less linguistically parochial than GB supposes, even though it has operations and principles of the kind that GB adumbrates. If MP is realizable, then FL exploits many generic operations and principles (i.e. operations and principles not domain restricted to language) in its linguistic computations and uses these for linguistic ends. On this view, Minimalism takes GB's answer to Plato's Problem to be largely correct though it disagrees with GB about how domain-specific the innate architecture of FL is. Borrowing terminology common in physics (perhaps grandiosely), Minimalism takes GB to be a good *effective* theory of FL but denies that it is the *fundamental* theory of FL. A useful practical consequence of this is to take the principles of GB to be targets for derivation by the more fundamental principles that minimalist theories will discover.

That's the program and that's how the Minimalist Program fits into the overall Generative research program. Has the program been successful? I believe it has been triumphantly so. I try to make this case in the chapters that follow.

---

[50] See Chomsky (2018) and references therein.

[51] We distinguish cognitively general from computationally general for there are two possible sources of relief from GB specificity. Either the operations/principles are borrowed from other pre-linguistic cognitive domains or they arise as a general feature of complex computational systems as such. Chomsky has urged the possibility of the second in various places, suggesting that these general computational principles might be traced to as yet unknown physical principles. However, for research purposes, the important issue lies with the non-linguistic specificity of the relevant operations and principles, not whether they arise as a result of general cognition/biology or natural physical law.

2 Tools and Particulars

2.0 The Generalizations Discussed in This Chapter

Here is a list of eight characteristic features of natural language Gs reflecting requirements of the FL/UG:

(1) a. Unbounded hierarchical recursion
  b. Binary branching
  c. Displacement (aka movement)
  d. Duality of interpretation: Gs generate natural formats for semantic interpretation (θ-roles and scope)
  e. Reconstruction/connectedness effects
  f. Movement targets c-commanding positions (e.g. no lowering rules, or sideward movement rules)
  g. Strict cyclicity
  h. G rules are structure dependent

2.1 The Merge Hypothesis

To this point we have discussed the broad goals of the Minimalist Program (MP) and shown how they fit with the overall Generative Program. Chapter 1 argued in detail that MP raises a novel question for consideration: Why does FL have the structure it has? Furthermore, Chapter 1 argued that it is only sensible to pose this question once earlier Generative questions have been (at least partially) answered. Once we have the outlines of FL's fine structure (and this is what GB provides), we can begin to sensibly ask why FL has *this* structure (incorporates *these* principles, operations and structures) and not another. In other words, given the success of GB (itself based on the success of earlier Generative inquiry), the time is right for a *program* of inquiry of the kind that MP proposes. In short, there is every reason to think that the question MP proposes is both well-posed *and* likely to lead to productive inquiry given its overall place in the larger Generative enterprise.

However, the real test of the fertility of MP (indeed of any program) lies not in the relatively abstract musings engaged in above but in the particular *theories* that MP considerations lead to. In particular, MP will be deemed successful to the degree that it leads to specific theories that derive the basic GB laws of grammar from simpler assumptions. Happily, MP has birthed such theories. The most prominent of these is the Merge Hypothesis (MH).[1]

Before getting into details it is important to appreciate what the MH is and how it relates to the MP. As noted, MP is a program, and as such is judged in terms of fecundity, not truth. MH, in contrast, is a theory and, as such, it aims for truth. We evaluate its verisimilitude by (in the first instance) seeing to what degree it can explain basic design features of FL as embodied in the GB laws of grammar. In short, MH is intended to be an explanation of why FL contains these kinds of laws.

Two more quick points and we begin. First, MH embodies a provocative theoretical intuition based on the observation that natural language generative procedures (grammars) are recursive. This, recall, is what underlies the obvious fact of linguistic creativity. MH builds on this observation by proposing that the correct explanation for the recursion found in natural language grammars will also serve to explain many (most? all?) of the other distinctive features that Generative inquiry has discovered them to have.

Second, MH assumes that the recursive operation that endlessly combines linguistic expressions is very very … very simple. We will see more precisely what this entails below.

If one combines these two assumptions, we get the broad outlines of MH: FL has the properties it has because the very simple combination operation that specifies the recursive nature of human Gs also delivers Gs with the other properties natural language Gs have. This is, to put it mildly, a very bold hypothesis. In this chapter we begin to show that this conjecture has legs.

In particular, this chapter argues that the "simplest" account of (1a) suffices to explain (1b–h). More specifically, MH postulates that FL/UG contains a very simple combination operation, Merge, that suffices to generate unboundedly many hierarchically structured objects (1a) and that these Merge-generated hierarchical structures come with the further properties (1b–h). The central theoretical idea is that the properties that make Merge a simple(st!) combination operation are the same properties that lead it to have the other listed characteristics. This chapter outlines how the logic of MH goes from (1a)

---

[1] This chapter is based on Hornstein (2017), which was an elucidation of Chomsky's conception of Merge. Thus, the version of MH you read here is not original with me (in fact, much of what you read in this book is not original with me!), though how I frame things might be somewhat different from the way Chomsky intended (though I hope not, as I was aiming for faithfulness). All of which is a long-winded way of saying that I should be the one you complain to if you *don't* like what follows and Chomsky should be credited if you do.

A friendly reviewer has pointed out that Epstein and his collaborators should be credited with first suggesting that Merge explain syntactic relations. This is correct. See Epstein (1999) and Epstein et al. (1998, 2015).

2.2 The Merge Hypothesis: Unbounded Hierarchical Objects

Unbounded hierarchy implies a recursive embedding procedure.[2] MH proposes that Merge is the requisite operation. The inductive definition in (2) uses Merge to recursively specify an unbounded domain of hierarchically structured *Syntactic Objects* (SOs). These SOs consist of lexical atoms (2a) and sets of sets of sets ... of these atoms ((2b) and (3)). The key theoretical idea behind MH is that (2) is about as "simple" an inductive definition as one could hope to find in that it exploits as simple a combination operation (Merge) as can be imagined.

(2) a. If α is a lexical item then α is an SO[3]
     b. If α is an SO and β is an SO then Merge (α,β) is an SO

(3) For α, β, SOs, Merge (α,β) → $\{\alpha,\beta\}$

The inductive step (2b) allows Merge to apply to its own outputs and thus licenses unboundedly "deep" SOs with sets contained within sets contained within sets ... within sets. The Merge Hypothesis is the conjecture that the "simplest" instance of this combinatoric operation (the minimum required to generate unboundedly many hierarchically organized objects) also generates objects with the other properties listed in (1). Thus *if* FL contains Merge and this is the sole recursive grammatical operation that FL allows, then we can explain why natural language grammars, being the products of FL, have the properties in (1).

The claim that Merge is the "simplest" combination operation and that the inductive definition in (2) that incorporates it is the minimum required to generate unboundedly many hierarchically structured objects is carrying a lot of weight here. It is thus fair to ask in what way Merge is the "simplest" combination operation and (2) is the sveltest way of getting unbounded hierarchy? Here is an attempt at an answer. Let's start with Merge.

---

[2] Recall that linguistic creativity implies recursive Gs, and linguistics has discovered ample evidence that G_1s can generate structures of arbitrary depth. This reflects the fact that native speakers are linguistically productive.

[3] The term *lexical item* denotes the atoms that are not themselves products of Merge. These roughly correspond to the notion *morpheme* or *word*, though these latter notions are themselves terms of art and it is likely that the naive notions only roughly correspond to the technical ones. Every theory of syntax postulates the existence of such atoms. Thus, what is debatable is not their existence but their properties.

The Merge operation directly and uniquely targets hierarchy by (i) specifying that two expressions form a unit and (ii) specifying nothing more than that they form a unit. In other words, Merge specifies the absolute minimum that a combination operation must specify if it is to be a combination operation at all. This very simple conception of combination has four consequences: (i) Merge-combined expressions are not ordered when combined by Merge, (ii) Merge in no way changes the properties of the atomic objects combined (Inclusiveness Condition), (iii) Merge in no way changes the complex objects combined (Extension Condition) and (iv) if, as seems natural, it takes at least two to "combine," then the simplest combination operation will combine two items (and no more).[4] Chomsky packages the Inclusiveness Condition and the Extension Condition together into the "No Tampering Condition" (NTC).[5] Thus, Merge recursively builds "binary branching" hierarchy (and only hierarchy) without "tampering" with the inputs in any way save combining them in a very simple way. It seems fair to say an operation that does nothing *but* combine pairs of objects without changing them in any way is simpler than an operation that combines objects *and does something else as well* (e.g. imposes a linear order on them) and one that combines the combinands and otherwise leaves them untouched is simpler than an operation that changes the objects it combines while combining them. Thus, it seems fair to say that Merge so understood is indeed a very simple combination operation and has fair claim to being as simple a combination operation as can be imagined, and thus, the inductive definition that incorporates it is a simple(st?)

---

[4] If one further assumes that the simplest operation does nothing more than conceptually required, then Merge will combine *at most* two expressions. I personally would not wish to put too much weight on this line of reasoning, but it has some attractions so I offer it here. Why the reticence? Because it might be argued that an operation that can combine arbitrarily many expressions into a unit is simpler than one that restricts the combination to two. One might. Is a screwdriver capable of screwing any of a dozen different screw heads simpler than one that can only apply to just a single head? I dunno (well actually, the multi-purpose screwdrivers I have seen are far more complex than the single screw head ones). However, to my mind, it is more convincing to observe that *any* adequate combination operation sufficient to deal with human natural language grammars must have the power to combine *at least* two expressions, and it is plausible that it needs no more. Does endowing the combination operation with greater latitude make it simpler even if that power is not conceptually required? Is a more abstract function that has a simpler function as a special case "simpler" than the special case function? I don't know, but it strikes me that there are grounds for doubting that it does. Again, that said, I do not place much weight on these ruminations except insofar as they aid in distinguishing 'generality' from 'simplicity,' a distinction I believe is worthwhile.

[5] Observe that Inclusion and Extension are not *conditions* on Merge. Rather they are properties of it. No Tampering is a property that expresses *how* a simple combination operation is simple. It is not a principle distinct from the operation that the operation obeys. Thus observing that merge "obeys" the NTC is just another way of saying it is simple, just as noting that it forms units from inputs is just another way of saying that it is a combination operation.

recursive definition sufficient to generating unboundedly many hierarchically organized objects.[6,7]

So Merge is simple. The chief theoretical insight of MH is that *if* FL has Merge as its primary generative mechanism, then FL will deliver language-specific G_Ls with properties (1a–g). And if this is right, it partially answers the question of *why* FL/UG has some of the properties we believe it to have. In other words, this would be a very nice result given the aims of the Minimalist Program (reviewed in the previous chapters). Let's see how Merge so conceived derives (1a–h).

2.3 Merge, Structure Building, and Unbounded Hierarchy

It should be clear that Gs with Merge can generate unbounded hierarchical dependencies. Given a lexicon containing a finite list of atoms α,β,γ,δ, ... we can, using the definitions in (2) and (3) form structures like (4).

(4)   a. {α, {β, {γ, δ}}}
        b. {{α, β}, {γ, δ}}
        c. {{{α, β}, γ}, δ}

Thus, we use (2) to generate (4a) as follows (the stuff in square brackets indicates the relevant parts of the definition):

(5)   a. Select γ,δ. Merge (γ,δ) → {γ,δ} [(2a) (3)]
        b. Select β, {γ,δ}. Merge (β, {γ,δ}) → {β, {γ, δ}} [(2b), (3)]
        c. Select α, {β, {γ, δ}}. Merge (α,{β, {γ, δ}}) → {α,{β, {γ, δ}}} [(2b), (3)]

The derivation involves selecting inputs and merging them. Note that the selected expressions retain their integrity in the outputs (i.e. their lexical and "constituency" properties) and, being formed into sets, no order is placed on the elements. Thus, for example, the set {α, {β, {γ, δ}}} and its mirror image {{{δ,γ,}, β}, α}) are identical sets.

This is just one example, but it should be clear that given the recursive nature of the operation as defined in (2), we can keep on going *ad libitum* (try it!). So Merge suffices to generate an unbounded number of hierarchically organized binary branching syntactic objects.

---

[6] In my opinion, MH does not require that Merge be the "simplest" possible operation. It suffices that it be natural and simple. The conception of Merge in (2) and (3) meets this threshold. Note that the hypothesis (in (3)) that Merge forms sets from inputs need not be freighted with much ontological significance. It is simply a way of formally reflecting the idea that Merge is a combination operation that targets hierarchy and obeys the NTC. Sets have the four features noted above and so are useful for representing what Merge does. Does this mean that phrase markers *are* sets or just that they are well represented as sets? I leave this question for budding philosophers, though see the appendix to this chapter for some discussion.

[7] Chapter 7 reconsiders this argument, without damaging the good work that Merge does theoretically and empirically.

Let's consider a less abstract example to illustrate how Merge functions to generate the requisite infinity of hierarchically structured objects. Consider the generation via Merge of sentences with complex subjects and objects like (6a), as in (6b–i).[8]

(6) a. The king of Georgia hugged the portrait of Lenin
 b. Select the SOs *of*, *Lenin* (both are lexical items and so SOs via (2a)). Merge them to the SO {of, Lenin} (licensed via (2b)).
 c. Select SO *{of, Lenin}* and the SO *portrait* to form the SO {portrait, {of, Lenin}}. [(2b)]
 d. Select the SO *the* and the SO *{portrait, {of, Lenin}}*. Merge them to yield the SO {the, {portrait, {of, Lenin}}}. [(2b)]
 e. Select the SO *hugged* and the SO *{the, {portrait, {of, Lenin}}}*. Merge them to yield the SO {hugged, {the, {portrait, {of, Lenin}}}} [(2b)]
 f. Select the SO *of* and the SO *Georgia*. Merge them to form the SO {of, Georgia} [(2a)]
 g. Select the SO *king* and the SO *{of, Georgia}*. Merge them to form the SO {king, {of, Georgia}} [(2b)]
 h. Select the SO *the* and the SO *{king, {of, Georgia}}*. Merge them to form the SO {the, {king, {of, Georgia}}} [(2b)]
 i. Select the SO *{the, {king, {of, Georgia}}}* and the SO *{hugged {the, {portrait, {of, Lenin}}}}*. Merge them to form the SO {{the, {king, {of, Georgia}}},{hugged, {the, {portrait, {of, Lenin}}}}} [(2b)]

This example should convince you that (2) and (3) suffice to generate unboundedly many hierarchically structured SOs with structures like those we find in natural language.

2.4 Merge and "Movement"

(2) and (3) also generate structures that model movement dependencies. Movement rules code the fact that a single expression can enjoy multiple relations within a sentence. Such dependencies are ubiquitous in natural language. So, for example, in questions like *Who did John say that Mary saw*, *who* is understood as both a variable binding question operator that scopes over the whole sentence and as the logical object of the embedded verb *see*. In other languages, elements are moved to indicate focus, topicalization, relative clause formation, comparative formation, and passivization, among other constructions.

Let's consider how movement structures might be formed using (2) and (3). Instead of deriving *Who did John say that Mary saw* (which I leave as an exercise for the reader) I will illustrate using αs and βs.[9]

---

[8] For simplicity I will treat each word as if it were an atom. We know that this is false, but it makes for easier reading. I also leave out mentioning (3) in every line of the derivation. (3) says that Merge forms sets and it applies to every step.

[9] A phrase marker is just a list of relations that the combined atoms enjoy. Derivations that map phrase markers into phrase markers allow an expression to have many different relations coded in the various dependencies it enters into in the varying phrase markers.

2.4 Merge and "Movement"

Here's how Merge generates movement dependencies: Given a structure like (7a) we can apply Merge to yield (7b) (as in (8)). Observe that in (7b), β occurs *twice*, once as a unit (binary set) with α and once as a unit (binary set) with $\{\gamma, \{\lambda, \{\alpha, \beta\}\}\}$. (7b) thus codes a movement dependency, as β is both sister of the SO α and sister of the derived SO $\{\gamma, \{\lambda, \{\alpha, \beta\}\}\}$.

(7)   a. $\{\gamma, \{\lambda, \{\alpha, \beta\}\}\}$
        b. $\{\beta, \{\gamma, \{\lambda, \{\alpha, \beta\}\}\}\}$

(8)   Select the SO $\{\gamma, \{\lambda, \{\alpha, \beta\}\}\}$ and the SO β (note: β is (within $\{\gamma, \{\lambda, \{\alpha, \beta\}\}\}$)). Merge them to form the SO $\{\beta, \{\gamma, \{\lambda, \{\alpha, \beta\}\}\}\}$

Note that this derivation presupposes that merging an SO does not rob it of its SO status. In other words, it assumes that once an SO always an SO. Thus, Merging an SO α to form part of a complex SO β that contains α does not change (tamper with) α's status as an SO. Consequently, because complex SOs are themselves composed of SOs and because SO-ness is preserved under Merge (a reflection of the NTC), Merge can licitly target a subpart of an SO for further Merging. This is how the NTC property permits Merge to generate structures with the properties of movement; structures in which an SO is a member of two different "sets."

There are (at least) two noteworthy features of the derivation in (8) and the one that underlies the derivation of (7a).

First, they illustrate one of the novelties of Merge-based approaches to structure building; ***it collapses the distinction between structure-building phrase structure rules and movement operations***. In virtually all earlier Generative theories of grammar (including GB, which, recall, we are taking as the target of explanation), phrase structures and movement dependencies are the products of two distinct kinds of rules.[10] For example, in all pre-MP accounts, phrase structure is the product of a context-free phrase structure (PS) component plus rules of lexical insertion that placed terminals into slots that the PS-rules made available.[11] In MP, they are different manifestations of the same operation (viz. Merge).

---

[10] Many current grammatical analyses also (implicitly) reject the unification, at least in part. At heart, the unification claims that local dependencies and non-local dependencies are products of the same generative procedure, i.e. Merge. Many contemporary accounts, in contrast, treat long-distance dependencies as effectively non-local feature-checking operations discharged by Probes inspecting the features of goals, while local feature checking piggybacks on Merge and does not involve an additional Probe/Goal operation. Movement on these approaches is, thus, a secondary process, additional to the feature checking itself, and some feature checking executed by the Probe on the goal is a different operation from the Merge operation that moves the checked element. In other words, (non-local) long-distance dependencies are different in kind from (local) phrase-building dependencies in that they involve an extra operation that does the grammatical heavy lifting. Thus my claim that the unification is set aside in such theories. The reader has likely (correctly) deduced that I believe this to be against the spirit of unification in MP and that it should be only reluctantly embraced. See Hornstein (2008) for some more discussion.

[11] For example, X'-theory assumes that there are distinctive phrase-building operations that project syntactic structure from heads following the X' template and inserting specifiers, complements and adjuncts into allowable "slots" in the projected templates.

Second, Merge so conceived *collapses the difference between phrase-building PS-rules and lexical insertion (LI) rules.* Let me explain.

In prior theories, PS-rules generated syntactic structures that lexical insertion (LI) rules lexically populated. The combination of these two different D-structure operations yielded phrase markers (PMs) with lexical terminals. These PMs were then manipulated by another set of operations (i.e. Transformations). We noted that MH eliminates the distinction between PS-like structure-building rules and movement transformations. However, it also unifies structure building and lexical insertion. The inductive definition in (2) builds complex structure from SOs, *some of which are lexical terminals.* However, there is no special rule of lexical insertion (though there is a base step that mentions terminals) that applies to populate "empty" syntactic structures with lexical contents. In effect, the Merge rule in (2)/(3) eliminates the structure/content distinction characteristic of earlier theories of phrase structure (including the X' version in GB).

And this is important. Why? Because one important technical feature of grammars that generate structure using the GB dual rule approach is that they distinguish a lexical terminal from the position that it occupies. This distinction is no longer viable in Merge-based accounts. And this has significant empirical/theoretical consequences, one of which is that *MH eliminates traces as definable grammatical constructs.* Thus, MH eschews traces. We return to this anon.[12]

As noted, MH collapses structure building (previously the province of phrase-structure rules) with movement dependencies (previously the province of movement transformations) and treats them as two possible outputs of Merge, a single basic operation. This has a very nice consequence for Darwin's Problem: *If* the emergence of grammar in humans is a function of the biological emergence of Merge, then we would expect the grammars that became cognitively available to humans to have *both* the capacity to form complex hierarchical (local) phrase structure relations *and* the capacity to establish (non-local) movement dependencies. Get one, get the other. In theories of grammar that treat the former as the province of phrase structure rules and the latter as due to transformations like Move α (e.g. as in GB) then

---

[12] More specifically, it eliminates the conceptual grounds for defining traces as G-internal objects. Traces, recall, are simply categories without lexical content (i.e. $[_x\ e]$, read as category of type 'x' without lexical content (i.e. 'e' = 'empty')). This is a definable construct in a theory that distinguishes structure building from lexical insertion as it can rely on a structure/content distinction to define traces (and PRO as well, as discussed in Chapter 4). Eliminate the structure/content distinction (as the definition of Merge does in (2/3)) and traces can no longer be defined as grammar-internal constructs. At best, they can be modeled as special kinds of lexical atoms. So in $[_x\ e]$, 'e' would name an atom (as 'dog' does) rather than marking the absence of an atom (as standardly assumed within Trace Theory). It is worth observing that GB rejected the latter option of treating traces as special lexical atoms.

2.4 Merge and "Movement"

explaining how natural language grammars came to have *both* phrase building and movement operations involves explaining how *two* different kinds of rules arose.[13] But, if both kinds of structures are merely different products of the same operation (i.e. Merge), then one need only explain how (2)/(3) arose to get both kinds of grammatical objects (both constituents and chains) in natural language grammars. On the plausible assumption that explaining how two different kinds of grammatical operations arose in our ancestors is more demanding than explaining how one did, then the unification of phrase building with movement is a nice feature of the Merge operation defined in (2) and (3) above.

Though constituents and movement dependencies (aka chains) are outputs of the same operation, it is useful for many expository purposes to distinguish these two applications of the operation. Following standard practice, I will call the phrase structure-building instance of Merge "E-merge" and the movement instance of Merge "I-merge." However, **to repeat** (while loudly banging fist on table), these do not name two distinct operations but denote two possible applications of the same operation.

A codicil to the reasoning deployed here: It derives the observed unification by assuming that Merge is as simple as stated in (2)/(3) above. It *is* possible to complicate the definitions so that structure building and movement are formally distinguished. However, this would require conceptually *complicating* the Merge operation (i.e. by adding further conditions on Merge so as to distinguish E- from I-merge). So, for example, one could stipulate that phrase building involves only SOs that are not in a containment relation while movement is defined as applying to SOs one of which is contained in the other. One *could* do this. One *could* complicate the definition of Merge so as to formally distinguish phrase structure building from movement. Or, to put this positively, keeping the Merge operation conceptually svelte allows for the unification of structure building and movement and to thereby explain why these two kinds of operations grammatically swing together in natural language (recall: get one, get the other). This then becomes a high-level *empirical* argument for favoring conceptual simplicity. Why so? Because insisting on simplicity allows these two kinds of dependencies to be unified and this unification *in the context of Darwin's Problem* is an empirical argument in favor of such conceptual simplicity.

---

[13] This is not quite right: Early minimalist theory treated movement as the combination of two more primitive rules, Merge and Copy. Some (e.g. yours truly) proposed that Copy was an operation available pre-linguistically. If so, then adding Merge alone to a primate's pre-linguistic repertoire would *in combination with its pre-linguistic powers* suffice to make movement available. That said, the unification of phrase structure and movement under Merge is, in my view, a far more elegant way of deriving this effect.

Let me re-emphasize one point before moving on: The key conceptual feature that allows Merge to generate movement dependencies is the "once an SO always an SO" assumption. And this follows from the more basic assumption that Merge is simple in that it does *nothing more* than take SOs and form them into units, otherwise leaving the combining objects unaltered. Thus, if some expression is an SO before being merged with another SO, then it will retain this property after being Merged, given that Merge in no way changes the properties of the combining expressions save for combining them. NTC (specifically the Inclusiveness and Extension Conditions) leaves all properties of the combining expressions intact. So, if α has some property before being combined with β (e.g. being an SO), it will have this property after it is combined with β. As being an SO is a property of an expression, merging it will not change this and so Merge can legitimately combine a subpart of an SO to its container.[14]

2.5 The Duality of Semantic Interpretation

Let's continue. As should be clear, Merge-generated structures like those in (5) and (8) also provide all we need to code the two basic types of semantic dependencies: predicate-argument structures (i.e. thematic dependency) and scope structure. Let me be a bit clearer. The two basic applications of Merge are those that take two separate SOs and combine them and those that take two SOs with one contained in the other and combine them. The former, E-Merge, is fit for the representation of predicate-argument (aka thematic structure). The latter, I-Merge, provides an adequate grammatical format for representing operator-variable (i.e. scope) dependencies. There is ample evidence that Gs code for these two kinds of semantic information in simple constructions like *Wh*-questions. Thus, it is an argument in its favor that Merge as defined in (2) and (3) provides a syntactic format for both. An argument saturates the predicate it E-merges with and scopes over the SO it I-merges with. If this is correct, then Merge provides the wherewithal for explaining (1c) (displacement, aka movement).

Let's add a little illustrative meat to these bare bones. There are two basic requirements for an adequate syntax of logical form. First, it must be able to

---

[14] Note that, as stated, there is no restriction on what expressions Merge can combine. As noted in the text, restricting Merge to non-embedded expressions allows one to rip apart what the simple definition of Merge has unified. However, this requires *complicating* the Merge operation (e.g. by limiting what can be selected to unmerged elements) and so is to be avoided if possible. Of course, simple operations always threaten to overgenerate. The question then becomes whether complicating an operation is conceptually worth the price of empirical coverage. For now, I assume that complicating Merge is not. That said, it is possible that derivations are more complex than here assumed and that operations are restricted in what they can select for merging and how they Merge them.

2.5 Duality of Semantic Interpretation

code for thematic structure. Second, it must offer a format for the representation of scope. Merge in its E and I versions does this.[15] Let's see how.

First thematic structure: since the earliest days of the Generative Program, thematic dependency has been coded in terms of sisterhood. We can, not surprisingly, reconstruct the notion "sister-of" in Merge-generated PMs. Thus two SOs α and β are sisters just in case they are members of the same sets. So, α is a thematic dependent of β just in case β is a thematic assigning head and α is sister to β. For example, in (9b), when *a bagel* E-merges with *eat* the resulting structure is one in which *eat* and *a bagel* are sisters: *{eat, {a, bagel}}*. Thus, the classical idea that θ-roles are discharged under sisterhood translates directly into the claim that θ-roles are discharged/assigned under (E)-merge (again modulo the caveat in note 15).

(9)   a. John ate a bagel
        b. {John, {Past, **{eat, {a, bagel}}**}}

Next, scope structure. This is easily coded in terms of I-merge. Take a typical question as illustration.

(10)   a. What did John eat
       b. {**what**{John, {Past, {eat, **what**}}}}

The syntactic structure in (10) lends itself to a trivial mapping into an operator-variable format wherein we can represent the scope of the question operator and the variable it binds. Following standard assumptions, we assume that an expression α scopes over what it c-commands.[16] Thus in (10b) *what* scopes over *{John, {Past, {eat, what}}}* and the copy of *what* in the θ-position

---

[15] Well almost. Here are two points that I discuss in later chapters. First, for the internal argument, it is quite straightforward. Less so for the external argument. For E-merge to work its magic in the latter case requires introducing labels, which we do in Chapter 3. For now, we concentrate on θ-marking the internal argument. Second, that E-merge supports the syntax of θ-marking does not mean that I-merge cannot license θ-marking (see Chapter 4). Nor does the fact that I-merge is typically pressed into service to explain what θ marks what mean that it cannot be useful in demarcating scope. I argue in later chapters that I-merge can license θ-marking in construal configurations. It is also obvious that E-merge can license scope relations (e.g. a propositional attitude verb will scope over the clause that it E-merges with). Thus, E-merge and I-merge are necessary to syntactically underwrite θ and scope relations, but this does *not* imply that all θ-relations are licensed under E-merge and all scope relations under I-merge. Indeed, given that E- and I-merge are mere outward manifestations of the same operation, it would be somewhat surprising to discover that E-merge could not license scope relations or that I-merge could not license θ-relations.

It is worth noting here that this view of E- and I-merge and its relation to the duality of interpretation is contrary to one that Chomsky seems to hold. He restricts θ-marking to E-merge, thereby preventing the analysis of binding and control discussed in Chapter 4. Rest assured that we will get to that.

[16] We can define c-command easily as well: α c-commands β just in case β is sister of α or is contained within a sister of α. As we shall see, the c-command restriction on movement follows from the NTC properties of Merge.

is interpreted as the variable that the copy in sentence-initial position binds. Thus, I-merge (like movement before it) can generate phrase markers that can serve as adequate formats for the coding of operator-variable dependencies.

Interestingly, just as (E-)merge provides structures respecting sisterhood, (I-)merge, as we shall demonstrate shortly, always generates structures in which the moved expression moves to a c-commanding position. In other words, the two applications of Merge can support θ-assignment and scope marking in virtue of generating structures that code for the properties of sisterhood and c-command, the first undergirding θ-assignment and the second scope.[17]

Chomsky has frequently noted the "dual aspect" of semantic interpretation (i.e. the fact that natural language grammars code for both thematic and scope information). Earlier Generative theories tracked this using two kinds of rules. Phrase structure rules plus lexical insertion coded thematic dependencies. Movement coded for scope in that the chains generated were very transparently understood in operator-variable terms. It is a virtue of the very simple Merge operation outlined in (2)/(3) that it suffices to offer ways of grammatically coding this duality without resorting to two different kinds of generative procedures. In other words, embodied in the very simple Merge operation is the capacity to generate syntactic formats sufficient for coding the two aspects of semantic interpretation that human grammars care about.

2.6 Copies and Reconstruction

The above (I-)merge analysis of movement is quite different from earlier Generative theories. One salient difference is that the (I-)merge analysis *entails* the Copy Theory of Movement (CTM). In particular, I-merge leaves copies of the "moved" (I-merged) expression in its wake. So, in contrast to GB, which incorporated traces into the definition of Move α, MH eschews traces entirely and generates chains whose links are copies. Indeed, as noted above, traces are not easily replicated in a Merge-based grammar. Let me elaborate these condensed claims.

GB accounts treat movement dependencies as the product of a dedicated movement operation, Move α, that (i) displaces the moving expression to some other position in the phrase marker and (ii) leaves a "trace" in the position from which the movement originates. As noted in Chapter 1, Trace Theory is motivated by a "conservation principle" (viz. the Projection Principle) that requires derivations to preserve syntactic information. Thus, traces serve to preserve the argument structure properties of a predicate (which are coded in D-structure) at

---

[17] To my knowledge, Epstein (1999) is the first paper that highlights the tight connection between Merge and c-command, albeit discussing a slightly different conception of Merge.

2.6 Copies and Reconstruction

every later level of the derivation. This, recall, is a GB innovation and contrasts with earlier Generative theories (e.g. the Standard Theory) where, for example, a predicate's transitivity information is not preserved in the derived PMs that are outputs of transformations like Passive and Raising.

Traces have several salient properties. They are phonetically silent formatives that mark the launch site of a moved expression.[18] However, though phonetically silent, traces are far from semantically mute. In particular, movement dependencies display well-studied connectedness effects wherein a displaced element can act "as if" it is still in one of its earlier derivational positions. Consider two examples for illustration.

Examples like (11a) have derived structures (roughly) like those in (11b) in GB and (11c) in a Merge-based system.

(11)   a. A unicorn seems to be on the roof
        b. [[A unicorn]$_1$ seems [t$_1$ to be on the roof]]
        c. {{a unicorn}, {seems, {{a unicorn}, {to be on the roof}}}}

Interestingly, the most natural reading of such sentences gives *a unicorn* a non *de re* reading, which naturally follows if it sits within the scope of (i.e. is c-commanded by) *seem*.[19] This requires that *a unicorn* be interpreted inside the complement clause of *seem* rather than in its phonetically overt matrix subject position. (11b) can support such a reading if we assume that traces can serve as interpretive proxies for their antecedents; for example, if we assume that there is an interpretive process wherein an expression can be interpreted in any of its trace-indexed positions. This would allow *a unicorn* to be interpreted in the position of t_1 and so be understood as in the scope of *seem*.

GB-style accounts that code movement via traces as in (11b) can execute this proxy function in several different ways. One is to have explicit rules of reconstruction whereby antecedents can be interpreted in any of their indexed positions. Another is to restate the rules of scope and binding so as to apply to chains rather than lexical items in specific positions. In retrospect, it is evident that these theoretical complexities arise within GB primarily in response to the technical fact that traces are structurally distinct from the expressions that antecede them. ***Were traces identical to their antecedents, the fact that traces can share the contents of their antecedents would trivially follow.***

---

[18] Technically, a trace is a grammar-internal formative defined as [$_\alpha$ e]$_1$ (e = empty, 1 = index of moved element). In effect, traces are syntactic categories without lexical content indexed to another expression. Within GB, these are natural enough constructs given the distinction between a lexical item and the position that it fills, a distinction that the division of labor between PS- and LI-rules supports. But, as noted earlier, this is *not* a distinction that survives the unification of these two rule types within Merge.

[19] Thus, the sentence is most naturally interpreted as saying that it seems that there is a unicorn on the roof, and not saying that there is a unicorn which seems to be on the roof. Why? Because there are no unicorns so the second *de re* reading is less natural than the first *de dicto* reading.

This is easy enough to see in (11c), a phrase marker generated by several iterations of Merge, the final application (I-)merging (aka moving) *a unicorn* to the head of the clause. Note that I-merge codes movement as a relation between copies. For the *de dicto* reading of (11a), the lower instance of *a unicorn* is the copy relevant for interpretation. In other words, because the MH version of movement based on Merge embodies the copy theory it can explain why traces can act *as if* they have the semantic contents of their antecedents. Why? Because traces *are* copies and so *do* have the contents of their antecedents.[20] Or, to put this another way, connectedness effects like those in (11) show that traces are not semantically null, though they are phonologically unpronounced, and MH, because it embodies the CTM, neatly ties together the facts concerning reconstruction and movement.[21]

Here's a second example. Reflexives (e.g. *himself*) need grammatical antecedents. These antecedents must be local and, important in what follows, must c-command the reflexive they antecede. Given this, sentences like (12) are problematic as *Peter* does not c-command *himself* in the derived structure. However, given a Merge-based treatment of movement, the structure of the question in (12a) is (12b). (12b) contains a copy of the moved expression in a position c-commanded by *Peter* and this copy can be used to license the relevant binding relation of the reflexive to *Peter*.[22]

(12)   a. Which picture of himself did Sara say that Peter loved?
        b. {{which picture of himself}, {Sara said that Peter loved {which picture of himself}}}

So, if we understand Merge to be an operation that creates syntactic objects as per (2)/(3) and movement is an instance of Merge, then copies of a moved expression must occupy its movement sites. And this is a theoretical virtue as connectedness effects provide evidence that natural language displacement operations show these effects and so act *as if* the launch site of movement is occupied by an expression with the same contents as the element that moved from said position. Put more simply, copies are what we want to explain connectedness

---

[20] More exactly, "copies" can be understood as "occurrences" of an expression. Thus, I-merge generates structures where an expression has multiple occurrences.

[21] An industry has arisen trying to explain why not all copies are pronounced (or, similarly, why not all copies are semantically interpreted), something that did not have to be explained in GB as this property of traces was simply *stipulated* to hold. Notice that such a stipulation cannot *explain* why traces are phonetically null (or why only one copy is semantically interpreted). Stipulations *never* explain. Indeed, one of the virtues of Merge-based theories of movement is that they have revealed some of the stipulations we took for granted in GB. Furthermore, the combination of the CTM and the idea that languages differ as to which copies can get pronounced lends itself to empirically novel predictions, many of which appear to be correct. We return to this in Chapter 4.

[22] In other words, (12) is acceptable with the relevant reading for the same reason that (i) is:
(i) Sara said that Peter loves this picture of himself.

2.6 Copies and Reconstruction

effects and the structures delivered by (2) and (3) *necessarily* code movement via copies and so allow for a simple account of such connectedness effects.

It is worth asking at this point what *feature of* (2)/(3) necessarily delivers the Copy Theory of Movement. It's the MH conjecture that Merge is the simplest possible combination operation and thus incorporates the No Tampering Condition, and thus the Inclusiveness Condition as a special case of the No Tampering Condition. In other words, Merge (α, β) yields {α,β} with α, β *otherwise unchanged.* Let's hammer this point home by considering how the NTC subsumes the CTM by comparing its operation with the Move α alternative.

To fix ideas, consider how we might code GB-style traces into a Merge-based account. Here's one way. We could treat I-Merge as a composite operation that first (I-)Merges the SO and then replaces it with a trace. So, returning to our original example, a GB version of Merge could add line (13c), where "$t_β/β$" means "replace β with trace of β."[23]

(13)   a. {γ, {λ, {α, β}}}
        b. {β, {γ, {λ, {α, β}}}}
        c. {β, {γ, {λ, {α, $t_β$/β}}}}

Clearly, on this coding, the Merge-based account that incorporates the CTM is "simpler" in that it does away with step (13c). The theory that encodes the CTM is also simpler in that it does not introduce new *formatives* into the derivation. GB traces are not copies. They are grammar-internal expressions distinct from the SOs that they are traces of. The Inclusiveness Condition (IC) prohibits the introduction of new formatives in the course of the derivation. So IC embodies the claim that grammatical operations that *do not* introduce new elements are "simpler" than those that do. As traces are by-products of G rules (like movement) then theories of movement that eschew traces in favor of copies are simpler than those that do not. Why? Because they do not change their inputs in any way.[24]

---

[23] There are other ways of incorporating Trace Theory. So we can think of movement as an operation that moves the contents of one category into another category in a structure-preserving manner. This is how substitution operations were actually defined, thus having movement vacate a phrase leaving behind the phrasal shell with no lexical content: [$_α$ e]. However, as noted previously, the distinction between an expression's position and its content is not available in a Merge-based theory and so the standard GB account cannot actually be incorporated into MH as is. Or, to put this more correctly, the simplest conception of Merge does not allow for a content/structure distinction so leaves no theoretical room for traces. And this, the argument above argues, is empirically the correct conclusion. Niiiiccce!

[24] Traces are reasonably natural constructs within GB for, as the discussion in notes 19 and 24 highlights, they exploit the GB distinction between an expression and a position that the phrase structure component coded. As noted in §2.4, MH eliminates the distinction by unifying structure building and lexical insertion, thereby banishing traces from the natural inventory of grammatical objects. The moral is clear (at least to me): *Radically simplifying* the combination operation severely reduces the inventory of possible theoretical constructs. As we will see in Chapter 4, PRO will suffer a similar fate within MH, and for roughly the same reason.

Compare the CTM and Trace Theory from a slightly different perspective. The latter is ontologically more expansive than the former in that it postulates a novel *kind* of theoretical object to code displacement. As is true for all such theory-internal objects, it requires empirical justification. Hence, *all things being equal*, if copies can do what traces do then swapping copies for traces is preferred as it does not require enriching grammatical ontology. However, things are not equal. The simpler option is also the superior one empirically. Given that natural languages display reconstruction effects, a theory of movement that incorporates traces must incorporate specific reconstruction rules to track such effects. So complicating the basic ontology with traces requires complicating the inventory of grammatical operations by adding a kind of rule that undoes what movement produces. Of course, this can all be avoided if we simply eschew traces and adopt the CTM and, happily, the CTM is a consequence of how Merge is defined. So, not only is the CTM preferable to Trace Theory, *all things being equal*, it is considerably better than that!

There is still another way to make the same point. Recall that traces in GB are motivated by the general idea that derivations are syntactically information preserving (i.e. the Projection Principle). So whatever information has been coded at an earlier derivational level is available at all later ones. Traces preserve the idea, for example, that if a predicate has an object at D-structure this information is preserved at S-structure and logical form (LF) by leaving a trace of the object in the object position. MH *strengthens* this assumption: Not only is the fact that a moved object was in a certain position prior to movement coded, the contents of that phrase in that position are preserved as well. So, whereas a trace in the object position of 'loved' in (12a) preserves the fact that 'loved' is transitive, a copy does this and also preserves the information that its complement contained a reflexive.

So IC embodies a *stronger* conservation condition than GB does. Moreover, it does so *intrinsically*. Here's what I mean. IC is not some condition *additional* to Merge; rather, IC embodies the principle that operations that do not "change" their inputs in any way are simpler than those that do. NTC, then, is a constitutive feature of simple operations, and Merge being simple embodies it. Thus, (I-)merge, by virtue of being simple, embodies NTC, which in turn entails IC, which in turn entails the CTM, which in turn provides the wherewithal to explain reconstruction effects. Yay![25]

---

[25] Note that I have not said that Merge via CTM explains *particular* reconstruction effects. These differ cross-linguistically and so should not follow from a theory of FL/UG. Rather, what CTM explains is the *possibility* of such effects. Moreover, it circumscribes the envelope within which such effects will arise: Reconstruction can occur where a copy from movement can appear. However, this still leaves open the question of determining which copies get semantically interpreted, analogous to the question of which copies get pronounced. The former issue is illuminatingly discussed in Sportiche (2005, 2017). For the latter, see Nunes (2004).

2.6 Copies and Reconstruction

In sum, there are good reasons to go with a Merge account of movement that embodies the CTM. There is a good sense in which such a theory of movement is simpler in that it incorporates the NTC, and generative procedures that are NTC compliant are less computationally or conceptually involved than those that are not. In sum, the CTM follows from the *simplest* conception of Merge, one that intrinsically incorporates the NTC.[26]

Finally, let me put this one last way. Generative grammar has shown the need for a system that generates unboundedly many hierarchically organized G objects. Every G ever proposed does this by combining atoms into more elaborate G structures. Thus, every theory of G has some "combination operation" that takes atoms and puts them together in larger structures. Merge is plausibly the simplest such combination operation as it arguably does *nothing but put (two) expressions together*. It doesn't put them in any particular order and it does not change them in any way in putting them together (e.g. it preserves their lexical and structural integrity while putting them together). In other words, *all* Merge does is combine them. In this sense, it is the simplest possible combination operation. What is intriguing is that this very simple operation when part of an inductive definition like (2) produces objects with many of the properties we want linguistic structures to have, including structure able to explain the existence of reconstruction effects.

There is plausibly one more nice feature of swapping copies for traces. Trace Theory *requires* an indexing operation that identifies the expression that the trace is a trace of. As traces are distinct from their antecedents, this indexing operation must be part of the grammatical process that underlies movement. Hence movement involves copying the contents of one position into another and co-indexing the two related positions. It is arguable that indexing can be eliminated from the syntax (i.e. the generative procedure that maps a selection of lexical atoms to a single-rooted hierarchically structured phrase) in a Merge-based account that incorporates the CTM. How so?

Well, indexing is required in a Merge-based grammar to distinguish two occurrences of a single (syntactic) expression from two syntactically different yet lexically identical occurrences of that expression (multiple repetitions of the same expression). Concretely, we need to distinguish *John likes John* from *John was admired (John)*. We do this by noting that these two sentences combine different atoms. The first uses two tokens of the lexical type *John*, one as subject and one as object. The second uses one token of that lexical expression and syntactically moves it. How does the computational system track this? One easy way is to formally distinguish the number of distinct selections from the

---

[26] This illustrates a general trope in Chomsky's discussion of such matters: Simple theories can carry great explanatory power by knitting together phenomena that seem on the surface to be disparate. This has become a general trope in minimalist theorizing.

lexicon by indexing the tokens selected. Any indexing will do. This is effectively how we distinguish distinct variables in an open sentence, for example. At any rate, this implies that the atoms that Merge manipulates are indexed on selection (or on their way to the numeration) *and so the atoms Merge manipulates are indexed as well*. As Merge preserves all information of the lexical elements it combines, it will preserve this too. Thus indexation is *intrinsic* to the computation, not an added operation. Of course, this implies that construal (control and binding) operations cannot be *indexing* operations, at least if they are the province of the syntax. Chapters 4 and 5 argue that such dependencies are determined via I-merge (construal "lives on" chains) and that construal dependencies are, in effect, movement (I-merge) dependencies. Note that this must be so if we assume that indexing is *not* a grammatical operation, that construal is part of the syntax, and that CTM is a by-product of Merge.

One more point: There are many Minimalists who consider indices to be theoretically unkosher interlopers (but see Collins and Stabler 2016) for a formalization that includes indexing as part of lexical selection). I have found none of the arguments in favor of this to be particularly compelling. So far as I can see, we need indices (or some analogous procedure/operation) to distinguish two selections of the same expression from the lexicon from each other. That two occurrences of the same syntactic expression can be distinguished from two expressions of the same lexical types I take to be something that is required in *any* computationally adequate theory of cognition, and hence not linguistically bespoke. Indeed, it appears that indexing holds quite generally cognitively (see Pylyshyn (1994) on FINSTs). Indeed, the type/token distinction and even the token/token distinction is best understood as a third-factor feature of FL and a general property of computational systems (see Marcus 2001).

Last point: So far as I can tell, *if* one exploits numerations (i.e. selects the atoms to be combined before combining them), then one needs to "count" multiple selections of the same expression somehow. The standard conception of numerations treats them as multi-sets *and these use indices to track the number of lexical selections of a given item*). So the multi-set/numeration for *John saw John* is something like {John^2, saw} whereas *John was seen* is something like {John, was, seen}. The little index-superscript in the first numeration codes the fact that we have selected two tokens of *John* for the syntactic computation. So indices are pressed into service to distinguish numerations via the multi-set technology. Now, if we simply code the different selections on the items themselves (as opposed to tracking the selections) we can treat numerations as simple sets. The two multi-sets can be coded as follows: {John$_1$, John$_2$, see} versus {John$_1$, was, seen}.

Caveat: I am not claiming that one way of doing things is better than another. I am saying that allowing indices to track selections is common to

2.7 Movement and C-command

both systems and that allowing two selections of the same item to be coded via indexations of the items is perfectly innocent theoretically and conceptually. Indeed, if Marcus (2001) and Pylyshyn (1994) are correct, this is the sort of thing any computational/cognitive system does as such. Or, to put this in current jargon, indexing "repetitions" is third-factor licensed.

2.7 Movement and C-command

I have shown that Merge delivers properties (1a–e). It can also derive the properties (1f,g,h). This time the relevant part of the NTC is the Extension Condition (EC). EC requires that the structural properties (i.e. constituent structure) of the inputs to Merge be preserved in the outputs of Merge. Slightly more formally, the items selected as inputs to the Merge operation must be units in the output. In other words, the selected inputs to the derivation must be immediate constituents of the outputs. Any other result would result in a loss of information and so violate the NTC. Interestingly, this implies (i) that all I-merge is to a c-commanding position, (ii) that lowering rules cannot exist, and (iii) that derivations are strictly cyclic.[27]

An illustration can clarify these claims. Consider (14):

(14)   a. $\{\{\alpha,\beta\},\{\gamma,\delta\}\}$
            b. $\{\{\{\gamma,\alpha\},\beta\},\{\gamma,\delta\}\}$
            c. $\{\{\gamma,\{\alpha,\beta\}\},\{\gamma,\delta\}\}$
            d. $\{\{\alpha,\beta\},\{\delta,\{\gamma,\delta\}\}\}$
            e. $\{\gamma,\{\{\alpha,\beta\},\{\gamma,\delta\}\}\}$
            f. $\{\delta,\{\{\alpha,\beta\},\{\gamma,\delta\}\}\}$

NTC prohibits deriving structure (14b) from (14a). Here we take $\{\{\alpha,\beta\},\{\gamma,\delta\}\}$ as input and *within this structure* we merge γ with α. The output of this hypothetical instance of Merge violates the EC by losing the information that $\{\alpha,\beta\}$ had been a unit/constituent in the input $\{\{\alpha,\beta\},\{\gamma,\delta\}\}$ (i.e. (14a)). More specifically, the derivational steps are: Select α, select γ, select $\{\{\alpha,\beta\},\{\gamma,\delta\}\}$. Merge (γ,α) within $\{\{\alpha,\beta\},\{\gamma,\delta\}\}$. The derivation "loses" the information that $\{\{\alpha,\beta\},\{\gamma,\delta\}\}$ was a unit as the output does not have this as a constituent.[28]

Nor can (14c) be licitly derived via I-merge from (14a). Here we try to (I-) merge γ with $\{\alpha,\beta\}$ within $\{\{\alpha,\beta\},\{\gamma,\delta\}\}$ deriving the complex constituent $\{\{\gamma,\{\alpha,\beta\}\},\{\gamma,\delta\}\}$. This derivation fails as $\{\{\alpha,\beta\},\{\gamma,\delta\}\}$, one of the necessary selected inputs to this derivational step, is no longer a unit in the output.

---

[27] The first conjunct only holds if there is no inter-arboreal/sidewards movement. For now, let's assume this to be correct (but see chapter 6 of Hornstein (2008) for discussion).
[28] Note, that leaving out mention of $\{\{\alpha,\beta\},\{\gamma,\delta\}\}$ being the domain of the merger of α,γ allows for a licit output, but not the one in (14b). What we would derive is simply $\{\gamma,\alpha\}$ not $\{\gamma,\alpha\}$ within $\{\{\alpha,\beta\},\{\gamma,\delta\}\}$, i.e. $\{\{\{\gamma,\alpha\},\beta\},\{\gamma,\delta\}\}$.

Nor is a derivation that violates the strict cycle (as in (14d)) possible. The envisaged derivation has $\{\{\alpha,\beta\},\{\gamma,\delta\}\}$ as input, and δ and $\{\gamma,\delta\}$ within $\{\{\alpha,\beta\},\{\gamma,\delta\}\}$ combine to get $\{\delta, \{\gamma,\delta\}\}$ within (14d). This is not possible as $\{\delta, \{\gamma,\delta\}\}$ is not a subpart of the input (14a) so (14d) cannot be properly factored into its inputs.

It is important to see exactly what the EC prevents. It is possible to derive a structure like (14d) from successive applications of Merge, just not *from* an input like (14a). Rather we need to build it up in some other way. For example, we can (E-)merge γ and δ to derive $\{\gamma,\delta\}$ then (I-)merge δ with (γ,δ) to get $\{\delta, \{\gamma,\delta\}\}$. Then (E-)merge α and β to get $\{\alpha,\beta\}$ and then (E-)merge $\{\delta, \{\gamma,\delta\}\}$ and $\{\alpha,\beta\}$ to get (14d) (viz. $\{\{\alpha, \beta\}, \{\delta, \{\gamma,\delta\}\}\}$). So the structure is derivable, *but not with (*14a*) as one of the selected inputs*. And note that this is the right result. After all, strict cyclicity allows movement to an intermediate Spec C. What is prohibited is movement to that Spec C when that embedded cyclic CP is properly contained within a higher cyclic domain. The output structure in (14d) is thus derivable, albeit with different inputs successively merged.

Only (14e) is a grammatically licit Merge derivation with (14a) as input, for here all the selected inputs to the derivation (i.e. γ and $\{\{\alpha,\beta\},\{\gamma,\delta\}\}$) are also proper sub-units in the output of the derivation (i.e. the inputs have thus been preserved (remain unchanged) in the output). Yes, a new relation has been added, but no previous ones have been destroyed (i.e. the derivation is info-preserving (viz. monotonic)).

Note that the same reasoning will prevent lowering operations from applying. In other words, though we can Merge δ and (14a) to derive (14f), we cannot Merge δ and γ in $\{\delta,\{\{\alpha,\beta\},\{\gamma\}\}\}$ to derive (14f). The former raises δ, the latter lowers it. The problem is that one of the selected inputs $\{\delta,\{\{\alpha,\beta\},\{\gamma\}\}\}$ is not preserved in the output (14f). This violates the NTC and the derivation is illicit.

Repeat the mantra: once an SO always an SO. In the illicit derivations discussed above, one of the inputs is no longer a unit in the output and so NTC/EC has been violated.

In sum, if movement is I-merge subject to NTC (because, **REMEMBER**, being subject to the NTC is a hallmark of a simple combination operation), then all movement will necessarily be to c-commanding positions, upwards, and strictly cyclic.

It is worth noting that the features here derived via the Merge Hypothesis are not particularly recondite properties of FL/UG. Indeed, they find a place in most Generative accounts (HPSG, LFG, RG, etc.) of movement. This makes their seamless derivation within a Merge-based account particularly interesting.

The elimination of these kinds of movements is interesting for another reason that I want to flag here (we return to this later on). Contrast how these movement restrictions are enforced in MH and in earlier GB-style theories. In GB-era theories, the Empty Category Principle (ECP) was what explained why movement is to a c-commanding position and why lowering rules don't exist. It is fair to say (ok, this is my opinion) that the ECP was not the most elegant sub-theory of GB. It is thus a virtue of MH that it opens the possibility of eliminating the ECP module. Of course, whether this conceptually desirable outcome is empirically tenable is something that we will have to return to.

One more point: The ECP is not only somewhat ugly (actually it is contrived, cumbersome and inelegant, as anyone who has ever taught it can attest to), it is not clear that it *can* apply within MP-style accounts. The reason is that it is a *trace* licensing condition and, as I've repeatedly noted, traces are *rei non grata* within MH. GB/ECP develops the intuition that traces are toxic unless grammatically licensed/identified. But MH replaces traces with copies/occurrences and there is no obvious reason why copies/occurrences need licensing/identification. Thus, the intuitive rationale for the ECP is unclear once copies replace traces. Furthermore, it is unclear how the available Merge technology could be revamped so as to apply only to some copies/occurrences and not others, as the ECP requires. For example, the head of a chain is not subject to the ECP. Rather it licenses all the other occurrences. The GB idea is that the head of the chain is *not* a trace. However it *is* an occurrence/copy no different from the other occurrences/copies. So why would it be exempt from the ECP if all other copies/occurrences were not? At any rate, it is a virtue of MH that the simple conception of Merge it incorporates allows us to secure some of the empirical benefits of the ECP without using the ECP (or traces) to do so.[29]

2.8 Structure Dependence

So, the simplest conception of Merge gives us unbounded structure building (why? The inductive definition in (2)/(3) is recursive), binary branching (why? A combination operation necessarily combines at least two things, the simplest one will combine at most two), movement (why? Merging a subpart of a phrase marker to the phrase marker is a special instance of the inductive definition in (2)/(3)), copy theory (why? The NTC), the duality of interpretation (why? E- and I-Merge suffice to specify the right formats for θ-marking and scope), c-command, a ban on downwards movement, and the strict cycle (why? All movement save to a c-commanding position violates the NTC). Any more? Yes. One more pleasant consequence.

Since the earliest days of generative grammar, it has been observed that syntactic operations are *structure dependent*. In other words, syntactic operations are sensitive to hierarchical relations in a phrase marker but not to sequential

---

[29] This is further discussed in Chapter 8.

ordering relations. Thus, in the classic discussion of polar question formation, rules easily expressible in terms of sequence (e.g. move the leftmost auxiliary) *do not exist* as possible G operations. So it appears that FL only exploits the hierarchical properties of phrase markers in syntactically manipulating them. The serial/sequential order relations among expressions seem not to matter. Why not? The theory of Merge in (2)/(3) above provides an answer: serial/sequential ordering statements are never exploited because syntactic objects don't code for serial/sequential ordering relations. Let me be more specific.

Recall that (3) analyzes Merge as an operation that produces *sets*. If this is correct, a syntactic unit or constituent is a set of some sort (one formed via successive applications of Merge understood as embodying the NTC). But sets do not serially/sequentially order their elements. Thus, the set $\{\alpha,\beta\}$ is identical to the set $\{\beta,\alpha\}$. But if phrase markers are sets and sets have no ordering information, then ordering information cannot be used to condition G operations if they are defined as operations on SOs (and what else could they be?). Thus, if the MH conception of Merge is roughly correct in that Merge delivers sets of SOs, we expect to see G operations sensitive to hierarchical notions of various sorts (e.g. α is closer to β than γ is because α is hierarchically more prominent than γ), but we do not expect to find operations conditioned by the serial/sequential order of elements within SOs. And we don't (well *by and large* we don't). Gs, for example, don't contain mirror-image rules; indeed, there is little evidence that Gs contain order-sensitive rules of any type.[30] This logically possible gap is explained if SOs are sets, which they are on the MH conception of Merge.

---

[30] There is some evidence that order sometimes counts. Larson and Jackendoff fought this issue out in the mid-1980s (see Bruening (2014) for more recent claims). It seems fair to say that there are some indications that linear order might matter in some cases (e.g. weak crossover (WCO) effects are often traced to a prohibition against indexing a trace with a pronoun to its *left*, 'to the left of' being a serial/sequential relation (for further discussion of WCO effects see Chapter 5)). However, the evidence is sparse and what there is can often be reinterpreted in hierarchical terms. Indeed, any theory that embodies some version of Kayne's Linear Correspondence Axiom (Kayne 1994) (as most MP accounts do) should expect a pretty consistent relationship between serial order and hierarchical order.

It is worth noting, however, that should it prove to be the case that serial order does sometimes matter, we could redefine Merge as a concatenation operation rather than one that forms sets. Hornstein (2008) does this for those that are interested. This would add a bit of order into the combination operation. We would lose the explanation above for structure dependence, but if indeed order can play a role in conditioning G operations, then the explanation above would be inadequate. See Chapter 7 for a longer discussion of this issue and a possible reanalysis of the data used to motivate structure dependence.

Last point, a reviewer noted that representing phrase markers as sets reflects Chomsky's long-standing idea that language is primarily for thought (the mapping to CI) and only secondarily for overt externalization (mapping to AP). As such, serial order should play no role at CI, and so the right *theoretical* move is to relegate such serial ordering relations to the mapping to AP. The suggestion seems to be that treating Merge as a set-forming operation might be understood as being grounded in this higher-level intuition (fact?) about what language as such is really for. Now, I have no principled objection to this line of thinking, though there is the caveat that it's not

2.8 Structure Dependence

Actually, let me be a bit pedantic and careful here. (3) formalizes Merge as a set-formation operation and this might seem to ontologically commit advocates of MH to the grammatical existence of sets. However, this, in my view, is an over-interpretation. Here's what I mean. MH postulates that a very simple combination operation lies at the heart of grammatical competence. What makes it simple? It does nothing more than combine what it combines. What does this mean? It *simply* combines them and does *nothing but* combine them. What do "simply" and "nothing but" mean here? Well, Merge combines expressions but does not order the elements combined (as this would go beyond *merely* combining them) and does not change the elements combined in any way (as this too would go beyond *merely* combining them).

Now let's return to sets. Such a simple Merge operation can be *coded* in terms of sets because combining elements into sets does not order the combined expressions and does not change them by creating sets from them. Therefore, formalizing Merge as a recursive set-forming operation will embody the simplicity conceptions like "no ordering" and the NTC. The real explanatory work is done by the postulated sparseness of the combination operation. Sets are just a notationally convenient way of formally representing these concepts.[31] The simplicity conception comes first, the set representation is a mere notational convenience.[32]

So, given the simplest version of (2) and (3) (i.e. subject to the NTC), we get a recursive system that can generate binary branching structures of unbounded size, whose rules are structure dependent, that encodes the copy theory (and hence allows for nice explanations of reconstruction effects), that requires that I-merged expressions obey c-command conditions on movement and provides grammatical formats for the transparent coding of the duality of interpretation. Thus, by adding one, arguably very simple, operation (a combination operation that does nothing more than combine the elements combined) delivers many core features of natural language grammars. In other words, as Darwin might

---

clear that language is *for* anything (this, btw, is, I believe, Chomsky's view as well). But I am not sure that it establishes the required relation between Merge and structure dependence. That CI is not sensitive to serial order does not *in itself* argue that the basic syntactic combination operation doesn't build phrase markers that embody serial information. On the other hand, if Merge builds sets (or set-like objects) then structure dependence follows immediately, regardless of what the facts about the interfaces happen to be. Thus, whatever the right view of what language is *for* is independent of whether G derivations are structure dependent.

[31] Stabler (2010) offers another more tree-like representational format. Truth be told, these are far easier to use than sets.

[32] It does raise an interesting question, however: What kinds of arguments would we look for to assert that sets are not notational convenience but *real* grammatical objects? Here's one idea: Merge is itself a set-theoretic operation. See the appendix to this chapter for a fanciful proposal for how this might be argued for. I am not personally convinced, but it was fun thinking about the problem.

have observed, add Merge to the cognitive system and out comes an FL with properties very like the ones attested in our FL.[33]

2.9 Conclusion

The core minimalist question concerns the structure of FL: What is linguistically bespoke and what cognitively and/or computationally general? The idea is that *if* we can answer this question we can also gain purchase on a closely related one: How did FL evolve in the species? The relation between the two questions is pretty clear-cut. The less linguistically specific the structure of FL, the easier it will be to tell a story of how it came to arise in the species. Novelty and complexity are problems for evolutionary accounts. Repackaging of available capacities with a smidgen of "simple" novelty mixed in is the standard route of a viable evolutionary explanation of any capacity. Thus, in the linguistic case we should be looking to find that the basic structure of FL (i.e. its operations and constraints) largely recycles what came before with perhaps a little extra. Merge is the proposed "extra," and the Merge Hypothesis is that Merge is the *only* extra we need to get a human-like FL. Or, more tendentiously: add Merge to the previous cognitive mix and we have all we need to construct a human FL. The Minimalist Program consists in seeing if this is a viable conception. It goes from hot air to something akin to science by identifying the core properties of FL and seeing how we can "deduce" them. This chapter is the first step in that direction. We have seen how Merge, a very simple combination operation, could explain several key features of FL and the Gs that it makes available. In fact, what makes Merge interesting is that it explains these

---

[33] I would like to here flag a problem that I discuss much more extensively in Chapter 7. The reasoning here assumes that the simplest available combination operation is the one used to inductively define the domain of SOs. This might be motivated if the requisite combination operation had not been part of the mental economy of our ancestors, for then we would need it to mutate into existence before being recruited as part of the inductive definition. And it does make some sense to assume that "simpler" operations have a greater chance of adventitiously mutating than do more complex ones. Simplicity, as I've remarked before, has evolutionary heft in this case. However, this advantage dissipates if we consider why Merge was selected as the basic combination operation rather than an *extant* one in the cognitive inventory of our ancestor. So, say that our ancestor had a way of mentally linking concepts that was more complex than putting them into sets, for instance via concatenation. Then *given* concatenation is there and could have sufficed to combine expressions, it is unclear why it should be passed over in favor of Merge as defined in (3). In fact, if both Merge and concatenation were both available in our ancestor's mental economies, there is no obvious reason why the "simpler" set-based operation should be preferred on evolutionary or methodological grounds. As I said, I will return to a discussion of this in Chapter 7; however, I flag it here for the explanation of structure dependence relies on the set-theoretic features of Merge, and why Merge should have these relies on a specific view of Darwin's Problem. It alone sorta/kinda ties together conceptual simplicity and evolutionary preference. And it is not at all obvious that it is able to carry the load it is being asked to bear.

2.9 Conclusion

features *because* it is so very simple (e.g. No Tampering and No Ordering plausibly follow from the very simple nature of the Merge operation). And, because it is so very simple, it is a plausible candidate for the adventitious novelty, the "extra," in our proposed Darwinian scenario (but see note 33).

Of course, these six features do not exhaust the properties we have reason to believe characterize FL. So, our next step is to push the MH further and see how to deduce other features of FL that Generative inquiry has discovered (see the list in (29) in Chapter 1). Deriving further "laws of grammar" requires adding a bit more structure to the basic combination operation. In particular, I will return to an earlier slightly more complex conception of Merge, one widely adopted in earlier minimalist theory. That conception of Merge not only combines elements, it also categorizes the resulting complex. This, in effect, captures the traditional notion of a constituent: a group of expressions forming a unit with a certain "label," (e.g. VP, PP, CP, etc.). The labeling operation respects endocentricity (i.e. the category label of the whole combined SO is a function of the label of one of the expressions combined). So endocentrically labeled "sets" will be at the center of the next chapter, which explores an extension of the Merge Hypothesis that I will dub (with a nod to early 1970s grammatical theory) the Extended Merge Hypothesis.

APPENDIX

Modeling Merge Set Theoretically

I claimed above that the set-notational representation of Merge is useful but does not imply that phrase markers (PMs) actually *are* sets. This said, it is interesting to consider what kind of argument would favor the more substantive view. What kind of evidence would we look for to establish the conclusion that PMs are sets rather than the weaker conclusion that PMs are usefully represented as sets? Here is one kind of argument that I would consider pretty convincing: The operation that forms grammatical structure and dependencies is set theoretic. In other words, *were* Merge itself a set-theoretic operation (or crucially invoke set-theoretic operations in constructing complex objects and dependencies), then the objects it applies to are sets and its outputs are sets. The question in this appendix is: What might such a set-theoretic conception of Merge look like?

Merge is often taken to be a non-set-theoretic operation that constructs sets. By non-set-theoretic, I mean that Merge is not a Boolean operation that takes sets as arguments and returns other sets. Rather, Merge takes lexical items and combinations thereof and forms sets therefrom. Thus, the objects Merge creates are sets, but the way it creates them is *not* set theoretic. In what follows, I would like to consider a system that factors Merge into two components, one, call it *Combine*, we identify with the set-theoretic operation union (i.e. U), and the other a function, let's call it *Select*, that maps an expression to its unit set, (i.e. S(elect)(α) → {α}). On this conception, Merge is a complex operation with two distinct parts: (i) a very general (i.e. non-linguistically parochial) set-theoretic U-operation, and (ii) a function that maps inputs to their unit sets. We can represent this complex operation as in (15):

(15)   Merge (x,y) = $_{def}$ U(S(x),S(y))

As with the standard definition, the domain of Select consists of lexical items and set-theoretic combinations thereof produced by (15).[34]

Before examining Merge's parts, let's consider how Select and Combine function together to derive sets with the by now familiar phrasal hierarchy characteristic of natural language expressions. Here's the derivation of a simple spec-head-complement phrase with α, β, γ lexical items.

(16)   a. Select α → {α}
       b. Select β → {β}
       c. Combine: {α} U {β} → {α,β}
       d. Select γ → {γ}
       e. Select {α,β} → {{α,β}}
       f. Combine: {γ} U {{α}, {β}} → {γ, {α, β}}

(17)   a. Merge (α,β) = U(S(α),S(β,)) → U({α},{β}) → {α,β}
       b. Merge (γ,{α,β}) = U(S(γ), S({α,β}) → U({γ},{{α,β}}) → {γ,{α,β}}

As (16) indicates, with the repeated iteration of Select and Combine we can create unbounded hierarchical phrases. I have separated out the two operations for perspicacity. (17) combines these "steps" into the Merge function. Note that the combination operation itself being simply U has the consequence that phrases will necessarily be binary branching. Why? Because the underlying combinatory power of Combine comes from its embodying the Boolean operation U, and U is a binary operator.[35]

As U's Boolean properties are well known, let's turn our attention to Select. Select is crucial if we are to distill composition from Merge. Why? Because lexical items (LI), *not themselves being sets*, cannot be combined by U. What Select does is map an LI into a set, the set containing only that LI (its unit set {LI}). This object, the unit set {LI}, is then a possible input to U. Note, until Select so applies to an LI, it is not formally able to be an argument of U.

---

[34] In other words, the domain of Select is the SOs. A useful question we ask later on is if there is a less gauzy specification of SOs other than whatever Merge and/or Select applies to. I will be suggesting that there is. The domain of these operations is labeled objects, which includes the lexical items (which label themselves) and phrases (which gain a label from their labeled expressions that enter into the combination operation. I return to a fuller discussion in Chapter 7.
[35] I owe this observation to Rick Lewis.

2.9 Conclusion

Select serves a second function. Or, more precisely, defining Merge as the combination of U and Select allows derivations to be information preserving (i.e. monotonic). Here's what I mean. Consider a derivation identical to (16a–d) continuing as follows:

(18)   Combine: $\{\gamma\} \cup \{\alpha, \beta\} \rightarrow \{\gamma, \alpha, \beta\}$

Note, that this is a perfectly fine application of U. However, Merge does not function this way. Why not? Because Merge is structure preserving: Structure that has been built cannot be destroyed. If we assume that Select must apply to *every* input to Combine (as (15) does), we end up with a system that is similarly structure preserving. Select, in effect, is a necessary condition for derivations to be information preserving if the combination part of Merge is U.

In sum, Merge as defined in (15) *must* form sets because it uses U to combine inputs and U outputs sets. Let's consider the subparts of Merge separately for a moment.

U seems like a very domain-general operation. After all, it is just set union. As such, it is hard to imagine that it is linguistically bespoke. What of Select? The domain of Select can be broken into two parts: (i) LIs, and (ii) the products of U. Without (ii), we could derive bigger and bigger sets using Select and Combine, but they would be flat rather than structured. If the domain of Select was restricted to LIs alone, then we could derive objects like (19a), but none like (19b):

(19)   a. $\{\alpha, \beta, \gamma\}$
        b. $\{\alpha, \{\beta, \gamma\}\}$

In fact, the size of the objects derivable with U and Select ranging over LIs is limited only by the size of the lexicon. When the domain of Select also includes the products of U, the size of a derived object is no longer limited by the size of the lexicon. The range becomes effectively unbounded. It is tempting to consider that the "miracle step" in the emergence of Merge as we know it is the widening of the domain of Select from LIs to LIs + products of Combine. So widening the domain of Select allows for structure preservation (i.e. monotonic derivations), and this allows for the generation of unboundedly hierarchical objects. These are the kinds of structures we find in natural language.

So what have we done? Not much actually. We have shown how to model Merge as consisting *in part* of the set-theoretical Combine operation 'U' and in part of a function Select that maps LIs and the products of Combine to their unit sets. If we analyze Merge as an operation that combines selected inputs via U(nion) we require that its inputs/outputs be sets. Thus, *if* Merge involves U, then PMs are actually sets, not merely objects conveniently represented as sets.

It is perhaps also worth observing that if we define Merge as in (15) then it is necessarily a binary operation that produces binary branching structures *and* it necessarily has the two NTC properties of Inclusiveness and Extension. Why? Because Select does not alter an element by mapping it to its unit set, and U does not alter its arguments in combining them. Merge as represented in (15) embodies the simplicity conditions that we want Merge to have. However, and this bears repeating, it is possible that other formalizations of Merge enjoy these same properties and do not invoke operations like Select and U. Or, to put this point another way: What makes (15) attractive is that it formally embodies the simplicity conditions we antecedently want Merge to have. And if this is the correct formalization, then Merge generates sets.

3 Adding Labels

3.0 The Generalizations Discussed in This Chapter

(1) a. Head-head (X°-Y°) Relations: Selection/subcategorization relations, very local relations that obey the Periscope Property
 b. Spec-head (XP-Y°) Relations: All θ-marking save that of the internal argument, criterial checking, case assignment, case and scope, many cases of agreement, and predicate-internal subjects
 c. Structure preservation: XPs are targets of grammatical operations, X's are not
 d. How to code rule variation across G_Ls

3.1 The Extended Merge Hypothesis and the Fundamental Principle of Grammar

Chapter 2 showed how a Merge-based theory of FL could derive eight distinctive features of natural language grammars. The derivations relied on the assumption that Merge combines two expressions as simply as possible. We interpreted "as simply as possible" to mean that Merge operates on the selected inputs without changing them in any way save in combining them. Merge does not "tamper" with the properties of the selected inputs in any way. It neither diminishes them nor adds to them in any way. It simply combines them. A key consequence of this is that all properties of the selected inputs are preserved in the outputs. Chapter 2 showed how the postulated simplicity of the recursive combination operation derives eight properties characteristic of natural language grammars.

This is an excellent start, but surely not enough. Generative research has discovered many other FL universals besides the eight discussed. For example, GB includes modules that regulate construal dependencies like binding and control, θ-marking, case marking, selection and subcategorization and more. We have a fairly good understanding of the principles that these GB modules incorporate, and this raises an obvious question: Do the distinctive properties of these dependencies also follow from the Merge-based system outlined in Chapter 2, or do we have to alter it to cover these kinds of data? In what follows, I am going to propose an *augmented* Merge-based theory and show how this (slightly?) more complex conception can explain other UG generalizations listed in Chapter 1. Concretely, I make two suggestions: (i) I complicate the Merge operation by adding endocentric labeling as an intrinsic feature. Thus, Merge not only combines two expressions it also labels the resulting combination. (ii) I also embed this richer conception of Merge in a more encompassing framework whose conceptual fulcrum is a principle that I modestly dub the "Fundamental Principle of Grammar" (FPG). The FPG adopts a very strong interpretation of the Merge Hypothesis: to wit, the FPG requires that all grammatical dependencies be Merge mediated.[1] Let's discuss these two features of the Extended Merge Hypothesis (EMH) in turn.

First, labeling: I propose that Merge not only combines elements into units as described above, but it also labels (i.e. names) the units so combined. Syntactic labeling has been a pretty standard assumption within Generative Grammar, and has only recently been questioned.[2] Indeed, the classic Generative conception of a constituent assumes that they are *typed* complex categories. For example, a V(erb) and a N(ominal) Phrase form a unit of the type V(erb) P(hrase). Generativists have coded this by labeling the unit consisting of the V and Nominal Phrase roughly as follows: $\{_{VP}$ V, NP$\}$. We read this notation as "saying" that the unit formed from combining a V and an NP *is a* VP. Alternatively, we can say that the V "labels" the unit, thereby categorizing it. The standard GB assumption, built into X'-theory, is that labeling is "endocentric," meaning that the label of the larger combined unit is always provided by the label of one of the combining expressions (the labeling expression being the "head"). I adopt this endocentric conception of labeling here. For concreteness, let's for now assume that Merge is a complex operation that incorporates labeling as a subpart. Thus, in what follows labeling occurs in the syntax, not in the transfer of Merge-constructed outputs to the interfaces. This is, as the cognoscenti will recognize, the earliest conception of Merge. It is currently less fashionable than it used to be. Indeed, it is downright unfashionable. And yet, I am going to urge the virtues of this retro conception and will revisit what this means for the larger minimalist project in Chapter 7.

I will, following current standard practice, further assume that labels are "bare" in the sense that they are not specified for bar level (see Chomsky 1995b). It is well known that a relational conception of labels (one that

---

[1] As previously noted, the FPG is not original with me. Both Epstein (1999) and Collins (2007) have earlier proposed very similar (if not identical) principles.

[2] A reviewer correctly points out that "recently" is doing some heavy lifting here. Collins (2002) already questions the need for labels in addition to Merge. More "recently," Chomsky (2013) denies that labeling is part of the definition of Merge (or even part of the syntax). See Hunter (2021) for some discussion of the classical conception. See Chapter 7 for a critical discussion of labels in "label-free" theories.

3.1 The EMH and the FPG

distinguishes phrases (i.e. XPs) from heads (i.e. X°s) and both from intermediate levels (i.e. X's)) allows one to recover different bar-level information without explicitly specifying this bar-level information as an intrinsic feature of the label.[3] This allows labels to be identified with the lexical atoms (terminals) into which complex phrases bottom out. In Chapter 7, I return to what this implies for the interpretation of the "is a" relation. But for now I simply adopt the classical endocentric conception: to wit, that a complex expression which is the product of Merge adopts the label of one of the two elements that are input to the combination operation that generates the complex expression.

Clearly, treating grammatical units as labeled categories is not minimalistically innocent. At the very least it complicates the Merge operation, for now Merge not only forms a unit from two more basic units, it further *names* the unit so formed. And this presents an apparent problem, or at least a challenge. Recall we *want* Merge to be very simple so that it could plausibly have mutated into existence. Requiring that Merge result in a *named* unit complicates the operation and so arguably renders this scenario less plausible.[4] I will not worry about this *for now*, though I promise to return to the problem in Chapter 7 (again, if you cannot wait, you have full permission to skip ahead (I won't look!)). For now, I adopt as axiomatic the assumption that Merge embodies a labeling operation and that the units of grammatical manipulation are *labeled* Merge-constructed objects akin to GB phrases with the codicil that the labels are bare.[5]

Consider now the FPG, the principle that all grammatical dependencies are mediated by Merge. This is a very strong principle. It imposes a very narrow locality condition on all grammatical operations. In fact, *it restricts all grammatical commerce to the constituent*. So, if some expression α θ-marks another expression β then it can only do so if α and β form a constituent *at*

---

[3] The observation goes back to Muysken (1982), I believe. It is incorporated into Bare Phrase Structure theory in Chomsky (1995b). The basic idea is quite simple (and, IMO, elegant). Bar-level information can be recovered as follows: An XP is a projection of X immediately dominated by a node labeled by some Z distinct from X. An X° is a lexical atom. An X' is neither an XP nor an X°. This relational specification of "bar levels" covers the main cases and renders an inherent (property) specification of bar levels unnecessary. This allows us to identify labels with the lexical atoms that "provide" them.
[4] Actually, for minimalist purposes we want whatever is language specific/bespoke to FL to be as simple as possible, not for Merge to be as simple as possible. If labeling is part of FL and Merge is part of FL and if both are irreducibly linguistically bespoke, then the emergence of both must be accounted for in any MP-style account. In other words, we want the *overall* simplest conception of FL, not the simplest conception of Merge. We discuss this in detail in Chapter 7. Those incapable of curbing their skepticism (and I deeply sympathize with you (really, I am not kidding)) are hereby granted permission to skip ahead and read the conceptual arguments deployed in Chapter 7 before proceeding further with the (merely) empirical justifications for incorporating labeling into Merge outlined in this chapter.
[5] This is the earliest notion of Merge outlined in Chomsky (1993, 1995b). Abandoning labels is a more recent innovation. I will be arguing that so streamlining Merge is a mistake.

some point. Ditto for case marking, agreement, binding, control, and any other dependency that Gs track. And there are many of these. Indeed, one way of thinking about particular Gs (e.g. lexicalized Gs) is that they track the dependencies that lexical atoms can enter into in syntactically kosher ways by tracking the configurations within which language-particular "features" can be grammatically licensed.[6] The FPG says that all such "feature" licensing takes place in constituents forged by Merge. I argue that an important consequence of the FPG is that it requires something like labeling to be adequately operationalized, at least if we keep all other aspects of Merge constant (in particular the No Tampering Condition). To see this, we will consider a couple of standard dependencies and see what kinds of analyses of these phenomena the FPG forces.

However, before we do so, let me rub your nose into one consequence of the penultimate sentence in the above paragraph. I consider the FPG to be a very very *strong* and *natural* consequence of the ur-intuition underlying the Merge Hypothesis. It makes explicit the fundamental idea behind MH; to wit that Merge is the secret sauce that explains the fundamental properties of natural language Gs. The FPG embodies this intuition by requiring all grammatical dependencies to be Merge mediated. If this supposition suffices to derive the basic properties of FL-compatible Gs, then it redeems the theoretical intuition behind the Merge Hypothesis in the strongest possible way. Talk about a "strong minimalist thesis"![7] But, if this is right *and* to operationalize the FPG requires incorporating labels, as argued below, then a minimalist theory *without* labels is conceptually weaker than one that incorporates them. Or, to put this as tendentiously as I can: If dumping labels weakens the strong minimalist thesis then dumping labels is a theoretical misstep to be avoided if possible. Now some of you should find this conclusion very annoying given the conventional wisdom concerning the methodological superfluity of labeling. What I am signaling here is that the conventional wisdom is wrong. If the claim that the FPG cannot do without labels is right, it buttresses this suggestion. Chapter 7 argues that the arguments against syntactic labeling were pretty weak to begin with, so the conventional wisdom, like much such wisdom, is rickety. We return to this. But for now, let's review some of the standard reasons for adopting labels and some of the reasons for thinking that operationalizing the FPG requires that Merge incorporate labels.

---

[6] See, for example, Stabler (2010).
[7] This line of reasoning (i.e. where the strong minimalist thesis is identified with a strong version of the Merge Hypothesis) was, to my knowledge (refreshed by reviewer C (thank you)), first explicitly developed in Epstein's (1999) discussion of the First Law. As should be clear, I find this line of argument completely convincing.

3.2 External Theta Roles and Predicate-Internal Subjects

Let's start with θ-marking. The FPG stipulates that the only way for one expression to θ-mark another is for the two to Merge. There are two rough configurations for θ-marking within GB. The internal argument (IA) is θ-marked under sisterhood with the predicative head (P) it merges with, as in (2a), and the external argument (EA) is θ-marked by merging as the specifier of predicate (P) that θ-marks it, as in (2b).

(2) a. {P, IA}
     b. {EA, {P ...}}

The FPG can unproblematically apply to (2a) as P and IA are sisters here. Not so with (2b). More specifically, *if* θ-marking is a relation between a predicate/head P and an argument/XP then the FPG requires that P and XP merge for θ-marking to take place. (2a) allows for this without labels. (2b) does not. Why not? Because EA does not merge with P in (2b). Moreover, if Merge (in virtue of its "simplicity") incorporates the NTC, EA *cannot* merge with P in (2b)! So given the FPG, either internal and external arguments are fundamentally different kinds of θ-dependents or EAs must be able to Merge with Ps in configurations like (2b) in some extended sense.[8] Labels support the extended sense. Here's how. If we allow that labels exist, then just as IAs merge with a label of

---

[8] There are arguments that treat IA and EA θ-marking asymmetrically. The former is analyzed as a relation between a head and a MaxP while the former is treated as a relation between a predicate and a MaxP. The argument goes back to Marantz (1984) and revolves around the observation that the EA's θ-role is compositionally derived. However, this argument, though interesting, is not very convincing. Here is why. The data revolves around contrasts like those in (i):
(i) a. John took the camera to school
    b. John took the bus to school
The claim is that John has two different θ-roles in (ia) and (ib) and this follows if these roles are not assigned by *take* but by the predicates *take the camera to school* and *take the bus to school*. Let's grant the facts. So in (ia) John has the "agent" θ-role while in (ib) it has some other θ-role, call it 'θ2.' The idea seems to be that we can explain the fact that the θ-roles assigned to the EA differ as they do by assuming the predicates are assigning EA's θ-roles. The problem is that this does not explain it, it just tracks it. Note that the same sort of data suggests that the IA's θ-roles also differ. So, *camera* is a "theme" while *bus* is something else, let's say θ3. So take+theme → agent EA while take+θ3 → θ2 EA. But this is entirely symmetric, meaning that agent+take → IA theme while θ2+take → θ3 IA. Does this mean that the IA should be seen as compositionally determined by the EA and the V? I doubt it. It likely means that determining the θ-values of EAs and IAs is a complex matter underdetermined by the heads that assign the grammatically relevant roles. The grammatically relevant roles are very bleached semantically speaking, likely little more than specifications of which nominal is IA and which is EA (i.e. the first and second argument of the predicative head). Nowadays, the standard wisdom is that it is *v* that assigns the EA role, and a very weak role it is, one with little content. Little *v* is just a "transitivizer" and it specifies the EA, and little else.

For a discussion of θ-roles as little more than specifications of the EA and IA, see Schein (1994) and Pietroski (2018).

P in (2a), EAs can merge with a label of P in (2b).[9] We represent this option in (3), where the constituent containing P as head carries the label 'P.' Labeling is then a way for expressions that have been merged to merge again without violating the NTC. They do this by labeling the complexes that contain them.

(3)   {EA, {$_p$ P ...}}

None of this is original. It simply regurgitates the assumptions about endocentricity, projection and labeling that are part of standard X'-theory. What is relevant here is that something like labels so understood is needed in order to make the FPG operational if we adopt the simple conception of Merge outlined in Chapter 2 (i.e. the one that embodies the NTC). So, unless we allow labels, specifiers cannot grammatically "talk to" heads under Merge. Once we add labels, so discoursing is trivial. If we adopt the FPG as *the* regulative fundamental ur-principle of grammar, we must assume that an operation like endocentric labeling exists. One might be tempted to conclude (snicker! snicker!) that labeling is virtually conceptually necessary *given* the FPG.

We can go a bit further. *If* external argument XPs are marked by predicative lexical heads or functional heads like v, then the FPG requires that external arguments be θ-marked within the domain of that predicative head. For example, take a transitive verb, if v θ-marks the EA, then EAs must merge (with a label of) v to be so marked. And this implies that EAs must begin their derivational lives internal to the maximal projection of v. In other words, the arguments of a transitive predicate must be generated internal to the vP, as in (4).[10] To repeat, this follows directly from the EMH/FPG and the assumption that EAs are θ-marked by vs. Thus, the observation that subjects are base generated within the verbal projection (even when found in Spec T on the surface) is a corollary of the EMH/FPG.[11]

(4)   [$_v$ EA [$_v$ v [$_v$ V IA]]]

Let me emphasize this point by noting a less general alternative. We can assume that θ-marking takes place under Merge and thus allow EAs to be generated predicate internally. However, if we have other kinds of grammatical operations (e.g. Agree/Probe-Goal, binding), then the fact that Gs require their

---

[9] Or, to put this more pedantically (thank you, reviewer number 4): Just as IA merges with an expression that has the label P, so too the EA merges with an expression with the label P. I will continue to elide this by saying that when α Merges with a β-labeled expression, then it merges with β.

[10] Let me be a bit more precise. The FPG requires that the external argument merge with a Predicate-labeled expression. If all arguments are XPs then, in (4) *if* v θ-marks EA and EA must be an XP, then v must project the label in (4) to the constituent containing v and EA. If EA were to project then it would not be an XP in (4). So *if* arguments are XPs then the predicate P must label the derived object.

[11] See Kuroda (1988), Koopman and Sportiche (1991), McCloskey (1997), and Hornstein et al. (2005) and references therein.

subjects to be generated predicate internally *does not yet follow*. It only follows if we can explain *why* θ-roles are not/cannot be assigned under Agree/Probe-Goal or binding. Were this an option, then the EA need not be generated internal to the vP.[12] It is precisely by obviating this theoretical option that the EMH/FPG explains why EAs must be base generated internal to the domain of the θ-assigning predicate. In other words, only by requiring that *all* grammatical dependencies be Merge mediated do we derive the fact that subjects must be base generated predicate internally. And this is why the EMH/FPG *explains* why Gs have predicate-internal subjects.[13]

3.3 Case Marking

The same argument to the same conclusion can be made for case marking, at least if we adopt the minimalist conception of case. Let me briefly review why.

The standard minimalist conception of case marking is that it is a head-XP relation.[14] The main innovation with respect to the GB approach to case is that minimalist theory replaces V with v as the accusative case marker. The effect of this is to assimilate the case-assignment configuration for accusative to that which exists for nominative in finite clauses. In particular, neither accusative nor nominative case is assigned with the case assignee as complement to the case assigner. Given the FPG, case assignment cannot be the reflex of a case assigning/checking head probing a case-needy nominal Goal.[15] Thus, the relevant case-assigning structures are like those in (5) in which the nominal expression requiring case licensing is specifier to a projection headed by the case licensing head. In (5), 'CM' stands for 'case marker.'

(5)   {NomP {$_{CM}$ ... CM .... }}

To repeat, given the FPG, (5) is the only licit case-marking configuration given the standard minimalist assumptions concerning the inventory of case markers. This does not entail that this is the correct approach to case. In fact, it is currently not at all fashionable, though it was the standard analysis in early Minimalism. As the reader no doubt knows, this is not how case marking is currently analyzed by many mainstream Minimalists. There are two

---

[12] Indeed, such a mechanism was suggested for control structures in Manzini and Roussou (2000) and could easily be extended to all cases of EA θ-role assignment.
[13] Observe that I have assumed that v θ-marks the EA. But say this is wrong. Say that V θ-marks the EA (as assumed before v was argued to be the relevant θ-assigning predicate). The derivation of predicate-internal subjects follows just as smoothly but with the EA being a specifier of V not v.
[14] See Hornstein et al. (2005) for review.
[15] Why not? Because *given* the FPG, long-distance Agree and the whole Probe/Goal architecture is theoretically superfluous (and so methodologically suspect). So too operations like feature lowering (e.g. v to V or C to T lowering of case features) as in Chomsky (2013).

mainstream approaches, neither of which is consistent with the FPG. Let me mention them briefly and show how they conflict with the FPG.

One standard approach treats case as a $Y°/XP$ dependency between a case-marking head and a nominal XP that requires case, as above. However, it differs in that the relation between the head $Y°$ and the nominal XP supervenes on an Agree relation established under a Probe-Goal configuration. The FPG is incompatible with this analysis as the FPG insists that *all* G dependencies are forged via Merge. The Agree dependency under Probe-Goal is not a Merge relation, and so it is not compatible with the FPG. So either we weaken the FPG and enrich the inventory of grammatical operations to include Agree/Probe-Goal or we abandon the Agree/Probe-Goal conception of case. I adopt the second option.[16]

The second mainstream minimalist approach to case is Dependent Case Theory, first proposed by Marantz (1991). This treats case as an XP/YP dependency (where XP and YP are DPs, typically the IA and EA). Suffice it to say that so analyzing case is hard to fit with the FPG as there is no obvious way of translating these case-assignment rules into ones wherein the two case-marked DPs merge at any point in the derivation. As such, I will assume for the rest of what follows that Dependent Case Theory is incompatible with the FPG.[17]

Let me make one thing clear before moving on: None of this implies that Dependent Case Theory or an Agree/Probe-Goal approach to case marking is wrong. Nor does it imply that the classic minimalist one adopted here wherein case is checked/assigned in a Spec-head configuration is right. It means exactly

---

[16] It should be observed that enriching FL to allow non-Merge operations is of questionable minimalist virtue. It becomes especially suspect if one agrees that Merge suffices to establish non-local dependencies, for then the addition of Agree/Probe-Goal looks very redundant as it covers the same configurations that Merge appears to cover. If Merge really does include I-merge as a special case, then adding Agree/Probe-Goal is methodologically undesirable. Hornstein (2008) observes that Agree/Probe-Goal architectures are incompatible with inter-arboreal movement. So, if such movement exists (and Hornstein (2008) reviews evidence that it does) then Agree/Probe-Goal theories have empirical problems. However, even if they do not, the general point stands: We should eschew consideration of operations like Agree/Probe-Goal unless forced to include them under considerable empirical pressure. If one assumes the Merge Hypothesis+the FPG, it is both unmotivated and unnecessary.

That said, Agree/Probe-Goal systems have one advantage: They do not require labels to license case. So, *if* one wants to dispense with labels (at least in the syntax) then one will be very inclined to add something like Agree/Probe-Goal technology to the inventory of basic G operations. Conversely, if one adopts a version of the Merge Hypothesis incorporating the FPG one will need labels and look grimly on Agree/Probe-Goal accounts.

[17] Dependent Case Theory assigns case to expressions in domains without directly linking them in any way. It exploits the logic of GB Principle B in the sense that and DP *cannot* get a specified case if another DP is in the same domain. There is currently a heated discussion about whether Dependent Case Theory is empirically superior to classical case theory and the relative methodological merits of each. There is even debate about whether case theory belongs in the syntax at all. These are interesting discussions, but I will leave them aside because Dependent Case Theory does not fit with the EMH that incorporates the FPG.

3.3 Case Marking

what it says: Both the former approaches are incompatible with the FPG, while the latter is not. The goal here is to investigate the properties of the EMH and show that its consequences are rich and interesting. That it can accommodate classical case theory is interesting from this perspective. Whether this theory of case is also correct is another matter, one that is important but will nonetheless be entirely ignored here.

Before moving on, however, it is worth tarrying a little to consider an interesting prediction concerning case marking and scope that *follows* directly from the FPG given the minimalist inventory of case-marking heads. As noted above, minimalist theories of case differ from GB theories in two respects. First, the inventory of case assigners replaces V with v.[18] The latter is an externalizing/transitivizing head that takes VP as complement. As Chomsky (1995a) argued, these assumptions suffice to regularize the structural configuration of case assignment, at least in the central cases. Let me remind you of the argument.

Chomsky (1995a) noted that to handle the standard instances of case licensing in English GB employed a rather baroque definition of government. This is not the place to go into the gory details, but suffice it to say that the definition required to cover the standard examples was, ahem, elaborate.

Chomsky's (1995a) re-evaluation and re-structuring of the GB approach centered on this. It noted that the GB definition of government unified three disparate-looking configurations: the simple head-complement relation wherein the case-assigning head and the case-licensed nominal are sisters (i.e. $[_{VP/PP}$ V/P NP]), the Spec-head relation where the case-assigning head licenses a nominal in its specifier (i.e. $[_{TP}$ NP $[_{T'}$ T°$_{finite}$ ...]) and exceptional case marking (ECM) configurations where a case-assigning head licenses the case of a nominal in the specifier of its complement (i.e. $[_{VP/CP}$ V/for $[_{TP}$ Nom $[_{T'}$ T°$_{-finite}$ ... .]]]). To the casual eyeball, these three configurations look very different. GB unified them by, effectively, taking the head-complement configuration as basic and defining government so that the apparent structure sitting between the case-assigning heads and their nominal assignees was disappeared in the last two cases. This was technically accomplished by substituting m-command for c-command and/or supplementing the definition of government to involve barriers and blocking categories as relevant to its calculation. Suffice it to say that the result, even when it worked, was as aesthetically pleasing as your typical dog's breakfast, as was first brought home to me in a terrific mid-1990s lecture by Sam Epstein. At any rate, Chomsky (1995a) proposed a reanalysis which I now outline.

---

[18] As in GB, the inventory of case-licensing heads differs across languages. We illustrate with English where it has been proposed that v, T_{finite} and P are case assigners.

The key idea is to take nominative case assignment in English as the basic configuration of case assignment. In other words, case assignment takes place in a Spec-head configuration with the case assigner being the head and the case assignee being a nominal in its Spec. Concretely, Chomsky (1995a) proposes that accusative case is assigned to a nominal outside the domain of the expression that θ-marks that expression (just as occurs with nominative case). So, nominative is assigned by a finite T° outside the verbal domain within which the external argument is θ-marked *and* accusative is assigned by *v* outside the domain of V that assigns a nominal the internal θ-role. In effect, Chomsky (1995a) assumes that a head cannot both θ-mark and case license the same nominal expression.[19] For nominative, this implies that externally θ-marked nominals receive their roles in the domain of the predicate (this is a consequence of the FPG, as noted above) *and* that internal arguments are case marked not by V but by something outside the domain of V (e.g. *v*). In effect, case assignment is a special case of criterial checking, but fed by A (rather than A')-movement.[20] This suggestion has been technically massaged over several iterations, but the end result is that *v* has replaced V as a case assigner and nominative/accusative case assignment takes place in configurations like (6), the trace indicating that the nominal has moved to the Spec of its licenser.

(6)   [nominal$_1$ [v/T$_{finite}$ ... t$_1$ ...] ...]

One very nice feature of this reconception of case (the desideratum that Chomsky (1995a) aimed for) is that it regularizes the configuration of case assignment. In particular, ECM cases now trivially unify with regular complement objects, the only difference being that the launch site of movement in ECM cases is the Spec of the embedded T rather than the complement position of V (sorta like the difference between Passive and Raising).

As should be clear, (6) is easily coded in terms of the EMH/FPG. It also comes with an interesting *empirical* consequence. Given this conception of case, underlying subjects and objects *always* move to some higher Spec position for case licensing. And given standard assumptions, this implies that the scope domains of nominals can be higher than the positions in which

---

[19] This is a kind of case/θ exclusion principle. Why heads should be able to assign θ or case to a given target but not both is a nice theoretical question that I will completely ignore here. But it is a nice question!

[20] There is, to my knowledge, no satisfactory non-stipulative explanation for the A vs A' distinction. Nonetheless, the distinction seems to be empirically crucial (A and A' dependencies have very different properties) even if theoretically opaque. Recognizing this, I will follow convention and assume that the CP layer is critical to specifying A'-dependencies but not A-dependencies. Chomsky (1993) provides features for distinguishing A' from A positions. These features are stipulative and so theoretically very unsatisfying. That said, it seems that this is the best we can do right now. For some weak attempts at doing better, see Chapter 5 where I mumble some things about rethinking the distinction in terms of phases.

they overtly appear to sit. Surprisingly, there is evidence in favor of so tying together case and scope.[21] Indeed, this was one of the earliest bits of *empirical* evidence in favor of the minimalist insistence on simplification. Simplifying the grammar leads to a more unified account of case licensing, and this unification leads to the prediction that case should impact scope. The EMH inherits this prediction. Specifically, the EMH/FPG argues that *if* finite $T°$ and v are the nominative and accusative case assigners, then case *must* be fed by I-merge and so case should impact scope. Note that adding Agree/Probe-goal to the mix of possible grammatical operations does not tie scope and case together, absent further assumptions.[22]

In sum, if we adopt the idea that v rather than V is the case-licensing head then the EMH/FPG implies that scope should track case. That there is some evidence that it does is a *novel* empirical consequence that follows if case licensing is fed by movement/I-merge. As the EMH/FPG requires that movement/I-merge feed accusative case licensing if v is the accusative case licensing head, the observed interdependency of case and scope follows.

Why do I keep beating this drum? Well, as noted in earlier chapters, one desideratum of a novel theory is that it derive the results of earlier ones. That's why we take the laws of GB as explananda for an admissible minimalist theory. However, we would also like our new theories to make novel predictions. The connection between scope and case is an example of a novel prediction that the EMH makes in virtue of embodying the FPG.[23] It's for this reason that I insistently bring it to your attention.

3.4 Constituency: Substitution and Labeled Expressions

The EMH/FPG places the classical notion of constituency at the center of grammatical theory. I confess to finding this feature very attractive as constituency has long been considered a fundamental feature of linguistic structure, one that most introductory syntax courses describe and motivate in loving detail. A Merge operation that both combines expressions and labels the resulting combination embodies the classical notion of constituency and thus fits

---

[21] See Branigan (1992) and Lasnik and Saito (1991). For a full discussion, see Hornstein et al. (2005).
[22] This holds for most other accounts of case as well. They can be made compatible with the observations but they rely on further assumptions to do so.
[23] Let me be clear about the logic here. That scope and case are conceptually related follows from two assumptions: (i) the θ/case exclusion principle (i.e. that a head X cannot both case and θ-mark the same YP, and so v rather than V assigns accusative case in English) and (ii) that case is assigned/checked in a Spec-head configuration. That these (or analogous) assumptions suffice to link (in particular, accusative) case and scope was noted by the references cited in note 21. What the EMH adds is that (ii) is the *only* way of checking case within natural language grammars once (i) is adopted. Thus, given (i) the EMH/FPG entails the link between scope and case.

86   3 Adding Labels

snugly with the classical data. To be concrete, a structure like (7) formed by a Merge operation that combines two expressions labeled α, β and labels the result β represents a complex object of the β variety:

(7) $\{_\beta \alpha, \beta\}$

As noted, Generative grammarians have amassed a lot of evidence that constituents are basic building blocks of natural language grammars. Let me rehearse some of the standard reasons for believing this, before moving on to show how the EMH incorporating the FPG can derive the further properties listed in (1). Let's start with some standard substitution tests for constituency.

Consider a sentence like (8a) in which we find a relatively simple nominal phrase in both subject and object positions.[24] Now, consider larger nominal phrases like those in (8b,c) built from *people* and *rutabaga*.

(8)   a. People love rutabagas
        b. many people, those three people, those three people from New Brunswick that I met last week at the rodeo, those many tall bald people that I met last week at the rodeo in New Brunswick for an hour and thirty-two minutes before the bull riding contest ...
        c. many tasty rutabagas, those three tasty ruby red rutabagas, those three tasty ruby red rutabagas that I bought for supper before I went to see the bronco busting exhibition downtown ...

Here is an interesting fact about how grammar works. If (8a) is a grammatical sequence of English, subbing any of the phrases from (8b) into the subject position occupied by *people* in (8a) and any of those in (8c) into the position occupied by *rutabagas* in (8a) will yield an equally grammatical sequence. In other words, phrases with the same heads are freely intersubstitutable in declarative sentences without affecting grammaticality. For example (9) is a fine sentence (albeit quite a bit more complex linearly and hierarchically than (8a) and yet it is no less grammatical).

(9)   Those many tall bald ***people*** that I met last week at the rodeo in New Brunswick for an hour and thirty-two minutes before the bull riding contest ***love*** those three tasty ruby red ***rutabagas*** that I bought for supper before I went to see the bronco busting exhibition downtown

The contrary holds as well. If a sentence sounds "weird" then more complex versions of the same phrase will not improve matters. For example, (10a) is weird presumably because rutabagas make lousy lovers. Fix this level of felicity. What is interesting is that complex nominals with the same heads don't remove this weirdness (see (10b)).

---

[24] I am not interested in plumbing the depths of the structural complexity of apparent simplex phrases. I have no doubt that they are more complex than just heads. However, the point I wish to make survives if we agree that the phrases in (8b,c) are more complex still.

(10)   a. Rutabagas love people
        b. Those three tasty ruby red *rutabagas* that I bought for supper before I went to see the bronco busting exhibition downtown *love* those many tall bald *people* that I met last week at the rodeo in New Brunswick last week for an hour and thirty-two minutes before the bull riding contest

Apparently, what matters for well-formedness in (8a) also affects that of (9). The (relatively) simple (8a) and (10a) suggest that what matters is the contribution of the three heads, *people, love, rutabaga*. (9) and (10b) argue that all the rest of the material in the relevant phrases is idle as far as syntactic structure is concerned. Phrases with the same heads fit into the same positions. Thus, if *people* is the head of the subject in (8a) and heads the more complex phrases in (8b) and ditto for *rutabagas* in (8c), then we can treat (9) as just a complex instance of (8a) and (10b) as a complex instance of (10a). In both (8a) and (9), a *people* headed phrase is the subject of the *love* proposition and a *rutabaga* phrase is the object. All the rest doesn't materially count. The same logic applies to (10a) and (10b). In effect, *phrases with the same heads distribute in the same way*. And this has two important implications: (i) heads count for these kinds of substitutions *and* (ii) nothing else does.

3.5   The Periscope Property: Head-to-Head Relations

Generative Grammar has explained these kinds of substitution data by restricting how syntactic atoms talk to one another. Take selection (and subcategorization) restrictions for example.[25] Some verbs select finite complements, some select non-finite complements and some select both:

(11)   a. John wants (Bill) to leave tomorrow/*that Bill will leave tomorrow
        b. John expects (Bill) to leave tomorrow/that Bill will leave tomorrow
        c. *John thinks (Bill) to leave tomorrow/that Bill will leave tomorrow

As far as we can tell, these restrictions can and do differ across languages and dialects. In other words, many such restrictions are diacritical facts (i.e. have no deeper principled explanations) about specific verbs and their complement structure within individual grammars.

Similar facts hold for adjectival complements (we say *interested **in*** not **interested **on/from/with*** and *angry **at/with*** but not **angry **from/against***) and nominal complements (an *interest **in*** not **on/out* and my anger *at/with* but not **from/against*). We even find idiosyncratic selection differences in expressions sharing a common root (e.g. *proud **of/*in*** versus *pride **in/*of***).[26] This also extends to functional material, with complementizers selecting specific

---

[25] I henceforth use 'selection' to describe all these head-to-head relations.
[26] See the excellent discussion in Merchant (2019).

sentential types (*for* selecting non-finite *to*-complements and *that* comporting only with finite ones):

(12)   a. John prefers for/(*that) Mary to leave
          b. John said that/(*for) Mary left

A related phenomenon occurs when considering how "bi-gram" word frequencies operate.[27] Thus, the probability of finding *apples* after *eat* in (13) is greater than finding *rutabagas* even though both are perfectly eatable.

(13)   John loves to eat apples/rutabagas

Furthermore, it seems that the statistics largely rely on the head information and not on much else. So (14) shows roughly the same profile as (13) even though *apples/rutabagas* is embedded in a larger phrase. Assuming that *apples/rutabagas* heads the larger phrase that contains it and that relevant inter-lexical statistical dependencies are computed over these head-to-head relations renders the statistical profile of the complex (14) as largely identical to that of the simplex (13).[28]

(14)   John loves to eat [$_{apples/rutabagas}$ the crisp juicy **apples/rutabagas** that I buy at the market]

These sorts of data are cross-linguistically robust. Some heads like to comport with other heads (both syntactically and probabilistically) for no apparent principled grammatical reason and speakers track and acquire this information and use it both grammatically and in performance. However, and this is the first interesting bit, the *window for these head-to-head interactions is very narrow*. It is restricted to the next head over:

(15)   A head X can only select the head Y of its sister.

To illustrate, whereas *interest* selects *in*, it imposes no restrictions on the nominal complement of *in* (any nominal complement will do (e.g. an interest in apples/astronomy/cooking/linguistics/ ...)). Similarly, though verbs and complementizers select their sentential complements, they do not select the subject of these complements. Any nominal (no matter how complex) can fit between *wants* and *to* in (16a) and between *for* and *to* in (16b).[29]

---

[27] Carl de Marken (1995) noted the close relation between subcategorization/selection and the probability dependencies between words in a clause. See Li et al. (2021) for some interesting arguments in favor of labeled expressions and their role in "learning" variation in NP recursion configurations.

[28] These facts, incidentally, suggest that the head of the nominal is not D as in a DP hypothesis, but N as in some current *n* accounts of nominal structure.

[29] Of course, not any nominal substitute will be acceptable. It must comport with the embedded verb that it is a subject of. However, the complementizer imposes no independent restrictions on these subjects, despite being linearly very proximate, indeed serially closer than the selected inflection head is.

3.5 The Periscope Property

(16) a. John **wants** ... **to** jump out of my ear
      b. **For** ... **to** jump out of my ear would make me smile

Consider another example of the same effect. In English, non-stative verbs are in the progressive in the present tense, while stative verbs are in the simple present and not in the progressive.

(17) a. John is now eating a rutabaga
      b. ??John now eats a rutabaga[30]
      c. John knows the answer
      d. ??John is knowing the answer

Importantly, the correlation of the present-tense form and the verb cares only for the head verb, not the subject nor the complement nor any possible modifiers of the verb.

(18) a. The tall man that I met last night is now at this very moment eating whatever you want him to eat.
      b. ??The tall man that I met last night now at this very moment eats whatever you want him to eat.
      c. The tall man that I met last night clearly knows the answer to my question
      d. ??The tall man that I met last night is clearly knowing the answer to my question

On the standard assumption that tense sits outside the VP and that the subject and object are inside the verbal projection replicates the configuration we saw above with complementizers/verbs and their complements. All that matters is the flavor of the verb. It alone determines the nature of the "right" tense form to use. The properties of the subject, modifiers and complement are irrelevant.

Incidentally, this present-tense restriction is idiosyncratic to English. In French, for example, the simple (non-progressive) present does not invidiously distinguish stative from non-statives. As such, it is very likely a fact about selection between T and V in English and not something more principled and interesting. What is grammatically noteworthy is that grammar only has a very narrow window for tracking these dependencies. And the interesting minimalist question is why. Why are selection, subcategorization and probabilistic inter-lexical effects limited to the small window to which they appear to be limited? In particular, why can a lexical item "see" the head of its *complement* and why is it *only* the *head* of its complement that it can see?

The assumption that Merge incorporates endocentric labeling coupled with the FPG provides a very simple explanation. Consider the details.

---

[30] Such sentences are acceptable, but not as present-tense assertions. They have a play-by-play flavor, in contrast to (17a).

Selection is a grammatical dependency. It applies exclusively between a head and the head of its sister. The FPG requires that all grammatical dependencies are forged under Merge. Thus, for a head X to select another head Y, an X-labeled expression and a Y-labeled expression must merge. More specifically, the FPG restricts selection dependencies to configurations like (19). In (19) the X-labeled expression merges with a Y-labeled expression thereby making Y "visible" to X for selection (etc.) given the FPG.

(19)   {X, {$_Y$ ... Y ...}}

So if selection is only possible between labeled elements under Merge then we derive the fact that heads can select other heads only if the relevant heads label expressions that are sisters (i.e. have merged). Thus, if the FPG regulates selection, then the fact that a head X *can* select the head of its sister Y (even if X and the head of Y are not, properly speaking, sisters) follows immediately if complexes are labeled endocentrically. In (19) an X-labeled expression merges with a Y-labeled expression thus allowing X and Y to "see" each other. Thus, given endocentrically labeled complexes, it follows from the FPG and the EMH that embodies it that a head can select the head of its complement.

There is a further consequence. The same logic accounts for the Periscope Property, the fact that the head is the only visible part of a sister constituent's structure (Hornstein et al. 2005: 178). In (19), whereas X can select for a particular Y, it *cannot* select for anything in the ' ... ' areas. In other words, the Periscope Property *restricts* a head's selection powers to the *head* of its sister and *no other contents of its sister*.[31] This is interesting because by many measures of proximity (e.g. serial order) the head X is closer to elements in the ' ... ' areas than it is to the head Y. Nonetheless, FL in the guise of the Periscope Property prohibits selection (etc.) between X and anything except Y. And the EMH/FPG explains why.

In fact, the explanation is very simple. In (18) X can see Y *and only Y* as X merges with a Y-labeled phrase and X does not merge with any labeled elements in the ' ... ' positions. In fact, X *cannot* merge with anything in the ' ... ' positions, for so doing would violate the No Tampering Condition. Consequently, X can only merge with the Y-labeled constituent '{$_Y$ ... Y ...}'

---

[31] Strictly speaking, the explanation presupposes that labeling is restricted to a single head. Thus the labeling in (i) is not permitted:
(i) {$_{XY}$ ... Y ... X ...}
In Chapter 7, I offer an explanation for this restriction in considering what labeling does. In a word, it closes the Merge operation in the domain of the lexical atoms. Thus, it maps every grammatical expression to an atom, thereby forming equivalence classes of expressions with atoms as moduli. If this is what labeling does then two heads cannot label an expression as there are no complex atoms. That's the idea. For now, let's just stipulate that at most one labeled expression provides a label to the complex it is part of via Merge.

3.5 The Periscope Property

and if selection is subject to the FPG, then X can "see" Y for the purposes of grammatical intercourse (because it merges with a Y label), and *nothing but* Y (because it cannot merge with anything contained in the large Y-labeled expression without violating the No Tampering Condition).

To recap: *if* syntactic objects are labeled endocentrically and *if* the EMH/FPG holds, then we derive (15). Specifically, the Periscope Property allows for a head X to select the head Y of its sister but does not allow for selection of Y's specifiers, complements or adjuncts. And the FPG explains why not: Because though the label X has merged with the label Y in (19), it does *not* (and cannot) merge with any labeled expression contained within the projection of Y. So, if the FPG governs selection (a grammatical dependency), then Merge restricts selection so that it can only hold between the heads of merged expressions *and nothing else*. And this is what we find; selection is restricted to a very narrow Merge-determined window. Selection has exactly the features we expect it to have *if phrases are endocentrically labeled and Merge provides the structural scaffolding for selection (as the FPG requires)*. So, *if* Merge is the *only* grammatical operation, then only it can support selection and so we expect to find the locality restrictions we do find if the Extended Merge Hypothesis that embodies the FPG is correct. Yay!!

Let me emphasize the point about lack of serial proximity. A head X can select another head Y that is arbitrarily distant from it serially.[32] As noted above, (16) allows subjects of arbitrary complexity to sit between the *want/for* and *to*. Given standard labeling conventions, *to* is the head of the embedded non-finite clause, so *to* labels the sentential complement. As such *to*'s label is what merges with *want/for* and so it is open to selection by *want/for* that merges with the complex that *to* labels. However, neither the specifier subject (nor the complement, nor an adjunct)) of *to* merges (or can merge) with *want/for*, so, given the FPG, neither can be selected by *want/for*. The correct locality restriction for selection, in other words, *tracks the history of Merge*, just as the combination of FPG and labeling requires. Or, to say this more directly, the Extended Merge Hypothesis explains the peculiar narrow locality restrictions FL imposes on selection.

So far as I know, no other explanation for the locality of selection or the Periscope Property exists. So let's be very clear about the assumptions that drive the conclusions.

First, the account relies on Merge being the *only* operation available for forming grammatical dependencies/structures (this is what gives the EMH

---

[32] For example, in (16), *if one disregards labels*, *want* and *for* are closer to a subject in ' ... ' than they are to *to*. This is so whether remoteness is calculated in terms of depth or in terms of linear proximity. Once labels are considered, however, this is no longer so. In (16) both *want* and *for* merge with a *to*-labeled phrase and so both are (in a straightforward sense) sisters with *to*, given that *to* is the label of the complex *to*-heads.

its oomph). To see this, consider how this explanation fails if we assume that, in addition to Merge, grammatical relations could piggyback on operations like Agree/Probe-Goal to form a dependency. In other words, say that a head could agree with another head that it probes under c-command (as is a standard assumption in much of the minimalist literature). Now take a look at the configuration in (19) once again. The FPG explains why specifiers and complements and adjuncts are not selectable by higher heads by noting that they do not merge with them. However, were it possible to select under Agree/Probe-Goal, it is quite unclear why specifiers (and adjuncts) are immune to selection. In (19) X c-commands everything within the projection of Y, including any specifiers, complements or adjuncts contained within it. So were Agree/Probe-Goal a licit grammatical operation capable of establishing grammatical relations, then one would expect these positions to be selectable by higher heads. Indeed, in Agree/Probe-Goal accounts, heads do typically probe far down into a phrasal sister to license, for example, *wh*-movement. But, as noted, FL/UG does not allow this species of selection. This would be somewhat surprising if selection could be executed under Agree/Probe-Goal. In contrast, the noted restrictions follow directly if one adopts the FPG, but *only* if one restricts the stable of admissible grammatical operations to Merge alone and bars potentially long-distance operations like Agree/Probe-Goal.

Let me be clear here. It is possible to *stipulate* that selection is restricted to hold exclusively between heads. And it is even possible to propose that a conspiracy of assumptions prevents Agree/Probe-Goal from selecting specifiers and complements (e.g. if we assume that specifiers can never be simple heads, it might be possible to prevent selection via some notion of economy wherein the selected head is always more proximate to the selecting head than anything else within the phrase could be[33]). However, the ancillary assumptions required are not, in my opinion, particularly well grounded and they do not follow from any general properties of grammar. In other words, though they can be made to "work," they involve quite a bit of special pleading and thus offer weak explanations, at best.

Second, the explanation of the Periscope Property offered here requires that Merge combine *labeled* expressions. Without them, in (18) X cannot get hold of Y via Merge, as merging X directly to the head Y would violate the No Tampering Condition. In fact, the only licit way of X selecting Y in structures without labels would restrict it to cases like (20) in which X and Y are lexical atoms. This is a coherent possibility. It *could* have been the case that selection

---

[33] Though even this assumption would not suffice. We would need to supplement it to evade the "relativized" part so that selection could not "ignore" non-featurally relevant interveners. Nonetheless, technically, I have no doubt this could be done (see, e.g., Collins 2002).

only occurred when lexical atoms merged. However, this hypothetical possibility does not actually hold. Though selection is structurally restricted, it is not restricted to bare heads.

(20)   {X,Y}

To sum up: selection, subcategorization and substitution are just three domains where grammars differ idiosyncratically. From what we know, this kind of diacritical difference between languages (and even speakers) is irreducible. The EMH and the FPG localizes this potential variation and restricts all such potential dependencies to a narrow window which governs inter-lexical effects. It is almost certain that the range of this inter-lexical idiosyncrasy is even wider than supposed here. For example, recently some have argued that there is at best a remote relation between semantic valence and argument realization, which, if correct, requires that we basically learn the complementation patterns of predicates and their arguments.[34] It is reasonable to think that restricting lexical dependencies to sisters would also be useful as regards learnability (as de Marken (1995) proposed long ago).[35] In other words, the noted restrictions on these kinds of head-to-head dependencies seem to be fundamental features of FL. The EMH explains them. To date, nothing else does.

3.6   EMH and Agreement as a Spec-H Relation

Consider another configuration within which heads appear to talk to one another.

(21)   a. $\{_\alpha \{_X ... X ...\}, \{_Y ... Y ...\}\}$
       b.   The *men* that we met at the show *are*/*is talking to Mary

To form (21a), the X- and Y-labeled phrases merge. This is a configuration in which X and Y can "talk" to one another (as in (17b)). Recall that the EMH/FPG assumes that Merge is the only available grammatical operation and thus that all grammatical dependencies piggyback on it. This requires agreement relations to be licensed in Spec-head configurations like (21a), the X-phrase being the specifier of Y or vice versa depending on whether α is Y or X. We know that agreement can occur in such configurations, as illustrated in (21b). We also know that what is relevant to this agreement process are the features on the head nominals rather than features on, for example, adjuncts to the head which are linearly more proximate (e.g. *show* in (21b)). This again is what we expect if indeed agreement is regulated by Merge. In particular, as in the cases of selection, what counts for agreement are properties of the heads and nothing

---

[34] See, for example, Pietroski (2018: 269ff).
[35] Also Li et al. (2021).

but the heads.³⁶ As with selection and subcategorization, we once again find that the Periscope Property is operative.

And the "checking" configuration depicted in (21) applies to more than ϕ-agreement. This is also the configuration for "criterial" agreement (Rizzi 1997), as found, for example, in cases of *Wh*-movement, topicalization or focalization. In these cases, a phrase whose head has the relevant features typically moves to the specifier of a higher head where its features and those of the head of its host are reconciled.³⁷ It is also the configuration for external θ-role assignment and case, as noted above.

Many readers will know that I am gliding over many complications here (e.g. see note 37). So it is well known that we find cases of ϕ-agreement in the absence of Spec-head configurations.³⁸ Indeed, cases of agreement where

---

³⁶ This presupposes a pretty stripped-down structure for nominal phrases, however. After all, what we are looking at is the agreement with respect to ϕ-features. If ϕ-features head their own projections, then the story presented here gets far more complex. I assume for now that this stripped-down phrase structure is tenable.

Let me also note another complication. In many languages, nominal specifiers agree with their head nouns. Thus, it will be hard to tell whether the agreement witnessed in cases like (21b) is driven by features of the determiner or those of the head noun. The FPG requires that it be the head noun (if what we have are NPs rather than DPs), but this will be hard to discern. In languages like English where the agreement tracks the visible features of the head nouns, this is quite obvious. But English is a very simple system and whether this view can be empirically maintained in more complex cases is beyond my meager typological competence to judge.

³⁷ This skips over a host of still unresolved puzzles, the main one being how the features of the phrase relate to those of the elements it contains. So, for example, consider *Wh*-movement. The apparently relevant features are the *Wh*-features. However, these need not reside on the head of the phrase. Thus, in *which book* or *whose book* the *Wh*-features reside in the specifier of the nominal expression. Even on a DP analysis, it is not at all clear that the *overt Wh*-features are located in the head. Rather, they can pied-piped from any constituent contained in the moving phrase. Indeed, these migrations can be quite complex under pied-piping: *reviews of pictures of **whose** mother annoyed Mary, to friends of whose friends did you send a formal invitation*. To my knowledge, there is no very good account of the process(es) by which the *Wh*-features in these phrases migrate to the containing moving phrase. The current account assumes that there is something like a higher WH head near the top of the complex (see Cable 2007). If this is the case, then the problems noted disappear if this higher WH is the head of the whole structure. With this waffling, I put aside these considerable complications with the understanding that they muddy the empirical picture presented in the main text.

³⁸ Note that I am using Spec-head here purely descriptively. One argument advanced for Agree/ Probe in place of Spec-head checking under Merge is that the latter privileges a particular kind of configuration (i.e. XP-Y) theoretically. I have never understood this point. A Merge-based theory like the EMH need not single out Spec-head configurations for special treatment. They are just instances of Merge that occur after some other instance of Merge has occurred. "First" Merge is always complementation, for the simple reason that there is no other structure before first Merge applies. "Second" merges will always be Spec-head structures, for the simple reason that the NTC allows nothing else. So, there is nothing privileged about specifiers or complements on this view. They are just descriptive names we give to configurations that reflect the fact that multiple applications of Merge regulated by the NTC result in different formal configurations. Neither relation is particularly privileged theoretically, or at least need not be. In fact, given labels, one can go further: Formally there is no distinction between head-complement and Spec-head configurations. Each is simply an instance of two labels in a sisterhood relation.

the relevant expressions are not in a Spec-head configuration are adduced as evidence that agreement is not regulated by Merge but must be accounted for in terms of Agree/Probe-Goal. I am going to put these examples aside here for two reasons.

First, I have discussed the purported inability of a purely Merge-based system to handle these kindsof effects elsewhere and argued that the failure is merely apparent (see Hornstein 2008).[39]

Second, I am interested in seeing how far we can get with a purely Merge+label-based system. Should inverse agreement phenomena prove to be the Achilles' heel of the effort, this would be an interesting result, not the least reason being that it would put an interesting question on the table: What is it about agreement that excuses it from the purview of the FPG?

3.7 Phrasal Movement, Labels and Minimality

Labels have one additional nice property in the context of a minimalist conception of grammar. MP widely assumes that grammars embody a general computational principle wherein shorter dependencies are favored over longer ones. This goes under the heading of "minimality." Superiority effects provide an illustrative example:

(22)   a. What impressed who?
          b. *Who did what impress?
          c. Who hugged who?
          d. *Who did who hug?

The greater acceptability of (22a) over (22b) is explained by noting that the movement of *who* to the +*Wh* CP in (22b) is "longer" than that of *what* to the same CP in (22a). Ditto for (22c/d). This is pictorially evident in (23) if one measures the distance from the two *Wh*s to the +*Wh*-marked C head:[40]

(23) $[_C C_{+Wh} [_T \textit{What} [_T \text{past} [_V \text{What} [_V \text{impress } \textit{who}]]]]]$

Naively, this picture suffices to illustrate the idea behind minimality, but it really is not enough. What we want is the *metric* that Gs use to measure (relative) distance. By what measure is *who* further from C_{Wh} than *what* is? If we respect the fact that phrase markers do not code for serial order and that this

---

[39] Hornstein (2008) argues that so long as one allows multiple specifiers, it will always be possible to translate any Agree/Probe analysis into one that involves movement with higher copy deletion. These systems are isomorphic. If so, then whatever an Agree/Probe theory can empirically "capture," a Merge-based account can as well. So unless one proposes replacing Merge with Agree/Probe as the basic operation, adding the latter to a theory of grammar that has Merge will be theoretically redundant, and hence strongly dispreferred.
[40] Measurement is from the head of the chain to C. As should be obvious, this is a very simplified depiction of the relevant structure.

is why grammatical operations must be structure dependent, it is clear that by "further" we must mean "deeper." So how is depth measured?

Before answering this, consider one more apparent fact about minimality. It appears to restrict comparison to expressions that stand in a c-command relation. Consider (24):

(24)   a. Pictures of what impressed who?
          b. Who did pictures of what impress?
          c. Whose mother hugged who?
          d. Who did whose mother hug?

The asymmetry in acceptability noted in (22) fades in this case. Why? The standard answer is that whereas in (22) the subject *Wh* (i.e. *who*) c-commands the object *Wh* (i.e. *what/who*), this is not so in (24), as here *what/whose* is buried within a larger nominal expression. To capture this, a c-command requirement is built into the definition of minimality:

(25)   In a structure ' ... X ... Y ... Z ... ' in which X c-commands Y and Y c-commands Z and in which both Y and Z have feature specifications relevant to X, no operation can involve X and Z.

Stated more felicitously, Z cannot grammatically relate to X over a featurally matched Y that intervenes. Crucially, however, intervention requires c-command and so it does not apply in (24) to block the movement of *who* over *what* (i.e. *what* does not intervene) or *who* over *whose mother* as the *whose* in *whose mother* does not intervene as it does not c-command *who*.

This describes the relevant facts. However, it does not really provide a satisfactory metric of distance. How is distance measured so that (25) follows. Here is one proposal.[41]

Let's define a path as the union of the nodes that dominate the expressions merged. In (23) this will be the set {C,T,V} if *what* is merged with C, and {C,T} if *who* is. Minimality requires that the dependency be the shortest one that meets the featural requirements. Given the notion of paths, we can restate this by defining distance in terms of subsets. Thus, the path {C,T} is shorter than the path {C,T,V} as the former is a proper subset of the latter.

Importantly, this metric also covers the cases in (24). Note that in these cases the path of the *Wh* embedded in the subject position will include the nominal phrase that contains it (i.e. roughly {C,N,T}), while the object *Wh* path is {C,T,V}. Importantly, neither is a proper subset of the other, so merging the object with C does not violate minimality.

In sum, if we measure distance in terms of paths, and relative distance in terms of the subset relations of these paths, we end up with the desired

---

[41] This is proposed in Hornstein (2008) based on earlier ideas developed in Pesetsky (1982).

3.7 Phrasal Movement, Labels and Minimality

conception of minimality for the basic cases. Interestingly, we get more. We get an explanation for why grammars target maximal projections (i.e. "XPs") for syntactic manipulation. Let's see how.

First, what do I mean by this? Well, it is well known that grammars move *phrases* and that construal relates *phrases*. Why should this be the case? Well, if Merge is the central (better still, *only*) grammatical operation, and Merge (specifically I-merge) respects minimality, and the FPG holds so that (the labels of expressions) check their featural requirements under Merge, and we adopt a bare phrase structure conception of labels (i.e. bar levels are not intrinsic but relational), then the central case of movement must be phrasal. Consider why.

The structure of a complex phrase will be something like (26), with X being the head of the X-labeled phrase.

(26) $\{_X \ldots \{_X \ldots X \ldots\} \ldots\}$

Say that this phrase is in a structure like (27) where Y and X must enter into a feature-checking relation.

(27) $\{_Y Y \ldots \{_Z \ldots \{_X \ldots \{_X \ldots X \ldots\} \ldots\} \ldots\} \ldots\}$

To do this, the FPG requires that we I-merge the labels X and Y. This I-merge must respect minimality.[42] The X-labeled constituent with the shortest distance to the Y-labeled root is the maximally X-labeled phrase. So this is the one that must be I-merged to the root. Every other X-labeled phrase will have a longer path to the root than this one has, for every other path will include an instance of X, whereas the path of the Max XP won't. Thus in (27) the path between X and Y of the largest X-phrase is {Y,Z}. The path of any other X-phrase is {Y,Z,X}. As the first path is a proper superset of the second, minimality will prohibit moving anything but the maximal X-phrase. So why do grammars target maximal projections? Because good computations minimize dependency length and Minimalism assumes that grammatical derivations are good ones computationally. Hence applications of I-merge will respect minimality. Or, to say this another way, if phrases are labeled and Merge is the fundamental rule of grammar and we adopt the EMH, then non-local dependencies will be mediated by I-merge and minimality will require that the I-merged elements be maximal.

---

[42] Note, Minimalism understands the minimality restriction as not linguistically specific but as a property of good computations more generally. So, for example, it is reasonable to think that shorter dependencies put fewer demands on memory resources than longer ones do. If this intuition is correct, then the minimality principle is not specific to FL and its existence can be taken to follow as a feature of good computational design. I return to a more general discussion of locality conditions and their relation to the EMH in Chapter 8.

Two remarks before I end this section.

First, this has obvious implications for how to analyze head movement. Minimality should prohibit it. Options for how to accommodate this are discussed in Hornstein (2008).[43] However, for present purposes, suffice it to say that there are ways of allowing it in if it is needed and there are alternatives in the literature that cover its effects without actually moving/I-merging heads (see Hornstein (2008) for some further discussion and references).

Second, so far as I know, this is the *only* account we have to date as to why it is that grammars generally target maximal phrases for manipulation. Indeed, one can go further. If Agree/Probe-Goal is a core grammatical operation then it is quite unclear why maximal projections are ever grammatically manipulated. Agree/Probe-Goal is quintessentially a head-to-head relation and can occur without any apparent Merge operation applying at all. So given Agree/Probe-Goal, *why* we have displacement at all becomes a puzzle. But even if we finesse this problem, in label-free approaches there is no current account as to *why* maximal phrases ever are grammatically involved in non-local dependencies, let alone why movement (more or less exclusively) targets maximal projections. There is occasionally some hand-waving about pied-piping which purportedly explains the ubiquity of non-local phrasal interactions, but this idea has never been satisfactorily worked out.[44] Consequently, the account above is currently the only game in town.

3.8 Variation

The proposal advanced here to incorporate labeling into Merge departs from a standard assumption in contemporary syntax that relegates labeling to the post-syntactic components (e.g. labeling being an aspect of Transfer). So far as I can tell, *all* current minimalist theories incorporate labeling, the differences reside in where the labeling occurs. The EMH requires that it appear as part of the syntax. Other theories regard syntactic structures *per se* as label-less, labels only appearing at the interfaces (particularly the CI interface).[45] One way of empirically distinguishing these different placements of labeling lies in finding the fingerprints of the operation within the syntax. One rather obvious place to look is in the variation specific Gs display as regards what they can grammatically manipulate. If such variation exists, then labels seem likely to be part of the syntax. Let me explain.

---

[43] Chomsky (2021) similarly argues against head movement as a syntactic operation.
[44] Nor do I believe it can be without invoking labels in some way. If this is so, then either phrasal movement/I-merge is not a basic syntactic operation or labels will be required in the syntax. I prefer the second horn of this dilemma, and I don't consider it very pointy.
[45] For further discussion, see Chapter 7.

It appears that some languages can move or delete *types* of expressions that others cannot. So, English allows for VP fronting (and VP ellipsis) while, for example, the Romance languages do not. This kind of variation is easy enough to state with labels. English allows I-merge rules like "Move VP" while French, for example, does not. As is well known, if the difference between English and French is to be accommodated in the way described, then we need something like labels to distinguish the Gs of the two languages. And if the variation attested is a *syntactic* one, as is standardly assumed, then it would appear that labels are required *in the syntax*.

Again, this line of reasoning is not dispositive (though I confess to finding it pretty convincing). It might be possible to recapitulate the G variation in some way that restricts the differences not to what is moved but by what the two Gs permit as licit interface configurations.[46] For now, I leave these observations concerning grammatical variation as puzzles for those inclined to adopt the current orthodoxy.

3.9 Conclusion

I have argued that by adding labeling to the basic Merge operation we can bring a host of grammatical dependencies under the purview of the Extended Merge Hypothesis. We do this by allowing the Fundamental Principle of Grammar to operate when constituents larger than heads are involved. Labels are a technical way of allowing heads within complex projections to talk to one another via Merge. In particular, it allows for a small extension of strict head-to-head locality in head-complement and Spec-head configurations. This allows for the FPG to condition external θ-marking, case marking, head-to-head selection, criterial checking, and agreement. And it does so all the while explaining why such relations are restricted by some version of the Periscope Property. Labels further allow for a minimalist conception of the classical constituent, thereby bringing classical distributional arguments involving constituency within its purview. In addition, (syntactic) labeling allows for a simple way of accommodating the apparent variation among the kinds of rules we find

---

[46] Though it looks like the relevant interface will be AP not CI. Recall that the standard assumption is that all Gs produce CIs that are largely identical. However, if the difference is one between different APs then it seems to require richer labels at AP than is standardly assumed. We have evidence that the phonology and phonetics of a language requires distinguishing heads from phrases, but there is little evidence that phrases need to be distinguished among themselves for the purposes of AP operations. This means that we might need to distinguish an X° from an XP, but we don't, it seems, need to distinguish a VP from an NP. If this is so, then it will be challenging to trace the kind of variation mentioned in the text to variant labels at the AP interface. This does not mean that it cannot be done. I never underestimate the ingenuity of syntacticians. However, at first blush, the simple fact of variation seems to pose a problem for theories that eschew labels in the syntax.

in different Gs. Last but not least, combined with a natural computational principle like minimality, we get an account for why grammatical operations like A/A'-movement target maximal phrases (and disallow movement of intermediate projections).[47] This, of course, leaves the question of *why* Merge involves labels (a question we return to in Chapter 7). However, even without an answer to this interesting question, it is worth noting the tight relation between the FPG and labels. In particular, any evidence in favor of the FPG is also evidence in favor of a Merge operation incorporating labels.

---

[47] As the EMH/FPG analyzes construal dependencies in terms of I-merge (see the following chapters), the same account in terms of minimality explains why the relata in construal dependencies are MaxPs.

4 Construal and the Extended Merge Hypothesis (1)
A-Chain Dependencies

4.0 The Generalizations Discussed in This Chapter

a. Classical A-chain structure
b. Obligatory control effects
c. Principle A binding effects

4.1 Setting the Stage

The Extended Merge Hypothesis (EMH) incorporates the Fundamental Principle of Grammar (FPG). As such, it implies that all non-local dependencies "live on" chains (i.e. are mediated by I-merge). Parts of this claim are staples of Generative wisdom.[1] Constructions such as Raising and Passive or *Wh*-question formation and Topicalization are understood to live on A- and A'-chains respectively. By this I mean that the properties of the construction are (in part) explained in terms of operations that move (aka I-merge) constituents with a certain feature structure to positions that check/match those features. Thus, nominals raise or passivize so that they can check/match case features. *Wh*-expressions and topics move to A' "criterial" positions so that they can check/match *Wh* or topic features in the relevant heads. Indeed, according to GB theory, part of what endows a language-specific grammar (G) with its language-specific properties are the distinctive feature specifications that its heads carry and that its grammars track. A fundamental conceit of GB theory is that it is possible to resolve the properties of constructions that the (pre-GB) Standard Theory identified and described into FL/UG general operations (like Move α) and language-specific feature checking (like Check Topic

---

[1] Manzini (1983) and Koster (1984) propose unifying control and A-chain dependencies within GB. Similar unifications were proposed earlier still by Bowers (1973) within the framework of the Standard Theory. These earlier proposals differ from this one technologically, but not in spirit. Thus, if there is something theoretically distinctive in the present proposal it is not that we should seek to unify Obligatory Control and Reflexivization with A-chains but the over-arching Fundamental Principle of Grammar that forces such a unification. Suffice it to say, I here follow pathways previously well laid out by others.

Feature). Applications of the general operations insert/move expressions with language-specific G features into positions that allow these features to be locally checked/matched by specified heads.[2]

Minimalist considerations endorse this theoretical apparatus and urge a generalization of its logic. In particular, EMH+FPG proposes that *all non-local* dependencies be cashed out in terms of "movement" (I-merge (which, recall, is just a specific application of Merge)). So not only *Wh*-movement and raising but also pronominal resumption, obligatory control, reflexivization, pronominalization and case marking are relations mediated by movement/I-merge. In fact, the EMH+FPG requires that *every* dependency be mediated by Merge. Consequently, every apparent non-local dependency must involve mediation by I-merge. That's the claim. This chapter is intended to show that there is non-trivial evidence in its favor, or to put the point more modestly, that it is not entirely crazy to think that it might be true. This chapter considers construal dependencies that live on A-chains, specifically obligatory control (OC) and Principle A effects as attested in Reflexivization structures. Construal processes that live on A'-chains are taken up in Chapter 5.

Here's how I will try to make the case that this is a plausible hypothesis. I take the generalizations that GB discovered and push them through the EMH/FPG grinder to see what kind of minimalist sausage we get. I then evaluate the tastiness of said sausage. I start with a brief discussion of how GB analyzes classical movement dependencies. I then see to what extent these apply to classic construal relations. The argument is that understanding construal relations as chain relations parallel to the classical GB cases of movement allows us to derive many of the empirical generalizations GB identified for construal dependencies and even allows us to explain some of (what GB took to be) their axiomatic (i.e. *stipulated*) features. Of course, taking this route will also generate problems that I will remark upon, leaving some (well, maybe most) of them behind (currently) unsolved.

Before moving forward with some details, it is worth noting that this project has echoes within GB itself. Recall (see Chapter 1) that GB tried to rein in the overgeneration of Move α by treating A-traces as anaphoric and hence subject to Principle A of the binding theory (BT-A). This maneuver

---

[2] An aside: This is how we should understand Chomsky's claim that constructions do not "exist." It does not deny that we can identify linguistic objects that have the construction properties described in prior research. Nor is it to deny that constructions are mental constructs that native speakers use in mental activities like production and/or comprehension. Rather the claim is that *constructions are not FL/UG primitives*. It is thus compatible with Chomsky's claim that native speakers compile constructions from more primitive structures that FL/UG makes available and even crucially use these compiled constructions in mental computations. Thus, constructions, if they do exist, are not fundamental features of FL's basic architecture.

4.1 Setting the Stage

served to unify A-movement and binding theory.[3] What is outlined below thus constitutes a return to this earlier theoretical ambition of unifying movement and construal.

Before diving in, here is a little roadmap. GB identified two kinds of chains: A and A'. Thus, the EMH+FPG leads us to expect two kinds of construal rules: those that live on A-chains and those that live on A'-chains.[4] In this chapter I discuss the former. In the next chapter I consider construal dependencies that live on A'-chains. The aim will be to derive as many properties of these kinds of construal from the supposition that they live on different kinds of chains with different kinds of properties. I also hope to show how the axioms that condition these construal processes themselves derive from the kinds of chains they live on. As these two chains are the only ones we have (though *why* this is so is not something we even dimly understand)[5], if I can do what I am proposing here, then we have a first-pass answer to two questions: (i) Why do natural language Gs have construal components at all? and (ii) Why do the construal modules have the properties GB discovered them to have?

The first question is family related to one discussed in Chapter 2: Why do FL-compatible Gs have movement rules? The answer given there is that any grammar that contains the simplest conception of Merge (i.e. one that delivers constituents and most simply allows for hierarchical recursion) will also allow another application of Merge, I-merge (aka movement), as well. I-merge/movement then is just an application of the more general combination operation that builds unbounded hierarchy. Get one, get the other! In other words, the simplest combination operation capable of addressing linguistic creativity brings with it movement operations. Or, to put this slightly more technically, the simplest combination operation that delivers constituents will also deliver chains.

Following similar logic, we can ask why does FL have construal rules? And as in the case of movement, one very good answer would be that they are also

---

[3] It is, perhaps, worth recalling that in the earliest days of GB, A'-traces were similarly understood as anaphoric and so the unification of A'-movement and BT was similarly anticipated. And indeed some interesting work aiming at such a unification developed (see Aoun 1986). This line of attack eventually petered out and the ECP replaced BT as the theoretical vehicle for licensing traces left by movement. That said, the *idea* that movement and binding are intimately related is part of the GB legacy.

[4] In what follows, I take A-chains to be those that only involve A-position links. A'-chains involve at least one A'-position link. A-positions are the grammatical function positions plus the θ-positions plus the case positions. A'-positions are those, roughly, in the C domain. As noted in Chapter 3, there is currently no non-stipulative way of distinguishing A from A' positions. Chomsky (1993) provides a feature specification in terms of V vs C involved positions. In my opinion, there is little to recommend this way of grounding the distinction as it amounts to little more than an opaque list. I will just settle for the list and hope that someone will come up with something better someday.

[5] Though I will feebly address the issue in some scattered remarks below.

an inevitable by-product of Merge, the simplest combination operation. That's my claim, or it is *almost* my claim. The full proposal is that Merge in a theory without D-structure suffices to produce chains that support anaphoric dependencies of the kind we find in reflexivization, control, and pronominalization constructions. Or, the EMH in the context of a G model without D-structure suffices to produce chains with multiple θ-links, and such chains are how FL represents anaphoric dependencies. As every MP theory rejects D-structure, then the EMH plus standard MP assumptions suffices to generate construal dependencies. In other words, once D-structure is discarded, a Merge-based conception of FL will necessarily represent construal-like dependencies. So why does FL have a construal component? Because its single operation Merge produces chains with multiple θ-links. Anaphoric dependencies, then, are the logical by-product of Merge in the absence of D-structure constraints preventing I-merge/movement into θ-positions.

I want to stop for a moment to smell this rose for it illustrates in what way MP questions are novel (and deep). MP is the first linguistic research program to ask why FL has the structure it has. Here, once again, is what this means.

If we take GB to be a pretty good description of FL's internal structure, then MP has tasked itself with the project of trying to explain why FL has GBish structure. One such question is: Why does FL have both structure-building and movement operations? Another is: Why does FL contain rules of construal? The answer to both questions is the same: because FL is simple in that it has a very simple combination operation, adopts only those levels that are required of a G theory (a level that feeds CI and one that feeds AP), and eschews the GB levels that are superfluous from this simple perspective (i.e. D-structure and S-structure). The claim embodied in the EMH (which incorporates the FPG) is that this simple set of assumptions suffice to produce unboundedly many hierarchically structured objects, suffice to model "movement" dependencies, **AND** suffice to produce construal structures. If true, this is really a beautiful story!

In fact, maybe too beautiful. Be skeptical! I am. Let's flesh out some details.

Some Basics: A-movement

Consider a simple case of A-movement. It creates a chain whose head is in a case position (+C) and whose tail is in a theta position (+θ). It may also involve an unbounded number of intermediate A-positions that occupy neither case (−C) nor theta (−θ) slots. This is illustrated in (1), α designating the moved nominal expression:

(1) $[\ldots \alpha_1 \ldots [\alpha_2 \ldots \alpha_3 \ldots]]$

The αs are occurrences of the same nominal expression (indices are simply for purposes of expository identification). Higher αs c-command lower ones.

4.1 Setting the Stage

α1 is in a case-marking/checking position, α3 is a theta position. α2 (of which there can be unboundedly many) is neither a case-marking nor a theta-marking position. Standard GB assumptions ensure that chains bear one case and one theta role. A chain bears each if one of its occurrences is in a position where each can be checked/assigned. There is no upper bound on the links of a well-formed chain. However, assuming something like D-structure (characterized by the twin requirements (i) that all and only theta positions are lexically filled there and (ii) that the output of DS feeds the movement (aka Transformational) component) results in chains which bear exactly one θ-role. Various other GB assumptions can be pressed into service to prohibit A-movement from case positions (hence chains will carry exactly one case), and to force movers exclusively to c-commanding positions (e.g. Binding Principle A (BT-A) or the Empty Category Principle (ECP)). This results in A-chains conforming to the format in (1) with each link c-commanding the ones below it and with the highest link sitting in a case position and with the lowest in a θ-position.[6]

In the earliest GB-style theories (e.g. Chomsky 1981), properties of A-chains rest on two basic theoretical assumptions. The first is that movements leave behind traces. The second is that the traces left by A-movement are subject to BT-A. In effect, GB unifies A-traces with reflexives under the auspices of the binding theory.[7] This unification has the pleasant property of explaining why raising from finite subjects is unacceptable (see (2) and (3)) and why Raising and Passive result in chains where higher links c-command lower ones (two of the distinctive properties noted above):

(2)   a. Mary$_1$ was believed t$_1$ to be intelligent
       b. *Mary$_1$ was believed t$_1$ was intelligent

(3)   a. Mary$_1$ believed herself$_1$ to be intelligent
       b. *Mary$_1$ believed herself$_1$ was intelligent

In effect, movement in (2b) is out for the same reason that reflexives in (3b) are illicit. In both cases the antecedent for the t/reflexive is too remote for it to satisfy Principle A (i.e. given standard definitions of binding domains, *Mary* and *herself* are in the same domain in (3a) but in different domains in (3b)).

The unification of traces with reflexives under BT-A also explains why links in an A-chain c-command lower ones (e.g. why A-movement is upwards not

---

[6] An important fact that I exploit later on is that A-chains are composed of links in A-positions. Again, as noted, we currently have no interesting (i.e. non-stipulative) theory as to what makes a position A or A'. However, as the distinction is central to much GB work (and has quite a bit of empirical backing), I will assume that it correctly describes a crucial grammatical distinction, even if at the moment, it is theoretically diacritical.
[7] As discussed in Chapter 1.

downwards).[8] As anaphors must be bound, and binding requires c-command, licit traces/reflexives must be c-commanded by their antecedents.

As time went by, this elegant line of theory began to leak. To my mind the two biggest problems were (i) that it seems to imply that A'-movement need not respect the c-command condition on chain links (why? Because A'-traces were not unified with BT-A) and (ii) it treats (3b) as a BT-A problem. (i) is false as A'-movement as well as A-movement is restricted to c-commanding landing sites. Furthermore, later work on binding (see Chomsky 1986a) argued that the binding domain for the reflexive in (3b) is actually the matrix clause.[9]

There is a further, more abstract, problem that arises in a minimalist context. The direction of unification above rests on a theoretical intuition that Minimalism abandons. A core GB idea is that traces are grammatically unruly and in need of taming. In other words, they must be licensed. Binding them licenses them. However, the Merge Hypothesis and its Extended descendant eschew traces as theoretical constructs. Links in a chain are just different occurrences of the same expression. Thus there is nothing wild about traces as they don't exist, and there are no obvious invidious differences between multiple occurrences of the same expression. Hence there is no apparent problem that licensing solves. All we have in a chain are multiple occurrences (copies) of the self-same item, with none more grammatically wanting than others.[10]

Happily, we don't require a unification with BT to derive the c-command condition on chains for it follows directly from the No Tampering Condition (NTC), specifically the Extension codicil.[11] On this conception, then, *all* chains formed by movement (aka I-merge), be they A or A', have their higher occurrences c-commanding their lower ones.[12]

---

[8] C-command is an axiomatic part of the definition of binding (i.e. it is a stipulation). So binding theory leaves unexplained *why* binding requires c-command. I mention this because this stipulation *is* explained by Merge-based analyses of construal, as we shall presently see. For the cognoscenti, observe that the combination of Move α and BT-A also prohibits sidewards movement. See note 9.

[9] The generalization that movement is restricted to c-commanding positions might also be false. I argue in Hornstein (2008) for the virtues of allowing sidewards movement (SW). If SW holds, then only movement within a single sub-tree must target a c-commanding landing site. This implies that A-traces need not be locally bound within the chain. This vitiates any unification of traces and reflexives under BT-A. It further scuppers any attempt to unify them under a principle like the antecedent government clause of the ECP. At any rate, as we shall see, unification in terms of BT-A is not required to derive the relevant observed c-command restrictions on movement.

[10] This line of reasoning applies to any trace licensing operation/condition. So, the ECP is no less minimalistically odd than is the assimilation of traces to A-anaphors. MP's rejection of traces requires rethinking a very large chunk of GB's greatest hits. See Chapter 8 for some further discussion.

[11] For those that have forgotten this, see Chapter 2, Section 2.2.

[12] But see note 9. This holds for *all* chains only in the absence of sidewards movement. In other words, it holds for all chains derived by I-merge in a single sub-tree.

What of the restriction in (2b)? Here versions of the Merge Hypothesis (indeed, minimalist theories in general) do little better than earlier GB. They invoke a stipulation; to wit that movement into a case (+agreement) position freezes further movement. Why? Unclear. Like all MPers, I will accept this stipulation and move on, hoping that someone someday offers something insightful.[13]

So to recap: A-chains which bear exactly one case and one theta role and in which the links locally c-command one another is one kind of grammatical object generated by movement. Furthermore, these properties follow more or less directly from the assumption that D-structures are input to the transformational component (hence the tail of a chain is $+\theta$), that A-traces are subject to BT-A/ECP (hence must have local c-commanding binders) and that occurrences in case/$+\phi$ positions are frozen. As these assumptions are discarded and replaced by more minimalistically acceptable ones, a wider typology of chains becomes available, ones that allow obligatory control and Principle A effects to be unified with movement. The most relevant enabling MP assumption for this unification is that D-structure does not exist. I consider this next.

4.2 Dumping D-Structure

One of MP's earliest theoretical achievements was its radical simplification of the derivational Y-model.[14] Recall, a GB derivation starts at D-structure (DS), moves to S-structure (SS), then splits and proceeds to logical form (LF) and phonological form (PF). Chomsky (1993) argues for the elimination of both DS and SS. It is now a fixed point of MP theory that Gs are without DS or SS levels. Why do I mention this? Because one consequence of eschewing DS is that it opens up the theoretical possibility of movement into thematic positions, and this in turn makes a movement (i.e. chain-based) approach to construal processes theoretically possible.[15]

---

[13] It is worth pointing out that case in general is quite odd given MP considerations. Why must nominals bear (abstract) case? Why are there case features at all? Who knows! This suggests that maybe abstract case should be eliminated and case effects reanalyzed. I would personally be sympathetic to this. However, to date, no obviously superior ways of dealing with the central phenomena have arisen so it looks like abstract case still has some utility.
   One more point: It is possible that the restriction to a single case per A-chain is empirically incorrect in general, though it seems to hold in specific Gs (see Bejar and Massam 1999). In what follows, I will assume it holds, at least parametrically.

[14] See Hornstein et al. (2005) for discussion.

[15] Why is the elimination of DS *required* for a Merge-based approach to construal? Because the central feature of construal operations like control and binding is that they relate at least *two* θ-involved expressions via I-merge. Thus, the proposal that construal lives on chains requires that movement into θ-positions be possible. And this is *impossible* if Gs involve a DS level which feeds the transformational component and requires that all and only θ-positions be lexically filled. This last is the classical view of DS that MP argued should be dropped. Hence, the proposals under consideration here are incompatible with the existence of DS as classically understood. This is not a bad result (indeed, it is a *good* one) if, as MP argues, DS does not exist.

Let me be clear about this, for the above claim is contentious.

Movement into θ-positions runs afoul of the Theta Criterion. This principle involves three separate claims:

(4) a. Every argument must have at least one θ-role
b. Every predicate must discharge all its θ-roles
c. Every argument can have at most one θ-role

(4a,b) are plausibly conditions on interpretability enforced by the CI interface, as they reflect requirements of full interpretation. (4a) amounts to the requirement that arguments must be integrated into propositions to be semantically viable, (4b) to a requirement prohibiting semantic features from being interpretively idle. This latter condition itself links back to the Principle of Full Interpretation, which plausibly explains the unacceptability of sentences like (5) wherein *who* is idle in that it is an operator without a variable to bind given that all the thematically available positions are already busy θ-marking other DPs.

(5) *Who did John see Mary

Of the three conditions in (4), (4c) is the interpretive outlier. Even if we concede that every argument must find a thematic home and even if we grant that all of a predicate's θ-roles must be expressed, it does not follow that a given expression cannot bind more than a single θ-position/variable. Indeed, in standard logical notations there is nothing semantically awkward about having multiple occurrences of the same variable bound by a single content. That is roughly what we get in (6), for example, where the multiple occurrences of *x* all get the same content as determined by the universal quantifier that binds them. Translating from logic-speak to ling-speak, (6) allows *x* to be a thematic dependent of *F* and *G* and *H*. Thus, semantically speaking, there is nothing wrong with endowing a given expression with more than one θ-role. So *if* (4c) holds, then it is not the obvious reflection of a Bare Out Condition (i.e. a condition enforced by natural requirements of the CI interface, discussed in more detail in Chapter 7, Section 7.1).

(6) $\forall x\,(Fx\ \&\ Gx\ \&\ Hx)$

And indeed, this is not (4c)'s provenance within GB. Rather (4c) arises as a *consequence* of GB's grammatical (in particular, its derivational) architecture. Specifically, it results from having a level like DS as a basic component of the grammar. Let me explain.

DS has two basic features: (i) It is a representation of "pure GF-θ," and (ii) the output of DS is the input to the transformational (i.e. Move α) component.

Point (i) enforces an isomorphism condition between semantic and syntactic form as regards argument structure. In particular, if some expression E is

4.2 Dumping D-Structure

interpreted as the "logical" object (i.e. internal argument) of P then, *at DS,* it is the syntactic object of P, and if some expression E' is interpreted as the "logical" subject of P (i.e. external argument) then, *at DS,* it is also the syntactic subject of P. In other words, DS is where semantic and syntactic roles neatly align.

Point (ii) requires that the thematic/syntactic alignment required by (i) *precede all* transformational manipulations. And this ensures that there can be no movement to a θ-position as there are no vacant θ-positions available once the derivational train has transformationally left the DS station. And if this is so, then there can be no transformational movements into thematic positions. Hence, we get (4c): A nominal expression cannot have more than one θ-role. In effect, given the GB understanding of DS incorporated into the Y-model, (4c) follows as a trivial consequence. Or to put matters more transparently, (4c) is a *syntactic* consequence of the organization of a GB-style grammar that incorporates DS.[16]

The astute reader (all of you, my dear friends) will now be asking what happens if DS is dispensed with (which, recall, is a common MP premise)? One immediate consequence is that movement into θ-positions is no longer *theoretically* ruled out. Let's see why this is so.

This conclusion reflects two basic features of MP. First, MP abandons the assumption that *all* DS operations precede all transformational operations. In particular, as Chomsky (1993) argues, it is *empirically* necessary to interleave structure-building operations (i.e. phrase structure (PS) and lexical insertion operations) and movement operations. Thus, it is false that *all* DS-like operations must precede *any* movement operations. As such, movement into a θ-position is now *logically* an option. Second, as Merge unifies structure building (E-merge) with movement (I-merge) (see Chapter 2), treating the two as instances of the very same Merge operation, it would be conceptually awkward to formally segregate operations that discharge thematic requirements from those that move expressions around. More specifically, it is hard to state (4c) as a prohibition against *movement* into θ-positions if I-merge (movement) is not an operation distinct from E-merge (structure building) and E-merge suffices for θ-role assignment. Thus, if E-merge can discharge θ-roles and E-merge is the same operation as I-merge, then I-merge should be able to do so as well. Or: If E- and I-merge are just two ways that Merge applies, then it would be theoretically mystifying if movement cannot do whatever structure building can.

---

[16] More accurately, it is a feature of every Generative theory prior to MP, as every one of them incorporated some version of DS as a basic component. This reflects the intuition that a derivation starts from a well-formed thematic base, which in turn reflects the reasonable idea that DS is where the lexical requirements of predicates interface with the syntactic requirements of grammar. I should add that this intuition is still very much with us, or at least very much with Chomsky. It is one prong of the Duality of Interpretation (DOI) and survives in the idea that θ-roles can only be discharged under E-merge. I will return to this below and in Chapter 8.

110   4 A-Chain Dependencies

Let me immediately assert that were it necessary to adopt (4c) on *empirical* grounds, there are ways of *complicating* the basics of the theory to accommodate this. Indeed, Chomsky (1993) proposes a way of incorporating (4c) relying on the (*extra*) assumptions that movement must be feature driven *and* that θ-roles are not features in the sense relevant for driving movement (in contrast to case and φ-features, which are so relevant). In my opinion, this is an ad hoc move and so should be resisted for standard minimalist reasons. However, the additional codicil *can* be added and so movement into θ-positions *can* be banned.[17]

Let me be a little more specific, for I will soon be proposing that movement into θ-positions is a pretty good idea. Chomsky (1993)'s specific theoretical proposal for keeping (4c) while eliminating DS preceded the unification of PS-rules and movement operations under the general conception of Merge (reviewed in Chapter 2) that incorporates both. If one adopts such a unification, which is now the standard practice, the Chomsky (1993) proposal requires extensive rethinking as there is no formal difference between E- and I-merge. Consequently it is unclear how/why E-merge could do what I-merge could not. In particular, how/why I-merge would require certain feature-checking requirements that E-merge would not.

We can add to this another problem. The greed-based approach to derivations (the first extra assumption noted above) characteristic of early MP accounts is currently far less fashionable (indeed, minimalist theory is currently largely revisiting the idea that operations freely apply) and so the question of how to force a wedge between E- and I-merge via feature-driven versus non-feature-driven instances of Merge becomes even more theoretically challenging.[18]

This said, I doubt that drawing an invidious distinction between E- and I-merge is formally difficult. Yet, two things seem clear, at least to me. First, it is far less trivial given current MP assumptions than it was in earlier MP accounts, and, second, it will require *additional* stipulations to accomplish.

---

[17] We can also stipulate that E-merge alone can establish a θ-dependency, pointing to a principle like the DOI. However, I do not see how this stipulation is better than the one noted in the text. The DOI is a fact. Given this fact, let's agree that there is a difference between establishing argument dependencies vs scope structures. Even given this, the fact is only elevated to an FL principle if we insist that grammars formally respect these two different interpretive functions. We can do this by restricting θ-marking to E-merge and scope marking to I-merge. But this then seems to be taking back with one hand what the MH wants to establish with the other. It appears to renege on treating both instances of Merge as different applications of the *same* operation. It, in effect, reifies a distinction between two operations that the MH has argued should be unified. Of course, we *could* do this, but shouldn't we consider this a second-best theoretical maneuver? (Hint: yup!)

[18] Again, theoretically challenging does not mean formally difficult. It is easy to add bells and whistles to derive desired empirical outcomes. The problem is not formal difficulty but theoretical attractiveness.

In other words, *the most direct consequence* of ditching DS is to abandon (4c). Reinstating it will require *extra* theoretical machinery and hence a less elegant theory. Thus, all things being equal, we should assume that (4c) is false and that movement into θ-positions is possible unless (pretty strong) empirical considerations motivate its theoretical reintroduction. In what follows, I argue that dumping (4c) has some further appealing theoretical payoffs. In particular, we can go a long way towards explaining the core features of obligatory control (OC) if we assume that DS does not exist and so movement into θ-positions is possible. We explain these by assuming that OC lives on A-chains with multiple θ-positions. In other words, OC chains are just like the A-chains underlying Raising and Passive but for their having more than one θ-related link.[19]

4.3 Obligatory Control, the EMH, and A-Movement

Consider an OC sentence like (7):

(7)   John expects to love a puppy

Here John (the semantic value of *John*) is interpreted as having both the external argument value of *expect* and the external argument value of *love*. In addition, *John* agrees in φ-features with *expects* and is case marked by the matrix finite T°. Lastly, it may (or may not) check some feature of the embedded non-finite T° (though what that feature might be has always been somewhat obscure). Given these descriptive facts, the FPG licenses a derivation like one in (8). Let's go through it.

(8)   [$_T$ John [$_T$ Present [$_v$ John [$_v$ v [$_V$ expect [$_T$ John [$_T$ to [$_v$ John [$_v$ v [$_V$ love [$_D$ a puppy]]]]]]]]]]]

John first E-merges with the lower *v* to receive the external θ-role of *love*. It then I-merges with the T projection of *to* to check whatever (somewhat obscure) feature non-finite T has.[20] *John* then I-merges with the matrix *v* and thereby receives the external θ-role of *expect*. Finally, it I-merges with the matrix finite T, thereby checking its case and the φ-features of finite T.

---

[19] Please observe: OC is *not* a species of Raising or Passive. Indeed, once one gives up constructions, as GB already has, the first sentence makes little sense, as constructions are not grammatically fundamental objects. Rather, all three constructions are formed by A-movement (the application of I-merge to form A-chains). All involve multiple applications of I-merge into A-positions resulting in complex A-chains with varying properties. Of relevance here is that OC chains differ from Raising chains in that the former's occurrences inhabit more θ-positions than the latter's do.

[20] This movement is not required for the present account and is included simply because it is standardly assumed that there is a PRO in this position.

It is worth comparing the structure of (7) with a closely related Raising analogue:

(9) a. John seems to love a puppy
  b. [$_T$ John [$_T$ Present [$_v$ v [$_V$ seem [$_T$ John [$_T$ to [$_v$ John [$_v$ v [$_V$ love [$_D$ a puppy]]]]]]]]]]

We can contrast the two different chains schematically as in (10):

(10) a. (John$_{+case}$, John$_{+\theta}$, John, John$_{+\theta}$)
  b. (John$_{+case}$, John, John$_{+\theta}$)

The chains differ only in the control chain having two θ-related links and the Raising chain having one. Note that both are derived via the iterative application of Merge with dependencies and theta/feature checking executed via merge with the relevant (projection) of the head (aka label), as prescribed by the FPG. The chain in (10a) depicts what I intend when I say that OC "lives on" an A-chains with multiple θ-positions as links.

If this is correct, then several features of OC follow at once. First, we expect what GB would describe as OC PRO to necessarily have a local c-commanding antecedent. Why? Because OC PRO is just a "trace" residue of A-movement, and all A-chain traces must have local c-commanding antecedents. Moreover, the fact that the antecedents *must* c-command OC PRO follows from the fact that the antecedent is a product of I-merge and I-merge *always* "moves" whatever it moves to a c-commanding position. Why? Because Merge embodies the No Tampering Condition which in turn incorporates the Extension Condition.[21] It is local because all A-movement is local (see Section 4.1 for discussion).

To recap: The EMH incorporating the FPG treats OC structures as products of Merge, both E and I. Consequently, OC properties reflect the properties of the A-chains with multiple θ-slots that they live on. A critical piece of this analysis is that I-merge (aka movement) into θ-positions is licit, an option that the MH's eschewing of D-structure makes available.

This is the kind of analysis of OC constructions compatible with EMH+FPG. Is this reasonable? Well, there is substantial evidence suggesting that it is, in addition to that just reviewed. Let me suggest a couple of salient data points suggesting that this analysis is empirically plausible.[22]

---

[21] See Chapter 2. As previously noted, this holds only for *standard* movement within a single rooted phrase marker.

[22] What follows is contentious. Many don't like the Movement Theory of Control (MTC). I and others (see e.g. Boeckx et al. (2010) and Hornstein and Nunes (2014) for discussion of the lay of the land) have trumpeted its virtues and argued that the problems identified for the analysis are not dispositive. However, here is not the place to go into these matters. The interested reader can look up the debates. What I want to do here is display the logic of the analysis (show that MTC *fits* with first principles (EMH+FPG)) and show that there is non-trivial empirical evidence supporting it.

4.3 Obligatory Control, the EMH, and A-Movement

I have already shown that treating OC as an A-chain relation easily explains why OC PRO requires a local c-commanding antecedent (aka controller). This follows trivially from the fact that on the Movement Theory of Control (MTC), PRO is just an A-"trace" and so must have a c-commanding local antecedent. Moving on, (11) illustrates that in cases where Raising fails, so does OC. (11a, where ec stands for empty category) is an example of A-movement from finite subject position and it is unacceptable. Ditto for (11b).

(11) a. *John seems ec likes Mary
     b. *John hopes ec likes Mary

More interesting, the restriction in (11) appears to be language particular. In other words, there are languages in which Raising from a finite subject are licit. One of these languages is Brazilian Portuguese. Consider (12):

(12) a. Os meninos$_1$ parcem que ec$_1$ fizeram a   tarefa
        The boys   seem that ec   did   their homework
     b. O Joao$_1$ disse que ec$_1$ comprou   um carro
        John   said that ec   bought   a car

(12a) is an example of Raising and (12b) of OC. Note that in both cases there is an empty category in the finite subject position of the embedded clause with an antecedent in the next clause higher up. Furthermore, these antecedents are required, must c-command the ec in embedded-subject position and must be local to that ec (i.e. in the next higher clause). In other words, in both cases, the ec displays all the characteristic properties of A-traces.[23] Note that the MTC leads us to expect this parallel behavior for it postulates that OC and Raising are both products of A-movement.[24]

As a final illustration, consider what is perhaps the most interesting consequence of the MTC, backwards control (BC). I say the most interesting, for if the empirical data are correct, *no PRO-based theory of control is viable*. Let's consider the basic phenomenon.

---

[23] These data were first discussed extensively in Ferreira (2009) and Rodrigues (2004). For a detailed critical review of the considerable subsequent literature, see Nunes (2019).

[24] It is worth noting that the MTC explains why "PRO" appears where it does. It can appear wherever an A-trace can appear. Generally speaking, in GB terms, these are non-case-marking positions (aka the subject positions of non-finite clauses (i.e. ungoverned positions in classic GB)). Early minimalist approaches to PRO tracked its distribution in terms of an ad hoc case that only PRO could carry. The stipulative nature of the account precludes any explanation of this fact. This has led some to rest content with a more direct stipulation banning PRO from all positions save the subject positions of non-finite clauses (Landau (2000) dubs this an "honest stipulation"). Though honesty is indeed a virtue, it does not endow the postulated stipulation with any additional explanatory power. To my knowledge, the MTC provides the *only* explanation of PRO's distribution. That the EMH+FPG entails a version of the MTC means that it inherits the MTC's explanatory virtues.

114   4 A-Chain Dependencies

In languages like English the controller is always pronounced in a position higher than the controllee.[25] However, this is not always the case. Relatively recent typological work has discovered languages where the controller sits in a position *lower* than the controllee.[26] Thus instead of (13a), we find (OC structures like (13b):

(13)   a. [Controller/DP ... [controllee/"PRO" ...
       b. [Controllee/"PRO" ... [controller/DP ...

These kinds of control configurations are surprising given standard PRO-based approaches to OC.[27] Note that in (13b) the controllee (aka PRO) is unbound. Furthermore, the controller is bound, thereby plausibly violating Principle C. Both of these are problems for standard PRO-based approaches to control. Happily, they are not problems for movement approaches to OC given other standard minimalist assumptions and technology. Let me explain.

The MTC treats OC as a fact about A-chains. A-chains, on this approach, differ in the number of θ-roles the chain has (i.e. the number of θ-positions its occurrences occupy). A simple standard Raising structure looks like (14a) and a simple standard OC structure looks like (14b), the difference being the number of θ-positions DP occupies (again, indices for expository purposes only).

(14)   a. [DP_1 ... V ... [DP_2 ... [DP_3 v [V ...]]]]
       b. [DP_1 ... [DP_* v [V ... [DP_2 ... [DP_3 v [V ...]]]]]]

The two DP chains are similar in that in both, DP_3 is a θ-position, in both, DP_1, a case position and in both, DP_2 is the Spec of a porous TP.[28] Where the two

---

[25] This is a very informal way of putting things. Pronounced structures are not phrase markers so 'higher/lower' doesn't apply. Rather, in the phrase marker that feeds AP the pronounced expression which corresponds to the controller sits higher than the position that it controls. You get the idea.

[26] There has been a lot of work on this topic, but the prime movers have been Masha Polinsky and Eric Potsdam. See their work cited in the bibliography and further references therein.

[27] Baltin (1995) and Kayne (2002) have argued that control is based on movement but that OC chains do not involve chains in which any expression occupies more than one θ-position. The relevant derivations start with the controller and PRO in a doubled configuration like [Controller PRO] and the controller A-raising to its surface matrix position. PRO assumes one θ-role and the controller another. This still involves movement into θ-positions but does not require the assumption that any expression occupies more than a single θ-position. More specifically, *if* one assumes that control configurations start their lives with the controller and PRO in a doubled nominal configuration like [Controller PRO], then BC seems to require lowering the controller, in violation of the NTC. This noted, the EMH+FPG looks to be compatible with this version of the MTC (see Hornstein 2008 for discussion). BC is the most interesting empirical puzzle for this doubling approach to OC.

There is also a theoretical puzzle. Generative Grammar has always treated the controllee as a theory-internal object. What I mean by this is that it has never been treated as a lexical item. There are good reasons for this which I will not go into here (see Hornstein and Nunes 2014 for discussion). See note 47 later in this chapter for a discussion of the pros and cons of treating PRO as a grammar-internal object vs as a lexical item.

[28] This is the typical case. It could also be a small clause or something clause-like but not a TP. I ignore these niceties here.

4.3 Obligatory Control, the EMH, and A-Movement

chains differ is with respect to DP_*. This is the "extra" θ-position one finds in OC A-chains. Just as interpretation supervenes on chain structure in (14a) so too it supervenes on chain structure in (14b). (14a) will be interpreted with DP having a single thematic function and (14b) will be interpreted with DP having two. Why? Because the (14a)-chain has one θ-role and the (14b)-chain has two. So far, so standard.

However, the chains we see in (14) require some massaging to get them to the AP systems. They require some PF adjustments when compared with the mapping of GB derivations to PF. Why? Because in contrast to GB, MP "traces" are full copies and not phonetically null empty categories.[29]

As you no doubt all know, MP accommodates the fact that (in general) only a single copy is pronounced at the AP interface by deleting copies in the mapping to AP. There are various interesting theories of how to do this, but for now, the details don't much matter.[30] What does matter is that all MP theories that adopt Merge inherit a version of the copy theory of movement and so require an operation that deletes copies in the mapping from the syntax to the AP interface.

Now, there are at least four ways to execute such mappings in (14): We can retain the top copy or a lower copy or all the copies or none of the copies. In the case of control, this means that no copy/occurrence is articulated, either the top one is or a lower one is, or both the top and bottom ones are. I am assuming, as is standard, that *at least one* copy must be expressed due to some principle (e.g. the Recoverability of Deletion) and I am also assuming that copies that are articulated must be licensed in some way (e.g. via case theory, see note 30). At any rate, we need some operation that prunes occurrences and leaves (at least) one to be pronounced. And this is required not just for control structures generated by the MTC, but for *any* account of how I-merge-generated phrase markers are interpreted at AP. So, as we need something like this, let's assume that something like this exists. Here is the interesting part: In combination with the MTC, this mechanism yields a straightforward analysis of BC structures. In fact, the MTC plus the simplest general theory of copy deletion (retain at least one copy) yields the following typology of grammatical possibilities (see Haddad and Potsdam (2013: 241–42) (H&P)). I use H&P's useful discussion and nomenclature to illustrate:

(15)   a. [John managed [~~John~~ to win]] (forward control)
        b. [~~John~~ managed [John to win]] (backwards control)

---

[29] Just to be clear, this is *not* an advantage of the GB perspective, for GB has no theoretical explanation for why traces are phonetically null. This is a stipulation. In this sense, the question of copy deletion that MP theories face is simply the question of why traces are phonetically null.

[30] The most developed version I know (and it is very good) is Nunes (2004). Additional interesting work can be found in Polinsky and Potsdam (2006, 2012) and Haddad and Potsdam (2013). Suffice it to say that case and economy play vital roles in these proposals.

c. i. [John managed [~~John~~ to win]] (alternating control)
   ii. [~~John~~ managed [John to win]]
d. [John managed [John to win]] (copy control)

H&P shows that all the possible theoretical options are in fact empirically attested. BC is thus one typological option among others. Consequently, there is nothing paradoxical or theoretically problematic about BC when one understands OC structures as living on A-chains and that BC is one of the standard deletion options. It fits into a full empirically realized set of theoretically predicted typological options.[31]

Note that given this logic, we should also expect to find cases of Backwards Raising as well. And apparently Backwards Raising empirically exists as a typological option. Not surprisingly, the same approach applied to BC also accommodates Backwards Raising.[32]

So, BC is not theoretically problematic given the MTC plus standard simple independently motivated approaches to copy deletion required by any MP theory. And this, in my very very humble opinion is a very very good result. Why? Because the structures in (13b) are a very serious problem for standard PRO-based analyses of control as they *systematically* violate the requirements (i) that OC PRO have a local c-commanding antecedent and (ii) Principle C. Anaphors always require binding and they seem to never bind their antecedents. Cases of BC are thus a real puzzle for PRO-based accounts, for the structures that should underlie them leave unbound anaphoric PROs and bound controller antecedents.[33] We thus have in this one construction two

---

[31] See Haddad and Potsdam (2013) for a much fuller discussion. The case of copy control is also discussed in Boeckx et al. (2007). We return to this in our discussion of Reflexivization and its relation to I-merge. Suffice it to say here that certain Principle C effects in English such as *John likes John* where the two instances of *John* are treated as co-referential (and which are relatively unacceptable in English) are fine in other languages, as Lasnik (1986) long ago observed. The astute reader should, by looking at (15d) be able to say why. This should no more induce a Principle C violation than cases of BC do.

[32] See Polinsky and Potsdam (2012) for discussion. It is worth observing that, as the current set of assumptions would lead us to expect, there is evidence that Copy Raising exists as well. For discussion, see Landau (2011) and Fujii (2005) reanalyzing Potsdam and Runner (2001).

[33] BC also provides another argument against D-structure. Theories that assume D-structure require expressions like PRO to syntactically accommodate the kinds of anaphoric dependencies we find in OC configurations. There is no real alternative once Equi-NP Deletion analyses of control fail empirically. Why? Because a syntactic analysis of OC must establish a dependency between two thematically linked positions. Given D-structure, this dependency cannot be forged via movement. Given the inadequacy of Equi analyses, it cannot be forged via deletion under identity. This only leaves a construal dependency between two base-generated positions, as we find in GB control theory. But BC shows that this is empirically inadequate also. This leaves us with movement theories of control as the only viable options. So there is a *very* intimate connection between D-structure, control, and PRO-based accounts.

Two further points: First, on minimalist methodological grounds, PRO is a very suspect entity. It is a purely theory-internal construct and, like all such, is suspect until proven innocent. In other words, on simple methodological grounds, PRO-less approaches to control are preferred

4.3 Obligatory Control, the EMH, and A-Movement

violations we should never see. Both the binding principle that requires OC structures to have a bound controllee (i.e. PRO), and Principle C, which requires an R-expression to be free (especially free of its anaphoric dependent), are very robust empirical principles. Consequently, we do not expect to see them systematically violated within the same construction in a given grammar.[34] Indeed, given standard assumptions, backwards control ought to be impossible.[35]

And yet it exists. So what does this tell us? It tells us that PRO-based accounts of OC are empirically very problematic and that we should look for PRO-less analyses of OC. To my knowledge, MTC is the *only* extant PRO-less approach to OC, and it is precisely this feature that makes the MTC theoretically viable given BC. I am tempted (and I can never resist temptation) to say yet more. In the context of both the MH and the EMH, the MTC is an immediate theoretical option. It follows seamlessly once one dumps DS (and *all* of its attendant properties) and endorses the EMH version of FL/UG that incorporates the FPG. Thus, the empirical successes of the MTC redound to the glory of the EMH+FPG. Less grandiosely, given BC, the MTC is an argument in favor of the EMH.

By now, there is a small minimalist industry on OC. Truth be told, the MTC is a minority position. However, my aim here has not been to defend the MTC against alternative PRO-based accounts of control (though the reader should be able to tell that I believe that this is an eminently viable enterprise) but to outline how the EMH leads to the MTC and to illustrate that this is not an *obvious* empirical dead end. Indeed, it has some very nice features which follow rather directly from the EMH.[36]

---

to PRO-encumbered ones. Second, the empirical inadequacies of Equi accounts disappear if one makes a distinction between two occurrences of the same expression versus two lexical selections of the same expression. This distinction is easy to establish given a copy theory of movement. Thus, Equi accounts are empirically problematic given theories that incorporate D-structure. For discussion, see Hornstein (2001).

[34] And indeed, languages that allow BC also obey other instances of Principle C.

[35] For precisely this reason, apparent cases of BC in the earlier literature were dismissed. And rightly so. For Polinsky and Potsdam to revive the issue required two important steps: (i) they provided strong novel evidence that BC indeed exists and (ii) they showed that *given current reasonable assumptions*, it could be theoretically accommodated. Interestingly, their approach also requires a rethinking of Principle C. In particular, it is not a principle whose applicability can be simply read off the surface string. We return to Principle C in Chapter 5.

[36] Consider just one more: The MTC embodies a simple version of Rosenbaum's Principle of Minimal Distance (PMD). As noted by him, and many others since, the controller is typically the most proximate local binder. Thus, in structures with two matrix-possible antecedents, a higher subject and a higher object, it is the object that typically is the binder. This follows from the MTC if, as standardly assumed, movement respects minimality. Of course, there are well-known counterexamples to the PMD. However, there are also plausible work-arounds that preserve the reduction of PMD to minimality. For some discussion, see Hornstein and Polinsky (2010).

118   4 A-Chain Dependencies

To sum up: I have illustrated some empirical benefits of taking OC as an A-chain phenomenon. First, we can derive its core properties as A-chain properties. Second, we can explain parallels between Raising and OC by observing that they share a common generative etiology. We can also account for some interesting cross-linguistic variation: for example, the fact that just as Brazilian Portuguese allows for finite control, it also allows for raising from apparent finite Spec TPs. And last of all, the MTC (in conjunction with a general theory of copy deletion) is able to account for backwards control, a very serious problem for classical PRO-based analyses of OC. The same mechanisms predict a typology of control configurations all of whose options are attested. These data follow from the MTC, which in turn follows from EMH incorporating FPG. Let's hear it for EMH!

4.4 Reflexivization, Movement, and the EMH

The logic of I-merge applied to OC extends pretty directly to Reflexivization. Both constructions involve a dependency between θ-bearing DPs. And in both cases the anaphoric OC PRO and the reflexive require local c-commanding antecedents (at least in English). It is thus natural to assume that (local) Reflexivization and OC have analogous grammatical analyses and so are products of the same operation and instantiate analogous structures. In particular, if OC lives on (A-)chains so must Reflexivization. I presently return to what differentiates them.

First let's illustrate their similarities. Consider the examples in (16), which illustrate OC PRO and reflexive structures:[37]

(16)   a. John$_1$ washed PRO/himself$_1$
        b. John$_1$ expects PRO/himself$_1$ to win
        c. *John$_1$ expects Mary to wash PRO/himself$_1$
        d. *John$_1$ expects PRO/himself$_1$ will win
        e. *John's$_1$ mother washed PRO/himself$_1$
        f. *For PRO/himself to wash himself is impossible

The verb *wash* in (16a) has an OC version. Note that both the forms with PRO and a reflexive carry the same θ-interpretation, with *John* interpreted as engaged in self-washing whether there is an overt reflexive present or not. I indicate the position as filled by a PRO, but this is just for notational convenience. If the MTC is correct, this is generated by movement of *John* through both θ-positions ultimately landing in Spec T for case valuation/agreement. The structure is provided in (17a). The difference on this analysis between

---

[37] (16a) implicitly makes a controversial claim; namely that PRO can appear in a position other than Spec T.

4.4 Reflexivization, Movement, and the EMH

control and reflexivization can be attributed to a (minor?) feature of the morphophonology.[38] It revolves around whether the object is deleted (i.e. left unpronounced) or pronounced as a reflexive.[39] The same holds for the other cases, which we will discuss in turn.

(17)   a. [John [T+past [John v [wash John]]]]
         b. [John [T+pres [John v [expect [**John** to [John win]]]]]]
         c. [John [T+pres [John v [expect [Mary to [Mary v [wash John]]]]]]]
         d. [John [T+pres [John v [expect [John [will win]]]]]]
         e. [[John's mother] T+past [[John's mother] v [wash John]]]

The derivation in (17b) is fine with *John* starting as the embedded external argument of *win* and moving through the embedded non-finite Spec T to the external argument position of *expect* to the matrix finite Spec T where case/agreement applies. The difference then between Reflexivization and OC amounts to whether ***John*** is deleted or pronounced as a reflexive.

This derivation contrasts with the one in (17c) in that *John* starts its life as the internal argument of *wash*, *Mary* being the external one. The derivation is illicit. To reach the external argument position of *expect* requires a movement that is too long (it must move over *Mary*, thereby violating minimality). This leads to ungrammaticality and hence unacceptability.

The derivation in (17d) is also illicit. This time *John* must move from a case-marked position. As we saw earlier (see (11a)), this kind of A-movement is generally unavailable in English (a violation of the tensed S

---

[38] Whether we find a clause with a deleted gap (i.e. PRO) or Reflexivization most likely revolves around the theory of case. Overt material requires case licensing. In English, the objects of verbs like *wash* are optionally case marked, allowing for the attested variation between the control and reflexive readings. This kind of variation is also seen with exceptional case marking (ECM) verbs like *expect*, where case marking is also optional. This is a far too simplified discussion of the variation, but I will leave it incomplete and move on.

[39] This analysis has obvious affinities with one of the earliest Generative analyses of reflexivization first offered by Lees and Klima (1963). There are various versions of movement analysis of reflexivization mentioned here, most of which differ in how they realize the reflexive morphophonologically. I here adopt the simplest one on offer initially provided by Idsardi and Lidz (1998). Other options are discussed in Hornstein (2001) and Zwart (2002). See Kayne (2002) for discussion as well.
Note 27 mentions a doubling option for the analysis of OC and suggests some problems. However, in the case of reflexivization, the noted problems might be a virtue. It seems that we don't find cases of backwards reflexivization analogous to backwards control. Why not? If reflexive structures begin their derivational lives with the antecedent and reflexive forming a unit and the antecedent then moving to saturate a θ-position, then this doubling analysis would suffice to block backwards reflexivization. The relevant theoretical issue is motivating the assumption that reflexives and their antecedents *must* start off together as a unit. If this requirement could be explained in a principled manner it would obviate the stipulation discussed in Chapter 5 that reflexives/pronouns mark the site from which I-merge/movement occurs.

condition). This makes the indicated movement ungrammatical and the sentence unacceptable.[40]

The derivation in (17e) is similarly unacceptable. *John* moves to the Spec of the complex DP/NP whose nominal head is mother. This is movement to a non-commanding position and is illicit as it violates the No Tampering Condition.[41]

Consider one last fact: like OC, reflexives require local c-commanding antecedents. (16c) and (16e) illustrate the locality and c-command restrictions. (16f) shows that an antecedent is required for OC/Reflexivization constructions. The unacceptability of these is because the PRO/reflexive in the subject position of the complex infinitival subject has no antecedent.[42]

Let's recap: The EMH forces a movement (aka I-merge) analysis of OC constructions. The relevant movement is A-movement, and OC constructions live on A-chains with multiple θ-positions. Treating OC in this way allows for the derivation of many of OC's salient properties, including the fact that OC "PRO" is (generally) found in non-case-marked positions, and requires local commanding antecedents. Reflexives fit a very similar profile, suggesting that they should be derived in the same way. Given the EMH, they too are analyzable as living on A-chains with multiple θ-positions. The main difference between OC and Reflexivization regards the licensing of overt morphophonological material, a matter on which I have little to say. What is critical for present purposes is that Reflexivization's core properties as enumerated in Principle A of the binding theory follow pretty seamlessly from the assumption that Reflexivization is an A-chain phenomena akin to OC.

There are also some anomalies that a movement analysis of Reflexivization and backwards control can explain away. Consider two.

First, Polinsky and Potsdam (2002: 272) observe in their paper on backwards control an interesting interaction between cases of backwards Reflexivization

---

[40] One might wonder whether the derivation is out for morphophonological reasons. The case assigned here should be nominative rather than reflexive. Many languages fail to have nominative reflexive forms (e.g. in English there is no *he-self* form of the reflexive). Some languages allow a reflexive in this position, but in these there is either no required agreement between the subject and predicate of a finite clause (Japanese) or there is no agreement because the subject is non-nominative (Icelandic). In these languages what is absent in English is attested: a reflexive in the finite subject position bound to an antecedent in the next higher clause. There is some very interesting discussion of these phenomena, called the *anaphor agreement effect*, dating from original work by Rizzi (1990a) and Woolford (1999). For some recent excellent discussion, see Preminger (2021). This is also discussed in Hornstein (2001).

[41] I am playing a bit fast and loose here. It does violate the condition if there is no sideways movement. If there is (and I believe there is), this case will require rethinking. Add another issue to the to-do list.

[42] Note the use of *himself* here in the object position. This forces the OC PRO reading by preventing the arb reading of PRO in subject position.

4.4 Reflexivization, Movement, and the EMH

and Reflexivization. In Tsez, for example, it is possible to find reflexives apparently c-commanding their antecedents:[43]

(18) nesa nesir₁ [_TP irbahin-a₁ halmaɣ-or ɣutku rod-a] Ø-oq-si
      Refl.I.dat Ibrahim.I-erg friend-dat house make-infin I.begin-past-evid
      'Ibrahim began, for himself, to build a house for his friend'

Given classical binding theory, this should be impossible. However, if we assume a movement theory of control and reflexivization then we can do for these cases what we have done in cases of backwards control. More specifically, assume that in Tsez the spell-out of the reflexive is more liberal than it is in languages like English. In English the foot of the complex chain gets spelled out, while in Tsez a higher copy can be the locus of this morphological conversion. And assume that backwards control obtains. Then we can account for the data in (18) by assuming that the underlying structure of (18) looks like (19), where the reflexive is anteceded by a c-commanding DP in Spec of the matrix T. The options are illustrated in (19):

(19) irbahin-a₁ nesa nesir₁ [_TP irbahin-a₁ halmaɣ-or ɣutku rod-a] Ø-oq-si
      Ibrahim   Refl.I.dat Ibrahim.I-erg friend-dat house make-infin I.begin
      past-evid
      'Ibrahim began, for himself, to build a house for his friend'

Second, there are languages where Reflexivization can be expressed without the use of dedicated reflexives. For example, in San Lucas Quiaviní Zapotec (SLQZ) and Hmong (to take two of many) it is possible to express Reflexivization via copies:

(20) John saw John

We know that this is a reflexive structure for it licenses sloppy identity under ellipsis. Thus, (21a) (can) mean that Bill saw himself, not that he saw John. Contrast this with (21b) in English, where only a strict reading is available:

(21) a. John saw John and Bill too (=John saw himself and Bill (saw himself))
      b. John saw John and Bill too (=John saw John and Bill (saw John) but
         *John saw himself and Bill (saw himself))

The movement theory of Reflexivization treats reflexive morphemes as the product of copy spell-out operations. Languages like SLQZ and Hmong do not avail themselves of this in cases like (20), preferring to leave the intact copy in place of a reflexive anaphor. It is worth observing that in both languages the copy must be an exact duplicate of the antecedent. This too follows naturally

---

[43] Polinsky and Potsdam (2002: 272 (72)) presents similar data for the licensing of secondary predicates. The antecedent of the predicate fails to overtly c-command the predicate it licenses.

from the assumption that Reflexivization lives on A-chains, as the copies that are articulated are a consequence of the formal properties of I-merge. It appears that grammars have the option of replacing these in spell-out (as in English Reflexivization), deleting them (as in OC configurations) or leaving them intact (as in copy-reflexive languages). So, modulo the morpho-syntax, these chains are basically the same and behave as grammatically expected.[44]

One last observation: Note that the English "translation" of (20) in (21b) is slightly "off." Their degraded status is standardly explained as a Principle C violation. Lasnik (1986) long ago observed that there were some languages that appeared to violate this instance of Principle C. However, we now see that this is not so. Rather these languages express Reflexivization using copies. Depending on how one analyzes Principle C effects, there need be no violation of Principle C here. I offer such an analysis in Chapter 5. For the present, note that the chain underlying reflexives in both English and copy-reflexive languages is the same up to the morphophonological expression of copies. Once we control for this, then it is easy to account for both the unacceptability of the English cases (English requires copies to surface as reflexives, as Lees and Klima long ago noted) and the acceptability of the copy-reflexive cases (these languages permit the phonological realization of multiple copies).

Very very last point. The astute historically informed reader should immediately have noticed that the movement approach to both OC and Reflexivization owes a lot to the earliest analyses of these constructions in the Generative literature. These early theories treated OC as a transformational operation wherein higher copies deleted lower ones and treated Reflexivization as transformations that turned a lower copy of a (nearby) nominal into a reflexive.[45]

---

[44] Before moving on, let me highlight a problem. I have not been able to find cases wherein an overt reflexive c-commands its antecedent without an intervening controller. So, for example, in the Tsez example, we need not assume that reflexives are themselves parts of chains to account for the data. We need simply assume that reflexives require binding and that the deleted copy of the antecedent in Spec T of the matrix serves as a potential binder. Note too that in copy-reflexive languages the data does not involve a morphologically overt reflexive. Thus, I do not here offer a pure case of backwards reflexivization; the analogue of (i):
(i) Mary believes himself$_i$ to like John$_i$
This means that it is possible that backwards reflexivization does not exist and that the overt realization of an expression plays a role in which copy can be retained. If Polinsky and Potsdam are right in their surmise that overt morphological expression should ultimately be tied to case, this means that when an expression ends up in a (obligatory) case-marked position it is realized as the moving copy and not spelled out as a reflexive. I am not sure why this should be so, but there are various ways of implementing the movement theory of construal as it applies to reflexives, one of which, as previously mentioned, involves a doubling strategy wherein the reflexive marks the launch site of movement. This assumption is pressed into further service in the discussion of pronominalization in Chapter 5. For some discussion of the doubling approach, see note 27, the discussion in Hornstein (2001) and Kayne (2002).

[45] We reviewed the Lees–Klima reflexive rule in Chapter 1.

The treatments here return to these earlier analyses.[46] In particular, like earlier versions, they treat the morphophonological adjustments of the copies (aka chain links) as free parameters. GB's reanalysis of OC and Reflexivization effectively retains the constructional properties of the earlier transformations by building morpheme-specific grammatical conditions on the licensing of reflexives (the *self* morphemes) and PRO. Within GB, these items are grammatically regulated. In movement approaches, reflexives are the morphological detritus that copies sometimes throw off. They are distractions. The locus of grammatical action is the OC/Reflexivization *relation*, not the morphemes that often accompany these relational dependencies. Treating both constructions as living on A-chains unifies these dependencies with A-movement constructions like Raising and Passive more generally. The cost is a few morphophonological spell-out rules (i.e. the identification of certain formatives as products of the grammar rather than products of lexical insertion). This important distinction between formatives that are by-products of grammatical operations and those that are denizens of the lexicon directly reflects the assumptions of these earlier grammatical analyses.

4.5 Conclusion

The EMH, incorporating the FPG, requires that all grammatical dependencies be mediated by Merge. If, as assumed since the earliest days of Generative Grammar, antecedence is a grammatical dependency, then the EMH insists that it be a Merge-mediated dependency. More specifically, if A antecedes a remotely located anaphoric dependent D, then (i) A and D must have merged (i.e. formed a constituent) at some point in the derivation and (ii) A must have moved away from D (I-merged into some other position) distant from D in some subsequent part of the derivation. In other words, there is a Merge-generated chain relation mediating A and D which is the product of various combinations of E- and I-merge.

Generative Grammar is well acquainted with chain structures. They have well described well-formedness conditions. Thus, analyzing (some) antecedence relations as "living on" chains brings with it pretty robust predictions concerning their properties. In the case of control and reflexives, the relevant chains are A-chains. I have presented some illustrative evidence that these expectations are plausibly realized. The supposition covers the main salient facts about the distribution of OC PRO and reflexives and many of the core

---

[46] Though there are some important technical differences that evade some earlier critiques of these analyses. In particular, the fact that copies are occurrences of chains allows the current versions to evade the implication that *Everyone expects himself/PRO to leave* means *Everyone expects everyone to leave*. This is a good thing as the former does not mean what the latter does.

locality and binding properties of control and binding-A configurations. For example, I have shown that *if* these constructions are Merge-generated then we expect anaphors to require antecedents and we expect these antecedents to c-command the dependent anaphors. *If* we further assume that OC and Reflexivization live on A-chains, then we also expect them to display the locality restrictions (Specified Subject and Tensed S condition) they seem to respect. This is what the EMH leads us to expect, and this is (pretty much) what we find.

There are, of course, complexities. A Merge-based conception of construal requires some housekeeping rules not unlike those that the earliest Generative approaches to binding and control postulated. Thus, we need rules that delete copies or convert them into other morphophonological forms. This means that some morphophonological material is grammatically derived (e.g. reflexives) rather than lexically inserted. We found some ancillary evidence in favor of this view by noting that there are languages that can express reflexivization without reflexives, phonologically pronouncing the "copy" that I-merge generates. We noted that this has the useful property of providing a rationale for why some languages appear to allow Principle C violations that other languages enforce. It turns out to be a surfacy fact about how many copies can survive to AP.

So, there are reasons in favor of adopting a movement account of both OC and Reflexivization and thereby unifying them with Raising and Passivization constructions. What I would like to once again emphasize is the very strong relationship between a movement account of OC and Reflexivization and the EMH+FPG. To the degree that we find the former empirically viable, it redounds in favor of the latter.

This strong connection is, in my view, theoretically very attractive. First, as discussed above, the EMH+FPG provide an account for why natural language has construal dependencies at all. It has them, because Merge in the context of a DS-less account of derivations allows for their generation. Merge without DS leads to chains with multiple θ-links, and such chains just are the grammatical representations of construal dependencies.

Second, a Merge-based approach to construal explains the properties we find in such dependencies. More specifically, it is one thing to describe control and binding phenomena, and quite another to explain their properties. GB, for all of its many contributions, did not *explain* why antecedents need to c-command their anaphoric dependents, or why anaphors require syntactic antecedents (aka binders), or why they need be close by (etc.). The movement theory (and hence the EMH+FPG) does offer an account of these features of anaphoric dependencies. The account is simple: They follow from how these structures are generated. In other words, they follow from general properties of Merge. If we take Merge to be the *only* way of establishing dependencies and we eschew D-structure and allow chains with multiple θ-positions, we derive the basic properties of these constructions. Not bad, right?

4.5 Conclusion

One second to last point that is worth making: This approach to construal is different from standard GB accounts in one critical way. The story above provides an account of how dependencies are formed regardless of what the morphemes that mark these dependencies are. The GB theory, for all of its virtues, is a theory of the requirements that specific morphemes impose on the grammar. PRO has one set of requirements, reflexives another, bound pronouns a third.[47] Why does PRO have the requirements it has? Well, because we stipulate that PRO must meet these requirements. There is no more to it than that. Ditto for reflexives, reciprocals and bound pronouns. They have the properties they have because of the morphemes involved, and the morphemes have these particular properties by stipulation.

The EMH has a very different take on these matters. There is nothing special about the morphemes involved. They do *not* impose demands on the grammar. Rather, these are morphological detritus that grammars can use (but need not) to meet other grammatical demands (e.g. case, agreement, etc.).

Why do I mention this? Because there is a straightforward sense in which earlier GB accounts treat reflexivization and control (and pronominalization) as *constructions*. The movement theory of construal (and the EMH) is radically *anti*-constructionist. Chains are built by Merge and they have interpretations in virtue of expressing general interpretive properties of chains. The problem with constructions as fundamental is that they cannot explain why constructions have the properties they have. Constructions preclude explanation as they pack the properties of the observed constructions in the (ad hoc stipulated) feature structures of the relevant constructional heads. The virtue of the EMH is that, via the movement theory of construal, it can offer explanations for the basic properties that these constructions have. If explanation, then, is what you want, then non-morpheme-based accounts of construal is what you need.[48] The EMH+FPG tracks the properties of all grammatical structures and dependencies via how Merge generates them. In other words, construal looks the way it

---

[47] Let me be careful here. Within GB there are various views of the ontological status of PRO. The first was that PRO was a lexical item just like any other, maybe a null reflexive. The second was that PRO was a theory-internal construct, e.g. a nominal category without lexically inserted content (i.e. [$_{NP}$ e]). This latter was the predominant theoretical version, and for good reason: It allowed the properties of PRO to be derived from *general properties of the grammar*. If PRO is just a lexical item then it becomes impossible to explain the properties of control structures. They just reflect the diacritical idiosyncrasies of a particular lexical item. It is worth observing that current MP accounts eschew the distinction between phrase structure rules that build structure and lexical insertion rules that populate these built structures. Thus, there is little theoretical room for the second conception of PRO. This leaves the first, where PRO is just a lexical item with its own peculiar features. This option, however, comes with a cost. It blocks all avenues to explaining *why* control structures have the properties they do. There is no grammatical explanation, just a description. This makes this understanding of PRO very MP repugnant.

[48] As some GB approaches to PRO recognized. See note 47.

does because the only operation available for building structure or establishing dependencies is Merge. This restricts the kinds of structures and dependencies we expect to find. Interestingly, what we expect to find (more or less) fits with what we do, at least in the central cases.

Let me make a slightly stronger claim. Generative Grammar has identified two kinds of movement rules and various kind of nominal positions. A-movement creates dependencies between A-positions. A-positions comprise +/−θ-positions, +/−case positions, and +/−agreement positions.[49] Now consider all the possible dependencies the A-movement analogue of I-merge can generate. It looks like FL allows Gs to realize them all. So we can get +θ to −θ dependencies in Raising and Passive (there are also −case to +case dependencies), +θ to +θ dependencies in OC and Reflexivization (the latter being −case to +case, the latter being +case to +case), and so on. In fact, so far as I can tell, we realize almost all of the possible options (big exception: +case +agreement freezes further movement).[50] In other words, there seems to be a Principle of Grammatical Plenitude at work here: Every possible dependency option is realized in the A-domain. In Chapter 5 we note that this is also the case in the A'-domain. And this is what we should expect from an EMH kind of theory with no additional restrictions as regards derivational options.[51]

And now the last point: I have suggested that some construal constructions live on A-chains. However, as we all know, A-chains is not all there is. Grammars have A'-chains as well. In the next chapter we allow this second shoe to drop and consider the possibility of pronominal anaphora as living on A'-chains. If you thought that this chapter was overly speculative, fasten your seat belts for you ain't seen nothing yet.

---

[49] And subject positions of non-finite clauses. These are "pure" intermediate positions regulated only by the Extended Projection Principle (i.e. the principle that requires sentences to have subjects). Nothing surfaces here, at least in English. At any rate, I will put these aside in the remarks that follow.

[50] This is the anaphor agreement effect briefly noted in note 40. So far as I know, the source of this effect is currently unknown.

[51] The discussion above of the typological variation in OC constructions noted by Haddad and Potsdam (2013) illustrates a similar point regarding plenitude. All the logical options are realized.

5 Construal and the Extended Merge Hypothesis (2)
A'-Chain Dependencies

5.0 The Generalizations Addressed in This Chapter

a. Resumptive Pronoun (RP) effects
b. Pronominalization/Principle B effects
c. The complementarity of Reflexivization and Pronominalization
d. Principle C effects
e. Strong and weak crossover effects
f. Long-distance anaphor effects

5.1 Setting the Stage

In the previous chapter I reviewed some of the central properties of some construal relations and showed how to derive them from a Merge-based system like the EMH. The key was to treat these relations as "living on" A-chains and thus similar in their derivational etiology to classical Raising and Passive constructions despite their divergent thematic properties. In particular, I suggested that certain core grammatical properties of obligatory control and reflexivization follow if we assume that a bound "PRO" or a reflexive is related to its antecedent via A-movement, a species of I-merge. In this chapter I would like to extend this logic to include other cases of construal. More specifically, I will consider constructions involving bound pronouns such as those in (1). (1a) is an example of Pronominalization, (1b) of Resumption.

(1)   a. Every woman$_1$ thought that she$_1$ was tall
         b. Which woman$_1$ did you wonder whether she$_1$ was tall

The bound pronoun products of Pronominalization in (1a) are quite standard in English, the resumptive pronouns in (1b) less so. Nonetheless both, I propose, involve (at least in part) an A'-chain dependency that relates the indicated antecedents with the indicated bound pronouns. As we shall see, technically implementing this proposal requires dropping some principles that GB and current MP approaches adopt. In other words, making things work out will require overturning the theoretical cart somewhat, and this should always raise (justifiable) suspicions.

Why then explore this possibility? Because this is the kind of analysis that the EMH incorporating the FPG leads to. So, if you like what the EMH/FPG has to offer, you will want to explore these kinds of analyses. As I do, I will. My plan is to show that there are explanatory gains to be made if we give in to these urges. More specifically, as with the cases of construal discussed in Chapter 4, I argue that we can derive many central properties of pronominal construal in both bound pronoun and resumptive pronouns constructions if we assume that they live on A'-chains.

The basic idea is a simple one. Following the logic of the EMH/FPG, the structures in (1) are roughly those in (2):

(2)   a. [$_{TP}$ **Every woman** [[every woman$_\theta$ v [thought [$_{CP}$ ***every woman*** that [every woman/she was [every woman$_\theta$ tall]]]]]]

    b. [$_{CP}$ **Which woman** did [$_{TP}$ you think [$_{CP}$ ***which woman*** that [which woman/she [was [every woman$_\theta$ tall]]]]]]

Note that in both cases we have chains that involve a (***bold italicized***) link in an A'-position (viz. the intermediate Spec CP). In both cases the lowest link of the chain is realized (at AP) as a pronoun (and at CI as a copy). The derivation in (2a) involves an instance of improper movement, as we move from an A'- to an A-position in generating the chain. Furthermore, (2a) involves Merge into multiple θ-positions (as indicated by the 'θ' subscript). Thus, Pronominalization cases like (2a) are being treated as the A' analogues of obligatory control and reflexivization (which, to refresh your memories, involves movement through multiple θ-positions). Pronominalization constructions similarly involve chains bearing multiple θ-roles. We return to this anon.

In contrast, (2b) structures are the A' analogues of Raising and Passive in that these chains contain a single θ-position. The key idea of the present proposal is that (at least some) bound pronouns live on chains which involve a link in an A'-position, and in this they structurally contrast with the cases of construal in Chapter 4 that live on "pure" A-chains, chains that do not contain any A'-links.

A few words before I start.

First, the idea of so treating bound pronouns is (sadly) not original to me. It was first mooted in Kayne (2002). I will not necessarily follow its details, but I do adopt its central idea.

Second, whereas the hypothesis that obligatory control and reflexivization realize A-chain structures has been somewhat explored in the literature, the idea that bound pronoun dependencies are products of movement has, with the exception of Kayne (2002), been relatively ignored. There are some suggestions that resumptive pronoun dependencies are based on movement, but extending these to standard bound pronouns seems not to have been widely investigated. As such, this chapter may be a bit on the longish side.

Third, whatever residue of problems and puzzles that the A-chain approach to control and reflexivization offered in Chapter 4 may suffer from, they are mild (what an understatement!) compared to the questions that the extension of the EMH/FPG to bound pronoun constructions generates. I will, again, mention some of them but leave most of them unresolved. My aim here is not to argue that these analyses are correct so much as to argue that they are plausible, that they follow from the EMH/FPG, and that they have a nice budget of explanatory consequences. That said, it is clear to me (and soon will be to you) that these extensions are far more fragile and contentious than those outlined in Chapter 4 (which, as the reader surely knows, are already plenty controversial).

5.2 Bound Pronoun Constructions and the EMH

A'-chains involve links in both A- and A'-positions. To illustrate, consider a standard example of long *Wh*-movement:

(3)   a. I wonder what Bill said that Mary bought
        b. I wonder [**what** C_{+wh} [Bill said [**what** that [Mary bought **what**$_\theta$]]]]

The underlying structure of the indirect question in (3a) is provided (roughly) in (3b). The A'-chain is composed of (at least) three links: The top one rests in an A'-position, the bottom one sits in a θ-position, and there is one in an intermediate A'-position.[1] This A'-chain is phonetically realized as (3a) by deleting all but the top copy.

This is not the only way of forming *Wh*-dependencies. In some languages the bottom link can be realized as a resumptive pronoun (RP). Generative Grammar has vigorously debated whether RP constructions are deeply different from *Wh*-constructions that have gaps in place of RPs. One view, due to Chomsky (1977), is that they are and that leaving a gap is a *diagnostic property* of movement operations.[2] However, recent research has suggested that

---

[1] Depending on your theory of case assignment, the bottom link is also case marked. Given the EMH/FPG, and assuming that accusative case is assigned by *v*, there should also be a link in the Spec of *v* in the most deeply embedded clause. GB case theory is different. In particular, a direct object is θ-marked and case marked in the base position. Some MP versions of case marking that involve feature lowering (Richards 2007) adopt a similar hypothesis for accusative case marking, but this approach has been replaced by accounts that require direct objects to move from their θ-positions (Chomsky 2013). These hypotheses are incompatible with the EMH and so I will ignore them in what follows. Of course, this may be a big mistake empirically speaking, but what the hell!

[2] Chomsky's (1977) proposal then requires that Resumption *not* be a movement-generated dependency but the output of some kind of construal process. This dual route approach to *Wh*-structures contrasts with Ross's (1965) proposal for how these structures are generated, which assumes that gaps are the product of a deletion operation distinct from the movement operation that generates the dependency. The main motivation for Chomsky's contrary proposal is the (apparent) observation that island effects, which Chomsky (1977) takes to be diagnostic of

RP constructions also involve movement and we review some of that evidence now. Why? Because this is the kind of analysis that the EMH/FPG requires. Recall, the central EMH idea is that all G-dependencies are Merge generated (viz. the FPG), and this means that if the dependent expressions are remote from each other, then I-merge is involved in separating them. So, RP constructions where some A'-element is interpreted as "binding" the RP must be formed by movement. There is no other option.

So what is the evidence for RPs being related to their antecedents via movement?

Demirdache (1991) provides evidence that resumptive pronouns are tails of regular A'-chains. First, in robust RP languages like Hebrew and Jordanian Arabic, RPs can occur in variation with overt gaps. Furthermore, like overt gaps, they are interpreted as bound variables, just like non-phonetic A'-traces. Both these facts follow if RPs, like A'-traces, are residues of movement (i.e. are identical up to some low level morphophonological adjustments).

Second, RPs can overtly move in Hebrew. They can sit at the left edge of clauses. Hence, we can find the Hebrew analogues of examples like (4):

(4) The man (**about him**) that (**about him**) I think that (**about him**) said-you that (**about him**) wrote Sara (**about him**) a poem

The bold copies indicate the various positions that the RP can occupy. Formally, this appears analogous to other kinds of stranding we find with A'-movement, and the distribution of these RPs follows if we assume that they are stranded under A'-movement of the operator that forms the relative clause.[3]

Third, RPs can "mix" with gaps in across-the-board (ATB) constructions. So the Hebrew analogues of (5) are acceptable.[4] If RPs are products of A'-movement then both conjuncts contain a residue of A'-movement and hence fit the standard profile of licit ATBs.

movement, seem to only surface when the *Wh*-constructions have gaps. Or, put more positively, when RPs tailed A'-chains, the *Wh*-dependency was taken to be acceptable.

Subsequent research has suggested that this observation may not be correct (we return to this). Furthermore, with the minimalist replacement of trace theory with the copy theory, it is not clear how to state the correlation that Chomsky (1977) wishes to make between movement and the gaps (i.e. trace residues) it leaves behind. Current Merge-based approaches to movement require something like Ross's (1965) original deletion mechanism in addition to whatever generates a movement/I-merge dependency. In a word, if traces don't exist then it is very hard (impossible really) to correlate island effects with *trace*-leaving movement operations.

All of this is additional grist for the EMH/FPG mill as the distinction between construal properties generated by grammatical operations and those that result from Merge cannot be made. In other words, the EMH is incompatible with Chomsky's (1977) suggestion of two distinct kinds of grammatical operations for the formation of *Wh*-chains. And the apparent fact that the desired distinction is not stateable given standard MP assumptions argues that this incompatibility is a theoretical virtue.

[3] See McCloskey (2000) for discussions of English Q-float off of A'-movement, and Doliana (2021) for *alles* float in German.
[4] Note (5) is improved in English if we delete the RP in the second conjunct. Not so in Hebrew.

(5)   The man₁ that Rina wants t₁ and loves him₁ more than anyone

Fourth, RPs can license parasitic gaps. The Hebrew/Arabic analogues of (6) are acceptable.⁵

(6)   The movie₁ that everyone who saw t₁ loved it₁

The parasitic t_j gap inside the relative clause island needs to be licensed by a "real" gap in a non-island position. The RP it_j serves as the licenser if it is the tail of an A'-chain.

Fifth, RPs display both strong and weak crossover effects, both characteristics of A'-traces. The argument is a bit involved, but the relevant cases are examples involving bound epithets. Demirdache (1991) notes that Hebrew examples analogous to (7) and (8) are unacceptable.⁶

(7)   *This is the guy₁ that I informed the idiot₁ that the teacher will flunk him₁

(8)   This is the guy₁ that I informed his/*the idiot's₁ parents that the teacher will flunk him₁

The critical assumption is that epithets are *not* residues of movement (though, as we shall see, they can be semantically bound).⁷ If this is correct, and if RPs are products of movement, then we expect (7) to instantiate a typical case of strong crossover (SCO) with the RP/trace/variable residue of movement bound by the epithet.

Similarly, (8) displays a weak crossover (WCO) configuration with the RP residue of movement having an antecedent (the epithet *the idiot*), to its left. The WCO effect disappears when the epithet is replaced by a pronoun, as in that case the leftmost pronoun might be the resumptive one and so no WCO configuration will be realized. It is worth noting that, as expected, the cases in (7) are all unacceptable if a gap/trace replaces the RP.

Sixth, there is some recent evidence that RPs *do not rescue island violations*. This is important. Why? Because the main motivation for Chomsky's (1977) proposal that gaps be taken as diagnostic properties of movement (i.e. trace/gap-leaving operations) is the purported contrast in cases like (9):

(9)   The man₁ who Mary met a woman who said that she admired *t/ok:him₁

---

⁵ Once again, in English, deleting the bound RP *it* improves acceptability.
⁶ Demirdache and Percus (2011: 377, (25)) show similar effects in Jordanian Arabic. And they demonstrate that the unacceptable (8) with a bound definite description to the left of the RP is a weak crossover effect by offering examples where the RP and the definite description swap positions and the sentence is acceptable. Thus while the order " ... Operator₁ ... Definite Description₁ ... Resumptive Pronoun₁ ... " leads to unacceptability, the order " ... Operator₁ ... Resumptive Pronoun₁ ... Definite Description₁ ... " seems fine.
⁷ I return later to cases in which epithets/definite descriptions function as bound variables and the distinction between syntactic vs semantic binding. The viability of the latter difference is critical if the story here has any chance of survival. Skeptics take note.

However, some recent experimental investigations of such long-distance dependencies have failed to confirm this contrast.[8] I should add that the data is mixed. What is clear is that most experiments show no contrast between regular *Wh*-chains and RP chains while some others do. The evidence, then, is decidedly more mixed than previously thought and it is fair to conclude that the ameliorating effects of resumption are unclear. What is relevant here is the following: *If* islands are diagnostic of movement, and RPs like "traces" are products of movement, *then* the acceptability profile of island violations for the two constructions should be the same.[9] And it seems that the bulk of the available evidence currently suggests that RPs do not much improve island violations.[10]

Consider one last rather sophisticated argument that will prove useful later on when I discuss pronominalization constructions.

Say that we are right in thinking that RPs are products of movement and thus subject to island restrictions. If this is correct then RPs within islands cannot be the residues of movement. In other words, they must be linked to their antecedents in some manner different from movement.[11]

A proposal along these lines is advanced for RPs in Lebanese Arabic (LA) in Aoun, Choueiri and Hornstein (2001) (ACH). Here's the gist of the argument. ACH takes reconstruction effects to be a useful diagnostic of movement.[12] Interestingly, in LA, RPs license reconstruction *unless* they sit within islands.

---

[8] See Sprouse (2007), Keller (2000) and Polinsky et al. (2013). But also see Ackerman et al. (2018).

[9] Actually, this assumes that island effects are analyzed roughly along the lines of Chomsky (1977) as a condition on movement. Ross (1965) did not so analyze island effects. There unacceptability results from illicit chopping within islands. Hornstein et al. (2003/2007) develop a version of this approach. For now, however, I will adopt the conventional view due to Chomsky (1977).

[10] Two caveats: First, when I introduce the distinction between semantic and syntactic binding, we will find some room for possibly accommodating the results that argue that RPs can rescue islands. The idea will be that semantic binding is not hindered by islands and that some might be able to use such binding to ameliorate the overall (un)acceptability profile. This story will be consistent with the idea that movement is sensitive to islands and that RPs are residues of movement. Second, RPs quite definitely do improve Fixed Subject Constraint violations (see Sprouse 2007). However, as these are not generally reduced to island effects, this fact does not bear on the current discussion.

[11] The reader is no doubt thinking that this contravenes the EMH/FPG. And it might. But I will suggest that it might not in that the dependency is established *extra-grammatically*. I will propose that semantic binding exists alongside syntactic binding and that semantic binding is *not* an operation of sentence grammar. Thus, the EMH holds as a principle of FL, but there are ways of effecting similar results using other non-grammatical means. The reader should be very very skeptical here, which I am sure you are. But I will try to make the case for this position below.

[12] See Chapter 2 for discussion of the Copy Theory of Movement (CTM) and how it follows from Merge and serves to provide an analysis of reconstruction effects.

5.2 Bound Pronoun Constructions and the EMH

If an RP sits inside an island, reconstruction fails. The contrast in (10) illustrates this (English analogue of LA sentences provided):

(10)   a. [Her$_1$ bad student]$_2$, we want to tell no teacher$_1$ that he$_2$ cheated on the exam
        b. * [Her$_1$ bad student]$_2$, we want to tell no teacher$_1$ about the girl with whom he$_2$ cheated on the exam

In LA, *her* in (10a) can be bound by *no teacher* via the copy of *her bad student* in the position of the RP *he$_2$*. This same interpretive option is blocked in (10b). It is blocked because there is no copy of *her bad student* inside the island because there has been no I-merge/movement of *her bad student* from the island because islands block I-merge/movement. Hence, whatever the relation between the fronted phrase and the pronoun, it is not an I-merge/movement-generated relation.[13]

Here's the take-home message: It looks like islands "turn off" reconstruction effects in RP constructions. They do this by blocking the movement that generates the copies necessary for licensing such effects.[14]

Demirdache and Percus (2011) (D&P) uses a similar kind of argument to show that islands can turn off crossover effects with RPs. If this is correct, then it suggests that these too are products of movement, though D&P does not make particularly clear exactly how islands turn off crossover effects (I offer a proposal below).[15] Here is the argument. It is based on Jordanian Arabic examples.

The examples (7) and (8) above demonstrate crossover effects in non-island contexts. D&P turns off these effects by embedding the epithet and putative RP inside a *because* island. Doing this renders the relevant indexing acceptable. Contrast (7) and (11) and (8) and (12).

(11)   SCO: *Every boy$_1$*, I got angry because *the donkey$_1$* thought that Layla loves *him*1

---

[13] An aside: Interestingly, the form of the pronoun within islands can differ from that found outside of islands. In particular, LA has both strong and weak forms of pronouns. RPs are always weak. Inside islands the pronoun related to the antecedent can be weak or strong. I take this fact to be of some importance below as I will suggest that it is a decent diagnostic for distinguishing those pronouns that are residues of movement and those that are not. We will, in fact, find analogous data in English with respect to where bound definite descriptions are allowed.
[14] Need I add that, *if* this is correct, then it is a hell of an argument for an (I-)merge based analysis of movement and a movement analysis of RPs! This argument was developed by Aoun and Choueiri before Hornstein jumped onto ACH as a third wheel.
[15] Here's what I mean. Why islands would obviate reconstruction is theoretically clear given the CTM coupled with the assumption that islands obviate movement. However, it is less clear why crossover effects should be sensitive to movement. Typically, crossover effects are theoretically managed representationally. A filter (ad hoc, I might add) is postulated to cover the restriction. However, if such effects prove to be sensitive to islands, as D&P argues, then a movement approach to crossover effects is called for. I will limn a *partial* analysis along such lines below.

(12)   WCO(: *Every boy$_i$*, I got angry because *this donkey's$_i$* mother hit *him$_i$*

This, in my humble opinion, is very very surprising, given standard assumptions. And yet, it fits nicely with the idea that RPs that are not contained in islands are products of movement. The logic of the argument parallels that of ACH, which demonstrates that islands can turn off an RP's capacity to license reconstruction effects. In this case, it seems that islands can also turn off crossover effects.

This said, there is one very important difference between the two cases. Given standard MP assumptions concerning Merge, the ACH story explains why reconstruction effects go away when movement is blocked (viz. sans movement there are no copies and so no possible reconstruction). In the case of crossover effects, we are missing an account of *how* islands obviate them because we are missing an explanation of *how* movement is relevant to crossover effects. In other words, we need a movement account of crossover which specifies how blocking movement would block these effects. And we don't currently have such an account (but see below!).[16] However, even absent such

---

[16] Let me phrase this a bit more carefully. One way of stating the WCO effect is to say that a pronoun cannot be interpreted as bound with a variable to its right. The SCO says that pronouns cannot bind variables they are co-valued with, as such variables/traces are subject to Principle C. Thus, in a structure like (i) we cannot interpret the pro(noun) as co-valued with the variable bound by the operator:

(i) Op$_1$ ... pro$_1$ ... t$_1$/x$_1$ ...

Note that (i) plays fast and loose with what counts as a variable. We might mean by variable something that is the residue of A'-movement (i.e. t$_1$ in (i)). Or we could mean what is interpreted as a variable semantically (i.e. x$_1$ in (i)). Or we could mean either or both. At any rate, if the filter in (i) understands variables to be residues of *syntactic* A'-movement (i.e. A'-traces) then the absence of S/WCO effects in cases like (11) and (12) when there is no A'-movement is explained, for t$_1$/x$_1$ cannot be residues of movement, and so whatever filters out S/WCO effects won't apply in such cases. The problem from a minimalist perspective is to figure out what constitutes a "residue of syntactic movement" once we get rid of traces. The obvious answer is an A'-bound copy. Thus, S/WCO effects obtain in configurations like (ii), where the DPs are copies and the left one is in an A'-position.

(ii) ... DP$_1$ ... pro$_1$ ... DP$_1$ ...

So, it is possible to reduplicate the required filters to accommodate the crossover effects. But (and you knew this was coming, right?) in the context of MP, this kind of filter is very suspect. Why? Because the only legitimate filters are Bare Out Conditions (BOCs). BOCs are interface-legibility conditions, requirements the interpretive interfaces impose in virtue of their inherent properties. BOCs should not refer to essentially *syntactic* properties. Rather, they should make reference to how such properties are interpreted. However, as is well known, there is nothing semantically odd about configurations like (i) where pronouns are co-valued with semantic variables to their right. Indeed, this is what we find in cases like 'Everyone$_1$ said that his$_1$ mother loved him$_1$,' where this means 'For All x, x said that x's mother loved x.' So there is no reasonable reading of filters like (i) as CI BOCs.

Where does this leave us? Well, we have a nice observational generalization and we even have a kinda/sorta explanation. But we need something other than the BOC treatment. I will propose something below that might fit. The idea is to understand crossover effects as by-products of how these structures would be generated under a movement approach to construal (i.e. an approach of the kind that the EMH/FPG would urge).

5.3 Pronominalized Bound Pronouns

an analytical link between movement and crossover, the mere sensitivity of crossover effects to islands suggests (in my view rather strongly) that RPs must be the products of movement.

5.3 Pronominalized Bound Pronouns

Let's now turn to pronominalized bound pronouns like those in (1a), repeated here as (13):

(13)   Every woman$_1$ thought that she$_1$ was tall

Cribbing from Kayne (2002), I suggested above that an analysis consistent with the EMH would be something like (2a), repeated here as (14):

(14)   [Every woman$_{(+case)}$ [[every woman$_{(+\theta)}$ v [thought [$_{CP}$ *every woman* that [every woman/she$_{(+case)}$ was [every woman$_{(+\theta)}$ tall]]]]]]]

The structure in (14) embodies the following proposal: Bound pronouns live on improper movement chains. The bound pronoun is the spell-out of a copy in the lower part of the chain (i.e. most likely the copy in the case position). The chain transits through A' positions (the italicized copy in Spec CP in (14)) and improperly moves to a θ-position. Thus, like obligatory control and reflexivization constructions, bound pronoun configurations involve chains with two or more θ-roles. Like Reflexivization, the chain contains a morphologically spelled-out copy. Unlike the A-chain construal processes, pronominalization chains have *at least one* A'-link.

It is worth making some analogies obvious. Chapter 4 proposed that Obligatory Control and Reflexivization live on A-chains and so are similar to Raising and Passive, *but for the additional θ-roles and, in the case of Reflexivization, some construction-specific morphological spell-out rules.* The core of the proposal is that all these constructions live on A-chains generated by multiple applications of Merge (both E- and I- instances). Bound pronominalization is to simple cases of A'-movement (like we find in regular *Wh*-questions and RP constructions) as Reflexivization is to simple cases of Raising and Passive. They involve multiple θ-links, (possibly) some spelled-out material realized as pronouns and at least one A'-link. On this view, bound pronouns are (i) like A'-traces in being A'-bound, and (ii) like A'-bound traces in being interpreted as (bound) variables. Indeed, A'-traces, A'-bound RPs and bound pronouns are all interpreted in the same way and are all syntactically (locally) A'-bound.[17]

---

[17] The interpretive parallels between RPs and traces are highlighted in Demirdache (1991) and form one of the more interesting (IMO) arguments for unifying RP constructions with "regular" A'-constructions. Kayne (2002) extends the unification to bound pronouns more generally by

That's the proposal. Let's examine the assumptions required to generate the requisite chains.

First, it requires I-merge into θ-positions. It is almost definitional that construal relations involve expressions semantically realizing multiple thematic functions.[18] An EMH-compatible account of Pronominalization can meet this requirement by allowing I-merge (aka movement) into θ-positions. As the astute reader will have noticed, we've already assumed this for the movement analyses of Obligatory Control and Reflexivization (and noted that this possibility follows pretty directly from dispensing with D-structure (as virtually all MP accounts do, as argued in Chapter 4)). So nothing new here with respect to θ-theory.

Second, we must allow A' to A movement. GB theory dubs such movements "improper." Why does GB bar A' to A movement? Because improper movement allows for the generation of some clearly unacceptable sentences. Thus, the GB ban on improper movement is *empirically* grounded. And this is important. Why? Because, *theoretically* speaking, we should expect improper movement to be licit! Consider why.

Standard theories of movement within Generative Grammar recognize three kinds of movement as licit: A to A movement (e.g. as in Raising and Passive), A to A' movement (e.g. as in simple clause-internal *Wh*-questions in English), and A' to A' movement (e.g. as in successive cyclic "long" *Wh*-movement). Given these three kinds of licit movement, symmetry would urge that we complete the pattern and allow A' to A movement. In short, on grounds of methodological simplicity (symmetry actually) we should expect to find cases of A' to A movement. Nonetheless, GB has blocked this natural theoretical move for empirical reasons. This is an entirely reasonable move if the empirical evidence in its favor is sufficiently strong. Time to review it to see how solid it is.[19]

Here's the empirical problem that the ban on improper movement is meant to solve. It seems to generate sentences like (15a) via derivations like (15b):

(15)   a.   *John$_1$ seems that Mary likes t/him$_1$
       b.   [**John** seems [***John*** that [Mary likes **John** →(t/him)]]]

assuming that they involve, *despite appearances*, syntactic A'-binding. This is, in my view, Kayne's (2002) essential insight. I should add that the paper does *not* assume that the bound pronoun is immediately A'-bound but it is part of a structure that is related to an A'-antecedent. As mentioned earlier, the details offered here differ from those in Kayne (2002), but its basic insight is retained. That said, the Kayne (2002) version is, I believe, compatible with the EMH and might have some other redeeming empirical values.

[18] This is not the same as saying that a single expression has multiple θ-roles. Binding can, for example, link two expressions in such a way that the "object" that both refer to has two θ-roles while the expressions that carry these roles have one each. Kayne (2002) permits movement into θ-positions while retaining the θ-criterion ban against an expression's bearing more than a single θ-role.

[19] A methodological point: The burden of proof rests with the claim that improper movement is banned. This claim carries the argumentative burden as, all things being equal, it is theoretically ugly.

5.3 Pronominalized Bound Pronouns

To my knowledge, these are the only kinds of cases cited for excluding improper movement.[20] So, despite the theoretical symmetry argument for recognizing A to A' movement as a licit option, it seems that empirically we must prohibit this possibility because of examples like (15a).

There are some possible replies. First, many have provided apparent examples of *licit* improper movement. For example, starting with Brody (1993), there have been persuasive analyses of *tough* constructions which exploit an A' to A movement step. Indeed, Brody (1993) argues that these constructions have exactly the structures of (15b):[21]

(16)   a. This book$_i$ was tough for Mary [PRO to review t$_i$]
           b. **This book** was tough for Mary [**this book** [PRO to review **this book**]]

Second, there are apparent Raising constructions that pattern a lot like *tough* constructions (see Potsdam and Runner 2001):

(17)   a. **There** seems like/as if Mary thinks that **there** are too many people in the auditorium
           b. ***There** seems that Mary thinks that **there** are too many people in the auditorium

The facts in (17a) are curious. Typically *there* must be locally related to an indefinite (in this case *too many people* as in *there are too many people in the auditorium*).[22] However, in (17a) we seem to have two *there*s. We could explain this apparent exception to the one-to-one relation between *there* expletives and indefinite associates if we treated the two *there*s as spelled-out occurrences of the same moved expression. This is not typically allowed in English, but we have seen that such copies are options in other languages (e.g. SLQZ and Hmong). If (17a) is a product of movement/I-merge we could say that the two *there*s are both tokens of a single expression whose associate is *too many people*.

Note that for this potential account to gain traction we need to assume that it involves improper movement as the two *there*s are quite far apart (i.e. further than the length of a licit A-chain). They could be related if we allowed movement via Spec C, as in (18):

(18)   **There** seems like/as if [**there** Mary thinks that [**there** are ...]]

---

[20] Note that these are bad even if one uses an RP in place of the trace. We return to this anon.
[21] I found his argument convincing and followed him in Hornstein (2001). Subsequently, others have made the same move. Note too that the standard analysis of *tough* constructions (see, e.g., Chomsky 1981) involves an operation incompatible with the EMH (effectively chain composition). This leaves the Brody (1993) analysis as the only current EMH compatible analysis. See note 23 for discussion. Also see Obata and Epstein (2011) for further arguments for allowing A' to A movement as a parametric option.
[22] Chomsky (1986a) shows that the span between *there* and its associate cannot be more than that of a licit A-chain.

We can also explain (17a)'s contrast with (17b). The contrast can be explained if *seems like/as if* constructions tolerate improper movement while *seems that* constructions do not. As noted above, the premiere evidence against improper movement comes from unacceptable structures involving raising predicates. This data, and the *tough* construction data suggest that improper movement is *sometimes* licit and sometimes not. In other words, it is a grammatical option with lexical restrictions (*seems like/as if* allow it, while *seems that* does not).

If this is correct, then perhaps we can keep to the best of all possible theoretical worlds and allow A to A' movement as an option and thereby allow analyses like (14) for bound pronouns. Going forward, I will assume that this is indeed the case.[23] In the following sections, I review some reasons for thinking that a movement theory of pronominalization might be on the right track.

5.4 The Complementarity of Reflexivization and Pronominalization

First, the supposition that bound pronouns live on improper movement chains allows for the derivation of one of the central properties of binding theory. From the earliest theories of binding (Lees and Klima 1963 (L&K)) through

---

[23] Though GB banned improper movement, it developed technology to allow the kinds of dependencies illustrated in (13)–(16). GB allows chains to "compose," and such composition serves to relate an expression in a θ/A-position with an A'-chain headed by a ∅-operator. For example, GB uses chain composition to generate *tough* constructions and parasitic gap constructions. Thus, sentences like (i) have analyses as in (ii):
(i) a. Which book did John review before you read?
 b. This book was tough for Mary to review
(ii) a. Which book$_1$ [John [[review t$_1$] [∅$_1$ before [you read t$_1$]]]]
 b. This book$_1$ was tough [∅$_1$ [for Mary to review t$_1$]]
Note that we have two composed chains with t_1/*this book*$_1$ linking to ∅$_1$ (coded as co-indexation). Importantly, composed chains function very much like movement-generated chains. Thus, t_1/*this* book$_1$ in (i) are understood to be θ-related to the lower trace position t$_1$. Moreover, the links in a composed chain are required to be subjacent to one another. In effect, the point of chain composition is to deliver a chain with the properties I noted above for "improper" movement chains but without the "improper" part. The impropriety is excised by relating the tail of one chain to the ∅ operator heading the other by allowing for indexation without movement. Interestingly, to my knowledge, nobody ever asked why chain composition could not serve to derive unacceptable sentences like (iiia) as in (iiib). The structure in (iiib) is quite analogous to that of the *tough* constructions in (16b).
(iii) a. *John$_1$ seems that Mary likes
 b. [John$_1$ seems [∅$_1$ that [Mary likes t$_1$]]
I see no obvious way for GB to ban chain composition in (iiib) and, if it cannot do so *in some principled fashion*, the apparent problem that such unacceptable sentences create for improper movement largely disappears. In other words, we can *stipulate* that improper movement in cases like (iii) are out for some reason just like we can *stipulate* that chain composition is out for some reason. Neither stipulation explains anything, but neither is worse than the other *theoretically speaking*.
Last point: So far as I know, chain composition has not been much scrutinized in the MP literature. Presumably, it is not the kind of operation we want to allow, at least if we adopt the Merge Hypothesis. Second, there are independently attractive accounts of parasitic gap constructions that employ improper movement/I-merge (see Nunes 2001, 2004; Hornstein 2001).

5.4 Reflexivization and Pronominalization

the GB theory, it has been observed that Reflexivization and Pronominalization are in complementary distribution. In Chapter 1, I reviewed how the L&K theory manages to explain this. It derives the complementarity by assuming the rules apply to distinct domains and are obligatory and ordered so that Reflexivization applies before Pronominalization does.

The GB approach adopts a similar kind of explanation but simplifies the assumptions. Principles A and B impose contrary requirements on the licensing of reflexives and pronouns. The former must be bound in their domains, while the latter cannot be. Thus, pronouns that occur where reflexives are licit must be syntactically unbound and reflexives that occur where bound pronouns are licit will necessarily be syntactically unbound. This derives the complementarity.

Despite the fact that both kinds of construal systems can (more or less) capture the complementarity facts, neither explains *why* Reflexivization and Pronominalization are in complementary distribution. They simply assume that they are because the facts indicate that they are and show how the complementarity can be formally coded. The current movement approach to binding does better. It derives the complementarity of the two processes. Here's how.

Generative Grammar has discovered that chains come in two flavors, A and A'. Given the EMH/FPG, then construal must be a Merge-generated process. Or, to state this another way, construal dependencies must live on chains. If there are two kinds of chains, this means that there can be at most two kinds of construal processes; ones that live on A-chains and ones that live on A'-chains. If we understand construal processes as those that involve relating two or more θ-positions, then if there are only two kinds of chains then construal dependencies are restricted to the two kinds of chains noted above. Let me be more specific.

Chapter 4 shows how to model Reflexivization as an A-chain dependency by movement into θ-positions. (14) shows how to model Pronominalization once we allow movement into θ-positions *and* improper movement. Now note that these two kinds of chains are the only kinds of chains sufficient to model construal dependencies if we restrict ourselves to a Merge-/chain-based account of construal. In other words, if all you have is Merge then these two kinds of chains must suffice to model the interdependence of (at least) two θ-marked expressions. Moreover, so far as I can tell, nothing but a movement theory will serve given the EMH/FPG. If correct, this *derives* the complementary distribution of Reflexivization and Pronominalization. Or, more exactly, we expect to find exactly two kinds of construal dependencies, and given that one involves no A'-links and the other requires at least one, they must be in complementary distribution. You won't get Pronominalization where Reflexivization is licit because the latter lives on chains that eschew A'-links and the former lives on chains that require at least one. You won't find Reflexivization where

Pronominalization is licit because the latter requires transiting via an A'-link to get to the θ-position of the antecedent, but the former's chain consists entirely of A-links. So, we derive the complementarity from the fact that the two kinds of construal processes live on *qualitatively distinct chains* and these are all and only the kinds of chains that will support multiple θ-links and thus be adequate for modeling construal constructions.[24]

To recap: Once you accept the EMH/FPG, you are in for construal properties living on Merge-generated chains. And once you accept that there are only two kinds of chains (which I take to be true even if we have no good theory at present as to why), then you are in for there being construal processes that involve either A-chains or A'-chains. And once you accept this you derive that the two kinds of construal properties will apply in mutually exclusive domains. As the EMH/FPG countenances *only* Merge-generated structures, there will be no other grammatical way to establish dependencies and so this will be what FL allows Gs to have, and nothing more.[25]

A few additional random remarks

First, there is a further theory-internal reason for taking a chain-based approach to Pronominalization *given* the fact that it is complementary with Reflexivization. More exactly, *given* the complementarity of Reflexivization with Pronominalization, then *if* you adopt a movement/I-merge approach to Reflexivization, then you are almost required to take a movement/I-merge approach to Pronominalization. Why? Because it is hard to see how to *theoretically* derive the complementarity unless both Reflexivization and Pronominalization exploit similar kinds of generative procedures albeit in slightly different ways.

The accuracy of this conclusion becomes clear when one considers the two previous Generative approaches to binding in L&K and GB. In L&K the rules of Reflexivization and Pronominalization are almost identical modulo their order and domain. Same for Principles A and B, which impose contrary binding requirements on pronouns and reflexives and thereby derive the complementarity. What this suggests (strongly, in my opinion) is that an adequate theory of the two processes must exploit similar generative mechanisms (i.e. types of rules) *so that they can be made to conflict*. The conflicting

---

[24] Please note, that we are here abstracting away from the morphological realization of the bound expressions. That is why I refer to reflexivization (not reflexive binding) for example. Recall (Chapter 4) that reflexivization can occur without reflexives and there is no FL/UG principle requiring reflexives and bound pronouns to be morphologically distinct. This is a long-winded way of saying that it is an accident of English that *him/her* are the bound pronouns rather than *himself/herself.*

[25] But see the discussion of *extra*-grammatical binding below.

5.4 Reflexivization and Pronominalization

requirements serve to derive the complementarity. What we don't want, for example, is a movement-based approach to Reflexivization and some other distinct kind of formal procedure licensing bound pronouns (say something like Binding Principle B). Why not? Because if we derive the properties of Reflexivization and Pronominalization using entirely different types of formal processes we will have no hope of explaining why the two entirely different kinds of formal processes conflict and thus we will have no theoretical way of deriving the observed complementarity. So, *if* one accepts that Reflexivization and Pronominalization are indeed complementary, then *if* one analyzes reflexives as by-products of movement, then bound pronouns should also be so analyzed. Thus, the two kinds of construal should come as a unified formal package, as proposed here.[26]

Second, note that I have been talking about Reflexivization and Pronominalization rather than in terms of Principles A and B of the binding theory. I do this for the reasons noted in Chapter 4. One can get Reflexivization without reflexives and, it appears, that one can get Pronominalization without pronouns (SLQZ allows copies to be interpreted as bound pronouns). Moreover, the theory outlined here is more like the one outlined in L&K than the standard binding theory in that with respect to pronominalization, the chains specify the antecedent of the bound pronoun rather than specifying the nominals from which the pronoun must be disjoint. L&K's rule of Pronominalization is a rule that establishes a binding relation. Principle B does not specify the binder of a given pronoun but specifies which expressions cannot be binders of given pronouns. Thus, strictly speaking, Principle B is *not* a theory of antecedence, while L&K's rule of Pronominalization is. The approach here does specify licit antecedence relations and syntactically specifies a class of bound pronoun relations. It thus isolates a class of bound pronouns as grammatically targeted and distinguishes them from non-bound pronouns (e.g. deictic, cataphoric, etc.).[27]

Third, again following L&K, the Merge-based approach to construal generates chains with copies/occurrences as links. This means that there is a process

---

[26] It is worth observing that mid vintage GB (e.g. Chomsky 1986a) formally understood Reflexivization as akin to cliticization, a movement operation. In other words, in this period, while Reflexivization was unified with movement, Pronominalization remained the province of Principle B. Given these different formal restrictions, the complementarity of Reflexivization and Pronominalization is no longer a *design feature* of the binding theory but results from a strange conspiracy of interacting principles that have nothing to do with one another. This, of course, could be the correct way to think of the matter, but it rejects the long-standing theoretical intuition within Generative Grammar that the complementarity of the two processes is not a haphazard accident.

[27] In this I follow the lead of Higginbotham (1985) and Reinhart (1983). There are some empirical puzzles that this conception tries to sweep under the theoretical rug and that Lasnik (1991) uncovers and rightly observes are empirical puzzles for the former view. They are also a prima facie problem for the EMH/FPG one outlined above.

that morphophonologically converts copies/occurrences into flesh-and-blood reflexives and pronouns (and gaps if one includes control and simple movement rules as generated by the same kinds of Merge-based operations, as I do here). L&K make this conversion process explicit. I have said nothing about how this might be accomplished, though I suspect that case considerations will be important.[28] That said, the present story follows L&K in taking this morphophonological process as largely an extra-syntactic affair and relatively tangential to the basic syntax of binding.

Once again, here L&K approaches contrast with that implicitly adopted in the GB theory.[29] And they do so by distinguishing bound pronouns, which are grammatical formatives, from non-bound pronouns, which are lexical formatives.[30] Interestingly, there is some interpretive evidence supporting this view.

Transformational pronouns introduced by the Pronominalization rule are semantically inert, while lexically inserted referential pronouns are not. What does it mean for a pronoun to be semantically inert/active? Well, as a pronoun is just a bundle of φ-features that have values for person, number and gender, in semantically active pronouns these φ-features will determine the semantic values these pronouns can have, while with pronouns that are semantically inert, the φ-features the pronouns carry should have no effect on their interpretation.[31] There is some evidence in support of this semantic cut.[32] Consider some data:

(19)   a. This proposal is boring. No, it/*she/*he/is not/*No they/we/you are not.
        b. Only John thinks he is smart.

---

[28] See Polinsky and Potsdam (2006) and (2012) for a theory along these lines.
[29] And in non-movement Agree-based theories of binding like those advanced in Reuland (2011). In these latter kinds of accounts binding is triggered by feature specifications of reflexives and (sometimes) bound pronouns. These expressions are taken to be defective in a way that requires their licensing via antecedence (e.g. they have some φ-feature defect that requires an antecedent to make them whole. See Preminger (2021) for a critique of this approach to binding phenomena). The L&K theory allows that these expressions are defective when compared with more standard lexical items in that they are *not* lexical but morphological detritus that the grammatical system throws off.
[30] There is a rather wide conceptual divide between the L&K theory of construal and the GB binding theory. The latter thinks of binding as a way of repairing featurally defective lexical expressions (especially Principle A). In this way, dependent anaphors are like traces in requiring licensing to be made grammatically whole. What drives construal derivations is the necessity of fixing up these toxic feature-deficient lexical items by relating them to antecedents that "repair" them and make them whole. L&K sees things differently. It treats reflexives and bound pronouns (and PRO) as "mere" morphology, with no impact whatsoever on the derivational process. In case it is not clear, my sympathies lie with the earlier L&K approach.
[31] For example, the φ-features could set presuppositional restrictions on satisfiers of the bound variable.
[32] To my knowledge, the observations concerning deictic pronouns outlined below were first made in Enc (1981). The more general point concerning the φ-nudity of pronominal variables is attributed to Kratzer by Heim.

5.4 Reflexivization and Pronominalization

      c. No, I think I'm smart, you think you are, Mary thinks she is and they think they are.
      c.' No, Mary also thinks he is smart.

(19a) illustrates a typical co-referential pronoun dependency. To pick up the referent of *this proposal* in the following clause, we must use *it*. The ϕ-features of *it* are singular, neuter, third person. This is why the other pronominal forms cannot be used to contradict the claim made in the first clause. (19b) is ambiguous. On the reading where *he* is bound by *only John* it is possible to contradict the claim ignoring the ϕ-feature values of *he*. This is indicated in (19c). Note: (19c) is a perfectly fine way of contradicting the assertion made in using (19b). However, this requires that the ϕ-feature values of *he* be semantically weightless. Its apparent values – third person, singular, masculine – are ignored by the conjuncts in (19c); *I* and *you* mismatch the third-person feature, *she* is not masculine, and *they* is not singular. Nonetheless, (19c) is a semantically appropriate contradiction of (19b).

There is a second reading for (19b). In this case, the ϕ-features of *he* are active. One cannot express this thought (viz. that Mary thinks that John is smart) by using any other pronoun form. In this, (19c') is like (19a). The two readings in (19c, c') correspond to the structures in which *he* is interpreted as a variable bound by *only John* and one in which it is understood as a co-referential pronoun with *John* as antecedent. Only in the first instance is *he* c-commanded by the DP it is dependent on (*only John* vs *John*).[33]

Corroboration for the dual semantic import of pronominal ϕ-features comes from considering the contrast between (20a) and (20b):

(20)   a. Only I believe myself to be intelligent
         b. Only I believe me to be intelligent

Reflexives are generally restricted to bound variable interpretations. If so, (20a) should have a range of contradictions as in (21), where the ϕ-features (person and number in particular) on *myself* are inert.

---

[33] This requirement appears to be purely syntactic. Note that *only I* is semantically equivalent to *nobody but me*. However, observe the following contrast:
(i) Only I think that I am intelligent
(ii) Nobody but me thinks that I am intelligent
The former is ambiguous much like (19b). The latter, however, is not. The only coherent contradiction is something like (iii), compare (iv):
(iii) No, Paul thinks that you are intelligent
(iv) #No, Paul also thinks he's intelligent
It seems that the semantic equivalence does not guarantee similar binding powers to expressions. Syntax counts. Whereas in (i) *I* can be the head of the complex phrase *only I*, *me* cannot be the head of the complex phrase *nobody but me*. In fact, the sentence that can be contradicted by (iv) has a third-person pronoun form:
(v) Nobody but me thinks he is intelligent
This indicates that *nobody* is the head of the complex phrase.

(21)   No, John believes himself to be intelligent, you believe yourself to be intelligent, they believe themselves to be intelligent …

This contrasts with (22), the contradiction of (20b), where to contradict the claim made, the pronoun must change its form to pick out the same individual that *me* picks out in (20b):

(22)   No, John believes you/#him/#me to be intelligent as well

All of this supports the data cut that L&K requires and that the above chain-based approach to pronominalization adopts. Not all morphologically similar pronouns are on the same interpretive footing. Those introduced lexically have active φ-features. Those that are products of morphophonological rewrite rules do not.

A final random remark: there was one lethal objection to the L&K theory that the present EMH reincarnation finesses. The L&K theory had a problem distinguishing two tokens of the same lexical type from two tokens of the same syntactic expression/type. And this distinction is critical when one considers examples like (23):

(23)   a. Everyone thinks he is intelligent
        b. Everyone thinks that everyone is intelligent
        c. Everyone thinks [everyone that [everyone is intelligent]]

The interpretation of (23a) is not that of (23b). But why not given the derivation in (23c), where we see two occurrences of *everyone* in the two subject positions? The original theory of Pronominalization (and for that matter the Standard Theory analyses of Control (aka Equi-NP Deletion) and Reflexivization had no ready answer. Minimalist theories do as they distinguish derivations wherein two selections of *everyone* from the lexicon are (E-) merged in the course of a derivation from those where just a single selection of *everyone* from the lexicon is first (E-) merged and then (I-) merged. In the former case we have two tokens of the same lexical item/type each with its own syntactic life in the derivation (i.e. and thus the derivation has two distinct syntactic items), while in the latter we have two tokens of the same syntactic atom/type (i.e. and thus have the same syntactic atom/type used twice, giving us two tokens of the same syntactic type). This grammatical difference suffices to distinguish the interpretive difference noted. It is a distinction that the Standard Theory does not deploy, but which all minimalist theories do. In other words, all MP theories, including EMH, distinguish between two tokens of the same lexical item/type and two tokens of the same syntactic item/type. Distinct tokens of the same lexical item are syntactically independent. Two tokens of the same syntactic item form chains. What we have in (23c) is an instance of the latter. The underlying structure of (23b) is an instance of the former. What the Partee criticism of L&K demonstrates (Partee 1971) is that we must respect this difference in our syntactic theories. Happily, all MP theories do so. Hence treating construal as living on chains does not succumb to Partee's objection given basic MP assumptions.[34]

Before plowing ahead, I would like to reiterate that I consider the above explanation of the complementarity between Reflexivization and Pronominalization (or (more or less) between Principles A and B of the binding theory) to be a very nice result. To my knowledge, there is no other explanation on offer. Indeed, to my knowledge, the question *why* the complementarity exists has never been mooted.

Let's keep moving. What other nice consequences can we credit to a movement theory of pronominalization?

5.5 More Nice Consequences of a Movement Theory of Pronominalization

First, we have already noted, following Kayne (2002) and Demirdache (1991), that treating construal as a chain relation makes it clear why traces/bound pronouns/RPs are all interpreted as variables. All these realize the same A'-chain configurations modulo the different morphological realization of the copies (here taken to be minor secondary effects).

Second, as Kayne (2002) observes, if bound pronouns live on (improper) A'-chains formed by I-merge then we account for the c-command restriction

---

[34] The MP distinction between tokens of a common *lexical* type versus tokens of a common *syntactic* type must be formally rendered. Logicians have a similar problem identifying occurrences of the same variable. They employ indices to make the distinction. Thus, the variable x1 is different from the variable x2 etc. Clearly a similar mechanism smoothly allows FL to distinguish one selection of an expression from the lexicon from two. And this allows for numerations to be identified as sets. Minimalists have been, IMO, overly obsessed with eliminating indices from FL. So, for example, numerations are often treated as bags (rather than sets), with the distinct selections a function of the bag rather than the items selected. I frankly do not see that any big issues are at stake here. We *know* that indices are required for any adequate treatment of quantification along Tarski-like lines (what Paul Pietroski (p.c.) dubs the Tarski trick). The ones we use to track selections from the lexicon can serve this interpretive function as well. Moreover, so far as I know, there is *no* interesting grammatical fact that hangs on the confusion of types and tokens. Thus, any linguistic phenomenon expressed in a sentence where multiple tokens of the same lexical type are used can be equally well expressed in structures in which no two expressions selected from the lexicon are of the same type. Or, to say this another way, I have no reason to think that FL would look any different than it does if no sentence in any language ever contained two atoms of the same lexical type. If so, but for bookkeeping, the type/token stuff is completely idle. To me that suggests that it calls for a technical fix, not a deep one. Indices are the ideal technical patch. This obvious technical fix is proposed in Collins and Stabler (2016).

on pronominal binding.[35] More accurately, the antecedent of a bound pronoun (typically) c-commands its anaphoric pronominal dependent:[36]

(24)   a. Everyone$_1$ made his$_1$ friends happy
         b. *My pictures of everyone$_1$ made his$_1$ friends happy

The c-command condition on bound pronominal variables follows directly from a theory where such anaphoric dependencies are generated via Merge given that I-merge is required to "move" the antecedent to a c-commanding position or violate the No Tampering Condition (NTC) (see Chapter 2 for discussion).[37]

Third, McCloskey (2006) has observed that languages do not have distinct pronominal forms for resumptive pronouns. More exactly, in a language with RPs, the form of a resumptive pronouns is always the same as the form of the bound pronoun in that language. Why? The current approach offers an answer. Structurally speaking, Pronominalization involves an RP-like subpart, as indicated in (25):

(25)   [... QP$_0$ ... [$_{CP}$QP ... [... QP$_0$ ...]]]

If we assume that the apparently similar-looking structures are indeed formally the same then we can explain why the morphological realizations of these structures is the same. Or, more accurately, if they are formally identical why should morphological processes discriminate between them?

We can go further. We don't find epithets and definite descriptions in RP structures that function as bound pronouns:

(26)   a. *Every boy$_1$ the donkey's mother$_1$ thought ...
         b. *Every kid$_1$ thinks Mary likes the kid/the cutie$_1$

It appears that RPs and bound pronouns express themselves morphologically using the same designated pronominal forms.[38] Why?

---

[35] It also explains why RPs are c-commanded by their antecedents. Indeed, it is the same explanation for why A'-operators bind their "traces." Specifically, the c-command requirement follows from the No Tampering Condition (NTC). In other words, if RPs are the morphological spell-out of copies formed via I-merge then they will necessarily live on chains where the links c-command one another because Merge incorporates the NTC (see Chapter 2).

[36] The accuracy of this generalization has been disputed, though the contrast in (24) seems correct. For a good defense of the generalization, see Drummond and Kush (2015). Also see discussion of the examples of (19)–(22), where syntactic c-command plays a critical role.

[37] I add all the usual caveats concerning movement within single-rooted sub-trees, thus abstracting away from the possibility of sidewards movement.

[38] This, despite the fact that definite descriptions *can* carry a bound interpretation:
(i) Orson Wells would drink no wine$_1$ before it/the damn thing$_1$ was at least 10 years old
These cases, I will argue, do not involve syntactic binding at all. So, though syntactic binding suffices for semantic binding, semantic binding can occur in the absence of syntactic binding. Of course, there is a cost when this occurs *and syntactic binding would have been possible*, generally decreasing the acceptability of the structure.

5.5 A Movement Theory of Pronominalization

Here is a stab at an answer. The above movement theory of binding follows L&K in treating the morphological realization of the dependencies (viz. reflexives and pronouns) as grammar-internal formatives. In L&K the specific morphemes that realize the binding are *stipulated* as parts of the rules of Reflexivization and Pronominalization. That the rule should specify a *specific* morpheme, rather than an open-ended number (as would be the case if any definite description could serve) makes perfect sense. It is quite typical to have closed-class items do grammatical work, typically one morpheme per task. This is what we find here. Similar chains use similar morphology to signal similar structure.

If this is right, this also allows us to understand a long-standing puzzle within binding theory. Why exactly are sentences like (26) somewhat unacceptable with the indicated syntactic binding? It cannot be because definite descriptions can't serve as semantic variables. They can.

(27) I gave every kid$_1$ a diploma after he/the kid$_1$ came to the dais

As (27) indicates, some definite descriptions can freely alternate with bound pronouns and can get interpreted as bound variables without affecting acceptability. What (26b) shows is that not all do.

This contrast has been treated as a Principle C violation in GB theory. But it is hard to see exactly why this should be so, at least if we assume, for example, that Principle C applies to R-expressions which are taken to be elements that already have an interpretation and so should not be bindable.[39] The problem with this explanation is that it is a little too good, for it predicts, counterfactually, that (27) should be unacceptable.

The current chain-based view offers an account. Definite descriptions *are* semantically bindable, as (27) indicates. However, they are unacceptable in contexts in which syntactic binding is the preferred grammatical option for expressing the antecedence relation *if it is available*. If syntactic binding is available in (26) but not (27) then we expect the difference in acceptability. What remains is to explain how (26) and (27) differ in their syntactic derivations. Below, I will offer some speculations on how to distinguish the two cases.

For the time being, note that the unacceptability of (26) is not semantically based but is rather the by-product of competing scenarios for establishing an antecedence dependency. The main idea is that an acceptability cost is incurred wherever syntactic/grammatically mediated binding is available and it is not used. Where establishing such a dependency is not grammatically available, other (non-grammatical) options can be freely used with no cost to acceptability. In other words, where the grammar can apply it does apply, and where an

---

[39] This is the explanation offered, for example, in Higginbotham (1985).

applicable grammatical option has been circumvented acceptability is reduced. Where grammatical options are unavailable then non-grammatical processes can apply costlessly.[40]

It is worth noting that the same distinction regarding bound definite descriptions crops up in RP structures. Aoun et al. (2001) observes that in non-island contexts, RPs have the (morphological) profile of weak pronouns in Lebanese Arabic. Interestingly, when the resumptive expression occurs within an island it is possible to swap the bound weak pronoun for a strong one or even with a "resumptive" definite description. This reiterates the observations in examples (26/27) if islands block movement.[41] Once movement cannot syntactically forge the RP dependency, the dependency can be established in some other way (which I will return to) *at no cost*. So, as expected given the current analyses of RP and Pronominalization constructions, we find the same restrictions in both as regards the use of a non-specific morphological expression (e.g. anything but a (weak) pronoun) to overtly signal the binding relation.

Let's keep going.

5.6 Principle C Effects and the EMH

With an additional assumption we can implement an EMH analogue of the L&K account of Principle C effects.

(28) a. *He$_1$ said that each guy/John$_1$ was tall
b. *Who$_1$ did he$_1$ say (who$_1$) was tall
c. [John/He$_1$ said [that John$_1$ was tall]]

L&K "explain" this contrast by stipulating that the bound pronouns must (anachronistically speaking) occupy the foot of the relevant pronominalization chain. The rules for Reflexivization and Pronominalization target the lower "copy" for morphological conversion to a reflexive/pronoun. This coding is empirically adequate but theoretically ad hoc (why can only the *lower* copy morphologically change?). That said, if we assume that the morphological pronoun marks the launch site of (A'-)movement, the data in (28a,b) follows directly. Both derivations violate the NTC, as both necessarily involve lowering

---

[40] It is worth noting that the logic here deployed contrasts with the economy logic of, for example, Merge over Move (MoM). The latter ranks grammatical alternatives and so the cost of ignoring MoM traces to using more expensive grammatical operations/derivations when cheaper grammatical alternatives are available. The logic regarding syntactic binding incurring a cost when available but not used states that grammars lead to expectations that reduce acceptability when they are unrealized. Or, to put this another way, when syntactic binding and semantic binding swing together all is copacetic. When these two diverge there is a cost in acceptability.

[41] Recall that Aoun et al. (2001) presents independent evidence for this idea as reconstruction into islands is forbidden. This follows if reconstruction effects piggyback on the copy theory of movement (see Chapter 2) and islands block movement.

5.6 Principle C Effects and the EMH

the non-pronominal "antecedent." Thus, if we assume that pronouns mark the "foot" of the chain (the position that is input to I-merge), then to derive (28c) with *he* understood as a bound pronominal, *John* must lower from the matrix subject position and I-merge into the embedded subject position. But this movement violates the NTC and so the derivation is illicit.

This account of Principle C effects has one very pleasant feature. It *explains* why Principle C effects are unbounded in their domain of application. Here's what I mean.

Unlike Principles A and B which apply to limited domains (i.e. clause-mates or "binding domains") and thus display locality effects, Principle C has no analogous locality restrictions.[42] Why not? What makes Principle C domain-less while Principles A and B are domain restricted? If we assume that antecedence dependencies are formed by I-merge, and we assume that the anaphoric reflexive/pronoun marks the launch site, then, however "short" the movement, lowering will violate the NTC. Thus, there should be no bound/domain delimiting the illicit dependency formation as there is none on the NTC. And empirically we really don't observe one. (29) is no better than (28):

(29)   He$_1$ said that Mary heard that John$_1$ was sick

Again, *why* Principle C is unbounded while A and B are domain sensitive is unexplained within earlier Generative accounts of binding relations. Indeed, to my knowledge, *why* there is a contrast with regard to domain restrictions/locality between Principles A/B versus C has not even been raised. I confess to very much liking this particular consequence of the EMH/FPG story.

So, a quick summary: If we treat binding relations as living on chains we can derive several heretofore stipulated properties of Generative binding theories. The first is the complementary distribution of Reflexivization and Pronominalization. The second is the unbounded domain (i.e. non-locally restricted nature) of Principle C effects. The third is that construal operations like Reflexivization and Pronominalization are domain restricted. This follows from the fact that they live on chains that are subject to locality restrictions.[43] And there is a fourth: We derive the fact that Pronominalization has a larger domain than Reflexivization by noting that the former lives on

---

[42] Thus, Principles A and B of the GB binding theory require that anaphors and pronominals be bound or free *within their domains*. Principle C, in contrast, simply states that an R-expression must be free. There is no domain restriction on the condition.

[43] In other words, the domain restrictions we find for Reflexivization and Pronominalization reduce to the fact that they live on A- and A'-chains respectively and so inherit whatever locality restrictions A- and A'-movement enjoy. Note, importantly, none of this explains *why* I-merge is subject to locality. Presumably, this follows from more general features of well-behaved computational systems (see Chapter 8 for some discussion). However, *given* that A- and A'-movement have locality restrictions, it follows that construal operations evident in reflexive and bound pronoun constructions will have them as well.

A-chains and the latter on A'-chains. As is well known, A'-movement has a longer span than the former. Hence, we expect, if this reduction of binding to chain properties is correct, that the domain of Reflexivization will be "narrower" than that of Pronominalization. Lastly, we also derive the c-command condition on construal dependencies. As the EMH/FPG forces a movement approach to construal, the fact that these properties drop out of a unified I-merge approach to binding/construal provides further evidence in favor of the EMH/FPG.[44]

Let's keep adding a few other assumptions and see what more the EMH might be able to explain.

5.7 The Merge over Move Principle and Weak Crossover Effects

The previous section offered an account of some Principle C effects given the assumption that grammatical operations must apply when they can and failure to apply them in cases where they can incurs a cost that is reflected in lower acceptability.

Consider now a grammar-internal economy condition, one mooted in the earliest days of MP, the Merge over Move principle (MoM). In what follows, I would like to explore how MoM offers an account of weak crossover (WCO) effects. Now, before you, dear reader, get over-excited, let me acknowledge that MoM is currently out of theoretical favor, and for some perfectly good reasons. Let me explain this by reminding you why it was *more* attractive in the early days of MP. Back then, movement was a composite operation made up of two more primitive operations, Copy and Merge. Back in the early days, Merge was just E-merge and movement was the combination of Copy plus Merge. Given this understanding of movement, there was a perfectly fine sense in which Merge was "cheaper" than Move as the latter involved more operations than the former. It included Merge *and Copy*. So the greater cost of MoM made some theoretical sense.

---

[44] That said, there remain "puzzles" (i.e. what we call data that don't fit the general schema). So, for example, there are cases of binding without c-command:
(i) a. Nobody's$_i$ mother loves him$_i$
   b. Someone from every city$_i$ admires its$_i$ subways
I do not have much to say about these at present. The best I can offer is the observation that the bound pronouns in these cases seem to be able to alternate with anaphoric definite descriptions:
(ii) a. (?) No suspect's$_i$ mother defended the brute$_i$
   b. Someone from every city admires the city's subways
This might point to the binding here *not* involving chains and so being cases of semantic binding. See below for a more elaborate discussion of semantic binding and its relation to the morphological observation above.
Here is a second bigger puzzle. If this analysis is on the right track we should expect to find pronominal and reflexive binding licensing reconstruction. This appears to be false. If so, we need an explanation for why we don't find such effects. I have none to offer.

5.7 The MoM Principle and WCO Effects

However, once movement and structure building are unified and E- and I-merge are taken to be instances of the same Merge operation, this no longer holds. I-merge is no longer composite and so there is no obvious sense in which E-merge is cheaper. Thus, there is no reason *why* structure building should be cheaper than movement. Indeed, many thoroughly modern Minimalists assume the contrary, that movement is cheaper than E-merge (as, for example, it putatively involves less "search"). The point is that MoM is not a particularly natural economy principle once we unify movement and structure building as different applications of the very same operation.

Are there other ways of getting the effects of MoM? Perhaps. So, for example, say (i) that derivations are phase based, they begin with a selection of atoms into a numeration, and (ii) that phases divide numerations into sub-numerations. MoM can then be taken to be the principle that says: All things being equal, E-merge an element from the current sub-numeration before merging expressions derivationally introduced in earlier sub-numerations. This would be a natural derivational economy principle if derivations had to integrate all atoms in the numeration into a single-rooted syntactic object in order to converge. If numerations are required (and this is not at all obvious, by the way) then this is a way of getting the effects of MoM differently than seeing I-merge as inherently more complex than E-merge. It is not their relative complexity that matters but how each advances the derivation towards completion (aka convergence). Using all the expressions in the numeration is a necessary condition for convergence. Thus the reason E-merge is preferred to I-merge, *ceteris paribus*, is that it advances the derivation towards convergence in an obvious way.

The upshot: It might be possible to motivate the effects of MoM without adopting the earlier minimalist ontology of operations. And this is a good thing if the EMH/FPG is correct as it prizes the unification of structure building and movement that later Minimalism developed. That said, it seems that MoM does have some interesting empirical consequences, and if they cannot be accommodated in any other way, then MoM will be worth retaining in some form, and so it will be worthwhile exploring natural ways of doing so. The approach in terms of numerations and their relation to derivations and phases is one possible way of adopting the contemporary conception of Merge without losing the virtues (if there are any) of the MoM.

Let me end this overly long digression, however, on a less sanguine note. It is not clear that theories that incorporate numerations are simpler than those that do not. They involve extra derivational steps – selecting expressions from the lexicon into a numeration and dividing them into sub-numerations. The evidence that numerations are required is very thin. Why not repeatedly access the lexicon as needed? Chomsky has some arguments that this is computationally profligate. Maybe, but I am not personally convinced. That said, it looks like MoM can play a constructive explanatory role and MoM requires something like numerations to be viable given current assumptions. If so, numerations it is! Just how grammars with them are simpler (if they are) than those without is a question that requires further thought.

All that conceded, *if* MoM can undergird an account of WCO effects then this is an *interesting* and *noteworthy* fact about MoM. Furthermore, *if* EMH in conjunction with MoM can do this, then it argues that there is something right about MoM and that we should try and figure out what kernel of truth is buried within it. With this in mind, let's *for the time being* make use of the MoM assumption. OK, to work.

Consider two derivations of (30) holding constant the EMH assumption that bound pronouns live on chains and the special (stipulated) assumption that overt pronouns mark the launch site of movement.

(30)   *His$_i$ mother loves everyone$_i$

Here is one derivation:

(31)   a. Numeration = {mother, everyone, loves, 's, v ... }
       b. Merge ('s, mother) → {'s, mother}
       c. Merge (Everyone, {'s, mother}) → {Everyone, {'s, mother}}
       d. Merge (v, loves) → {v, loves}
       e. Merge ({Everyone, {'s, mother}}, {v, loves}) → {{Everyone, {'s, mother}}, {v, loves}}

After (31e), the derivation is stuck. We cannot move/I-merge *everyone* to the complement position of *love* as this would violate the NTC. There is thus no way to derive (30) with the indicated derivation.

Consider one more derivation, but this time involving sidewards movement. I know, I know, sidewards movement, yech! However, humor me for the time being and I will presently explain why this might not be so execrable. The derivation is in (32):

(32)   a. Numeration = {, mother, everyone, loves, 's, v ... }
       b. Merge ('s, mother) → {'s, mother}
       c. Merge (Everyone, {'s, mother}) → {Everyone, {'s, mother}}
       d. Merge (loves, everyone) → {loves, everyone}
       e. Merge (v, {loves, everyone}) → {v, {loves, everyone}}
       f. Merge ({Everyone, {'s, mother}}, {v, {loves, everyone}}) → {{Everyone, {'s, mother}}, {v, {loves, everyone}}}
       g. {{(Everyone→his), {'s, mother}}, {v, {loves, everyone}}}

If the pronoun marks the launch site of I-merge (as assumed previously) then this is realized structurally as (32g). So the derivation converges. A bad result, as WCO configurations are unacceptable with the required binding. How then to stop this derivation?

5.7 The MoM Principle and WCO Effects

Well, if MoM holds, then it blocks step (32d) where *everyone* merges with *loves*. How does MoM do this? Note that the derivation I-merges *everyone* with *loves* but at that step we could have E-merged *{{everyone, {'s mother}}}* with *loves* instead. Thus, if MoM regulates derivations, it blocks this derivational option.

Interestingly, the MoM-compatible derivation converges with an acceptable output: *Everyone loves his mother*. Moreover, the structure generated by the MoM-violating derivation in (32) is grammatically blocked not because it leads to an uninterpretable structure but because it outputs a different interpretable structure in a more optimal way. In other words, the problem in (32) is that the WCO configuration requires a *non-optimal* derivation. Thus, *if* MoM (or some functional equivalent) holds, we can derive the unacceptability of WCO derivations like this even if we tolerate sidewards movement.

So, there are two ways of deriving WCO effects; one traces the effect to the NTC and the other hangs the effects on MoM. Why not just accept the first approach and forget about the MoM account? Here is one reason. There is an obvious difference between WCO and SCO effects, the strength of the unacceptability of the violation. *Weak* vs *Strong* says it all! Now, in Section 5.2 I noted that SCO effects can be derived as violations of the NTC. If this is so, then we should prefer to derive WCO effects *in some other way* so as to reflect the fact that WCO effects lead to much less unacceptability than SCO effects do. If you buy this, then the second derivation is the preferred one. The first option mimics the SCO derivation by attributing WCO effects to an NTC violation. But then this leaves no (theory-internal) room for distinguishing WCO from SCO effects. In contrast, the second derivation (which allows sidewards movement as an option) traces WCO effects to MoM, an economy violation. The WCO derivation converges with a fine output, it just does not do so optimally. So we have a peg to hang the acceptability differences on.[45] Thus, if the difference in acceptability strikes you as important, and I confess to finding it of some relevance, then the explanation of WCO effects in terms of MoM should appeal to you.

One last thing. Both accounts have one positive thing in common. They provide a *derivational* explanation of S/WCO effects. In other words, both accounts analyze S/WCO structures as derivationally (and hence, syntactically) problematic. This differs from the standard GB accounts which trace

---

[45] Of course, there may be other non-grammatical ways of distinguishing SCO from WCO effects. Always keep in mind that unacceptability is a measure of more than just the effects of the grammar. We all assume that ungrammaticality contributes to unacceptability. But other factors that go beyond the grammar do as well. Thus, it is possible that what gives SCO a more severe unacceptability has something to do with processing or production or memory or whatever. If so, this would neutralize the considerations I gave above for supporting the MoM approach to WCO rather than the NTC analysis.

the unacceptability to some kind of logical form (LF) interface condition (e.g. a constraint against a syntactic variable anteceding a pronoun to its left, or a bijection violation blocking an operator from A'-binding two variables). These conditions, being output conditions, must, given minimalist logic, reflect Bare Out Conditions of the CI interface. However, there is no independent reason to think that there is anything CI-problematic about these configurations. There is no apparent semantic reason why an operator should not be able to directly bind two variables, nor any reason why left/right should mean anything for CI structures. The lack of semantic motivation for any of this is reflected in the semantic literature on binding, where WCO effects are *ad hocly* coded into the rules of interpretation. In other words, there is no plausible Bare Out Condition rationale for S/WCO effects. This boosts the appeal of the present proposals. *Here S/WCO effects are tied to how grammatical dependencies are generated.* In other words, here S/WCO effects can be described as semantically arbitrary but syntactically principled. Just what the linguistic doctor ordered! Let me add a familiar refrain: So far as I know, this is the only syntactic account of S/WCO effects that does not hand-code them into FL/UG. And like the other principles derived earlier, the explanation critically relies on treating binding as a product of I-merge, which, as noted repeatedly, is the kind of approach the EMH/FPG promotes. Pretty satisfying, huh?

5.8 MoM and Long-Distance Anaphors

MoM can also be pressed into service to explain another curious interpretive effect, the subject orientation of so-called long-distance anaphors (LDAs). It has long been observed that LDAs are subject oriented.[46] In sentences with structures like (33) involving LDAs, it is possible for the LDA to have either of the two non-local subjects (i.e. Subject-1 or -2) as antecedents but not the intermediate object:

(33)   [Subject-2$_{ok1}$ V Object$_{*1}$ [Subject-1$_{ok1}$ V [Subject V LDA$_1$]]]

Why? Motomura(2002) provides a very clever explanation that exploits the idea that LDAs are the tails of chains. The account has four premises: (i) LDAs are tails of chains with the antecedent as head, (ii) MoM regulates derivations, (iii) derivations proceed in phases and (iv) improper movement is licit. Motomura's (2002) big insight is that if one divides the numeration into subarrays and assumes structure is generated respecting MoM, then the only places available for an expression moving up a tree to move to will be unoccupied subject positions. To see how this works, consider the derivations of the two

---

[46] See Motomura (2002) and references therein. That LDAs are bound pronouns is first proposed in Sportiche (1986).

5.8 The MoM and Long-Distance Anaphors

possible readings of (31), one where Subject-1 is antecedent and the other where Subject-2 is.

First the reading where Subject-1 is antecedent: Assume LDAs are the morphological residues of movements/I-merges that form "improper" chains with the moving expression as the head of the chain (i.e. the antecedent of the LDA). The derivation of a sentence like (33) with Subject-1 as antecedent would proceed as illustrated in the structure in (34) (DP = Subject-1):

(34) $[_{TP3}$ Subject V Object$_{*1}$ $[_{CP}$ $[_{TP2}$ DP $[_{vP}$ DP v [V $[_{CP}$ DP $[_{TP1}$ Subject V DP(→ LDA)]]]]]]]

DP first merges with the embedded V then moves to the local Spec CP on its way to the Spec of v (to assume the external-argument θ-role of the medial predicate) and then to Spec T. The foot of the chain gets spelled out as an LDA.

Now consider the move from Spec C to Spec v in a little more detail. The above account abstracts away from the issue of phases. If we take the standard view, then derivations are produced bottom-up phase by phase. In a phase-based derivational schema, MoM implies that expressions in the current phase must all be merged before expressions from the previous phase can be utilized. Consequently, in (34) after we have built up the embedded CP, we access {v,V} from the medial clause's sub-numeration. As there are no DP elements available in this sub-numeration, we can move the DP in Spec C *from the earlier phase* into Spec v. It moves again to Spec T in the next sub-numeration. We then access the matrix clause's sub-numeration which includes two DPs, one merged as object and one as subject and the derivation converges.

What happens if Subject-2 in (33) is the antecedent of the LDA? We then derive a chain like (35):

(35) $[_{TP3}$ DP-1 V DP-4 $[_{CP-2}$ DP-1 $[_{TP2}$ DP-3 $[_{vP}$ DP-3 v [V $[_{CP-1}$ DP-1 $[_{TP1}$ DP-2 [DP-2 v [V DP-1(→LDA)]]]]]]]]]

As in (34), we merge DP-1 as complement of the lowest V and DP-2 as external argument. DP-1 then moves to Spec C_1. The next phase up is accessed and it contains {v,V, DP-3}, all of which merge. When all these expressions in the medial sub-numeration are E-merged, DP-1 moves from the embedded CP_1 to the medial CP_2. We then access the next higher phase. Its numeration contains {DP-4, V ... }.[47] We merge V with CP_2 and then merge it with DP-4 to discharge that θ-role. We then have the external argument position to "fill." We have used up all the DP elements in the numeration that are fit for purpose, so MoM allows us to access DP-1 from the previous phase and move it to the external-argument position of the matrix clause. After some further standard

---

[47] I am leaving lots of functional stuff out to make the argument clearer. Suffice it to say, that there is a v and other stuff like T hanging around that gets merged in the regular way.

movements, the derivation converges with DP-1 "subject" of the matrix clause interpreted as antecedent of the DP-1 occurrence that is complement of the lowest V (and which is ultimately phonologically realized as an LDA).

Now consider the absent reading in which the matrix object in (33) cannot be interpreted as antecedent of the LDA. In particular, why couldn't DP-1 have merged as the internal argument of the matrix V rather than as its external argument? Were this to occur then the object in (33) would be the antecedent of the LDA. MoM prevents such a derivation. Here are the details.

Recall that at the point of the derivation where we are building the matrix clause, DP-1 is sitting in the Spec of the structure built in the earlier phase. MoM requires that we use up the elements in the numeration of the phase being built before we use material from earlier phases. Recall that DP-4 is an element of the matrix numeration. Thus, we must use it before we use DP-1 in CP_2. And thus moving DP-1 to the object position of the matrix V is blocked as DP-4 is available from the numeration of the current phase for this purpose. MoM requires that it be used, and so the only available slot left for DP-1 is the external argument of the matrix verb. And that is where DP-1 goes. This derives the subject orientation of LDAs.

Motomura's (2002) line of reasoning is beautiful. Given phases, some version of MoM relativized to phases, and a movement theory of LDAs, we expect to find a subject orientation effect, and we do. The subject orientation of LDAs thus provides interesting evidence in favor of a movement-based theory of LDAs, as well as for phase-based numerations and MoM.

5.9 LDAs and Split Antecedents

LDAs have another interesting property that lends additional support to a movement analysis.[48] Consider a sentence with two LDAs, as in (36). This structure has two LDAs in the bottom clause with three potential antecedent subjects, DP-1,2,3.

(36)   [DP-3 V [DP-2 V [DP-1 V LDA-1 LDA-2]]]

Here is the relevant fact: In structures like (36) the two LDAs must have the same non-local antecedent. In other words, in (36) the two LDAs can both have DP-3 or DP-2 as antecedent but one cannot have DP-3 and the other DP-2. Why?

Consider the structure that would arise if the LDAs had split non-local antecedents. For illustration, assume LDA-1 takes D/1 and LDA-2 takes D/2.

---

[48] This section is based on research by Yuki Ito (2010). Ito was the first, so far as I know, to appreciate that a movement theory of LDAs should induce certain kinds of island effects. The present section reports these findings.

5.9 LDAs and Split Antecedents

The structure we get with LDA-1 anteceded by the embedded subject D/2 on a movement account would look like (37) (for readability I will annotate the copies with respect to their antecedents and designate them as 'D/1' (meaning: D antecedent to LDA/1)). Now we need to get LDA/2 to DP/2, and here we run into a problem. To get to D/2, we need to move via the embedded CPs, first via the medial CP* and then to CP** and then to the external θ-position in the matrix. The problem is that the medial Spec CP* is filled by (a copy of/trace of) D/1. In other words, splitting the antecedents means moving two expressions via the same CP edge and this is illicit.[49]

(37)   [D/2 V [$_{CP**}$ [D/1 ... [$_{CP*}$ D/1 [$_{TP}$ DP V [D/2 (=LDA/2)] [D/1 (=LDA/1)]]]]]]

Is having different antecedents always grammatically illicit? No. Let's see why. First some facts.

In Japanese, which is the language Ito (2010) discusses, LDAs and local anaphoric reflexives can have the same form. Thus in (36), split antecedents *are* permitted so long as *one* of them is the local subject DP-1. This is permitted, for then only one of the LDAs exploits movement through the local CP in forming the (improper) A'-chain, the local reflexive being a product of simple A-movement. A relevant instance is illustrated in (38):

(38)   ... [$_{CP}$ [$_{TP}$ D/2 V [$_{CP}$ D/2 [$_{TP}$ D/1 V [D/1 (=LDA/1)] [D/2 (=LDA/2)]]]]]

As establishing the DP/1 (=LDA/1) relation does not need to transit via CP, nothing blocks D/2 from using that CP to establish the D/2 (=LDA/2) chain.

It is also possible for both LDA/1 and LDA/2 to have D* as antecedent, as in (39):

(39)   [DP V [$_{CP}$ [$_{TP}$ DP V [$_{CP}$ [$_{TP}$ D* V [D/1 (LDA/1)] [D/2 (LDA/2)]]]]]]

Here we have DP-1 E-merge in the first LDA-2 position, I-merge to LDA-1 and I-merge again till it stops in Spec T of the embedded clause (D*). So the two LDAs are actually *local* (rather than long-distance) reflexives and there is no movement through Spec C at all. Of course, this same apparatus allows D/2 or D/3 to start in the lowest clause and move, as in (40), both LDAs taking the matrix subject as antecedent:

(40)   [D* V [$_{CP}$ D* [$_{TP}$ DP-2 V [$_{CP}$ D* [$_{TP}$ DP-1 V [D* (=LDA/1)] [D* (=LDA/2)]]]]]]

So, by having the same antecedent, there need be only one expression in the relevant intermediate CPs and so there will be no filled phase edge blocking the relevant I-merge/(A')-movement via the intermediate CP edge.

---

[49] This is, effectively, a *Wh*-island violation with the copy of one of the moved elements preventing any other element from moving through the occupied phase edge.

Again, the explanation of these LDA effects uses standard reasoning concerning (*Wh-*)islands in conjunction with the hypothesis that LDAs are generated by movements with links in Spec C. There is nothing novel here except the assumption that LDAs, like other instances of pronominalization, live on pronominal (improper) chains. And this assumption is a consequence of the EMH/FPG.

5.10 Bound Pronouns and Island Effects

Let's now consider a proposal concerning bound pronouns in Kannada developed in Lidz and Drummond (2012). I include it here because it illustrates how the various assumptions we have been using hang together to produce a (to me) surprising set of consequences that appear to have some empirical grounding. The argument is complex, but in an interesting way. Here goes.

The previous section shows that LDAs can generate island effects. It concluded that if *Wh-* island effects are diagnostic of A'-movement then their appearance in cases of LDAs argues that bound pronoun dependencies are formed via I-merge resulting in (improper) chains with links in Spec C. I am going to use this diagnostic again here and I am going to then combine it (in section 5.11) with the Demirdache and Percus (2011) (D&P) discovery that one can "turn off" some WCO effects using islands. This will serve to make several points: First, it reinforces the claim that bound pronouns are products of I-merge and that WCO effects reflect improper applications of movement/I-merge. I am not sure that I expect anyone to be convinced by the argument as it is quite involved. However, I like the cascade of reasoning so I thought I would regale you with it here. Let's begin.

All good Generativists know that *Wh*-islands restrict movement. A strong version of this restriction can be seen with *why* questions:[50]

(41) a. *Why$_1$ ... .[*Wh* ... t$_1$ ...]
 b. Why did John tell me to go to the travel agent?
 c. Why did John tell me when to go to the travel agent?
 d. It was to pick up the tickets that John told me to go to the travel agent
 e. #It was to pick up the tickets that John told me when to go to the travel agent

---

[50] Adjuncts like *why* cannot extract out of islands. This is a very strong effect. The result is not mere unacceptability. Rather the interpretation of the *why* inside the island is simply unavailable. The reading is missing. I believe that this distinction between unacceptable yet interpretable versus unacceptable plus interpretation-unavailability is an important one. The former case holds when the derivation is illicit but there is an available CI that is well formed. The latter holds when the derivation is illicit and there is no well-formed CI. So the difference is between derivations that were they doable would lead to interpretable outputs versus those where the outputs at CI are illicit. I will return to this soon, but thought I'd raise it here so that it could burrow into your mind/brain.

5.10 Bound Pronouns and Island Effects

One standard account of this restriction is that the lower *Wh* in (41a) clogs up the left edge of the CP, thus blocking any further movement of *why* from the embedded clause.[51] (41b–e) illustrate the effect. (41d) is a fine answer for (41b) with *to pick up the tickets* modifying the embedded predicate *go to the travel agent*. (41c) is a fine question, but (41e) is a totally weird answer because the only verb that *pick up the tickets* can modify is *tell* and the combination is hard to interpret. And this is fixable: substitute *to lord it over me* and the sentence is fine as an answer to (41c) for this is a fine modifier of *tell*.

But you know all of this. I just wanted to remind you to set up the next step of the argument. If bound pronouns are locally A'-bound then we should expect them to induce similar kinds of island effects. Lidz and Drummond (2012) shows that this expectation is met in Kannada.[52] Here is some data that indicates that the same holds true in English.

(42)   a.   *$Why_1 \ldots QP_2 \ldots [_{CP} QP_2 [\ldots pronoun_2 \ldots t_1 \ldots]]$
           b.   Why did everyone say that Lola loves me
           c.   OK: Everyone said that Lola loves me because I am handsome and witty
           d.   OK: It is because I am handsome and witty that everyone said that Lola loves me
           e.   Why did $everyone_1$ say that Lola loves him_1
           f.   It is because $he_{2/*1}$ is handsome and witty that $everyone_1$ said that Lola loves $him_{2/*1}$
           g. $Everyone_1$ said [that Lola loves him_1 because he_1 is handsome and witty]

The relevant reading is the one in which a matrix (quantified) expression binds a pronoun inside the embedded clause (42e). Given the movement theory of pronominalization, this requires a syntactic structure like (42a). Note the embedded Spec CP is filled. (42b–d) show that without a (quantificational) expression binding a pronoun in the embedded clause, long movement of *why* is available and the modification of the embedded verb in (42c,d) is fine. The important case is (42e) and its contrast with (42b) with the interpretation (42g). It is not available. (42f) has a fine interpretation, but not if the pronouns are interpreted as bound by *everyone*. If interpreted referentially (i.e. with a 2 index), the sentences are fine. But not if interpreted as bound. And this is the effect we witnessed in (41) but this time with bound pronouns plugging the Spec C slot rather than a *Wh*.

Let's take a look at the same effect but with *how* in place of *why*:

(43)   a.   How did Mary hear that $most men_1$ washed $their_1$ cars?
           b.   It was with Turtle Wax that Mary heard that most men washed their cars

---

[51] Minimality is another option. The *Wh*-operator in Spec C blocks movement of the lower *Wh* across it. Given standard approaches to minimality, however, this assumes that *why* cannot first move to Spec C and then move further. The first move would obviate minimality. Thus, both the subjacency story and the minimality one rely on the common assumption that a filled Spec C gums up the movement works.

[52] To be accurate, there is a class of bound pronouns in Kannada that so function.

c. How did most men$_1$ hear that Mary washed their cars$_1$?
d. #It was with Turtle Wax that most men heard that Mary washed their cars.

(43b) is a fine answer to (43a). (43d), in contrast, is a weird answer to (43c). Why? Note that in (43a) *most men* binds *their* within the embedded clause. Hence there is nothing in the lower Spec C hindering movement of *how* through it. With (43c), however, *most men* is in the matrix clause and *their*, the bound pronoun, is in the embedded one. Given the movement theory of pronominalization, there must be a copy of *most men* in the embedded Spec C, and this hinders extraction of *how* from the lower clause. As *with Turtle Wax* is a lousy modifier of *hear* (I assure you TW does nothing to improve one's audition), and as the lower clause cannot be the source of *how*, we end up with a sentence with a weird reading. The relevant structures are provided in (44).

(44) a. How$_2$ did Mary hear [how [that most men$_1$ [washed (most men/their$_1$) cars] how]]
  b. How did most men$_1$ hear (#how) [most men [that Mary washed (most men/their) cars$_1$] (*how)]

5.11 Islands and Crossover Effects

Finally, let's consider some evidence that islands *block* pronominalization. Recall that I noted that effects like (45), in which an epithet or definite description (DD) cannot be bound by a quantificational antecedent, reflect the fact that where pronominalization can apply it must, and when it fails to apply the output incurs a cost reflected in lower acceptability.

(45) Every young scientist$_1$ (EYS) believed that he/*the scientist$_1$ would marry young

This effect disappears when the DD is inside an island.

(46) EYS$_1$ married the girl who **he/the scientist$_1$** knew as a child

Recall that Aoun et al. (2001) shows that this same contrast is found with RPs in Lebanese Arabic. Thus, if pronominalization involves something structurally akin to RPs as a subpart, then the contrast in (45)/(46) should come as no surprise. It indicates that islands affect pronominalization just as they affect resumption, and this follows if both are formed by the same kinds of movement.

We also saw another interesting effect of islands. D&P presented evidence from Jordanian Arabic that RPs induce S/WCO effects and that these disappear when the S/WCO configuration sits within an island. The same seems to hold of WCO involving pronominalization.

(47) a. EYS₁ thinks that **his/*the scientist's**₁ mother wants **him**₁ to marry
b. EYS₁ thinks that **he/*the scientist**₁ should announce that **he**₁ would marry
c. EYS₁ married the girl who the **scientist's/his**₁ mother wanted **him**₁ to marry
d. EYS₁ married the girl who **he/the scientist**₁ said **he**₁ would marry
e. * ... Op₁ ... DD₁ ... RP₁ ...

(47a/b) with the pronoun is fine. A bound DD, in contrast, is not. Recall that DDs cannot be directly (syntactically) A'-bound (see Section 5.6) and bound pronouns must be so bound when possible. D&P illustrates this for RPs in Jordanian Arabic. (47a,b) show that the same thing holds for bound pronouns in English. (47a) illustrates a WCO effect and (47b) a SCO effect.

D&P further argues that RPs are products of movement by showing that islands can turn off these S/WCO effects. So when the S/WCO configuration occurs within an island the unacceptability disappears. (47c,d) show that islands turn off S/WCO effects with bound pronouns as well. Note that both the DD and the pronoun are felicitous here inside a relative clause. So, just as with RPs, it seems that islands can "turn off" S/WCO effects, and this follows if bound pronouns (i) must be formed by movement when they can be and (ii) that S/WCO effects are by-products of grammatically illicit movement derivations. Again, this is what we should expect if pronominalization lives on complex chains that involve subparts isomorphic to what we find with RPs. And, as I have been arguing, these are the kinds of grammatical structures we should expect if we adopt the EMH/FPG.

In sum, we find evidence that RP and pronominalization constructions show a similar profile as regards crossover effects and their suspension. The parallel is expected if we assume that bound pronouns transit through an intermediate Spec C position on the way to the higher θ-position. Further, the EMH/FPG leads us to expect both RP and pronominalization relations are Merge generated, and this means that they should "live on" chains with A'-links. In other words, the parallels noted above are what we expect if the EMH/FPG is on the right track.

5.12 Some Loose Ends

There is one big loose end. Even if we agree that pronominal binding shows the marks of movement, how come we get *what looks like pronominal binding into islands* (as in (47c,d))? How do we establish the indicated semantic dependency if islands block movement?[53] The only acceptable

---

[53] This is especially problematic given the EMH, which postulates that *all* G dependencies are Merge mediated.

answer if one adopts the EMH/FPG is that the dependency is established *non*-grammatically. In other words, there must be a form of binding that is not a product of the grammar, and this form of binding allows for acceptable dependencies (without cost) when Merge cannot apply to generate the relevant binding.

Before saying what this might be, let me again note that what holds for bound pronouns holds for RPs as well. Recall that Aoun et al. noted that RPs within islands had different morphological profiles from those outside islands. In particular, in Lebanese Arabic strong pronouns and DDs can serve as RPs ***only*** in island contexts. Outside islands ***only*** weak pronouns can serve as RPs. This is exactly what we see in (47). My tentative suggestion is to use the presence of a non-weak pronoun (e.g. a bound DD) as a diagnostic of non-grammatical binding. For convenience, let's call this non-grammar-based species of binding "semantic binding."

So does semantic binding exist? Or more exactly, do we have reason to think that there is a non-grammatically restricted system of semantic binding? I think there is. And it appears in many natural deduction systems.[54] Consider, for example, cases like (48):

(48)   Every doctor$_1$ in town has a nurse$_1$. [She/the nurse]$_2$ makes [his/the doctor's]$_2$ appointments.

Note five facts. First, the natural reading is one where there are different nurses per doctor. Thus, *a nurse* is in the scope of *every doctor*. Second, the pronouns/DDs shift reference with that of the interpretation of the antecedents. Thus, the discourse says that Dr. A's nurse makes Dr. A's appointments and Dr. B's nurse makes Dr. B's appointments, and so on. In other words, these bound expressions are acting just like standard bound variables. Third, these antecedents clearly can do their work without c-command. There is no sense in which the quantifiers in the first sentence c-command the anaphoric dependents in the second. There are restrictions on this process, but they involve precedence rather than hierarchy. Thus, for example, reverse the order of the sentences in (48) and the indicated semantic binding is impossible. Fourth, note that in these cases we can swap pronouns for DDs without degrading acceptability. In other words, we see here what we see with pronominalization and RPs inside islands. And last but not least, these cases show no S/WCO effects.

(49)   Every doctor$_1$ in town has a nurse. Nonetheless, the doctor$_1$ believes he$_1$ should make his$_1$ own appointments

---

[54] These systems are staples of many intro logic books (see Quine 1982). They were investigated in natural language settings most extensively in Jeff King (1986) and George Wilson (1984).

5.12 Some Loose Ends   163

Note the serial order here – 'operator ... DD ... pronoun ... ' – is the one that generates crossover effects within non-embedded clauses (see (47e)). Yet they do not appear in examples like (49). Why not? Because in cases like (49) the relevant dependencies are not grammatically generated. In particular, the quantificational antecedent *every doctor* does not bind the pronoun in the next clause over *syntactically*. There is no cross-clausal movement, and so crossover effects *if they are products of movement* (as argued above) should not appear. And they don't.

So what's the upshot? If FL is structured along the lines required by the EMH/FPG it will greedily and reflexively analyze any linguistic dependency it runs across as Merge generated ***if it can.*** This last caveat is critical, for given general computational principles like locality (e.g. islands) and the apparent fact that grammars concern themselves with sentences (and not paragraphs), the domain of application of Merge will be restricted to intra-clausal local dependencies. This is where we expect to find grammatical dependencies with the properties that we are familiar with (e.g. A-/A'-movement, binding, control, resumption, subcategorization, selection, etc.). And we expect them to have the properties they have because they are Merge generated and live on Merge-generated structures.

However, we also expect another consequence: Structures that *don't* show these effects because the dependencies they instantiate are not Merge generated. Here we expect the signature properties of grammar to be absent. And we find this as well.[55] The cross-sentential semantic binding noted above is,

---

[55] Consider one more example of this reasoning. Recall, we account for illicit binding of definite descriptions in cases like (26) above by claiming that pronouns are the morphological residue of movement/I-merge and that where grammar can establish a dependency then it must do so or there will be a cost in acceptability. Thus the examples in (26) are unacceptable because we could have formed the binding dependency syntactically, as the acceptable analogue with a bound pronoun swapping for the bound definite description indicates. If this is correct and if something like MoM regulates derivations of antecedence, then we might expect to find bound definite descriptions acceptable when MoM is violated. This appears to be correct:
(i) A boy$_1$ persuaded every girl$_2$ that the budding politician$_{*1/ok-2}$ would soon become student council President
(ii) A girl$_1$ introduced every boy$_2$ before (the gal$_{*1}$/the guy$_{ok-2}$) came to the dais
The subject/object asymmetry in acceptability in (i)/(ii) follows if MoM regulates antecedence formation. The unacceptable subject "binding" is simply an instance of the Principle C effect discussed in Section 5.6. The acceptability of the object being antecedent to the DDs in (i) and (ii) follows if MoM holds. Movement to the object position in the derivations of (i) and (ii) would violate MoM. Thus, there is no licit syntactic derivation of the indicated dependency between the embedded subject and the matrix object. If this is correct, semantic binding can apply without incurring a grammatical penalty. We thus expect an anti-subject orientation effect. In other words, the subject cannot bind the definite description because this *is* a binding relation that a G incorporating MoM could licitly derive (note the sentence is perfectly OK with a bound pronoun in place of the definite description). Not respecting the grammatical option incurs a cost which appears in the relative unacceptability when semantic binding is attempted.

I believe, an example.[56] So too is binding into islands, as in (47). What is critical here is that semantic binding seamlessly applies (i.e. without an acceptability cost) precisely when grammatical binding cannot. And if the above is on the right track, this means precisely when I-merge cannot apply to form the requisite chains (e.g. because islands bar the movement, or G rules do not apply across sentences, or because some economy principle would be violated (see note 55)).

Say this is correct. It then provides another argument for the EMH/FPG. Let me lay it out.

There is an obvious sense in which the system above is functionally redundant. It postulates *two* ways of establishing antecedence. There is a non-grammatical process of semantic binding and a grammatically regulated Merge-based process of syntactic pronominal binding. Moreover, the former has a more expansive range than the latter. This raises an obvious question: Why does FL contain an operation *less* general than an independently available one? Why not just stick with the more general operation and dump the less general redundant one? In other words, why does FL have a process of syntactic binding at all given that semantic binding, which humans also have, would have sufficed. Worse still, why have a process of syntactic binding which interferes with the more general process of semantic binding and degrades the acceptability of the otherwise perfectly fine structures it generates. Who ordered that?

Well, nobody did. What we see here is simply the by-product of a Merge-based system of FL that respects the EMH/FPG to the max. Call it the Principle of Grammatical Plenitude (PGP). Once FL embodies the EMH/FPG, it reflexively treats whatever it can as a product of Merge. It doesn't care that there are other cognitive ways of doing things, for it blindly, relentlessly, and greedily analyzes whatever it can in terms of Merge. That's what FL does. You cannot turn it off. So, it applies where it can and lets you know when it is being thwarted by degrading the acceptability of expressions where it could have applied but didn't. A consequence of this is that one looks for its signature properties both in places that it does apply and in those that it does not. And now here is the punchline: If the EMH/FPG did not hold we should not expect to see the two kinds of binding profiles noted above. We should not expect their

---

[56] Another is non-obligatory control (NOC). Boeckx and Hornstein (2007) discusses this. What's important about these cases is that they contrast with OC along virtually every dimension. For example, NOC "pro" does not require an antecedent and can have a non-local non-c-commanding antecedent. Importantly, NOC pro is generally restricted to island contexts and so NOC dependencies cannot be generated via (I-)merge. As such, they *should not* display the characteristic properties of OC, which are so generated. FL applies its computational powers whenever it can. But when it cannot, it appears that other options become available. Yet these too reveal the shadow cast by FL by failing to bark with a grammatical accent.

properties to be disjoint. We should not expect one to interfere with application of the other. Actually, we should not expect to find syntactic binding at all as there is already a perfectly serviceable alternative. Furthermore, we should not expect their mutual interference to disappear when the grammar is prevented from applying (either because rules cannot apply across islands or must respect economy principles like MoM or …). So, the if pronominal binding (in both RP and pronominalization) is indeed the product of I-merge/movement, then their existence as such implicates the EMH/FPG. The EMH/FPG forces FL to give birth to syntactic pronominal binding, even when such binding is superfluous and serves to trip up the application of the more general process.

That's it, except for a quick recap.

5.13 Recap

In Chapter 4, I briefly reprised evidence for a movement theory of Obligatory Control and Reflexivization. I pointed out that the EMH/FPG in the context of the elimination of D-structure should allow movement into θ-positions and thus the generation of A-chains with multiple θ-links. These kinds of chains could form the grammatical scaffolding for dependencies like OC and Reflexivization which display the locality conditions characteristic of A-movement *because* they, like A-chains, are generated by Merge. Thus, if the EMH/FPG is on the right track and we assume something like the Principle of Grammatical Plenitude, we expect to find construal phenomena that live on A-chains.

I further observed that *if* we accept the GB observation (first coded by Lees and Klima) that Reflexivization and Pronominalization (or Principles A/B) apply in complementary structural environments, then *if* Reflexivization is a product of I-merge/movement, then Pronominalization should be as well. The reason is that it is very hard to see how the complementarity could be explained if Pronominalization dependencies were formed in ways totally unrelated to movement. Moreover, once we model Reflexivization as A-chains, it is hard to resist the possibility that Pronominalization lives on A'-chains. This, as noted, serves to derive the long-noted complementarity in a smooth way. Of course, some apparently dicey assumptions are required: We must allow improper movement and we must explain why apparent Pronominalization into islands is licit. This chapter tries to show the benefit of living with these assumptions and argues that they may not be as lethal as one might first think. At any rate, the result is that the EMH/FPG plus the Principle of Grammatical Plenitude suffice to yield an FL with the characteristics outlined in the GB construal module. It manages to unify these non-local dependencies as Merge-generated A-/A'-chains and allows for the derivation of many of their properties and accompanying effects. In short, we have a Merge-based theory of construal of a piece with the standard Merge-based theory of classical A- and A'-movement.

Is there a cost? Yes. There are details that need a lot of working out. Why are some cases of improper movement fine while others are not? Why do some chains realize overt morphology at their tails and some don't? Why is the morphology (often (but think backwards control)) at the tail of the chain (e.g. RPs, reflexives, bound pronouns)? All reasonable questions. None of them answered here. These noted, I have taken my job to be to show the benefits of rampant unification under Merge and to argue that it is a worthwhile project to explore such a unification. Why? Because EMH requires such unification and the EMH, incorporating the FPG, embodies a version of one of MP's central conjectures (viz. the strong minimalist thesis). Hopefully, the results of the last two chapters have made a case.

6   A Partial Wrap-Up and Segue

6.0   The Story So Far

The aim of Chapters 2 through 5 has been to show how to realize the minimalist goal of reconciling Plato's Problem with Darwin's in the domain of language. The strategy adopted has been to derive the GB laws of grammar illustrated in Chapter 1 from the simpler, more general assumptions of the Extended Merge Hypothesis (EMH). The two basic assumptions have been (i) a very simple combination operation (Merge) which combines expressions into labeled sets and (ii) the Fundamental Principle of Grammar (FPG) which requires Merge to mediate *all* grammatical dependencies. I have tried to outline how these two assumptions could be pressed into service to derive many of the mid-level generalizations (Laws) that the prior sixty years of Generative research had discovered. This chapter is intended to serve as a quick overview of the basic results. More specifically, the aim here will be to list the derived laws and to specify the assumptions used as premises for the derivations. The two noted above, a simple conception of Merge and the FPG, are central. However, others were also pressed into service, and it behooves us to note exactly what they are and which laws they are used to explain. This way, future empirical and theoretical improvements will have a place to start (i.e. something specific to criticize).

6.1   The Simple Conception of Merge

Chapter 2 shows how a simple conception of Merge is able to derive eight central properties of the faculty of language (FL).

Assumptions:

A. A simple conception of the syntactic combination operation, Merge:
   i.   Merge is recursive.
   ii. Merge is a very simple combination operation in that *all* it does is combine its inputs. This means:

a. No Tampering: It does not change the inputs in any way in combining them
      - It does not change lexical atoms in any way
      - It does not change complex objects in any way
      - It does not impose any serial order on the objects combined.
   b. Combination is minimally a two-place operation. It takes two to combine.
B. The specific inductive definition of Syntactic Object (SO) incorporating Merge:
   i. If α is a lexical item then α is a Syntactic Object (SO).
   ii. If α is an SO and β is an SO then Merge (α,β) is an SO.
   iii. For α, β, SOs, Merge (α,β) → {α,β}.

Properties Derived:

1. The Basic Property: The inductive definition in B yields an unbounded number of hierarchically structured SOs.
2. Movement: The inductive definition in B allows for at least two sub-instances:
   a. Neither α nor β contains the other (E-merge)
   b. One of α or β contains the other (I-merge)
   The first case (2a) delivers the analogue of phrase structure building (E-merge). (2b) provides an analogue of movement (I-merge).
3. Duality of Interpretation: The SOs provide adequate formats for the representation of argument structure and scope:
   As noted in (2), (B) supports the generation of SOs that are the Merge analogues of phrase structure and movement. θ-roles are assigned under sisterhood when a predicate and an argument (E-)merge. I-merge suffices to generate syntactic formats adequate for representing scope. An expression scopes over its sister and its sister's contents. Thus, the inductive definition in (B) generates SOs with formal structure sufficient to code the duality of interpretation (i.e. argument structure and scope) observed in natural language.
4. Reconstruction/connectedness effects:
   The "simple" conception of Merge in (A) produces syntactic formats that suffice for representing reconstruction/connectedness effects. (A) reflects the assumption that a combination operation that leaves its inputs unchanged is simpler than one that changes them in the course of combining them (Aiia). Simplicity, then, includes a No Tampering Condition (NTC) that has two consequences:
   a. Inclusiveness: lexical atoms that are combined by Merge are left unchanged by being so combined.
   b. Extension: Complex expressions combined by Merge are left unchanged by being so combined.

6.1 The Simple Conception of Merge

An immediate consequence of the NTC is the Copy Theory of Movement (CTM), the hypothesis that the links in I-merge-generated (movement) chains are identical. This Merge-based conception contrasts with the earlier GB theory of chains in which all links of the chain but the head are traces. The presence of copies in place of traces provides a simple format for reconstruction/connectedness effects. In sum, Merge as defined in (B) implies the CTM which in turn offers a structural basis for reconstruction/connectedness effects in natural language.[1]

5. The c-command requirement on movement (i.e. movement is upward and targets a c-commanding position):[2]

    That movement is upward and to c-commanding positions follows from movement being I-merge and I-merge embodying the NTC, specifically the Extension Condition (4b). If α contains β, then given the definition of Merge in (A) and (B), the only legitimate output combines β with its container α. This necessarily places β in a c-commanding position with respect to the copy of β in the launch site. Thus, the c-command condition on movement follows from the NTC which follows from the "simplicity" of Merge. Similarly, if Merge is the only grammatical operation (see assumption D below), then there is no operation corresponding to lowering that is grammatically legitimate. Thus, we derive that the only kind of movement allowed in configurations in which α contains β is upwards to a c-commanding position.[3]

6. Strict cyclicity:

    This also follows from the NTC, specifically Extension. Non-cyclic movement violates Extension as expressions are merged inside (rather than at the top of) a previously formed structure.

7. Binary branching:

    Assume Merge is the simplest possible combination operation. Conceptually, a combination requires at least two inputs (Aiib). The simplest assumption

---

[1] Let me repeat an important caveat. CTM allows for reconstruction/connectedness effects but does not require them. Rather the chains I-merge forms provide an envelope of interpretive possibilities. Which possibilities are realized within a given construction or grammar is determined by ancillary factors.

[2] To repeat, this holds within single-rooted structures. It does not hold if sidewards (inter-arboreal) movement is a grammatical option.

[3] Recall that GB explained this feature of movement in terms of the Empty Category Principle (ECP) (or at least part was). As noted, there are many empirical problems with an ECP-based explanation aside from its baroque character. A Merge-based theory of grammar has the very pleasant consequence of deriving the observed fact about movement without requiring a theory like the ECP. More interesting still, the ECP appears to be un-stateable in a Merge-based system because the ECP is a *trace licensing theory*. But I-merge does not have traces as it incorporates the CTM. And it *cannot* have traces as it embodies the NTC. Thus the ECP is idle in a Merge-based theory. So, not only is the ECP not required (or at least this part), but it is not even stateable. In my opinion, this is an important *theoretical* consequence of the Merge Hypothesis (and extensions thereof). For further discussion, see Chapter 8.

is that the necessary operation is also the only operation (i.e. a two-place combination operation is both necessary and sufficient). If this is so, then Merge will generate binary-branching structures.[4]

8. Structure dependence:
   This follows from the assumption that Merge does nothing to its inputs save combine them (Aiia). In particular, it does not linearize them *in* combining them, for linearizing the inputs is more complex than simply combining them. The output of Merge, then, is a grouping of elements with no left–right order. As the outputs of Merge are also inputs to further Merges, this means that the inputs to Merge carry no information concerning their linearization.[5] But this implies that syntactic rules cannot advert to such information in their application as such information is unavailable from the inputs. This derives the conclusion that syntactic operations are structure dependent.[6]

These eight properties, then, follow from the assumption that Merge is part of an inductive definition of the basic combination operation and that it is very simple in that it does nothing more than combine the objects it combines when it combines them. "Nothing more" is doing a lot of conceptual work here. It is understood to mean that it does not change the inputs in any way in combining them and adds nothing to the inputs in combining them. Thus, Merge does not change the properties of the lexical atoms it can combine with other syntactic objects (i.e. the Inclusiveness Condition) and it does not change the properties of the complex syntactic objects it combines with other syntactic objects (i.e. the Extension Condition). Further, simplicity enjoins that Merge does not order the elements combined, as all it does is combine them. These three features of Merge are understood to follow from the fact that it is *as simple as possible* and

---

[4] This reasoning has been challenged. One might argue that the simplest combination operation combines any number of inputs N, two being a special case when N = 2. This reasoning understands 'simplicity' as 'generality.' The combine-N version of Merge is more general than the combine-2 version. The relevant question is whether the more general version is also simpler. Decisively answering this is beyond my pay grade. Suffice it to say, that if one categorizes operations by their logical syntax, then operations of greater addicity are plausibly more complex than those of lesser addicity. As Merge with addicity 2 seems the least complex combination operation that could suffice to generate the hierarchical structures required in language, it is plausible that Merge with addicity 2 is the simplest such combination operation. For discussion of these matters in the context of the theory of types, see Pietroski (2018).

[5] This is why representing Merge as a set formation operation is apposite (Biii). Elements of a set have no left–right order: {a,b} = {b,a}.

[6] Note, this assumes that there are no syntax-like operations that apply *after* linearization has applied. Thus, only the syntax is generative. The interfaces are merely interpretive. They take the structures that the syntax generates and interpret them. Without this assumption, operations that are left–right sensitive should be available, logically speaking. Note that if this is correct, then it argues for the venerable assumption within Generative Grammar that *only* the syntax is generative and that the interfaces must be purely interpretive. This is a very interesting architectural conclusion about FL that seems to directly follow from the nature of Merge and the fact that generative procedures within Gs are structure dependent.

simple combination operations should not do more than combine their inputs. The effect of this is to recursively define an operation that can form larger and larger structures with complex structures as subparts. The general properties of the objects (i.e. syntactic objects/constituents) generated by the recursive specification are adequately represented as sets containing sets containing sets containing ... as members

In sum, if we assume that FL incorporates the simplest recursive combination as outlined in (A,B) then we can derive the facts in (1–8). Or, to put this another way: If we consider what is the simplest way of satisfying the Basic Property (1), we find a system with the properties (2–8).[7]

6.2 Merge with Labels

Thus far, the derivations focused on how elements that combine are combined. Chapter 3 complicates the combination operation. It adds labels. This revives the earliest conception of Merge wherein that output of the combination operation yields a complex object (set) with a label, the label being supplied by one of the two elements combined.[8] As noted, this is an *extra* assumption and it complicates the combination operation. This, thus, requires some justification, which I defer to Chapter 7. For now, observe that the assumption that Merge produces *labeled* syntactic objects treats the classical constituent as the central grammatical/syntactic object.

Theoretically, labeling allows for a very strong version of the Merge Hypothesis (MH), which I dubbed the Extended Merge Hypothesis (EMH). In particular, the Fundamental Principle of Grammar (FPG), which states that the only way to establish a grammatical dependency is via Merge, requires labels.[9] The EMH (i.e. MH+FPG), then, proposes a very strong version of the Merge Hypothesis (and thus a very strong version of the strong minimalist thesis), the cost being the addition of labels.

---

[7] As noted in Chapter 2, the line of thinking outlined here is due to Chomsky.

[8] Importantly, this complicates Merge as the operation now does *more* than simply combine two inputs. It does this *and* invidiously selects one as label to the exclusion of the other. In the *very next chapter* I return to this and suggest that labeling is the linguistically special operation. Merge is, thus, more computationally/cognitively general while labeling is the real secret sauce that, we shall see, yields hierarchy.

Please note the emphasis of 'the very next chapter'. The excellent reviewers correctly jumped onto the possibility that we could derive the relevant effects without labels in the syntax, and that this was both theoretically and methodologically superior to what is offered here. The *very next chapter* argues that this line of thought is incorrect. If you are someone that just needs to see these arguments before moving on, feel free to skip ahead. You have my permission. Don't hold back.

[9] The FPG eliminates all dependency-forming operations other than Merge from FL. In particular, Probe/Goal Agree is not a possible FL operation.

Assumptions:

C. Labeling:
   i. The output of Merge is a labeled set.
   ii. Labels are heads (i.e. syntactic atoms).
   iii. The label of the output of Merge is the label of one of the inputs.
D. Fundamental Principle of Grammar (FPG):
   All G(rammatical) relations are Merge mediated: If α is G-related to β then Merge (α,β).
E. The Case/θ Exclusion Principle (θ/CEP): If α θ-marks β then α does not case mark β, and if α case marks β then α does not θ-mark β.
F. Minimality:
   i. Shorter dependencies trump longer ones.
   ii. Paths measure distance:
      a. The path from α to β is the union of labels dominating α and β.

Properties Derived:

The locality of head-to-head relations (such as selection and subcategorization):
9. If a head α selects a head β then β or a projection of β is sister to α:
   This follows from C and D: the assumptions that *all* grammatical dependencies are mediated by Merge, that merge-formed SOs are labeled and that labels are heads. Thus, a head α can select/subcategorize a head β only if an α° merges with a β labeled SO: {α, {$_β$ ... β ...}}. Here α and the β-labeled expression are sisters. Note, given the No Tampering Condition (Aiia), α could not directly merge with β under Merge and so head-to-head relations in general would not obey the FPG (D). The only way to adhere to the FPG in general, then, requires labels. In other words, labeling is necessary for the strong version of the Merge Hypothesis embodied in the EMH.
10. The Periscope Property:
    A head can *only* select/subcategorize the head of its sister. In particular, heads cannot select specifiers, complements or adjuncts of β. This too follows under the assumption that selection/subcategorization piggybacks on Merge. Why? Because the *only* SO that α merges with is the β-labeled SO. No structure *inside the projection of β* is visible to α because α cannot Merge with structure inside the projection of β without violating the No Tampering Condition (Aiia). In particular, the NTC prevents α's merging with specifiers, complements or adjuncts of β and thus blocks any grammatical interaction between α and these SOs contained within the β-labeled SO. This explains why the Periscope Property restricts selection/subcategorizations to head-to-head relations.

11. YP–X° relations: Case marking, external argument θ-marking, and agreement:
The domain of θ-marking is also hyper-local. In particular, if a head α θ-marks an SO β (B and XP) then α and β are sisters.[10] For internal arguments, the relevant structure is {α, {$_β$ ... β ...}} (α θ-marks β). For non-internal arguments, the relevant structure is {{$_β$ ... β ...} {$_α$ ... α ...}} (α θ-marks β). Note that in both cases the α and β-labeled expressions are sisters, so the generalization that θ-marking is under sisterhood is derived given the FPG in D. Hence, the narrow locality restriction on θ-assignment follows from the FPG plus labels (C). Note, labels are critical for θ-assignment to non-internal arguments. Without labels, heads could only θ-mark internal arguments.
12. The Predicate Internal Subject Hypothesis (PISH): The FPG (D) plus the assumption that external arguments are θ-marked by the predicates they head (or some externalizing functional head that takes the predicate as an internal argument) implies that external arguments are base generated inside the projection of the head that assigns the external θ-role (e.g. v or V).
13. The same {{$_β$ ... β ...} {$_α$ ... α ...}} configuration supports case marking. Given the standard assumption that certain heads are case assigners/checkers and the minimalist assumption that a head cannot both θ-mark and case assign/check the same SO (E), all case assignment/checking is realized in a Spec-X° configuration. Labels (C) are required to allow α to "see" a β-labeled projection in its Spec if line of sight is limited to merged sisters (D).[11]
14. Case and scope: The discovery that an expression's case marking affects its scope options (Lasnik and Saito 1991) follows as well. The relevant assumptions are (i) that certain heads are case assigners/checkers, (ii) case is assigned/checked syntactically, (iii) it is assigned under sisterhood (D), (iv) SOs are labeled (C), (v) the θ/CEP (E) and (vi) the interpretive assumption that an expression's scope is restricted to what it c-commands.[12] The requirement that case features be discharged forces expressions to I-merge with a case-labeled SO (and thus become Specifier to that SO). This expands an expression's c-command domain, thereby expanding its potential scope. This is effectively the Lasnik-Saito explanation rephrased in terms of the EMH/FPG.

---

[10] Chomsky (1981) restricts it to the government domain of the head. Chomsky (1986a) restricts it to sisterhood.

[11] θ/CEP (E) does not follow from anything principled so far as I can tell. There is no reason why a head could not both θ-mark and case mark the same expression. Indeed, this is what transitive verbs do within GB. Most minimalist accounts of "standard" case theory (i.e. not dependent case theory), however, reject this GB option and adopt E.

[12] (i), (ii) and (vi) are standard in the literature. (iii) and (iv) follow from the EMH. (vi) is a standard interpretive assumption linking c-command and semantic scope. (v) has no interesting theoretical motivation, but it seems to be correct.

15. Agreement is discharged in the same Spec-X° configurations under I-merge with the relevant functional heads.[13]
16. XPs move, X's don't:
    This follows from labeling plus minimality (F). (F) states (i) that shorter dependencies are preferred to longer ones and (ii) that paths measure distance, a path being the union of the set of labels that dominate the SOs that merge. Minimality (in some form) is standard within minimalist theories. It is hoped that it reflects a non-linguistic property of our cognitive/computational capacities (see Chapter 8 for discussion). In other words, it is taken to reflect a principle of cognitive computation not specific to FL. (Fii) concretizes (i) in the domain of language. It provides a measure of distance "natural" for hierarchically labeled objects. It is important to observe that there are other conceivable measures that are equally natural (e.g. count the branching categories). However, there are two considerations that make the path conception particularly apposite. First, it does not rely on counting in any way. A path P1 is shorter than a path P2 just in case P1 is a proper subset of P2. It has long been observed that grammars don't count so we would expect a grammatical distance measure not to count. Second, I argue in Chapter 7 that labeling is the innovation that loosed unbounded hierarchy into cognition.[14] If this is correct, then it is natural that grammatical distance be measured in terms of labels. Neither of these "arguments" is dispositive, but I hope they are mildly convincing. At any rate, if paths measure distance, then given labeled SOs, we can explain the two facts above in terms of minimality. In particular, I-merge occurs in configurations like (1) (the numerals in brackets are for expository convenience only):

(1) $\{_{Y(1)} Y \ldots \{_{Z} \ldots \{_{X(1)} \ldots \{_{X(2)} \ldots X(3) \ldots\} \ldots\} \ldots\} \ldots\}$

What is the "shortest" kosher I-merge (movement) that can relate an X-labeled SO with a Y-labeled SO? It is one that moves the X(1)-labeled SO to merge with the matrix Y-labeled one (Y(1)). Why? Because this

---

[13] Thus, long-distance Agree under Probe/Goal is not *technically* required to accommodate long-distance agreement. Hornstein (2008) shows that Agree/Probe-Goal systems are isomorphic to ones with I-merge plus free copy deletion. Thus, there is no *technical* reason for requiring long-distance Agree operations in FL. More pointedly: If the Merge Hypothesis is correct, then FL has Merge as a basic operation. If the simplest conception of Merge has both E and I, then FL will necessarily contain both E-merge and I-merge. As I-merge and Agree/Probe-Goal largely track one another, having both is redundant. Every theory of FL must have an operation like E-merge. But the simplest version of E-merge will also permit I-merge. Hence, Agree/Probe-Goal is a redundant methodologically idle operation. It should be dumped!

[14] There is also a theoretical reason to assume this conception of paths: see (17).

6.2 Merge with Labels

path is the only one that contains no X-labeled SO. Thus, X(1) will move and X(2) won't.[15,16]

17. C-command and minimality:

    The definition of minimality incorporates a c-command restriction: In a structure ' ... X ... Y ... Z ... ' in which X c-commands Y and Y c-commands Z and in which both Y and Z have feature specifications relevant to X, no operation can involve X and Z.

    If minimality is understood in terms of paths as in (16), we derive this c-command restriction on minimality. The path from Y to X is not a proper subset of the one from Z to X if Y does not c-command X.

    The c-command restriction on I-merge/movement (5 above) follows from the No Tampering Condition (Aiia). The c-command restriction on minimality follows from the definition of paths. We show later that the c-command conditions on construal follow from the movement theory of construal, which in turn is a consequence of the EMH/FPG. It thus appears that we can derive *all* the c-command restrictions in FL. If correct, c-command is not a primitive relation of FL. Though it is (largely) descriptively adequate, it is not theoretically fundamental. Thus, a central relation employed by FL seems to be fully derivable from a Merge+label-based theory of FL.

So, recapping the assumptions. We added labeling to the Merge operation so that the output of Merge is a labeled two-element set, the label being the "head" of one of the two inputs. In addition, we strengthened the Merge Hypothesis (MH) by adding the Fundamental Principle of Grammar (FPG), the requirement that Merge is the only FL operation available for establishing grammatical relations. MH plus FPG comprise the Extended Merge Hypothesis (EMH). EMH serves to explain various linguistic generalizations directly; specifically locality restrictions on selection/subcategorization, the Predicate Internal Subject Hypothesis, and locality restrictions on θ-role assignment.

We then added some common assumptions about classical case assignment given standard minimalist assumptions. We assumed that heads could not both θ-mark and case mark the same SO. This results in a version of the movement theory of case proposed in Chomsky (1993) and refined in Lasnik and Saito (1991), where case and scope are shown to interact. The locality of

---

[15] Note that head movement is prohibited on this account. For discussion, see Hornstein (2008). That head movement is not a licit grammatical operation is less aberrant now than it was a decade ago. See, for example, Chomsky (2021).

[16] Hornstein (2008) observes that analogous assumptions suffice to derive a version of the Proper Binding Condition. The reader can appreciate this by noting that (1) effectively reduces to assuming the A-over-A condition as a condition on licit derivations. For discussion, see Hornstein (2008).

scope reduces to the locality properties of the theory of I-merge that underlies it. Suffice it to say that if case is fed by I-merge of the A-movement variety, the standard locality restrictions will fall out, just as they did in earlier MH accounts. EMH does little to change the basic movement explanation save to make it the *only* FL option. This is where the EMH via the FPG does some real theoretical work. Restricting all grammatical dependencies to Merge-mediated ones has real bite, for it forecloses options that grammars with more expansive rule options leave open.[17]

The last assumption that plays an explanatory role is minimality. This has long been a staple of minimalist theory and we follow standard practice in assuming that it reflects some general properties of cognitive computation. Like the literature at large, we do not specify what exactly these might be. Gesturing wildly to things offstage is all that we have managed (and to which we return in Chapter 8). We do, however, note that assuming a version of minimality defined in terms of shortest dependencies measured via sets of labels has some nice theoretical and empirical consequences, including deriving the fact that grammatical movement restricts itself to XPs and eschews X's (we punted here on head movement but see the notes). We also note that this approach allows for the elimination of c-command from the standard definition of minimality, pointing again to the possibility that c-command is not a primitive relation of FL but derivable from simpler assumptions like the No Tampering Condition and Shortest Dependency.

So, our assumptions are now the following: (i) a simple combination operation, (ii) a simple labeling operation, (iii) the FPG, (iv) a minimality condition, and (v) a θ/case exclusion principle. Of these, in my opinion, the oddest one is (v). The others are all standard fare, but (v) strikes me as the one that will be hardest to explain away internal to the logic of the program. Of course, we are not done yet. On to construal.

6.3 Construal

The construal module of the GB grammar comes in two parts: binding and control. These two sub-domains also divide. Binding conditions specify three sub-cases: (i) Principle A that covers anaphoric dependencies, (ii) Principle B that covers pronominal dependencies and (iii) Principle C that specifies the distribution of non-dependent R-expressions. Control comes in two flavors: (iv) obligatory control (OC) and (v) non-obligatory control. The thrust of Chapters 4 and 5 is that construal relations and their basic properties follow if we assume that these dependencies "live on" chain structure. In other words,

---

[17] Thus, the FPG plays the role of a theoretical forcing mechanism: suggesting some options and ruling out others.

6.3 Construal

antecedents relate to their anaphoric dependents in precisely the way that heads of chains relate to their traces.

The assumption that construal is a chain relation is a consequence of the FPG (D). An antecedent binds an anaphor when it heads a chain with multiple θ-links. There are several ways of executing this basic idea. Here is one: Syntactically, OC and Reflexive chains have a nominal argument heading an A-chain with two or more θ-links. Morphophonological rules can delete copies or convert them into designated morphemes when the chain is interpreted at the AP interface. Deletion of copies yields OC structures. Conversion of copies into reflexives yields Reflexivization constructions. In both cases, at CI we have an A-chain with copies in multiple θ-marked links.[18]

Pronominalization is analogous but has one important difference. There is at least one copy of the antecedent in an A'-position. Thus, pronominalization chains are derived via improper movement and have multiple θ-links.

If A- and A'-chains are all that FL allows, then we expect these two kinds of multiple θ-linked chains to exhaust the grammatical inventory of possible construal dependencies. This seems to be empirically plausible.

So, the FPG implies a version of the Movement Theory of Construal (MTC), the FL restriction of chain types to A and A' limits the basic kinds of grammatical construal structures to two, and language-specific morphophonological housekeeping processes allow for the various surface manifestations of these chains, leading to constructions like Obligatory Control, Reflexivization and Pronominalization.

Assumptions:

G. I-merge into θ-positions is grammatically licit.
H. There are only two kinds of links/Merge positions: A and A'.
I. "Improper" A' to A movement is grammatically licit.
J. Language-specific grammatical processes can delete or morphophonologically "rewrite" copies.
K. Merge over Move (MoM).
L. `Phase theory.

A word about these six assumptions.

All MP accounts eliminate D-structure (DS) as a level. Historically, the definitions of DS and movement have resulted in Generative theories that

---

[18] That construal chains have multiple θ-links does not follow directly from the FPG. All that follows is that the antecedent–anaphor relation be Merge mediated. One could have a doubling approach to construal that respects the θ-criterion. However, a theory incorporating the θ-criterion is, *ceteris paribus*, more complex than one that eschews it. The burden of proof is thus on those that wish to complicate the theory. The simplest EMH, then, will treat construal in terms of multi-θ-linked chains.

block movement into θ-positions. An important consequence of eliminating DS is to make movement into θ-positions a theoretical option. It is possible to block this theoretical option but only by complicating the overarching MP theory. This is clearly methodologically dispreferred.[19] (G) *rejects such complications* and uses the option of I-merge into θ-positions to build a chain-based movement account of construal. What is important about the assumption is that it is the default theoretical move; blocking such movement requires extra assumptions. Thus the burden of proof lies with those that reject G.

Now consider H and I. There is considerable empirical evidence for the A/A' distinction. Sadly, theoretical grounding is largely non-existent. What "theory" exists largely consists of stipulations identifying which positions are A and which A'. I have nothing substantive to offer here, but I take the distinction to be ineliminable and a core feature of FL.[20]

Given the A/A' distinction, there are four possible kinds of I-merge/movement: A to A, A to A', A' to A' and A' to A. The ban on improper movement prohibits the last of the four. Why? It appears to be empirically problematic.[21] Theoretically, however, it is what we should expect given that the other three possible kinds of I-merge/movement are kosher. A movement approach to pronominal binding requires rejecting the ban on improper movement. Again, this is the simplest theoretical assumption as it rejects *adding* this prohibition to FL thereby complicating it. Again, this makes I the preferred MP option.

Assumption J is again standard within MP. Once copies replace traces there must be operations that delete copies to get well-formed phonological outputs. Thus, given the CTM, deletion is an obviously necessary operation. J adds to deletion the option of converting copies into a small number of designated expressions, such as pronouns and reflexives. This is reminiscent of the kinds of rewrite operations found in the earliest Generative theories of construal (Lees and Klima 1963). The operations appear to be idiosyncratic in that different languages allow different options regarding which copies delete, whether copies must be rewritten and what they are rewritten as. Thus, *that*

---

[19] It is worth reiterating that a standard way of complicating the theory is also not available if Merge unifies structure building and movement, as in 2 above. If E- and I-merge are both applications of the same combination operation then it is hard to see how E-merge could create a θ-dependency but I-merge could not.

[20] Let me indulge in a very fuzzy piece of speculation. Phase theory distinguishes A- from A'-chains. The former chains represent intra-phase dependencies. The latter are (largely) interphasal. This suggests grounding the A/A' distinction in the theory of phases. Note, there is one agreeable consequence of so locating the distinction. It might explain why the distinction is two-way and not three-way or four-way (as is possible of feature-based definitions (see Chomsky 1993)). It is a two-way cut because a given phase dependency will necessarily be within a phase or across phases.

[21] But see discussion in Chapter 5.

6.3 Construal

such operations exist seems uncontroversial given MP assumptions. Of course, all things being equal, we want such rules to be simple and learnable. We also expect these operations to be grammatically regulated (e.g. by case requirements).

Assumption K is quite definitely out of fashion nowadays, and I am not that wild about it either. That said, it appears useful in explaining some subject vs non-subject pronominal binding asymmetries attested in the literature, especially as regards the subject orientation of long-distance anaphors and certain prohibitions against the binding of definite descriptions often attributed to Principle C. Given this, why the reservations? Because K has questionable motivation within a theory that unifies structure building and movement as different applications of the same operation (viz. E-/I-merge). How can E-merge be preferred over I-merge when the two operations are the same? Thus, K, though empirically useful, is nonetheless theoretically opaque. It would be nice to reconceptualize K theoretically while retaining its empirical consequences. For now, I have nothing interesting to offer so I simply assume K as stated.[22]

The final assumption (L) is similarly widespread. That phases regulate derivations has been a standard assumption within Generative Grammar since the early 1970s when Subjacency Theory was first developed. Phase theory is, so far as I can tell, the latest version of this kind of theory. Virtually every Generative theory of syntax assumes something along these lines. That said, many theoretical mysteries remain, all of which I will put aside. For current purposes, assumption L has the following content: There are locality restrictions on Merge that force derivations to be successive cyclic and that prohibit movement out of islands. Though the exact theoretical grounding for Phase theory (and its antecedents Subjacency and Barriers) is opaque, the existence of such a condition is empirically well grounded.

---

[22] Let me offer two possible routes to theoretically domesticating Merge over Move (MoM). First, as suggested in Chapter 5, one can get the basic empirical benefits of MoM by requiring that within a given phase, elements in its sub-numeration be used before accessing elements from the prior phase. This, in turn, might be motivated by a principle that treats expressions in a phase as more accessible than expressions in earlier phases.

Second, a path-theoretic motivation is also possible. Hornstein (2008) suggests that E-merge always involves a shorter path than I-merge. This is easy to see. If E-merge(α, β), then nothing dominates α or β. This implies that Path(α, β) = $\emptyset$. Thus, any application of E-merge will involve shorter paths than any application of I-merge. If derivations prefer shorter path formation to longer path formation, this will imply that E-merge is always preferred to I-merge. Note that this is not quite the requirement that shorter dependencies are preferred to longer ones, as this, in the case of minimality, is relativized to the discharge of particular features. Here it is not feature checking that is optimized but rule application in general. It suggests that the two shortest-path requirements be unified, though whether this is possible is something I leave for future consideration.

Properties Derived:

18. Basic properties of Obligatory Control (OC) constructions:[23]
    i. OC PRO requires an antecedent.
    ii. The antecedent must be local.
    iii. The antecedent must c-command OC PRO.
    iv. OC PRO sits in non-case-marked/"ungoverned" positions.

    These four features of OC follow on the assumption that OC constructions are underlyingly A-chains with multiple θ-links (G). All A-chains have heads (i). The head locally binds its links (ii–iii). Only the head of an A-chain is case marked. As OC PRO is, on the MTC, an intermediate link, it must be in a non-case marked position. Interestingly, as we discussed in Chapter 4, in a grammar in which A-movement from a case position is tolerated, so too is OC. Note too, the c-command property that links in a chain c-command one another follows if derived via I-merge (see property 5 above).

19. Reflexivization/Principle A effects:
    i. Reflexives like OC PRO have properties 18i–iii.
    ii. Reflexives differ from OC PRO in requiring case licensing.

    Reflexive chains are OC chains with additional case requirements. What distinguishes reflexives from OC structures is that in the former a copy in a case position is rewritten as a reflexive. Importantly, both reflexives and OC PROs are (usually) banned from the subject positions of finite (case and agreement positions) clauses, as these are positions from which A-movement is quite generally illicit.

20. Pronominalization/Principle B effects:
    i. The anti-locality of Pronominalization (a pronoun must be free in its domain).
    ii. The complementarity of Reflexivization/A effects and Pronominalization/B effects.
    iii. C-command condition on Pronominalization.

    The FPG (D) implies that Pronominalization is a movement dependency and so pronominal binding "lives on" chains. Pronominalization chains must have at least two θ-links (G), at least one A'-link (H) and involve improper movement (I). Their anti-locality (they are only licit in domains larger than the binding of reflexive anaphors) follows from the fact that Pronominalization chains contain at least one A'-link, and so involve an A'-chain as part of their sub-structure. This also explains why Pronominalization and Reflexivization are in complementary distribution.

---

[23] These are some of the properties the MTC derives. For a fuller discussion, see Hornstein (2001), Boeckx et al. (2010) and Hornstein and Nunes (2014).

6.3 Construal

The latter live on A-chains and hence contain no A'-links. The former have at least one A'-link. As A'-links sit higher than A-links, A'-chains are bigger than A-chains. In particular, A-chains don't fit where A'-chains do and vice versa. 20iii follows from the fact that Pronominalization is a chain relation, which in turn follows from I-merge being restricted to c-command positions (property 5 above), which in turn follows from the No Tampering Condition (assumption Aiia).

21. Crossover effects:
    i. Weak crossover (WCO)
    ii. Strong crossover (SCO)

    If I-merge is restricted to single-rooted sub-trees, then WCO violates minimality (F) if Pronominalization is an instance of I-merge. If inter-arboreal movement is allowed as an option, then WCO violates Merge over Move (K). On either option, WCO effects are the reflex of a derailed syntactic derivation. Critical to this explanation is the assumption that pronominalized pronouns are spell-outs of occurrences/copies at the foot of the chain (J). In other words, the bound pronoun marks the launch site of I-merge.

    The assumption that anaphors identify the launch site of movement, in conjunction with No Tampering, explains SCO effects. In effect, SCO effects involve lowering, which is an illicit operation as it violates No Tampering (Aiia above).

22. Principle C effects

    Principle C effects obtain when a pronominal anaphor c-commands its antecedent. If anaphoric pronouns are tails of chains (as per the FPG, D) (and hence mark the launch sites of movement), then they cannot be higher than their antecedents, as this would involve lowering the antecedent to its derived position, in violation of No Tampering (Aiia).

    Two remarks: First, Principle C is theoretically an outlier within the context of the GB theory as it applies without a domain restriction (in contrast to Principles A and B). The present account explains why. Lowering is an illicit application of I-merge no matter how shallow or deep the lowering may be. Second, Principle C is here treated as a feature of *bound* pronouns. If binding is distinguished from co-reference, we expect to find cases of Principle C violations where binding is not attested. Evans (1980) and Reinhart (1983) provide plausible examples of such. If this is right, then Principle C is a fact about the derivation of chains rather than about the intrinsic semantic properties of nominal expressions.

23. Three kinds of nominal elements subject to the binding theory:

    All binding lives on chains (FPG, D). Chains differ along two dimensions: (i) they can involve single or multiple θ-links and (ii) they can have an A- or an A'-structure (i.e. links can involve zero A'-links or one or more A'-links). If every nominal chain must have at least one θ-link (for purposes of full interpretation) then we have three kinds of chains: (i) non-construal chains (one θ-link), (ii) two or more θ-links with zero A'-links (Reflexivization/OC chains), and (iii) two or more θ-links with at least one A'-link (Pronominalization chains). Thus, there are three binding-relevant chains, only two of which allow for construal-relevant dependencies.

24. Resumptive pronoun (RP) effects
The FPG (D) implies RPs are formed via I-merge with spell-out of lower/occurrences copies. We thus expect RP constructions to exhibit movement-related restrictions, including island sensitivity (L) and crossover effects (property 21). There is interesting evidence that RP constructions do indeed exhibit such island and crossover sensitivities as well as demonstrating the marks of successive cyclic movement (L). This is all reviewed in Chapter 5.

25. Long-distance anaphor (LDA) effects:
The FPG (D) treats long-distance anaphors as the spelled-out tails of pronominalization chains formed via improper movement. If one assumes derivations are cyclic with phasal periodicity (L) and obey the Merge over Move condition, it is possible to derive the subject orientation of LDA, as well as various restrictions concerning potential antecedents in multiple LDA constructions.

26. Principle C effects with bound definite descriptions
There is a subject/non-subject asymmetry concerning bindable definite descriptions. This follows if we assume Merge over Move (K) and preference for Pronominalization where it is grammatically available. In effect, definite descriptions can be interpreted as bound just in case they are not in positions where a bound pronoun could be licitly licensed.

6.4 Conclusion

Recall the goal of a minimalist theory. The aim is to reconcile Plato's and Darwin's problems. Concretely, one way of doing this is deriving the generalizations of GB given simpler minimalist assumptions. The above goes some way towards showing how this might be accomplished. It shows that given the EMH (which is itself based on Merge plus labels plus the FPG), we derive many of the basics of standard GB grammar. We have reconstructed structure-building rules (E-merge) and movement rules (I-merge). We have unified movement and construal, the latter simply being multi-θ-bearing chains. We have identified two kinds of chains, A and A', and identified two kinds of construal that live on these two kinds of chains. Chain properties explain the basic features of Reflexivization, Pronominalization and

6.4 Conclusion

Obligatory Control constructions.[24] In other words, the EMH derives the bulk of the GB construal component. The simplicity of Merge (i.e. No Tampering) plus basic properties of computation (e.g. minimality, phases) explain the basic properties of A- and A'-chains (e.g. island sensitivity, locality). In other words, it seems possible to derive many of the basic properties of GB from simple assumptions concerning Merge plus locality conditions traceable (one fervently hopes) to more generic principles of efficient computation.

Moreover, adding a few more assumptions about how computations function (in particular Merge over Move and rules for converting chains with copies into objects interpretable at the AP and CI interfaces) provides plausible derivational accounts of crossover effects and Principle C effects. We even derive analyses of resumptive pronouns, long-distance anaphors and inverse control constructions that track many of their central features. Or, to put this tendentiously: The EMH provides a theory with the desired theoretical properties. If something along these lines is correct, then it resolves (or comes close to resolving) the tension between learnability and evolvability that drives the minimalist problematic. Evolvability is traced to the underlying simplicity of FL, or at least its linguistically bespoke parts. Learnability follows from the fact that the simple evolvable system leads to an FL with the basic properties of the GB conception of FL. In other words, from simple plausibly evolvable operations like Merge added to computationally/cognitively general restrictions (e.g. locality) arises a faculty of language as rich as that in GB which provides the basics required for grammar learning.

---

[24] Certain salient cases of non-obligatory control are also explicable. For discussion, see Boeckx and Hornstein (2007) and Boeckx et al. (2010).

7 Labels

7.0 Once More unto the Breach

As the astute reader no doubt recalls, I have an outstanding theoretical IOU. My discussion of the virtues of the Extended Merge Hypothesis (EMH) relies on a conception of Merge that incorporates labeling, an operation wherein one of the mergees provides a label for the merged complex. This is in line with earlier specifications of Merge but departs from the contemporary one in two ways: (i) the classical proposal treats labels as part of the syntactic representation, whereas more contemporary approaches relegate labels to the CI interface by treating labeling as part of the Transfer/Spell-Out operation, and (ii) in the classical approach labels are endocentric in the sense that they are supplied by one of the two mergees, while contemporary labeling rejects endocentricity and treats labels as products of a labeling algorithm. Thus, in the syntax, whereas classical Merge generates hierarchically structured *labeled* phrase markers, the current Merge operation yields hierarchically structured *non-labeled* objects. So, though at CI both approaches deliver structured labeled objects, in the syntax they crucially differ.

Now, earlier chapters (see Chapter 3) have presented empirical and theoretical reasons for thinking that syntactic phrase markers are indeed labeled. For example, this allows for a simple understanding of the locality that underlies selection and subcategorization. It also is part of an explanation for why grammars move XPs rather than X's. And it allows for the standard distributional accounts of constituency to carry over seamlessly to Merge-based grammars. However, as observed, there is a cost. The classical conception *is* more complex and thus, *ceteris paribus*, is methodologically less preferred than its more slimmed-down label-less successor. However, in this case, I will argue, ceteris is not paribus. So, on methodological grounds, the svelter conception is, at best (and IMO, not even this much) favored weakly rather than decisively preferred.

There is a second reason, however, that one might prefer the label-less conception. Recall why Minimalists want a simple conception of Merge. The idea is that the simpler the combinatoric operation underlying human grammars

7.0 Once More unto the Breach

(Gs), the easier it is to imagine how the faculty of language (FL) might have emerged in the species and so the easier it is to imagine how the Basic Property (viz. unbounded hierarchical recursion) might have popped into being biologically. As this is the central puzzle the Minimalist Program (MP) wants to address, we want a simple combination operation, and Merge without labels is simpler than one with them. In other words, removing labels from Merge might seem to more easily explain how hierarchical recursion, the Basic Property, could have come to be biologically endemic to our species. That is the hope. I wish to critically discuss this argument before circling back to defend the view that labels, not Merge, are the secret sauce that undergirds our recursive Gs.

But before proceeding, a word. I don't know if anyone has explicitly made this argument. I am offering it here because I have no other way of explaining why stripping Merge of labeling *in the syntax* is a step forward given that *all* minimalist theories of grammar retain labeling as part of FL. Theoretical disagreement is limited to *where* labeling occurs and *how* it is executed, not *whether* the structured objects generated by human Gs are labeled or not. So why *not* allow labeling in the syntax? Or more exactly, how is labeling as part of Transfer (the mapping from the syntax to the CI interface) "simpler" than labeling as part of the syntax? It cannot be that the latter requires a labeling operation that the former eschews as both approaches incorporate a labeling operation. The only reason that has been hinted at for preferring the first story to the second is that the CI interface *as such* demands labels while syntax *as such* does not. And if this is so, then we can treat labeling as a Bare Out Condition (BOC) imposed on syntactic structures as they are mapped to the CI interface. Labeling is then an operation forced by CI to apply in order to make otherwise illegible structures readable by the CI interface. On such a view, then, labeling does not complicate Transfer, because labeling is a legibility requirement that the CI imposes on syntactic objects so that CI can interpret them and applies when CI legibility is at issue. In sum, labels are "free" in the mapping to CI but costly when present in the syntax. That is why labeling should be eliminated from the latter but incorporated into Transfer.

The view I defend in what follows is almost the exact opposite: (i) there is no reason to think that labels are required for CI interpretation, (ii) labels explain how hierarchical recursion gets off the ground and (iii) Merge, with or without labels, is the wrong place to look for an explanation of the Basic Property.

One last point: This view has some consequences, not the least of them being that looking for CI interface conditions to motivate labeling is the wrong place to look. Labels do have effects on meaning interpretation, but this is because the syntax provides labeled objects that the "semantics" interprets and not because CI *as such* demands that expressions be labeled. Hopefully, this, no doubt cryptic, comment will be clearer by the end of this chapter.

7.1 Why Does FL Contain a Simple Combination Operation Like Merge?

Why do we want a simple combination operation? Here's the narrative. To the MP question: "how did the Basic Property emerge in the species?", the Merge Hypothesis (MH) answers: "Via adventitious mutation, Merge entered the computational repertoire of Homo Sapiens and Merge, in combination with the cognitive operations already present in our ape ancestor, sufficed to generate the kinds of grammatical structures we now associate with the products of FL." So why does FL contain a simple combination operation like Merge? Because simple operations are more likely to have adventitiously mutated into existence than complex ones. And for purposes of adventitious mutation, the simpler, the better. So, *ceteris paribus*, Merge without labels is better than Merge with labels, *if the emergence of Merge is what explains why FL looks the way it does, in particular why FL generates Gs with the Basic Property of hierarchical recursion.*

Now, it is common ground that the simple combination operation is not *enough* to explain the core features of FL. After all, every current account recognizes the need for some kind of labeling operation. The current label-free Merge proposal does not do away with labels, it simply strips labeling from Merge and relocates it to Transfer. In other words, in contrast to the earlier minimalist understanding of Merge as incorporating labeling and hence generating hierarchically labeled constituents/phrase markers (more specifically, sets) as Syntactic Objects, the current idea is to generate non-labeled constituents/phrase markers in the syntax, but to label these un-labeled sets as part of the operation that transfers these objects to the interfaces (or at least to the CI interface) for interpretation. I make this point to emphasize that the complexity of the current conception of FL is no simpler overall than the earlier one. Both involve a combination operation and both involve a labeling operation.[1] The difference resides not in the complexity of the overall system of operations but in their location in the generative procedure.

---

[1] A reviewer made the following point: The labeling operation in contemporary theories is a third-factor process (i.e. Minimal Search), while endocentric labeling presupposes some other method of labeling, presumably not Minimal Search. Even if correct, this is not relevant to the discussion above. First, the point made above is that in both theories labeling is part of the overall system and so neither is simpler than the other in this regard. Second, there is no argument that a Minimal Search version of labeling cannot be incorporated into the theory that locates labeling in the syntax. If this is possible (and frankly, it is hard to see that it would not be), then the nature of the labeling operation will not distinguish the two approaches. The only issue of contention will be the locus of the application of the operation, the syntax or the Transfer operation. The reader will know where I stand on this issue given the arguments in Chapter 3.

One more point: None of this should be taken as conceding that the labeling algorithm based on Minimal Search is any good. I criticize it below. Moreover, the algorithm that says "the label of the whole is one of the labels of the parts combined to make the whole" is pretty minimal. The

7.1 Why Does FL Contain an Operation Like Merge?

Why mention this? Because there is another argument in favor of a label-less Merge operation, a methodological one: All things being equal, simpler operations are preferred to complex ones. Merge plus labels is more complex than Merge simpliciter, so, *ceteris paribus*, the current conception is preferred to the earlier one. It is this kind of argument that the above paragraph is intended to parry. Whatever the virtues of methodological simplicity (and I for one esteem them highly), they do not apply in this case. What we want are the simplest overall theories, not the simplest individual operations. The earlier version of the Merge Hypothesis that includes a Merge operation that incorporates labeling is no more apparently complex than the later theory that segregates Merge from labeling yet includes both as parts of the grammar. Both theories have two operations and so are, so far as I can tell, equally complex or equally simple. What we have, methodologically speaking, is a tie.

Consider one more possible reason for preferring the contemporary label-free conception. As noted, it removes labels from the syntax. They appear in the mapping from the syntax to the CI interface. Why CI? Because labels appear to play no role on the AP side of the grammar.[2] And this might be explained (if correct, but see note 2) if labeling reflects a Bare Out Condition imposed on SOs by the CI interface.

There are two responses to this line of reasoning.

First, we have provided evidence that syntactic dependencies like selection/subcategorization and phenomena like structure preservation and constituency tests follow naturally if we assume that labels are part of the syntax. Labels are similarly useful in coding some of the grammatical variation we find across grammars. Languages differ, for example, in whether they permit VP fronting or VP ellipsis. This variation is easy to code grammatically with labels. It is less than obvious how to code such variation if labels are only available as part

---

search is restricted to the immediate inputs of the Merge operation. This leaves the question of which of the pair of labels is chosen to label the whole, but perhaps we can leave this to extra-syntactic factors (i.e. it is free, but more often than not, the wrong choice leads to gibberish at interfaces). So free labeling with the interfaces factoring out the "wrong" ones. Once one moves away from early minimalist assumptions concerning free rule application, this option is very natural.

[2] This is not strictly speaking correct. AP does appear to distinguish XPs from non-XPs for certain kinds of operations (e.g. intonational contour). However, so far as I know, AP (e.g. phonology) does not distinguish kinds of XPs from one another. There are rules for phrasal phonology and ones for smaller units, but there are no special rules for NPs versus VPs versus PPs versus APs, etc. So AP needs to distinguish maximal projections from non-maximal parts but does not need to distinguish one kind of phrasal category from another. What does this imply for Transfer as it applies to the mapping to AP? I am not sure. It is not clear how XPs are to be identified without labels of any kind. But the rich labelling we typically adopt seems to offer information that is not used. I will drop the issue here, but it is worth bearing in mind for, if correct, the claim that Spell-Out does not label SOs sent to AP is incorrect.

of transfer to CI.[3] So, the claim that labels are only operative at CI is tendentious, and plausibly incorrect.

Second, if it is the case that labels are important in the syntax, it is not clear that this reflects a fact about the structure of CI or reflects the fact that CI interprets Syntactic Objects that are labeled. Here is what I mean.

Collins (2020) has noted, for example, that currently there is no good semantic explanation for why we understand (1a) to be "about" the color blue while (1b) is "about" the firmament above:

(1)   a. Over there is sky blue
       b. Over there is blue sky

Standard semantic accounts treat modified phrases to involve conjunction. So *brown cow* denotes something that is a brown thing and a cow thing. But this does not tell us that for native speakers 'brown cow' picks out types of *cows* while 'cow brown' picks out a type of *brown*. In other words, there is an inherent asymmetry between modifiers and the heads they modify in natural language, and this semantic asymmetry does not follow from the logic of predicates or their conjunctions. So whence the asymmetry?

Labeling provides a source for the asymmetry and, with it, a possible explanation.[4] In 'sky blue' and 'cow brown' *blue* and *brown* are the heads of the larger projections. While in 'blue sky' and 'brown cow' the opposite is the case. In other words, standard labeling conventions distinguish heads from modifiers (and arguments)[5] and thus introduce the kind of asymmetry that we see semantically realized in the interpretation of phrases. Of course, it is possible that CI enforces this property, but if it does, there appears to be no independent semantic/interpretive reason for this, or at least none that we know of. Labeling, however, is inherently asymmetric (at least endocentric labeling is, the one that is part of standard X'-theory) and so we should not be surprised that the CI interface *in interpreting asymmetrically labeled constituents* interprets them asymmetrically.

The logic here is similar to that of weak crossover (WCO) effects. We observe that WCO effects occur when a pronoun is to the left of its antecedent. However, there is no reason why left/right should play any role in the semantic interpretation of bound pronouns. The effect seems semantically arbitrary, though it might have a principled syntactic source (see Chapter 5 for

---

[3] Such variation would have to be handled as *post* Transfer phenomena. So far as I know, nobody has outlined an account of how this might be done. And it won't be trivial. For example, how exactly is VP fronting (standardly understood as an instance of I-merge) to be understood as a CI effect?

[4] Or, as Paul Pietroski noted, "at least a promising description of the phenomenon" (p.c.).

[5] Collins (2020) discusses the same point as it applies to predicates and their arguments in a conjunctive Davidsonian semantics.

7.1 Why Does FL Contain an Operation Like Merge?

discussion). At any rate, the WCO effect can be built into CI, but placing it there seems wrong, as the effect has no apparent semantic basis. Better, then, to search for a syntactic source reflected in the semantic output. The same logic applies to the asymmetry noted by Collins (2020). It appears to be semantically arbitrary and so treating it as a CI BOC is the wrong move to make methodologically.

Consider one more argument against labeling in the syntax and in favor of labeling as part of transfer to CI.[6] Note, that this argument accepts that labeling is an additional operation but argues that *if* it is part of the Transfer operation then it comes "for free." In other words, the argument is that labeling is conceptually costless *in virtue of* being part of Transfer. Thus, *where* labeling applies affects its conceptual cost; costly in the syntax, but costless if part of the mapping to the interface. Here is the argument:

(2)   a. To be interpreted at the interfaces, SOs must be "identified" (aka labeled).
        b. Minimal Search is an independently available third-factor process.
        c. Minimal Search is how objects are identified/labeled.
        d. As third-factor processes are free and labeling is executed by Minimal Search, labeling is, theoretically speaking, "free."
        e. Endocentric label projection is not a third-factor operation.
        f. Thus, Merge plus label at Transfer is "simpler" than Merge plus endocentric labeling.

So, given (2), why does where labeling applies matter so much? For two reasons: (i) unlike the syntax, in which labels are conceptually superfluous, the CI interface demands that objects be labeled so as to be legible (i.e. for CI, labels are Bare Out Conditions, (2a)) and (ii) labeling at CI is an application of Minimal Search (a third-factor process and hence conceptually costless (2b,c)),[7] whereas labeling in the syntax is feature projection by the head (i.e. endocentric projection). So what makes the label-less account of Merge superior is that CI contains independently needed Bare Out Conditions (i.e. CI legibility conditions) that require labeling of SOs, and a costless operation (Minimal Search) executes that labeling whereas labeling in the syntax does not. Interesting argument. Let me cast some aspersions on it.

First off, observe that points (i) and (ii) are independent. Here is what I mean.

---

[6] This excellent argument was provided by one of the anonymous reviewers. Thanks a lot. Made me think.

[7] Here "conceptually costless" just means that it is not a linguistic proprietary feature of FL, but part of any well-constructed computational system. As MP assumes that FL is well designed, and as all MPers assume that FL begets computational systems (aka grammars/generative procedures), then as Minimal Search is part of any well-designed system, it must, of course, be a part of FL. The same, it is claimed, is not the case for endocentric projection. For pushback on the last point, see below.

Chapter 3 proposes that labeling is endocentric projection. It is there motivated largely on empirical grounds. The main argument is that such labels allow for a nice explanation of the peculiar locality restrictions of selection/subcategorization in terms of the Fundamental Principle of Grammar (FPG, i.e. that *all* grammatical commerce be conducted under Merge). However, say that this is wrong and that labeling is actually an instance of Minimal Search rather than endocentric projection. So long as it occurs in the syntax, the arguments in Chapter 3 would stand. What is important for these kinds of data is that SOs are labeled in the syntax. It does not matter whether the label is provided by projection or search, only that the label *be* a $Y°$ of one of the mergees. So, strictly speaking, if labeling is indeed an instance of Minimal Search (which I doubt, see below), then having it apply in the syntax would be compatible with the claims made in Chapter 3.[8] And if Minimal Search is indeed costless, then it costs no more to apply it earlier in the syntax rather than later in Transfer to CI.

If this is so, then the argument in (2) for relegating labeling to Transfer rather than the syntax reduces to (2a), the claim that labeling is a Bare Out Condition. Unfortunately, this claim, even if correct (but see below), implies only that an SO can only be interpreted at the CI interface *if it is labeled*. The fact that CI require SOs to have labels in order to be legible (if this is indeed a fact) simply requires that labeling take place *before* SOs meet CI. But this is as consistent with labeling taking place in the syntax as it is with labeling being part of Transfer. Last I checked, both precede the mapping to CI. What needs arguing to conclude that labeling *must* be part of Transfer and *not* in the syntax is that labels be *problematic* in the syntax (i.e. that they cause problems there) and that *therefore* the syntax should not have them.[9] But this is a very hard

---

[8] Let me go a bit further. Minimal Search is not even incompatible with the claim that phrases are endocentrically labeled. Rather it is incompatible with the proposal that endocentric labeling is the result of a process called 'projection' which is distinct from Minimal Search. Indeed, the claim that constituents are endocentrically labeled is compatible with the claim that labeling is a species of Minimal Search. The two fit together if the labels Minimal Search "finds and assigns" happen to be the endocentric ones even if Gs have no distinct operations like projection. To my knowledge, exactly how phrases are labeled (i.e. how labeling is formally executed), beyond noting that labels are heads that name the constituents that contain them, is hardly discussed. We tend to understand projection as a kind of percolation, but this is seldom argued for or even defined. See Stabler (2010) for a formal proposal that incorporates labeling without what appears to be a process of percolation.

[9] It might be possible to enhance the argument with the assumption that operations apply in a just-in-time manner. So, *if* labels are required for CI legibility *and* are not required in the syntax, then labeling should apply at the point that legibility becomes relevant *and not before*. Note, this is compatible with labeling being syntactically unproblematic but application of labeling should be delayed until needed. This argument could lead to the right conclusion (that labeling applies at Transfer), but it is quite weak. It becomes weaker if there are empirical payoffs of having labels in the syntax (as I have argued). And weaker still when we see that there are few (no?) arguments for thinking that labels are properties of CI as such (as I will argue presently). That said, a just-in-time principle could, if developed and motivated, have the right properties to delay labeling until Transfer even if it could have applied earlier unproblematically.

7.1 Why Does FL Contain an Operation Like Merge? 191

argument to make (and note, it is an empirical argument, not a conceptual one) and, so far as I know, nobody has made it.[10]

In sum, even if the argument in (2) is bulletproof, the conclusion (2f) does not follow. All that follows is that labeling is an instance of Minimal Search and that it is required by a CI Bare Out Condition. From these two conclusions it follows that labeling must obtain before the mapping to CI. But, this is entirely consistent with labeling being a part of the syntax and even with labeling producing endocentric structures. Of course, none of this implies that the premises in (2) are correct. It only argues that even if they are correct, the conclusion drawn does not follow. In my opinion, they are quite tendentious. Let me spend a few paragraphs indicating why I believe this to be the case.

First, it is not at all clear that SOs need to be identified to be CI interpreted.[11] Let's agree that SOs are specified by the syntax and are label-less. These SOs constitute the set of Terms (i.e. well-formed objects generated by the syntax). Why does being a Term not suffice to identify an SO at CI? Why are labels required and what is it that labels do that needs doing? Presumably if labels are required then being a syntactic term (which is what SOs are) is insufficient for CI interpretation. How so? In what way are label-less terms deficient and how do labels make up for these deficiencies? Let me polish this question to make it shiny.

A standard type-driven theory of interpretation does not require labels to apply. Interpretation proceeds bottom-up, successively applying rules of interpretation (e.g. function composition) to larger and larger units until a full interpretation is attained. Labels have no apparent role to play in such accounts. If they exist, they are idle. All one needs are for the terminals to be typed and rules of composition to combine them in accord with their types. So, as far as this kind of interpretive procedure goes, labeling plays no role and there is no obvious need for "identification" beyond what a label-less syntax already provides.

Of course, these kinds of interpretive theories may be wrong and the right ones might require labels. However, to make this case requires offering the relevant interpretive theory. As noted in the 'brown cow' discussion above, no current semantic account endogenously *requires* labels to deliver *an* interpretation, though *empirically* there is evidence that the interpretive procedure respects something like labeling given the 'brown cow' data reviewed above. Thus, contrary to assumption (2a), there is no current theoretical reason for

---

[10] Such kinds of arguments do exist. In fact, the argument for structure dependence reviewed in Chapter 2 is exactly this kind of argument. It argues that having the syntax produce objects with serial order is *empirically* problematic given the kinds of G rules we find, and so Merge does not impose serial order on its merges. Rather, such order arises from the mapping to the AP interface. It does not obtain in the syntax. This is the kind of argument we would need against labels in the syntax, and this is the kind of argument I don't believe has yet been provided.

[11] See note 2 for some comments regarding the labels at the AP interface.

thinking that CI *per se* requires labeled SOs. Indeed, the fact that labeling seems to be operative is something for which current semantic accounts of CI interpretation have no explanation.[12]

Second, let's say that nonetheless we discover that CI needs to identify the units it interprets. Why think that the relevant labels will be *syntactic*? Here is what I mean. I can imagine that CI needs to distinguish arguments from predicates, for example, as these are the kinds of units semantic composition deals with. Let's grant this for the sake of argument. Then if CI imposes a legibility condition (i.e. an identification process), presumably it will be one stated in a vocabulary suitable for CI legibility. But this is *not* the kind of labeling Generative grammarians are typically fussing about. The kind of labels we want are ones that distinguish, say, NPs from VPs from PPs, from APs, from TPs, from CPs (etc.). These are the kinds of labels that we need to handle the kind of standard distributional data linguists have traditionally used to motivate labeled constituency and the kind of cross-linguistic variation we see concerning what a language-particular G can move or delete (see Chapter 3). So even if CI needs to identify SOs why would CI not identify the kinds of SOs *it* needs (e.g. argument phrases and predicate phrases and modifier phrases, and propositional phrases rather than NPs, VPs, etc.)? In fact, as is well known, semantic categories crosscut syntactic ones. N, V, A can all designate properties even though they are syntactically different. NP, AP and PP can all be predicates in copular constructions despite being syntactically distinct categories. Both PPs and APs can serve as modifiers of the same heads/phrases even though they are syntactically distinct. The fact is that *syntactic* categories do not match *semantic* ones (and are not reducible to them) and it is hard to see why an interpretive interface like CI would have as a Bare Out Condition on CI legibility that SOs come with *syntactic* labels. How does that make sense? In sum, even if CI has Bare Out Conditions of the type hypothesized, it leaves unexplained why we find that constituents have *syntactic* labels like NP, VP and the like rather than more appropriate "semantic" ones.[13]

---

[12] See Collins (2020) for an excellent discussion of this point. Indeed, a takeaway from his discussion is that labels are an artifact of the syntax that the semantics deals with rather than a condition that the semantics places on the syntax. In this, it is a little like how GB-style theories handled WCO effects (they built a syntactic restriction into the interpretive rule interpreting bound pronouns). The syntax does things, and the semantics handles what it does in whatever way it does because it is handed objects with the properties the syntax assigns. The syntax proposes and the semantics makes do! The fact that structural properties of the syntax have interpretive effects does not mean that these effects explain the properties of the syntax. It is, in my opinion, usually the other way around. As it is here.

[13] Again, we should all be able to agree that there are syntactic features irreducible to semantic and/or phonological ones. The syntax manipulates objects that carry such syntactic labels. That the features the syntax manipulates are not reducible to properties of the interfaces is a venerable assumption within Generative Grammar. It is the Autonomy of Syntax Thesis (or, should I say, observation). Thus, the claim that there are *syntactic* labels reflecting *syntactic* properties of

7.1 Why Does FL Contain an Operation Like Merge?

Third, the assumption that Minimal Search is the optimal way to label expressions and that it comes "for free" is quite tendentious. Indeed, I would argue that the labeling algorithm (Chomsky 2013) is quite a clunky (i.e. inelegant, unnatural) procedure and requires many ancillary assumptions to work out right. Here is what I mean.

First, it requires distinguishing among terminals. Roots are not potential labels even though they are syntactic terminals. Why can't roots be labels? We are never told. Second, the algorithm stipulates that only lexical atoms (well atoms that are not roots) are potential labels. Why? Why can't any term be a label? What is it about non-terminals that excludes them from being labels? Third, the algorithm is stymied by ambiguity. Thus, it does not label {XP, YP} the way it labels {X°,YP} structures because both X and Y are equally accessible in the former. Why does this stymie the regular labeling procedure rather than allow either X or Y to be targeted by the algorithm? Of course, the labeling algorithm supplies a label in such "exocentric" structures but this time via agreement. Whether this is correct or not empirically, it does not follow from Minimal Search as such.[14] Fourth, Minimal Search is a top-down operation and thus, plausibly, anti-cyclic (like lowering) despite the fact that CI compositionality, which labeling purportedly serves, is bottom-up and cyclic.

In sum, even if we grant that the labeling algorithm embodies Minimal Search and that it is a third-factor "free" operation, in order to deliver the empirical goods, the labeling algorithm requires many other assumptions that do not follow from any obvious conception of Minimal Search (or anything else, so far as I can see), and so labeling, even if it involves Minimal Search, is not *entirely* a third-factor product.[15]

---

the grammar is a very very conventional position. The idea that such features are reducible to interface properties is the exciting position, and being exciting, it carries the burden of proof. Considerable proof, IMO, as it would refute the Autonomy Thesis (ahem, observation).

[14] To be more precise, the labeling algorithm requires separate assumptions to label (at least) the following four configurations:
  (i) {X°, √Y}
  (ii) {X°, YP} (where YP is a complex branching constituent)
  (iii) {XP,YP} (where XP and YP are complex branching constituents)
  (iv) {ZP, {X°,YP}} (where ZP = Z° (i.e. a lexical head))
For each of (i)–(iv), the labeling algorithm requires assumptions *beyond Minimal Search* to find and affix a label. Thus, the labeling algorithm does not reduce to Minimal Search. In my humble opinion, this makes the unification of labeling via the labeling algorithm about as elegant as the unification of islands in *Barriers* (Chomsky 1986b).

[15] Let me add, tendentiously, that the labeling algorithm that most naturally underlies endocentric labeling is quite simple: the label of a complex is provided by the label of one of the (two) expressions merged. Very local, very simple. Of course, the syntax does not *by itself* determine which of the two provides the label for the whole (just like syntax by itself does not say what copies are retained in a complex chain), though proposals that focus on what features are checked in an application of Merge might go some way in narrowing down the options.

One last point: I suggest below that endocentric labeling might be a third-factor requirement regarding closure as a desideratum on computational operations and domains. If so, it might enjoy the same conceptual (viz. computational) advantages that Minimal Search is supposed to enjoy. In addition, as we shall see, it explains why labels are always lexical atoms and why terms cannot be labels. Moreover, as shown in Chapter 3, such labels deliver the kinds of constituents required to cover the distributional data linguists have long cited as characteristic of language. Finally, endocentric labeling is plausibly a cyclic bottom-up procedure and so fits snugly with Merge-based bottom-up derivations.

So where does this leave us? I have argued that issues of simplicity (both as regards evolutionary scenarios and methodological concerns), though important, do not suffice to choose between accounts that fold labeling into the Merge operation versus those that treat it as part of the mapping to CI (i.e. Transfer). That said, I find it compelling that we should try to reduce the linguistic specificity of FL to a single novelty. Right now, we have both labeling *and* a combination operation. I would like to suggest (yet again) that labels are the secret sauce that gave us FL, while the combination operation is far more computationally generic.[16] In particular, I am going to revisit the argument made in the earlier chapters and try to dissect exactly what cognitive/computational powers our ancestors needed for Merge to play the role envisioned for it. My suggestion will be that Merge understood as the bare combination operation has been given too central a role and that the evolutionary scenario mooted in the opening chapters doesn't really work. I then provide another.

7.2 Labels as the Secret Ingredient

FL contains a recursive specification of the notion *Syntactic Object* (SO). The specification is contained in the following two postulates:

(3)   a. If α is a lexical item then α is an SO.[17]
          b. If α is an SO and β is an SO then Merge (α,β) is an SO.

(4)   For α, β, SOs, Merge (α,β) → $\{\alpha,\beta\}$

(3) recursively defines SOs inductively. (4) specifies what the Merge operation consists in (i.e. what kind of complex object the combination operation

---

[16] See Hornstein (2008) for an earlier argument to this effect.
[17] The term *lexical item* denotes the atoms that are not themselves products of Merge. These roughly correspond to the notion *morpheme* or *word*, though these notions are themselves terms of art and it is possible that the naive notions only roughly correspond to the technical ones. Every theory of syntax postulates the existence of such atoms. Thus, what is debatable is not their existence but their features.

7.2 Labels as the Secret Ingredient

creates). The big idea behind the Merge Hypothesis (MH) is the following: the simpler the conception of Merge, the easier it is to explain the etiology of the Basic Property (viz. the fact that humans have the capacity to acquire Gs that generate an unbounded number of hierarchically structured objects that have a meaning and "sound" profile). But the link MH forges between Merge and the Basic Property is somewhat misleading. The key cognitive power behind the Basic Property is the capacity to construct inductive definitions like the one in (3). This, in turn, rests on (i) the capacity to take a (finite) set of atoms (viz. the lexical items) and combine them *AND* (ii) the capacity to take the resulting combined expressions from (i) as inputs for further combination. (3) does this by stipulating in (3a) that atoms are SOs and by stipulating in (3b) that combinations of SOs constructed by Merge as specified in (4) are themselves SOs. What is important to note is that what is doing most of the work in explaining the Basic Property is not (4) but (3). In fact, *any* combination operation would suffice to generate an unbounded number of hierarchically structured objects.

Here is what I mean. Let's, for example, substitute another combination operation, say concatenation, for the set-forming operation Merge in (4). The result similarly yields an inductive definition able to generate an unbounded number of hierarchically structured objects, though the objects generated would now have different characteristics. For example, the concatenated expressions would have a serial order in virtue of being combined via concatenation rather than Merge. In other words, replacing (4) with (4') and coupling (4') with (3') would also allow the generation of unboundedly many hierarchically structured objects. Again, these objects would be different from those generated by (3) and (4), but the alternative system would still generate unboundedly many hierarchically structured objects.

(3') a. If α is a lexical item then α is an SO
      b. If α is an SO and β is an SO then Concatenate (α,β) is an SO

(4') For α, β, SOs, Concatenate (α,β) → $<\alpha,\beta>$[18]

What's this tell us? It tells us that the *simplicity of Merge is tangential to explaining the Basic Property*. The explanation of the Basic Property above rests with the supposition that humans are able to construct inductive definitions. The combinatorial specifics are a side issue. And, if this is correct, then the specific details of the combination operation are really beside the point if the goal is to offer an account of the Basic Property. What we want explained is the source of the cognitive power to construct inductive definitions like (3), more particularly a definition wherein outputs of a computational procedure can become inputs to that procedure. What pulls *that* trick off?

---

[18] Read $<\alpha,\beta>$ as α concatenates with β. This yields a unit $[\alpha,\beta]$ with the serial order $\alpha^\wedge\beta$.

Or, maybe another way of making the same point, given that we have a combination operation defined over the domain of lexical items/atoms, what makes the product of combining two lexical items/atoms something that can itself be further combined?[19] The answer, I suggest, is an operation that allows one to treat a combination of lexical items *as if it were a lexical item with respect to the combination operation*. Were the outputs of the combination operation treated *as* atoms then it is no surprise that they can be combined in the way that atoms are. And what is the operation that makes combinations of atoms act *as* atoms? Well, labeling. By labeling the output of the combination operation and interpreting it as Generative Grammar has always interpreted labels (i.e. via the "is a" relation), labeling allows us to understand the combination operation as creating endlessly many equivalence classes with the lexical atoms as the bases. So, if the combination operation is Merge and we assume that labeling is endocentric (i.e. one of the inputs supplies the label for the output) then we derive objects like (5a) read as (5b,c).

(5)   a. $\{_\alpha \alpha,\beta\}$
        b. $\{\alpha,\beta\}$ "is a" α
        c. $\{\alpha,\beta\}$ is in the equivalence class of α[20]

As expressions in the same equivalence class formally behave identically, labeling can account for why the combination operation plus labeling together can generate an unbounded number of hierarchically structured objects. What labeling specifically does is allow an expression in the range of the combination operation (an output of the combination operation) to be treated as an element in the domain of that operation (an input to that combination operation). In effect, (endocentric) labeling **closes** the combination operation in the domain of the lexical items because combination plus labeling suffices to license taking the outputs of the combinator as further inputs to that combinator. Or, to say this another way, the labeling hypothesis is the thesis that the SOs in (3) and (4) or (3') and (4') are

---

[19] Paul Pietroski has pointed out to me that there are two points being run together here. One is the presumed source of a *general* capacity to form inductive definitions, the other is the source of a *specific* capacity to take outputs of syntactic combination as inputs to syntactic combination. One possible approach to explaining the second capacity is to see it as a special application of the first capacity. However, to address the Basic Property, a more focused approach is also possible, one that explains how outputs of a linguistic combination operation become potential further inputs of *that* operation. Specifically, we would like an explanation of what it is that allows children to formulate generalizations like (3b) regarding SOs. I believe that labeling offers an account.

[20] To prevent confusion: treating a complex as an atom as regards further combination does not imply that it is like atoms in every respect. Equivalence classes of items are expressions that are treated similarly with respect to some specified operations. This does not imply that the elements in the equivalence classes are identical in every other way.

7.2 Labels as the Secret Ingredient

simply equivalence classes of expressions based on a finite lexical inventory of syntactic atoms.[21]

This way of construing matters has the following important consequence: The secret to unbounded hierarchical recursion is labeling for it is what theoretically licenses the crucial inductive step of taking the outputs of the combination operation as a potential input to that operation. Labels effectively specify what an SO is: an expression in the equivalence class of one of the syntactic atoms.

Some remarks: That phrases are equivalence classes of syntactic objects with the lexical atoms as their moduli is a venerable assumption within Generative Grammar. This is what constituents are. There is plenty of substitutional evidence for this, some of it reviewed in Chapter 3. That labels just *are* lexical atoms follows once we realize that bar levels are not intrinsic properties of labels but are relational, as, for example, Bare Phrase Structure proposes.[22]

Lastly, if labels serve to close the combination operation in the domain of the lexical atoms, then it *follows* that labels will always be atomic and never complex. Here is what I mean. One question that arises for any labeling operation is *why* it seems that only *one* of the inputs labels the combined output. In particular, why not both, as in (6)?

(6) $\{_{\alpha\beta}\,\alpha,\beta\}$

The labeling in (6) maps the combination of $\{\alpha,\beta\}$ to $\alpha\beta$. In other words, the combination has two heads. But we don't find this in FL grammars. Only one of the two inputs labels the output expression, never both. Why? Because labeling closes the combination operation in the domain of the lexical atoms, and though there are α atoms and β atoms, there are no $\alpha\beta$ atoms because $\alpha\beta$ is not an atom. So why are phrases singly headed? Because labels serve to close the combination operation in the domain of the lexical atoms.

This reasoning might be pressed further. If labels must map complexes to atoms, and Boolean combinations of atoms are not themselves atoms, then

---

[21] A useful example of equivalence classes is provided by "clock-arithmetic." Here the basic elements are the numerals 1–12. The equivalence classes of 1 include 13, 25, 37 etc. That of 2 is 14, 26, 38 etc. And so on. For any given number its equivalence class is determined by dividing that number by 12. The *remainder* determines the equivalence class. So 13/12 = 1 remainder 1, hence 13 is in 1's equivalence class. The idea offered here is that the lexical atoms determine the equivalence classes of SOs. They do so by labeling the expressions they are part of. So $\{_{\alpha}\,\alpha,\beta\}$ is a complex expression in the equivalence class α, α being a lexical atom.
[22] Bare Phrase Structure is outlined in Chomsky (1995b). It is one of the earliest (and, in my view, one of the most elegant) applications of minimalist simplicity reasoning.
[23] Nor can $\{\alpha,\beta\}$. As noted earlier, the labeling algorithm must stipulate that only heads (aka, atoms) are potential labels. This is derived if one understands labeling as serving to close Merge in the domain of the lexical atoms, as proposed here.

neither 'α&β' nor 'ανβ' nor '-α' nor '-β' can be labels either.[23] Labels can *never* be complex combinations of lexical atoms because these complex combinations are not atoms. If this is on the right track, then labels must be simple because they must map to lexical atoms.[24]

Here is a yet more radical inference: This suggests that labels cannot be exocentric. Let me be a bit fussy here. If the above line of reasoning is correct, then labels *must be lexical atoms*. Exocentric labeling countenances the possibility that in some cases of labeling (cases of exocentric labeling in structures like {XP,YP}) the label is not a lexical item. For example, Chomsky (2013) proposes that in exocentric {XP,YP} cases, agreement features serve as labels. However, Chomsky (1995a: chapter 4) argues (convincingly in my view) that agreement features are not lexical atoms. And if this is correct, then given the above reasoning, exocentric labeling seems impossible.

There is one conceivable way around this conclusion: Exocentric labeling maps a complex to a lexical atom, but one that is neither of the combinands. So, for example, say that labeling is a constant function that exocentrically maps {α,β} to γ where γ is a lexical atom distinct from α or β. This is possible, but what would γ be? Would γ be the unique exocentric label? Unlikely, for this would seem to suggest that TPs and CPs and vPs all have the same label. So, it must assign different labels to different inputs. If so, then the labeling must be *some* function of the labels of the inputs. But what is this function? It is not the simple one that says choose one of the labels of the inputs as label for the output as this would simply be endocentric labeling again, not an exocentric alternative. In short, we need some suggestion as to what the lexical atoms are that the different combinations of atoms select as label, *and* it seems that the labels would have to be expressions distinct from the atoms Merge has combined and yet be lexical atoms (contra Chomsky's (2013) suggestion that agreement features can be labels). It is hard to see what atoms these might be. In other words, if one assumes that labels are lexical atoms and that labeling is a function of the labels of the combinands, then it seems to me that endocentric labeling is the only conception that will fit these two desiderata. At the very least, proponents wishing to add exocentric labels to the mix need to flesh out the alternative, and I wish them luck because it looks like it won't be easy.[25]

---

[24] Paul Pietroski (p.c.) points out that these facts have no natural explanation if labeling is driven by CI requirements, nor for that matter a labeling algorithm like the one in Chomsky (2013). There is nothing conceptually untoward with having complex labels. Consequently, their absence requires explanation. To my knowledge the one above is the only one on offer.

[25] To repeat, the above assumes that we hold constant two desiderata: (i) labels are lexical atoms and (ii) labeling is a function of the (labels of the) inputs merged. Chomsky (2013) forgoes (ii). I suspect that *any* theory of exocentric labeling will have to forgo one of the two assumptions. Hence the conclusion that labeling is endocentric!

7.3 The Combination Operation and FL

To recap, inductive definitions can serve to recursively specify an unbounded set of hierarchically structured objects. But if used to explain the Basic Property, the etiology of this inductive capacity needs to be addressed. Where does this inductive capacity come from? What is clear is that it doesn't "come from" Merge. Rather, given a (general) capacity to form inductive definitions, Merge can be used in combination with the capacity to inductively specify a set of hierarchically structured expressions (i.e. SOs). However, without that capacity, Merge alone cannot specify such an unbounded set. So, Merge is not really where the action is if one's interest is in the Basic Property.

Rather, the action is with labels. Why? Because labels understood in terms of the "is a" relation can be understood as mapping complexes of lexical atoms to lexical atoms. In other words, labeling closes the domain of the Merge operation in the domain of lexical atoms and forms equivalence classes of expressions with these atoms as moduli. And this suffices to generate unbounded sets of hierarchical expressions of the right kind. In effect, adding labeling together with the combination operation serves to explain the Basic Property. Labeling is the secret ingredient FL pairs with a combination operation to give us unbounded hierarchy.

7.3 The Combination Operation and FL

Let's get back to the specifics of the combination operation. Even if the above is correct, we can still ask which combination operation FL combines with labeling to generate the SOs. Is there any reason to think that the right combination operation is one that forms sets as in (4) rather than, say, concatenates as in (4')? Some might be tempted to answer that simplicity, once again, favors (4) over (4'). Some might also note that there is some empirical evidence for (4) over (4') when we consider one of the basic features of FL, structure dependence. Let me discuss both of these points in turn.

Before proceeding, one caveat. What follows does not argue *against* the view that the combination is Merge-like in forming sets. Rather, the claim will be that the arguments on offer *for* this position are weak. Importantly, however, whether the following arguments are true is immaterial to the previous claims made about the role of Merge in explaining the Basic Property. Nothing I say below precludes the possibility that the combination operation is indeed something like (4); an operation that forms sets. My claim below is simply that the arguments offered in the literature (and reviewed in Chapter 2) for the conclusion that Merge forms sets are weak.

Let's now turn to the arguments. There are two.

The first argument is one of simplicity. We need some combination operation so why not assume the *simplest* one and see where that gets us. This presupposes that set formation is conceptually simpler than concatenation.

For purposes of the present discussion, let's grant this.[26] Does this lead to the conclusion that FL's combination operation is as in (4)? No, I don't think so. Here's why.

Potential explanations of the Basic Property are exercises in speculative evolutionary biology. The Basic Property is a feature of FL. We explain the Basic Property by explaining how an FL embodying the Basic Property arose in humans. The right combination operation for such an evolutionary scenario is the one that our FL *actually* incorporates.

Now, a combination operation can get into FL in two ways. First, it could be part of the inventory of cognitive operations of our pre-linguistic ancestors that was repurposed by FL for the specific function of combining lexical atoms. Second, the combination operation might have adventitiously arisen as a mutation which was then recruited to be part of FL. If the latter is the correct scenario, then simplicity (measured in terms of conceptual complexity) might be important if we assume that conceptual simplicity tracks mutational availability. So, if conceptually "simpler" operations are more likely to adventitiously arise via mutation than conceptually more complex ones, then there could be an argument in favor of the set-formation conception of combination *if we assume that the source of the combination operation found in FL is some kind of mutation*.

But what if the cognitive repertoire of our pre-linguistic ancestors already contained a perfectly respectable combination operation? Why wouldn't our potential FL recruit *it* rather than wait around for a simpler one? We know that evolution recycles available parts and puts them to novel uses (think exaptation and descent with modification). So say that there was an extant operation like concatenation available, then wouldn't a simple evolutionary trick (maybe the *simplest* evolutionary trick?) be to use *it* if combination is desired? Why wait around for set formation if concatenation is already available?[27]

I mention this because there is every reason to think that concatenation is part of the cognitive inventory of many many many animals, even ones that don't have any apparent linguistic capacities. If this is so, then the presumption that conceptual simplicity is an important consideration given the speculative

---

[26] This may be so, but it is not like concatenation is particularly complex conceptually speaking. In earlier chapters I fudged by saying we want a simple operation as opposed to the simplest operation. I did this because I have little sense of how to measure conceptual simplicity so that it can decide between, say, set formation and concatenation. Here for the sake of argument, let's concede set formation is indeed the simplest combination operation there is, recognizing that this is very much a contestable claim.

[27] Another conceivable scenario would have both set formation and concatenation cognitively available prior to the emergence of FL. In that scenario perhaps the simplicity of set formation favored its inclusion in FL over concatenation. Perhaps. However, now we need an argument or a principle that states that given a choice, evolution favors the simpler option among available ones. I know of no such principle. At any rate, it is not a proposal that has been (even implicitly) offered.

7.3 The Combination Operation and FL

evolutionary scenario being considered seems, at best, unclear. Even if we grant that set formation is simpler in some sense than concatenation, there is every reason to think that the cognitive inventory of operations of our pre-linguistic ancestors included something as basic as concatenation and, as we noted above, this operation in conjunction with labeling (and a finite lexicon of syntactic atoms) suffices to characterize the FL that explains the Basic Property. Conclusion: The line of argument that the combination operation is Merge-as-set-formation (i.e. (4) above) is weak given the evolutionary context in which it is deployed.

There is a second route to the same conclusion, this one empirical. As we noted, one feature of our FL is that it has the property of structure dependence. Now, the term "structure dependence" can signify many facts about Gs. One that Chomsky has consistently focused on (see e.g. Chomsky (2021) for a recent example) is that Gs don't make use of certain kinds of notions, notions like *to-the-left/right of* or *precedes*. Rather, G operations are governed by restrictions specified in hierarchical rather than linear terms. Chomsky has given several illustrations of this claim. I want to focus on a representative few here because they well illustrate the logic. Consider the two examples in (7) and (8).

(7) a. Can't eagles that fly swim?
     b. Yes, eagles that can't fly swim
     c. No, eagles that fly can't swim

(8) a. Very quickly, eagles that fly can swim across ponds
     b. Eagles that fly very quickly can swim across ponds
     c. Eagles that fly can swim across ponds very quickly

The question (7a) can be answered by (7c) but not (7b). Similarly, (8a) has (8c) as a paraphrase but not (8b). The standard Generative explanation is that (7a) and (8a) share structure with (7c) and (8c) and this structure allows *can* to move to the front of the clause from its base position in the structure underlying (7c) but not in (7b). Similarly, (8a) is formed by moving *very quickly* from its base position in (8c) but this movement is prohibited in (8b). The obvious question is why are the (7b)/(8b) sources illicit? This question can be sharpened by noting that *can't* and *very quickly* are, as regards serial position, closer to the left edge in (7b) and (8b) than they are in (7c) and (8c). So it seems that we do not compute where something has moved from by measuring distance in terms of serial order. Of course, as any good linguist knows, there is another measure: the closest source measured hierarchically. So *can* in the underlying form of (7c) is closer to the root of the tree than is *can* in (7b). Thus, if one measures distance hierarchically then we see that the relevant movement rule does relate the moved expression *can't* to the closest source in (7b,c). Ditto with *very quickly* in (8c) and (8b). Further, as Chomsky has rightly noted, if this is the correct way to frame matters, then we want an explanation for *why* movement rules *do* measure distance hierarchically and, even more importantly, *do not* measure distance using serial order. And the answer that G rules are structure dependent, in the sense that depth not distance in terms of serial order is what G rules are sensitive to, is a fine first step to an answer. Furthermore, *if the combination operation is like Merge-as-set-formation in (4) then the **only available measure of distance** is hierarchical because sets do not specify the serial order of their elements*. And this is a great explanation for *why* G operations are structure dependent in the sense exhibited by (7) and (8).

To repeat, **this is a very nice explanation for the problem as posed**. My objection is that it is not clear that this is the right way to pose the problem. Here is what I mean.

In both (7) and (8), the illicit source is contained inside a subject relative clause. These structures are well known to be islands, structures immune to extraction. What this implies is that even if the expressions inside the subject relative were serially ordered, extraction from these structures would be independently excluded. Putting this another way: The fact that movement operations from subject relative clauses are grammatically prohibited is independent of the question of whether the combination operation produces constituents whose innards are serially ordered. Thus, these data are not particularly useful in determining whether the outputs of the combination operation are set-like or not. Whether they are or they aren't, the data in (7)/(8) can be explained in the same way: Movement from a subject relative clause is grammatically prohibited. And this constraint is, at least *prima facie*, unrelated to the question of whether the combination operation serially orders its combinands.

Note, this does *not* gainsay the claim that G rules are structure dependent. Island facts are facts about hierarchically organized syntactic structures, so island prohibitions are structural prohibitions. However, these prohibitions do not imply anything much about the serial ordering of the outputs of the grammatical operations. Hence, these particular empirical arguments based on examples like (7) and (8) to the conclusion that Merge is a combination operation that forms set-like phrases do not go through.

Again, this does not mean that the combination operation (Merge) does not form set-like objects, just that the argument surveyed above does not require that it do so. Rather, the question is more subtle: Do grammatical operations *ever* advert to linear order in conditioning their applications? Unfortunately, this is a far more complicated question, one that I will refrain from answering here because it is beyond my meager expertise. There have been claims that G rules only ever care about hierarchy. But there are also arguments in the literature that argue that linear order conditions play a key role in the syntax.[28]

---

[28] See Jackendoff (1990), Larson (1990) and Bruening (2014).

At any rate, should there be no decent examples of linear order effects conditioning grammatical rule applications then we would want to know why and the proposal that phrase markers don't carry such information would be the perfect answer. My claim is that the specific examples used to substantiate this claim to date are not dispositive.[29]

7.4 Conclusion

Where does this leave us? I have argued that contrary to appearances, the main idea behind the Merge Hypothesis is unsupported. The big idea is that the emergence of Merge in the inventory of human cognitive operations is what explains the emergence of FL in humans. Merge arises adventitiously due to some mutation. The simpler the mutation, the easier it is to explain how it might pop into existence. This argues, in a roundabout way, for a very simple conception of Merge, binary set formation being the poster child for a conceptually simple operation. The problem is that this line of argument fails to explain much. Or rather, it presupposes one deeper capacity and one evolutionarily implausible guess. The deeper capacity is the capacity to form inductive definitions. Without this, Merge would not suffice to explain the Basic Property. Furthermore, with this inductive capacity, virtually *any* available combination operation could be pressed into service to yield an inductive definition of S(yntactic) O(bject) that would generate an unbounded number of hierarchically structured objects. The properties of the grammatical products of such an FL would differ in some ways from what we find with a Merge-as-set-formation-based inductive definition, but either would yield grammars displaying the Basic Property. In sum, the argument above does not really work.

In its place I suggested another possible explanation of the Basic Property. It starts from the assumption that our pre-linguistic ancestors had some relatively simple combination operation capable of grouping lexical atoms into units. The Basic Property arises when this combination operation is *closed* in the domain of the lexical items. The big idea, then, is that closure of the combination operation in the domain of the basic atoms yields grammars that generate unboundedly many hierarchically structured objects. Closure effectively allows the outputs of the combination operation to become inputs to that same operation.

---

[29] A possible argument for the conclusion that phrase markers are set-like is made in Moro (2016). He considers two possible rules for neg placement in artificial languages and argues that only the structure-dependent one is learned *as* a grammatical rule. Moro does not argue that the other rule is not acquirable, only that it uses cognitive resources distinct from those of FL to acquire it. Here is not the place to discuss his subtle reasoning, except to say that its bearing on the simple claim that FL creates *only* sets relies on assumptions concerning the brain loci of FL that are easily contested.

In effect, it maps the range of the combination operation into its domain, thereby rendering the combination operation recursive in that domain. The key grammatical factor underlying closure, I suggested, is labeling, in particular endocentric labeling. Labeling understood in a bare phrase structure idiom suffices to generate an unbounded number of more and more complex syntactic objects each in an equivalence class with one of the lexical atoms (i.e. the bases/moduli of these equivalence classes). In sum, it is proposed here that the closure property embodied in labeling is the key to understanding the Basic Property.

Interestingly, closure is just the sort of property a well-behaved computational system should have. Gallistel (2018 (§ 2(b))) says the following of closure as regards arithmetic calculations:

On the operational side, an arithmetic operation performed on two numerons by the brain's implementation of arithmetic should always yield another numeron, that is another symbol for a magnitude. In formal developments of number (number theory), this operation is called closure. The numbers in number theory form a system that is said to be "closed under the basic operations of arithmetic". The need to develop such a system drove much of the historical evolution of what are today regarded as "the numbers" by those who work with numbers professionally (mathematicians, engineers and computer scientists). Failure to satisfy closure constraints would cause the brain's computations to break down whenever its computational machinery was fed two numerons for which that machinery could not generate an output numeron. In the design of computing machines and computing software, much thought and effort go into obtaining as much closure as possible, even though it is well understood that complete closure is impossible.

So closure is a very nice property for a computational system to have precisely because it allows for functions to compose (i.e. for "the results of one computation [to be] routinely fed to further computations"). If one assumes that computational "efficiency" of the kind that Gallistel (2018) alludes to is one of the forces that drive the design of computational systems (a common enough minimalist assumption) then it would be no surprise if closure was something that a system of linguistic computations aimed to realize in virtue of being computational.[30] And if natural language computations start with combining lexical atoms then closure amounts to treating these combinations of lexical atoms as potential inputs to further combination. There is no easier way of assuring this than assigning each such combination to the equivalence class of some atom. And this is exactly what labeling does. If this is correct, there is at least a prima facie argument to be made that labeling is motivated on the grounds of computational efficiency (aka, closure), a third

---

[30] The widespread minimalist assumption is that computational systems as such have a bias for (computational) efficiency and that this bias is a third-factor natural effect. We return to this bias for efficiency in a very very very brief (and inadequate) discussion of islands and minimality effects in Chapter 8.

7.4 Conclusion

factor property. The fact that linguistic objects form labeled constituents is then, a consequence of the computational efficiency of FL.[31]

I don't expect anyone but those who have completely embraced the minimalist ethos to find this reasoning at all compelling. But then again, I don't expect anyone but someone interested in minimalist questions to find most of this book interesting. For now, I am satisfied outlining the argument for labeling as the quintessential way that linguistic computation strives for efficiency.

One last point: If this is an adequate way of conceiving of the problem of the origins of the Basic Property, it does away with the requirement that we ascribe to pre-linguistic humans the *generic capacity* to form inductive definitions. FL consists of a Merge operation that combines expressions in the equivalence class of the lexical atoms. The inductive leap is not packed into an inductive definition but into the operation that forms unboundedly many expressions of the same equivalence class. Once we have this, then the fact that atoms combine suffices to license the combination of more complex labeled expressions. We need no inductive definition to specify the class of SOs. Or more exactly, though *we* can specify this class inductively this is *not* how *FL* specifies that class. FL specifies SOs in terms of combination and labeling operations. Their joint efforts result in a function (i.e. a grammar) with the Basic Property. This property can be *extensionally* specified using an inductive definition as we have done above. However, the *intensional* specification of the computational procedure is in terms of the combined efforts of the combination plus labeling operations. In other words, the inductive specification of the set of Syntactic Objects is extensionally adequate but it does not reflect the actual inner workings of FL's generative machinery. This machinery does not exploit inductive definitions, just functions closed in the domain of the lexical atoms.

So where does FL come from? From a generic combination operation defined over the atoms (possibly set formation, possibly concatenation, possible something else) and labeling of its outputs to close the combination operation in the domain of the atoms. With this we get grammars that have the Basic Property.

APPENDIX

The appendix to Chapter 2 provided a formal set-theoretic specification of Merge in terms of set-theoretic union operation (U) and an operation Select (S) that maps expressions to their unit sets (i.e. $S(elect)(\alpha) \rightarrow \{\alpha\}$). Both U and

---

[31] It is worth mentioning that Generativists have long noted that one cannot take for granted that the outputs of G operations are *ipso facto* potential inputs to these same operations. For example, Chomsky (1955) spends quite a bit of mental effort showing that transformational outputs can serve as inputs to further transformations in virtue of their formal properties.

S are simple operations. Given these, it is possible to restate the discussion in §7.3 in the following way.

Merge combines two operations: the domain-general set-theoretic U(nion) operation defined for sets and a domain-general operation that maps objects *in a given domain* to their unit sets. These two operations applied to a domain of linguistic atoms allows the derivation of bigger and bigger sets, bounded only by the number of basic atoms. Thus, the repeated application of Merge defined as in (9) derives objects as in (10) given that $\alpha,\beta,\gamma,\delta$ are basic lexical atoms.

(9)   Merge $(x,y) =_{def} U(S(x),S(y))$

(10) $\{\alpha\}, \{\alpha,\beta\}, \{\alpha,\beta,\gamma\}, \{\alpha,\beta,\gamma,\delta\}$ etc.

Note, all the objects in (10) are "flat" (as in without hierarchy). This is because S is defined as mapping lexical atoms to their unit sets. This means that the expressions in (10) are *not* in the domain of S and so cannot be mapped to their unit sets by S so defined. The proposal in §7.3 is that labeling changes the domain of S very slightly, from lexical atoms to elements in the equivalence classes of a lexical atoms, equivalence classes defined in terms of labeling. So $\{_\alpha \alpha,\beta\}$ is in the α equivalence class and so now in the domain of S. This shift from lexical atoms to labeled expressions understood as elements in the equivalence classes of lexical atoms suffices together with (9) to generate unboundedly many hierarchical objects with the properties we want SOs to have.

So what is the trick required to get from flat sets to hierarchically organized objects? Labels. All the rest is plausibly *generic* computational machinery. That's the proposal.

8 Odds and Ends

8.0 Introduction

To this point, I have argued that the Extended Merge Hypothesis (EMH) incorporating the Fundamental Principle of Grammar (FPG) can derive many of the generalizations (what I also called the "laws of grammar") that GB ascribes to the faculty of language (FL). The goal has been to demonstrate that an inductive definition of Syntactic Object (SO) that incorporates a simple definition of Merge (or, more accurately, a conception of Merge that highlights labeling) can, in combination with the FPG, derive the basic syntax of natural language grammars. If correct, the EMH unifies the disparate phenomena that the modular GB account of FL segregates. Movement, phrase structure, reconstruction, selection/subcategorization, construal, and case are different expressions of the self-same Merge operation. From the perspective of the EMH, FL has no internal modularity. Modulo the identity of the features being checked, everything is always and everywhere just an output of Merge.[1]

That was the agenda. Though the postulated assumption that Merge is all there is may have seemed radical, the overall goal of the project has been conservative in the specific sense of aiming to *conserve* the prior results of GB, while still identifying some novelties that arise from the very spare assumptions of the EMH. One consequence of simpler theories is that they leave less wiggle room. They thus force analyses that unify phenomena and countenance dependencies among expressions that prior theory was happy to leave

---

[1] I have assumed, following conventional wisdom, that the specific characteristics of language-particular Gs consist in the features checked (see, e.g., Stabler 2010). Feature checking *as an operation* I take to be cognitively/computationally general (and so not linguistically bespoke). "Feature checking" is what we call operations that regulate cognitive well-formedness conditions. What seems specific to language is not feature checking per se but the specific features checked. Unfortunately, IMO, the etiology of these features and their range and complexity is currently a complete mystery. We have good evidence for specific features (e.g. ϕ-features, case features, categorial features) and how individual grammars check them. However, to my knowledge, we have no general theory of features (e.g. what is a possible feature? How are features in general structured?), no general account of the limits on possible linguistic features, how they are acquired or how they arose in the species. Our lack of knowledge concerning these matters is profound. We await enlightenment.

uncoupled. In Chomsky's felicitous phrasing, simplicity *forces* certain kinds of explanations, and EMH (and most especially the FPG), being based on specific simplicity claims, forces in spades, or so the earlier chapters have hopefully illustrated, even if they may not have been completely persuasive (haha). In this chapter I want to sketch the picture of FL that emerges if the line that I have pursued is on the right track and bring to your attention points of contact this perspective on FL might make with other interesting questions concerning the structure of FL. Needless to say (though I say it anyway), these remarks are even more speculative than those in preceding chapters.

8.1 It's Merge All the Way Down

I have already mentioned the biggest change between the presented conception of FL when contrasted with earlier GBish conceptions. It is deeply *non*-modular. Perhaps the defining characteristic of GB conceptions of FL is their high degree of internal modularity.[2] Different types of dependencies track different primitives, are generated by different kinds of operations, and are regulated by different well-formedness conditions. Thematic dependencies differ formally from case dependencies, that differ from binding dependencies, that differ from movement dependencies, that differ from control dependencies .... The primitives manipulated differ, the rules that establish the dependencies are different and the locality conditions that they must respect are different. Hence the internal modularity of FL.

EMH replaces this GB conception with one in which all grammatical dependencies and relations are Merge mediated. There is no fundamental difference between movement and structure building, between binding and movement, between selection and movement, between obligatory control and binding. They are all generated via Merge, the differences residing entirely in what the merged elements are. In effect, EMH unifies all the modules of the GB conception of FL, thereby radically eliminating the last vestiges of "constructionism" from grammatical theory. Let me elaborate on this last point a bit.

---

[2] I contrast the "internal" vs the "external" modularity of FL as follows. FL is *externally* modular in that it is informationally encapsulated with respect to other cognitive faculties. In practice, this means that there are some properties of FL *proprietary* to FL, and so not shared with other cognitive modules. This amounts to saying that FL is not just an expression of our general cognitive powers. There is something special and specific to language that FL embodies and makes FL its own module. Of course, if MP is on the right track, there is only a smidgen of difference. But there is something special. If EMH is correct, then that something special includes labeling.

GB's description of FL adds the claim that FL is *internally* modular. Specifically, FL contains subparts that are informationally encapsulated from each other. GB has modules that deploy distinctive primitives, operations and dependencies and that are all part of an interactive FL that is also externally modular. EMH shrinks this internal modularity to a small point. GB's theory of FL, in contrast, is highly internally modular.

8.1 It's Merge All the Way Down

One of the main goals of GB was to eliminate constructions as fundamental primitives of FL. In this, GB contrasts with earlier versions of Generative theory wherein operations like Passive and Raising and Topicalization are the basic "rules" of the Grammar. The move from these kinds of rules to operations like Move α eliminates such rules from the FL's basic inventory by reanalyzing constructions as compiled complexes with simple non-constructionist parts. On this view, constructions (should they be cognitively active) are built from simpler formal parts whose properties in combination exhaust the properties that (complex) constructions have.[3]

However, even if this point is conceded, GB is chock-full of constructionist features. Thus, different types of dependencies are licensed by different kinds of operations. Most prominently, movement is fundamentally distinguished from structure building, and both are fundamentally distinguished from construal. Thus, GB incorporates three very different kinds of operations to serve three (purportedly) different grammatical functions: the construction of phrases, the displacement of expressions, and the establishment of antecedence relations. The constructions GB countenances are often more general than those envisioned in prior theory, but FL still cuts the operations up functionally to a significant degree in much the way that prior construction-based grammars did. Indeed, when it comes construal rules, the cuts are about as fine as they were in earlier Standard Theory proposals. When viewed as construction-specific operations, there is really very little to choose from between rules like Reflexivization and Pronominalization on the one hand versus Principles A and B of the binding theory on the other. Ditto for the difference between Obligatory Control and rules like Equi-NP Deletion or Non-Obligatory Control and Super Equi. Whatever the virtues of theoretical simplification that attend eliminating constructions, they are at best partially realized in even the most sophisticated versions of GB.

And in this, there is a stark contrast with the EMH! For better or worse, there is no serious formal difference between these apparently different dependencies. If FPG is correct, then the grammar's formalism respects no functional differences. Thus, for example, it's not the case that construal is formally a feature of binding rules while structure building is formally a product of phrase

---

[3] This is important. GB does not deny that constructions might be cognitively active features of a language-competent mind. Rather it denies that constructions are *primitives* whose properties must be axiomatically stipulated. This contrasts with primitive operations like movement rules or phrase structure rules whose properties are fundamental in that they *are* axiomatically established.

This noted, an empirical issue remains: Are constructions cognitively active even if not grammatically primitive? Much of the evidence for constructions can be seen as arguing that complexes of operations larger than simple grammatical rules are linguistically operative. Even if this is correct (and it would be interesting if it is), it does not gainsay the central anti-constructionist claim advanced by GB.

structure (X') rules. All dependencies, whatever functions they serve, are realized formally in the same way. It's Merge all the way down and all across the grammar. Or, to say this another way, the formal properties of grammars vastly underdetermine their disparate functions. Thus, the formal properties of G rules cannot be categorized by the functions served by the application of these G rules. There is only one formal kind of G dependency, the one established by Merge, and that serves every linguistic function, however disparate these appear to be. That's the picture that emerges.

I want to stress that this radically anti-constructionist conception is not a fundamental feature of most current minimalist accounts. For example, most minimalist theories distinguish formal processes based on the Duality of Interpretation (DOI). Let me elaborate.

Early Minimalism distinguished Merge from Move (the latter being the combination of Copy+Merge). Against this background, Chomsky argued that θ-discharge is mediated by Merge while scope is determined via Move. With the unification of structure building with movement in later minimalist theory, the formal distinction between Merge and Move could no longer be pressed into service to functionally express a θ/scope duality. Nonetheless, Minimalists still stuck to the idea that θ-roles are discharged via E-merge while scope was the province of I-merge.[4] Chomsky (2021) retains the same basic idea. The paper proposes barring movement (I-merge) into θ-positions based on the idea that it would clash with the DOI. Thus, the DOI has teeth in that it formally restricts the kinds of operations that are available to regulate dependencies.

This contrasts with the story offered here. In particular, as the FPG requires that all dependencies be Merge mediated, the control relation must be as well. And given that control descriptively involves an expression's bearing more than a single θ-role, it requires that I-Merge into θ-positions be licit. In fact, as Merge is the only grammatical operation it becomes impossible to functionally distinguish between formal operations as there is only a single formal operation available. Or, to say this another way, if the DOI is a grammatical principle regulating FL and if the DOI requires the dual nature of interpretation to be formally expressed, then the DOI is incompatible with the FPG. One of them must give. If the EMH is correct, then FL is radically non-constructionist in the sense that formal features of the grammar are not regulated by *any* functional desiderata (including the DOI). Of course, the DOI might well correctly describe one of the functional dependencies that Gs track. However, that Gs track both argument structure and scope has no formal teeth as both θ-marking and scope marking are grammatically parasitic on a single operation: Merge.

[4] As the reader no doubts realizes, I have no idea how this is supposed to work. There is no formal distinction between E- and I-merge as they are simply two instances of the same Merge operation. That said, the dictum was (and is) that arguments must be E-merged into their θ-positions and scope is determined via I-merge.

I would like to further emphasize this point. Even if one allows the distinction between E- and I-merge to have some ontological heft (i.e. one does not treat it as a notational convenience of no theoretical standing), then the EMH still does not neatly divide things the right way. If the EMH is along the right lines, then one can move into θ-positions and can form chains that have multiple θ-links. Moreover, elements may well bear scope properties even if never moved (e.g. Neg and Q morphemes bear important scope properties even though they are generally E-merged into their scope positions). So though it is correct that in some standard cases (mainly as regards the θ-roles of internal arguments) E-merge licenses θ-properties and I-merge determines an expression's envelope of scope options, this is not so in the general case. And this is not a problem *unless* one adheres to a vestige of constructionism. Conclusion: Learn to love radical anti-constructionism.[5]

8.2 The EMH and Locality

Syntax revolves around four basic concepts: (i) constituency, (ii) hierarchy, (iii) dependency and (iv) locality. The EMH deals with the first three. Or, to be more precise, earlier chapters have tried to show how to derive the linguistic properties associated with the first three notions. Thus, the EMH offers a notion of constituency based on Merge and label that largely tracks the traditional conception. The "simplicity" of Merge embodied in the unification of E- and I-merge and the No Tampering Conditions (largely) derive the ubiquity of c-command (the quintessential hierarchical concept) in regulating hierarchical dependencies in the grammar. The unification of construal and movement operations as species of I-merge derive the c-command requirements on non-local dependencies. This, and quite a lot more (or so I have argued), follow pretty directly from the EMH, and, if correct, this is a very good thing.[6]

That said, the EMH has remained largely mute concerning the locality properties also characteristic of natural language grammars. Not completely

---

[5] Chomsky is very committed to the DOI and has been since the earliest days of Generative Grammar. Recall, in earlier epochs of Generative Theory, first Deep Structure, then D-structure was the locus of θ-relations. Movement followed once these were determined in the base and, as work in the 1970s and 80s showed, movement affected scope options. This hypothesis was retained within Minimalism even after the D-structure was jettisoned for theoretical reasons. DOI was retained in the assumption that θ-roles are the product of E-merge/Merge and *could not* be discharged via I-merge/Move. Some version of the DOI has been retained in virtually all subsequent theory, and its retention has been the sole motivation for barring movement/I-merge into θ-positions.

[6] To remind you, it is not the EMH alone that does the derivational work. There were some ancillary assumptions pressed into service as well, such as Merge over Move and the Principle of Grammatical Plenitude as well as some pure stipulations like pronouns and reflexives spell out copies in the tails of chains.

mute, however. For example, EMH unifies the locality domains evident in movement operations together with those of binding operations. Thus, there are no separate binding domains and movement domains if the EMH is on the right track. They are one. True, there are two kinds of non-local dependencies depending on the type of movement involved (A vs A') but *given* these two kinds of I-merge, the EMH unifies the domains of Obligatory Control and Reflexivization with that of Raising and Passive (all species of A-movement/I-merge) and unifies Resumptive Binding and Pronominalization with that of *Wh*-movement and Topicalization (all species involving A'-movement/I-merge via Spec C). So the EMH has *some* consequences for the kinds of locality we find in natural language grammars.[7] However, the EMH has nothing to say as to *why* we find the locality restrictions we do find for A- and A'-movement/I-merge.[8] Here is what I mean.

Standard cases of movement are subject to minimality. The EMH exploits this, for example, to offer an account as to why XPs are targets of movement and X's are not.[9] However, the EMH says nothing about *why* movement should be subject to minimality at all. Why are movement dependencies subject to locality restrictions like minimality at all? This is a typical juicy minimalist question. And yet, the EMH has nothing to offer in reply.

Nor does the EMH say much about the locality restrictions (viz. island effects) we find with long A'-movement. There is a lot of empirical evidence that A'-dependencies are subject to island conditions. And these conditions have been extensively investigated and excellent theory has developed that describes them in detail (rather beautiful detail, IMO). Yet, the EMH says nothing as to *why* island conditions exist, or why unbounded dependencies of the A' variety are governed by them. Nothing. Really. Nada, zip, gar nicht, bubkis, zero! As with minimality effects, why island effects exist is outside the purview of the EMH.

Nor do I believe that this will ever change. In other words, I see no reason to think that the EMH (or any other version of the Merge Hypothesis) will ever explain *why* these kinds of locality conditions exist. Let me explain why I think this.

---

[7] Here is another consequence for locality. As I have mentioned several times, Merge-based theories will have a hard time incorporating a licensing condition like the Empty Category Principle. See §8.3 for elaboration.

[8] Henceforth, I simplify 'movement/I-merge' to simply 'movement.' If the reader prefers to hear 'I-merge,' I am fine with that. My formative syntax education is to blame for the archaism.

[9] The EMH is also comfortable with the conclusion that there is no head movement, though the astute reader might well consider this a serious problem rather than an obvious benefit. To assuage discomfort, I noted that Hornstein (2008) offered a couple of ways of permitting head movement. Of course, these are patches and the world would be a prettier place were they not required. However, they are useful in that they indicate that the existence of head movement would not be lethal for the general approach.

8.2 The EMH and Locality

If one inspects proposals within MP, they factor the properties of FL into two broad categories: (i) those that reflect the distinctive combinatorics of natural language grammars (in particular that generate unboundedly many hierarchically structured SOs (aka the Basic Property) and (ii) those that reflect generic features of well-designed computational systems (or, at least, the generic features of extant *biological* computational systems). I have argued that the province of the EMH falls under the first kinds of concerns. In particular, I have followed minimalist practice in arguing that there are simple Merge-based theories of recursion that accommodate the Basic Property and that also have many of the other properties we find in natural language grammars.

I have also followed minimalist practice in relegating locality to the second pot of concepts. Locality, on this view, is to be understood in terms of the kinds of properties well-designed computational systems should have. On this view, minimality effects and island effects reflect *generic* properties of (well-designed) computational systems as refracted through the particular prism of grammar. The MP question is whether this very general hunch can be worked out in sufficient detail to be convincing (or maybe more accurately, to even be contentful). If it can, then the locality conditions found in FL are not linguistically bespoke. The important minimalist question then is the following: Can the locality restrictions found to be operative within natural language grammars be understood as just particular applications of more cognitively generic or computationally general principles of mental computation? Can this idea be empirically and theoretically cashed out? I have no idea, but what follows are some random comments meant to suggest that this might be feasible.

Let's first consider minimality. The Minimality Condition can be stated as in (1):

(1)   In a structure ' ... X ... Y ... Z ... ' in which X c-commands Y and Y c-commands Z and in which both Y and Z have feature specifications relevant to X no operation can involve X and Z.

Note the condition basically says that where two expressions Y, Z share features relevant to entering into a checking relation with X, then the closer of the two must be the one that enters into that relation. In effect, the Minimality Condition in (1) says that shorter feature-checking dependencies trump longer ones. That something like this *should* hold is natural if establishing dependencies exacts a cost. Something like this makes sense if, in some sense, shorter dependencies can be understood as being less cognitively onerous than longer ones. If they are, then the Minimality Condition can be understood as a grammatical strategy for minimizing such cognitive costs. Why would FL function to minimize such costs? It would do so if FL (indeed, cognitive modules more generally) has a bias towards computational efficiency. Or, to say this another way, if grammatical rules/operations are written so as to ease computational burdens, then we might expect a locality condition similar to the Minimality Condition.

The story can be developed further, and it has been. Ortega-Santos (2011) notes that biological memory is very sensitive to the features that cognitive objects (including linguistic objects) bear. Thus, there is a large literature that indicates that parsing is cue-based, the cues including various syntactic features. It is also well known that different SOs with similar cues/features regularly interfere with one another. Why? Well, this is a feature of content-addressable memories, memory structures in which memory registers are indexed by their contents. It appears that biological memory is of the content-addressable variety and that is why we commonly see interference effects in tasks that involve cognitive computations. Importantly, these effects are not restricted to language computations. They are ubiquitous. Put this all together and we arrive at the idea that memory of the human variety will run into trouble when cognitive computations want to relate contents with similar feature structures. In such cases other cognitive contents with these same feature structures will normally interfere and screw things up. Say for the moment that this is indeed the case. In particular, say that human/biological memory is largely content addressable and that it displays these kinds of interference effects. If this is so, *and there is a bias towards computational efficiency*, then it might explain why G rules are grammatically constrained to apply so as to avoid these sorts of problems. In effect, (1) is a way of avoiding interference effects that arise from having to compute over SOs with the kinds of memories humans/animals have. This is a nice story, IMO.

Some caveats. There are at least two ways of understanding the interaction between properties of a grammar and properties of human memory, both of which start from the (obviously correct) observation that real-time computations of grammatical structures will require performance systems with memory structures.

The first way of relating the two sees minimality effects as simple performance effects. On this interpretation, FL, as such, has no analogue of the Minimality Condition. Rather, minimality effects reflect the fact that SOs when parsed/produced (i.e. when worked on by the performance systems) will run into problems when they engage the sensitivities of a performance system that incorporates this particular kind of memory. Minimality effects so understood are *not* the result of a Minimality Condition that is part of FL but are the by-products of the actual interaction of the properties of the SOs performed upon plus the memory structure of the performer. On this view, there are minimality effects but no Minimality Condition.

There is a second way of construing the relationship between the two, and this one is more of what I (and I believe Ortega-Santos) had in mind when I

8.2 The EMH and Locality

limned the general story a few paragraphs earlier. Here the Minimality Condition is a constitutive part of FL, not simply an interaction effect of the competence system embodied in FL and the performance system that has content-addressable memory. That said, I would like to understand the Minimality Condition as reflecting the exigencies that arise in performance due to the specific organization of the performance systems. The problem is how to do this without confusing competence and performance issues. Or, less tendentiously, why should matters of competence reflect factors of performance? Here is one kind of possible answer: (i) some grammatical formats are "easier" than others for some performance systems to use and (ii) the Bias for Computational Efficiency favors those formats.[10] FL, in other words, is biased to reduce computational complexity in a sense of complexity to be presently specified. Let me elaborate with a little story about typing and keyboards.

QWERTY (the first Six letters of the top line) is the standard English typing keyboard. Why this layout? Here is one story. The layout turns out to be efficient in that it is easy for a typist to get to the letters that often go together. This makes typing quicker and typos less common. Thus, given the configuration of typical human hands and the spelling of the most common words in English, this keyboard layout leads to fast and accurate typing.

Now, as it turns out, this story is somewhat incomplete. A third factor has been regularly cited as relevant (this addition might not really be correct actually), the mechanics of the typewriter itself. The story goes that once upon a time, before the IBM Selectric and way before our current computer word processing systems, a typewriter's typing mechanism would frequently jam if typists typed too quickly. Consequently, there was a desire to *slow typists down* especially when specific combinations of letters needed to be typed. The QWERTY keyboard, it has been claimed, is a good layout for preventing jamming while also allowing for fast and accurate typing. In other words, *given the technology available*, the QWERTY layout was the best fit in the sense of maximizing speed and accuracy.[11]

There are two properties of the above account sketch that are relevant for the present discussion of computational efficiency. First, it provides a measurable sense in which one layout is better than another layout *given* human physiology,

---

[10] One might see this bias as a third-factor feature of computational systems; such systems tend toward computational efficiency in the representational formats of their cognitive sub-systems. Note that saying this does not explain it. This is an axiom, and a rather mystical one at that, for it says that computational systems as such tend toward efficiency. Why should this be true? In earlier days when we had arguments for benevolent deities, the simplicity of nature and the efficiency of natural computation could be offloaded onto YOU KNOW WHO. Nowadays all we have is Darwin and it is unclear why Darwinian tinkering should lead to optimal design. This is an old issue, and one that I will now scurry away from quickly having mentioned it.

[11] See David (1985) for this account. See Stamp (2013) for a more recent discussion which questions this charming account.

typing techniques and typewriters.[12] One might even say that given these *performance* factors, the QWERTY layout is computationally efficient.[13] Second, it is clear that this sense of computational efficiency relies on assumptions of how the keyboard's layout is *used*. Thus, the competence theory (the layout) is efficient with respect to (among other things) the machine+typist that performs typing on it. Efficiency, in this sense, takes a peek at how the system is used to evaluate the efficiency of the layout itself. One might object to this being misleading. It is not the layout that is efficient, but the layout+machine+typing-technique+human physiognomy that is. Correct. But, it is not *too* misleading. And it is informative to say that the layout can be evaluated for efficiency (in a way that one can actually measure) once one holds the other factors constant.[14] With this as background, let's unpack the analogy in the domain of grammar.

Grammars, like layouts, are competence theories. Humans use them to perform tasks like production and parsing. Such performances require human memory and attention resources in addition to grammars. Thus, it is plausible that some kinds of grammatical formats are more efficient than others *once one fixes the properties of these other resources*. In particular, let's return to the Ortega-Santos conjecture considered above. The claim is that human memory being content addressable favors grammatical formats that incorporate the Minimality Condition in (1). How so? By eliminating the potential problems that humans would encounter were they to perform computations using the content-addressable memories they have when linguistically performing. Or, FL grammars eliminate such problems by *grammatically* prohibiting syntactic structures that would induce them.

If we further assume that FL (or, more reasonably, any cognitive system) has a bias for eliminating this kind of performance complexity by adjusting competence theories to avoid structures that would invite them, we can "explain" the Minimality Condition as the by-product of reducing computational complexity.

The same kind of story applies to locality effects (e.g. island effects or successive cyclicity effects) like those one describes with bounding/barriers/

---

[12] Technique is important. Stamp (2013) discusses a new layout, KALQ, that is superior for thumb-typing on smartphones and tablets; a different machine allows a different typing technique, and a different layout proves better.

[13] Other "competence" layouts have been investigated. The most common being the Dvorak layout. It has been claimed that it is superior. Maybe it is. Stamp (2013) reviews some of the data. What is relevant here is that we can imagine testing this claim holding the indicated parameters constant.

[14] This notion of complexity contrasts with the understanding of computational complexity common in the Computer Science literature. The latter tries to categorize the complexity of different kinds of problems and abstracts as much as possible from the details of the "machines" that do the computations. For an accessible discussion of this and its relevance to matters linguistic, see Berwick and Weinberg (1986).

8.2 The EMH and Locality

phase theories. These systems impose locality restrictions on long-distance dependencies. In effect, they force unbounded dependencies to be factored into bounded subparts that add together to allow for the full unbounded effect. For example, long-distance dependencies in sentences like (2a) are the product of shorter movements involving comp to comp movement (2b).

(2)   a. What did John say that Mary heard that Sheila won
      b. [what [John said [**what** that [Mary heard [**what** that [Sheila won what]]]]]]

Grammars that embody some version of bounding/barriers/phases will generate structure akin to (2b) with the indicated intermediate copies of *what*. Why do FL grammars have this locality requirement? One possible answer mimics the one above for the Minimality Condition: Such Gs are computationally a good fit for the kinds of memory systems we have. For example, if we assume that holding things in memory incurs a cost and that holding them over long distances requires that the memories be "refreshed," then one way of accomplishing this would be to have copies of the elements retained in memory periodically called from memory, thereby boosting their activation.[15] If this is correct, then a grammatical format that obeys locality conditions like the ones we find in grammars that adhere to bounding/barriers/phases formats can be seen as offering a solution to these kinds of problems. Once again, we advert to properties of the systems of performance (in particular, the cost of holding things in memory) to account for why grammars used by such performance systems have the grammatical formats they do.

Now please note: These are *at best* account sketches not accounts. To become empirically interesting we need a lot more detail about how exactly memory works in humans. We should look for similar effects in other cognitive domains that compute with non-linguistic cognitive objects. In particular, if this line of thinking is on the right track, then we should find effects similar to minimality effects and bounding effects in other domains. We should find confusability due to proximity effects and memory degradation due to distance effects. We might even hope to find cognitive patches within these domains that serve to ameliorate these problems representationally within different cognitive domains. Unfortunately, working any of this out is way beyond my pay grade, so I will leave matters in this faintly sketched state.

Wrapping up, let me make two points. First, I do not expect any version of the Merge Hypothesis to explain locality effects. That they are attested within

---

[15] I am sure that there are other conceivable mechanisms. What I rely on here is the idea that holding something in memory is costly and that such memories fade. So the fading or cost must be addressed, and reactivating it by linking it to a copy that is "not too far away" is one way of doing so.

grammar is indubitable. The evidence is overwhelming. I also believe that the evidence is overwhelming that the effects are grammatical in the sense of being tuned to grammatical structure.[16] Thus, for example, distance for the Minimality Condition invokes c-command, and in bounding/barriers/phase theory in terms of bounding nodes, barriers and phase heads. These are grammatical measures, not generic cognitive ones. However, what I hope to have at least conceptually demonstrated is that these issues of cognitive format *could* reflect generic computational desiderata of the systems that use these formats for various ends, and that by peeking at the properties of the systems that use these formats, we might be able to understand why the formats that are used have *some* of the properties they appear to have.

Second, the Bias for Computational Efficiency is the name of a rather mysterious process. Why should FL embody it? I don't know. Here are some handwaving remarks. If this property exists, it is not restricted to FL but is a more general feature of biological systems. Naturalists have long marveled at how exquisitely constructed animals are. How well their parts fit together. There is, after all, an observational basis for the argument from design! It would not be surprising if cognitive organs (modules) fit together as neatly as non-cognitive ones, at least to a significant degree. If not perfect, then damn well. But why? Selection pressures? Some master principle that favors organs that play well together? I dunno. But whatever holds in the domain of physical organs I want to assume holds for cognitive ones as well. I have assumed something along these lines here (viz. the bias for computational efficiency) and have used it to illustrate how locality conditions might be fitted into an overall MP setting centering a Merge-based system of computation.[17]

8.3   Farewell ECP

In earlier sections of this book, tucked away in elaborate footnotes, I have been making the argument that an important consequence of the Merge Hypothesis (MH) is its poor fit with the ECP. In this section I would like to reprise this argument and bring all the scattered comments together in one place. I think that this result is an important one given the centrality of the ECP to later versions of GB theory and given the substantial acceptance of GB results to the development of MP theory. If the line of reasoning that follows is correct it offers an important way in which minimalist theory as developed in versions of MH differs substantially from GB. So despite the general conservative

---

[16] See Sprouse et al. (2013) for discussion.
[17] There is a specifically linguistic topic that I have not addressed. Why do we have the bounding nodes/barriers/phase heads we do? For example, why are CP, DP (and possibly vP) the nodes relevant for measuring locality? As I have nothing of even mild interest to say on this topic, I will simply mention that it exists and leave it untouched.

8.3 Farewell ECP

nature of the relationship between GB and MP, here is an important point of divergence, a place where MP appears to be inconsistent with some important GB generalizations. Interestingly, there is evidence to suggest that as regards the ECP, MH is right and GB is wrong. We will review it anon. But first let's review the argument against the ECP, taking as fixed MP accounts that center versions of the Merge Hypothesis.

Let's begin at the beginning. What is the ECP? There are two parts. One part addresses subject/object asymmetries such as those in (3) and a second addresses argument/adjunct asymmetries such as those in (4):

(3)   a. *What did Mary wonder who bought
        b. **Who did Mary wonder what bought

(4)   a. *What did Mary wonder why Bill bought
        b. **Why did Mary wonder what Bill bought

First, a little description of the judgments above. All the indicated sentences are quite unacceptable. The relevant data point is that the second b-example in each pair is considerably *more* unacceptable than the a-example. Second, there is an important contrast between (3b) and (4b). The latter is acceptable, but only on the reading in which *why* originates in the matrix clause. The reading in which *why* is questioning the reason/cause of the buying event denoted in the embedded clause is simply unavailable. This contrasts with (3b), where, if you allow your brain to squint, it can bring into focus the reading of the unacceptable sentence. This is just not so for (4b). Screw your brain as hard as you can, the reading will not come into focus. Let's stipulate that this is indeed the correct description of the facts.

I will have very little to say about the data in (3). The reason is that there are ample ways of accommodating the differences in (3) without the ECP. (3) violates the *Wh*-island condition while (3b) violates that and the Fixed Subject Condition (effectively the generalized version of the *that*-t effect). This is an independent restriction on movement illustrated by the unacceptability of the examples in (5):

(5)   a. *Who$_1$ did Mary say that t$_1$ left
        b. *Who$_1$ did Mary wonder whether t$_1$ left

Thus, there is a way to accommodate the indicated differential unacceptability in (3) without reaching for the ECP. As such, I will leave these cases aside in what follows.[18]

---

[18] There is another reason I ignore them. Even within GB, the consensus view (IMO) was that the unification of Fixed Subject Condition effects with the rest of the ECP was a mistake. These effects looked to be related to overt phonological gaps in ways that the data in (4) were not. Thus, examples like (5) are improved with the addition of resumptive pronouns even in a language like

Within GB the contrast in (4) was theoretically accommodated in terms of the ECP's conditions on acceptable antecedent-government relations. The ECP stated that traces needed licensing via their antecedent-governors, and the relevant relation could not be established in the derivation underlying (4b), while it could be in the structure underlying (4a). There were several ways of coding the relevant differences but they largely shared the technology developed in Lasnik and Saito (1984). This sort of story is not readily transferable to a minimalist theory incorporating the Merge Hypothesis. And the reason for this is fundamental. In GB, the ECP is understood as a *mechanism for licensing traces*, and traces are not licit grammatical constructs within MH (see Chapter 2).[19]

Let me massage the problem a bit more so that you can get a feel for the incompatibility. The antecedent-government licensing condition crucially distinguishes the different links of a movement chain. In particular, the head of the chain is a lexical expression while the other links are traces. This is *why* the latter need licensing and the former do not. In brief, the GB intuition is that there is something toxic about traces and they require licensing by a lexical antecedent (the head of the chain in which they are links) in order to defuse their ill effects. In a theory like MH, however, this intuition is problematic. Why? Because, there is no formal difference between the head of a chain and the other links. They are all simply occurrences/copies of the self-same lexical expression. Thus, antecedents and "traces" are structurally identical and so it is unclear why either would require any more licensing than the other. If lower links need it and they are identical to higher ones, then heads of chains are in as much need of licensing as lower links are. Conversely, if heads of chains are in no need of licensing, then given that lower links are identical to higher ones as they are all occurrences/copies of the same expression, then lower links are licit without licensing too. The asymmetry the ECP built into antecedent-government licensing finds no footing within minimalist accounts incorporating the MH as MH has no place for traces as formal grammatical objects. Thus, an MP theory centered on MH has no way of incorporating the ECP principle as an integral part of FL's fine structure.

English where these do not generally improve island violations (see Sprouse 2007). That said, there is no standard minimalist explanation for Fixed Subject Condition effects. The GB version that leverages the phonetic nullity of traces is not immediately available for MP accounts given the elimination of traces with the adoption of MH. That said, I suspect that it would be easy to code an analogue of the *that*-t filter as part of Transfer to AP, effectively prohibiting the deletion of a copy/occurrence next to a filled C°. This would chime with early approaches to these effects that located them on the PF side of the Y-model derivation (see Aoun et al. 1987). For another interesting approach also compatible with current technology that places the restriction inside the grammar proper (rather than in the Transfer operation), see Pesetsky and Torrego (2000).

[19] The licensing condition also occurs late in the derivation, before transfer to CI. This further complicates any hoped-for translation of the basic mechanics in MP-acceptable terms.

8.3 Farewell ECP

There are further reasons for suspecting the ECP from a minimalist perspective. First, antecedent government looks very like binding and yet it is not readily reducible to it.[20] Second, the domain of licit antecedent government is virtually identical to that of standard A'-movement (Subjacency and Phase Impenetrability Condition effects) and yet it is distinct from these. Put another way, theories of licit A'-movement that accommodate successive cyclicity and island effects (e.g. Subjacency, Barriers, Phase theory) incorporate a locality condition on movement that is identical to the domains that license licit antecedent government. Thus the ECP is highly redundant with the theory of Bounding incorporated into theories of A'-movement that descend from Chomsky's (1973, 1977) original Subjacency Theory. And yet, by hypothesis, ECP effects are not Subjacency effects. Need I add that minimalist scruples bridle at such redundancy and suggest that one of these need to be dispensed with? The plausible candidate for elimination is the ECP.[21]

In sum, the ECP fits poorly within minimalist theory and it should be eliminated. Or, to put this more provocatively, minimalist theory implies that the ECP does not exist and its effects need another explanation.

And wouldn't you know it, there is recentish data arguing exactly this. How nice. The argument is offered in Lu et al. (2020). Let me review the main gist.

The paper reports a formal judgment study and argues for two main conclusions. The first is that *wh-in-situ* constructions (e.g. in Chinese) show island-effect profiles similar to those found in overt movement grammars (e.g. in English). And second, that the additional ECP effects found with adjunct (un)acceptability judgments (in comparison with arguments) is not because they are more sensitive to islands than arguments are but is likely due to the fact that long adjuncts like *why* don't like to move long distance at all.[22] In other words, Lu et al. (2020) argues that the additional unacceptability found in cases like (4b) is a feature of the restricted capacities of adjuncts to move far rather than a reflection of the structures that they move from. Thus, if Lu et al. (2020) is right then the significance of the data in (4) has been misanalyzed and there is no need for a layer of theory additional to that required to accommodate argument island effects. In sum, we can drop the ECP.

---

[20] Though see Aoun (1986) for an attempt to treat antecedent government as a species of A'-binding.

[21] Nor, truth be told, is the ECP among the more elegant sub-theories of GB. The technology required to make the ECP trains run on time is imposing, and not in a good way. For details of what is required, see Lasnik and Saito (1984). All in all, aesthetic grounds alone suggest that there is something amiss with the ECP.

[22] Why this is so is left unexplained. But, and this is the key point, it does not need to be explained to debunk the idea that adjunct effects reflect greater island sensitivity than arguments. The greater unacceptability of adjunct extraction from islands is a complexity effect wherein adjuncts don't like to move from their base-generated clauses. In the context of long movement out of islands this suffices to explain their additional unacceptability *without* postulating further grammatical licensing requirements like those embodied in the ECP.

To repeat, this is a very nice result from the purview of minimalist theory. MH theoretically argues against trace licensing conditions like the ECP, and Lu et al. (2020) provides an empirical argument against such a licensing condition as well. If this is correct, it is another win for minimalist theories that incorporate some version of the Merge Hypothesis. Yaaay!!

8.4 *Wh-in-Situ* Constructions

Before moving on to another topic, let me note one further important consequence of Lu et al. (2020). As the authors note, argument *wh-in-situ* constructions display island effects identical to those found with overt movement. If this is correct, then it too comports with what we would expect from the EMH. Let me explain.

Prior to Lu et al. (2020) the standard view was that *wh-in-situ* constructions were insensitive to islands (roughly for the same reasons that RP constructions were thought to be (i.e. they left no phonetic "gaps")). Several theoretical options have been deployed in order to accommodate this purported difference. Early theory proposed that Subjacency applied to overt movement only (see Huang 1982). Another theoretical accommodation distinguishes between dependencies established via movement and those formed via some kind of agreement or binding (in this case, between a Q-morpheme in CP and a *Wh*-expression it c-commands). Importantly, these more "interpretive" options are not subject to locality conditions on movement (e.g. like the Subjacency Conditions) as they don't involve movement. Thus, by restricting Subjacency and the like to movement-formed dependencies, it is possible to distinguish different kinds of *Wh*-licensing operations and subject only a subset of these to the locality requirements that underlie island effects.

The EMH (which incorporates the FPG) blocks these options for circumventing Subjacency-like locality effects. Recall that the FPG requires that all grammatical dependencies be established via Merge. There is no other licit formal way of establishing them. This implies that *if Wh*-question formation is a grammatical dependency, then it must be established via Merge. As the relation between the Q-morpheme and a *Wh* within a clause is non-local, this means that it must be established via I-merge (aka movement) and so should be subject to island effects following from the locality conditions embedded in subjacency/barriers/phase theories. Lu et al. (2020) shows that Chinese *wh-in-situ* constructions conform to this requirement despite the absence of any apparent movement, *just as the EMH predicts it should*. And the EMH predicts this because it incorporates the FPG and so disallows all non-Merge-based workarounds for establishing grammatical relations. In effect, the FPG eliminates the theoretical option of some kind of agree or binding relation mediating the dependency between Q and *Wh* in *wh-in-situ* languages.

8.4 *Wh-in-Situ* Constructions

Nor is the other option available, the one which distinguishes covert from overt movement and subjects only the latter to conditions like Subjacency. The reason is that it is not at all clear how to code for covert movement (i.e. I-merge) in a minimalist grammar. Doing so within GB exploited the possibility of evaluating chains for Subjacency at S-structure prior to splitting the derivation along a PF and LF track (see Chapter 1 (17B)). However, minimalist theories don't have levels like S-structure, so they don't have the theoretical wherewithal to distinguish pre-S-structure and LF movement. So it is not clear that the analogue of the GB option of restricting Subjacency to *overt* movement can be incorporated into a minimalist theory like the EMH.

In short, because the EMH is less expansive in its theoretical options than is GB it drastically narrows the formal options available for establishing grammatical dependencies and, in this case, this forces the following conclusion: *wh-in-situ* constructions establish the dependency between Q and Wh in the same way as overt movement languages do, and so this dependency in these two types of languages should be subject to the same conditions. And this, to repeat, is what Lu et al. (2020) finds. Once again, the restricted range of the theoretical options that the EMH allows forces analyses with the right empirical properties and thus leads to strong explanations precisely because the EMH limits the range of analytical options that are grammatically available.

To sum up the last two sections then: Standard minimalist reasoning would lead us to dispense with the ECP and its theoretical apparatus because this apparatus is redundant with Subjacency Theory. In particular, the domain of licit antecedent binding is the same as that for licit movement/I-merge, and the antecedent-government relation is simply a species of A'-binding. Methodological parsimony suggests that we treat such redundancy suspiciously, and this is bad news for the ECP. Lu et al. (2020) drives an additional nail into the ECP's theoretical coffin. The paper argues two important points: (i) that the empirical data supporting the core of the ECP (the so-called argument/adjunct asymmetry) does not reflect an additional structural effect (i.e. the ECP) added on top of a simple island effect and (ii) that regular *wh-in-situ* constructions display the same island effects found in overt *Wh*-movement languages. The former point follows if there is no ECP effect additional to bounding/island effects. The latter result follows directly from the EMH. If this line of reasoning is correct, it is a major departure from earlier GB theory and it greatly simplifies the structure of FL. Of course, nobody should *yet* be convinced that the ECP should be dispensed with. What one *should* be convinced of is that eliminating it is a theoretically desirable move on grounds of simplicity and that there is interesting evidence supporting this best of all possible methodological worlds. Ditto with generating *wh-in-situ* and overt *Wh*-movement constructions in the same way. That is enough for now.

224   8 Odds and Ends

8.5   The Merge Hypothesis and the Y-Model

Here is another consequence of the Merge Hypothesis. It is incompatible with GB's Y-model (see Chapter 1, (17B) repeated here as (6)). Let's see why this is so.

(6)   The Derivational Y-model:

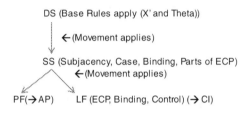

First, what is the Y-model a model of? It is a model of a grammatical derivation. It says that a licit derivation involves four distinctive levels, DS, SS, PF and LF, at which various well-formedness conditions are checked. DS is the level at which the grammar interfaces with the lexicon. SS is a grammar-internal model derived from DS via the application of numerous applications of Move α. It is also the point at which derivations split into two branches that feed the two interfaces AP and CI. The one that leads to a structure that feeds AP is PF and the one that ends in a phrase marker that feeds CI is LF. GB did not discuss the route from SS to PF very much. However, it had lots to say about the derivation from SS to LF. LF is derived from SS by further applications of Move α. Because the derivation splits at SS, the applications of Move α on the SS to LF leg have no AP effects despite being applications of the same operation that has AP effects when applied before the SS split.

Now as you, my readers, no doubt know (but let me be pedantic here and repeat what you know), many features of the GB model of derivation no longer hold in MP theories. For example, MP accounts dispense with both DS and SS and so these levels cannot play the role they played in GB. In addition, the conditions that apply at these levels have been rethought so as to regulate derivational processes (rather than outputs of these processes) or have been reanalyzed as Bare Out Conditions that apply as legibility conditions at the interfaces and so are not properly parts of the grammar.

There is more. MP accounts generally incorporate an operation Transfer that peels off the information relevant to AP from that relevant to CI and sends these informationally specialized phrase markers off to the AP or CI for interpretation. Multiple Spell Out (MSO) versions of Transfer do this periodically. In contrast, a non-MSO version of Transfer would do this once

8.5 The Merge Hypothesis and the Y-Model

when the entire derivation converges.[23] Importantly, Transfer sends a derived grammatical object to the interfaces for interpretation. Importantly, the interfaces are not part of the grammar. That would seem to imply that after Transfer, grammatical operations should no longer apply to the objects that have been transferred. The standard view is that the interfaces are interpretive rather than generative, which means that they read/interpret what they have been given using whatever non-grammatical principles and operations are unique to them. And if this is right, then MP theories cannot treat covert movement as post-Transfer applications of I-merge because I-merge does not apply post-Transfer, Merge being a grammatical operation, not an interface operation. And this suggests that covert movement in the GB sense cannot be a feature of minimalist theories.

Things are actually more complicated still. It is not clear that standard applications of covert movement of the GB variety *could* apply even if we allowed Merge to apply post-Transfer. Think of Quantifier Raising or *Wh*-Raising in *wh-in-situ* languages. In embedded clauses, these operations would target embedded positions. Thus, say that Quantifier Raising moved quantified expressions to the edge of vP or TP. This sort of movement would be illicit in embedded clauses as it would seem to violate the No Tampering Condition (recall, the NTC requires that Merge always be at the root, and by definition an embedded position is not at the root). Similarly, *Wh*-raising could move *Wh*s to embedded Spec C positions and this too would violate the NTC. If correct, this alone suffices to argue that there is no analogue of covert *movement* in an MP theory (at least if movement is I-merge). And if this is right then much of the information coded via covert movement in GB accounts must be handled in some other way in MP theories, for the only way to do movement in MP theories is via I-merge, and such movement must obey the NTC and *therefore* such movement must apply before Transfer.

In sum, MP accounts that center the MH look to be incompatible with the Y-model.

So, how might covert movement effects be incorporated in a Merge-based minimalist theory? Here is one way.[24] Covert movement is simply overt movement *plus* the deletion of higher copies in the phrase marker interpreted at AP. All movement is "overt" in the sense of applying in the syntax before Transfer.

---

[23] MSO is the dominant view of Transfer nowadays. Thus, interpretation occurs phase by phase with completed phases "sent to" the interfaces for AP and CI interpretation. However, there are puzzles that arise from this way of viewing things. For example, there are many interpretive operations that seem to involve the whole phrase marker (e.g. think pronominal binding, or reconstruction effects, or rising intonation for questions). These cannot be calculated until more or less the whole output sentence is available. Such phenomena vastly complicate the idea that interpretation proceeds phase by phase. That said, I leave these issues to one side here.
[24] See Bobaljik (2002).

What distinguishes movement with and without AP effects is which copies are retained for AP interpretation. If we understand copy deletion as part of Transfer then when Transfer applies to a syntactic phrase marker, all but one of the copies that are the products of I-merge are deleted (this, at least, is the standard case) and only one survives to the interfaces to be interpreted there. Thus, for example, in overt *Wh*-movement languages the *Wh*-copy that survives for CI interpretation is the same as the one that survives for AP interpretation. This contrasts with a *wh-in-situ* language where the *Wh* that is AP interpreted is the bottom copy while the one relevant for CI interpretation is the top one. Importantly, this approach gets the frequent "mismatches" between sound and meaning that motivated covert movement proposals in GB but without a covert movement operation. In effect, covert movement effects do not require covert movement operations and so don't require the Y-model. All that is required is that the interfaces treat copies differently.

If this is correct, then MP theories reject the Y-model of derivations that is central to GB, and they do so quite radically. Not only does MP dispense with DS and SS and the conditions that apply to each, it even rejects the idea of covert movement. Indeed, it appears to be theoretically incompatible with this kind of operation. In place of covert movement, Merge-based accounts have differential copy deletion in Transfer to AP and CI.

In sum, the MH conception of a derivation is radically different from that of the Y-model in GB. In place of D-structure, there is the selection of expressions from the numeration.[25] These are combined to form complex hierarchically structured objects via repeated applications of Merge. At some point, these complex constructed objects are Transferred to AP and CI and as part of this process, copies/occurrences are deleted. The analogue of the split in the Y-model derivation is that Transfer to AP is not the same operation as Transfer to CI as different copies can be deleted in the two applications of Transfer. Thus, Transfer is not a unitary process. But then it was never thought to be, for everyone has always believed that what gets transferred to AP is not the same as what gets transferred to CI. What gets transferred to AP is linguistic information relevant to the "sound" system. What gets transferred to CI is

---

[25] More exactly, if there is a one-time selection of atoms then we have a numeration. But nothing said here is incompatible with a model where selection from the lexicon can occur repeatedly and the numeration is dispensed with. There are various theoretical and empirical arguments that have been made *for* numerations. Chomsky has claimed that these reduce computational complexity because accessing the numeration is onerous and multiple retrievals of lexical atoms from the numeration is more onerous than a one-time retrieval of multiple atoms. I have never understood these arguments and do not see why repeated access to the lexicon is worse than a one-time selection of all the atoms to be merged. As for the empirical arguments, they largely revolve around the empirical utility of the Merge over Move condition and whether phase regulates derivations. If derivations are phase based in some rich sense then it would seem that access to the lexicon is not completely free. At any rate, I leave these issues aside here.

what is relevant to "meaning." And these two kinds of information are very different, as Saussure long ago pointed out. So in a generic MP theory that takes Merge to be the basic combinatoric operation, there is little left of the theoretical structure offered in GB. All there is are lexical atoms that combine via Merge and that get interpreted at two distinct interfaces after some copy deletion. This is all pretty minimal (in the sense that any theory needs at least this) save for the requirement that (all but one of the) copies delete. Why we don't eschew deletion and just interpret *all* the copies at AP and CI is quite unclear (theoretically, not empirically). What would be wrong with that! I could speculate (others have – Chomsky has suggested that this too is an effect of computational efficiency (maybe)) but not in an interesting manner. So I won't. Feel free.

8.6 The EMH and Language in the Brain

Consider now one more nice consequence of the MH should it prove tenable. As I have repeated repeatedly, the Chomsky program in Generative Grammar takes the aim of linguistics as being to provide a description of the faculty of language, in particular, those properties of FL that are specifically linguistic (rather than cognitively and computationally general). The general idea has been that providing a decent description of these bespoke mental properties would facilitate the *further* project of discovering how FL is realized in brainware. However, as Poeppel and Embick (2005) have argued, coordinating the mental concepts from linguistics with neural concepts has not proven to be particularly easy. The main problem has been that there are too many of each and the required concepts seem to be of the wrong grain size to snugly match. One nice consequence of the Merge Hypothesis (or at least the Extended Merge Hypothesis outlined here) is that it provides a path for bridging the gap between the two sets of concepts, making their mutual mapping potentially easier.[26] Here is what I mean.

The basic architecture of GB is very busy. It contains lots of basic concepts, and the project of showing how they are each realized in brain matter is correspondingly very demanding. The MH version of MP greatly simplifies the problem. How? Well, if the EMH is correct, then all of the myriad effects identified by GB are functions of the operation of Merge. That is what the Fundamental Principle of Grammar asserts, and it is at the core of the EMH. So if the EMH is roughly right, then finding out how FL is realized in brains

---

[26] Note the guarded locutions. This is very hard stuff, and right now the best we can do is point to possibilities rather than argue for specific realizations. That said, I mention this here because I believe the problem to have been made substantially easier if the offered unification of GB's properties as all instances of Merge is essentially on the right track.

amounts to finding out how Merge is incarnated in wetware. And if the version of Merge adopted here is on the right track, then one way of zeroing in on how Merge is realized in brains is to discover how brains track constituents. Why so? Because the products of Merge are unboundedly complex hierarchically ordered constituents, constituents being labeled sets, and labels being lexical atoms. So if the EMH is on the right track then we should expect humans to be exclusively (i.e. species specifically) adept at identifying constituents of arbitrary complexity precisely because we have Merge as part of our cognitive repertoire and other animals do not. And if being constituency-competent is what makes us linguistically capable (which is a consequence of the EMH) then we can start looking for those parts of the brain that respond to constituents and we can then investigate how brains do it.

A couple more remarks.

First, it is important to see that this directed quest for the neural markers of constituents as the key to understanding the neural basis of human linguistic competence only makes sense if some version of the EMH is correct. What I have tried to show is that the EMH suffices to explain a good chunk of what Generative Grammar has taken to be the distinctive features of linguistic competence, and hence the linguistically proprietary features of FL. The book has argued that we can unify a pretty large number of grammatical effects that Generativists have understood to reflect the basic architecture of FL if we assume them all to be products of Merge (understood to include labeling). And as this conception of Merge places at its center the classical notion of the constituent, then focusing on constituents allows us to zero in on what is linguistically specific about the language-ready brain.

Second, this kind of investigation is not premature. There is already interesting work that provides brain measures that appear to be sensitive to constituency (see Ding et al. 2016). This is exactly what we would hope to find if the EMH is on the right track. Of course, this work is still at the early stages, but it is of the right kind. That said, we would want more. We would not only like to show that human brains track constituency, but we would like to know how they do this. In particular, we would like to understand how brain circuits embody the Merge operation itself, for Merge is what underlies the capacity to generate unboundedly complex hierarchical structures (i.e. constituents) that include smaller constituents as subparts. Merge is the prize, for once we see how brains embody it, we will understand what it takes for brains to be language ready and for humans to be syntactically competent.

Third, the particular contribution of the EMH to these neuro investigations is that it identifies *one* target for investigation. Without the EMH, syntactic competence appears to involve a whole slew of capacities that appear to be quite different from one another. The virtue of the EMH is that it unifies these

8.6 The EMH and Language in the Brain

into one simple notion, Merge (again, understood as incorporating labels), whose product is, at bottom, a well-known object, the constituent (labeled sets). If the EMH is basically right, then most of the core dependencies Generative Grammar has identified over the last sixty years (e.g. movement, binding, control, reconstruction), and the conditions on these (c-command) and the relations it has discovered that grammars exploit (A-/A'-binding, selection, subcategorization) can all be understood as aspects of Merge. And it is this unification that makes the exclusive focus on constituency in the hunt for the neural substrates of grammar a reasonable one. Absent this kind of unification, there is no reason to believe that constituency per se is the key to unlocking the secret of linguistic competence and the central notion that we want the neuro-science of language to ground.[27]

---

[27] There is one topic that this book has avoided discussing, though mention of it is sprinkled in the footnotes. That topic is sidewards movement. I have restricted discussion to examples where derivations take place within single-rooted sub-trees and where dependencies are regulated by c-command between links. However, there is a literature that I am very fond of that argues that derivations can be more expansive than this and that one can have dependencies between non-c-commanding expressions. See, for example, Nunes (2001, 2004) and Hornstein (2001, 2008), and Bleam and Hornstein (2018). If the EMH is correct, then almost certainly grammars countenance derivations *between* sub-trees. (i) offers two examples of constructions that have such dependencies:
(i) a. Which book$_1$ did you read t$_1$ without Fred's reviewing t$_1$
   b. Mary$_1$ was hugged t$_1$ by John before PRO$_1$ leaving the dais
I, following others, have analyzed these constructions (and others) as requiring sidewards movement between unconnected sub-trees. And I still believe these arguments have merits. However, I will not discuss them here. For extended discussion, the interested reader is referred to the indicated references, and especially Hornstein (2008), where I make the case at length.

9 Conclusion

This book had three main goals.

The first was to identify the set of problems that the Minimalist Program (MP) took as its own. I tried to realize this objective by locating MP in the wider Chomskyan version of the Generative enterprise. I reviewed how two big facts (viz. linguistic creativity and linguistic flexibility) set the problem space for the first four decades of research and how the (relatively successful) solutions to these two problems set the scene for Minimalism. I also focused on how in an important sense the subject matter of MP is different from (though intimately related to) that of the earlier periods. The explananda of the first forty years of Generative investigation were the structure of particular grammars and the structure of the faculty of language (FL) that explained why particular grammars take the general shapes they do. The target of minimalist explanations is the structure of FL itself. The central minimalist question is the following: Why does FL have the particular properties Generativists discovered it to have and not other conceivable ones? In other words, whereas early Generative work aimed to describe the properties language-specific grammars have and to explain why they have them, Minimalism aims to explain why FL has the peculiar properties it has. MP thus takes as its own a very abstract question, one whose appropriateness rests on assuming that prior work on the first two questions was largely correct. It does not pay to ask why FL has (for example) GB-like properties if it is *wrong* to think that it does. In other words, on my telling, MP *presupposes* that earlier theoretical work essentially correctly identified the core properties of language-particular grammars *as well as* traced the key structural features of FL. With this firmly assumed, and only with this firmly assumed, does it make sense to ask the MP question. Hence the forty-year wait, or so I argued.

Let me hit this point harder still. One of the points I have tried to make is that it is very hard (if not impossible) to construct decent theory in the absence of having a clear explanandum. Methodology alone will not get one far. Pursuing simplicity or elegance or naturalness will lead to largely airy assertions in the absence of specifying exactly what we aim to simply, elegantly, and naturally explain. IMO, too much of minimalist "building theory from the bottom up"

9 Conclusion

has led to fluffy remonstration and simplicity mongering. Don't get me wrong, there is NOTHING wrong with aiming for simplicity, elegance and naturalness. No good theory eschews these three virtues. However, they are idle slogans in the absence of a specified target of explanation. To paraphrase Kant: Simple, elegant, natural theory without an explanandum is aimless, while an explanandum without simple, elegant, natural theory is pointless. If this is right, then too much minimalist research has suffered from the absence of a clear target of explanation, no clear specification of what the proffered theory is a theory of. This book has proposed that the proper target of minimalist investigation is the structure of FL (i.e. why does FL look the way it does?) and has operationalized this by taking GB and its relatively well-specified description of FL as the concrete target. Given this target, we can ground our theoretical proposals.

Taking this tack also serves a second useful purpose. An important one, at least as it relates explaining Generative research to the wider scientific public. It highlights the cumulative nature of the Generative Program. And this cumulativity is very important. Why? Because a distinctive mark of a successful research program in the sciences is that it builds on its successful past discoveries. In contrast, one good mark of a degenerate program is that it looks like every change in theory means discarding what we thought we knew and starting afresh all over again. After a few such "successful" revolutions who can blame an onlooker for concluding that the field is simply confused. Too much minimalist research appears to condemn all prior Generative work to the flames, suggesting it to have been almost entirely worthless, without explanatory value and at best "mere" description. Not only is this false if the story I have outlined above is on the right track, but it is also self-defeating as it plays right into the hands of those that think the Generative Program has been one big con job. What better mark of sterility than a new "revolution" every decade! This needs to stop for the very good reason that it is false (i.e. as indicated here, MP directly builds on the prior sixty years of Generative research and is the next obvious step for the Generative Program to take given the success of this earlier inquiry) and a public relations disaster. Sterile and self-defeating – not a great combination.

So, in sum, I have argued that MP has often received a rocky reception because it has not been clear about its core research question. It should not be surprising that people do not understand answers to questions that they don't know have been asked. But so it is. I hope that what I have written clears up this confusion. I also hope that this will put to bed any general hostility to MP research, though this is likely asking too much.

The second goal has been to outline what I take to be the best answer to the core minimalist question: the Merge Hypothesis (MH). In contrast to MP, which is a program, MH is a theory. Programs are fecund or sterile, theories are true or false. At root, MH conjectures that the structure of FL can be largely understood in terms of the properties of the generative procedure that underlies the recursive properties of the grammars that FL licenses. Or to put this another way, MH is the theory that says once you understand exactly how FL delivers grammars that are linguistically productive (that generate unboundedly complex hierarchical structures of the kind we find), you will also understand most of the other properties that FL has.

This is a really bold thesis. It gets most of its interest from an intriguing argument form we can trace back to Chomsky (1995a). Here is the conjecture: Unbounded hierarchy is the product of a very simple combinatoric operation (i.e. Merge). What makes a combination operation simple? It takes two linguistic objects and puts them together as simply as possible. And what is "as simply as possible"? Well, it doesn't do anything other than combine them. It doesn't change them in combining them and doesn't order them in combining them. It just combines them! That's how simple. We explore how far this idea gets us in Chapter 2 (which is surprisingly far). And I further elaborate MH to allow the Extended Merge Hypothesis (EMH) to cover yet more properties Generative Grammar has attributed to the basic architecture of FL.

The extension I propose reduces to taking the classical notion of the constituent as the basic building block of grammar. I implement this idea by enshrining the very old idea that the basic combinatoric operation does two things. It combines two objects together and uses the name of one of the two objects combined to name the resultant combination. In effect this adds a (endocentric) labeling operation to the process of combination. I then propose a Fundamental Principle of Grammar (FPG) that requires that all grammatical dependencies be mediated by this specific Merge operation. Let me reiterate one more time that in this I have followed the lead of others, in particular Noam Chomsky, Sam Epstein and John Collins, each of whom has proposed what I see as similar versions of the FPG. At any rate, the FPG articulates a version of the strong minimalist thesis, the idea that the core features of FL can all be explained in terms of the principle that all grammatical dependencies are Merge-mediated dependencies. Chapters 2 through 6 argue that this conjecture has a lot going for it (despite the many obvious problems (some of which I canvass) that I set aside as puzzles to be solved by future sedulous graduate students). Chapter 7 returns to refocus on labeling and argues that the apparent complexity of my revised version of Merge (in fact the earliest version of Merge) has a lot going for it and suffers from none of the methodological problems that initial inspection might suggest.

In sum, EMH is a Merge-based account intended to address the central question posed by MP. In particular, the development of the EMH operationalizes MP so that it goes beyond programmatic pronouncements. Programs that fail to do this are of little value. EMH is intended to illustrate exactly how

9 Conclusion

the programmatic basics of Minimalism can lead to specific empirical theories with good empirical coverage and substantial explanatory power. In other words, MH and EMH are proof that the MP pudding is worth eating and is not just a bunch of pretty (empty) words.

The third aim of the book should be satisfied if the first two have been (even partially) achieved. The third aim is to defend the legitimacy of the minimalist questions and the progressivity (in Lakatos's sense) of the Generative Program. The success of the Generative Program (and its last minimalist phase) is manifest by the fact that it has allowed us to formulate increasingly abstract questions concerning human linguistic competence *and* to offer reasonable, empirically justifiable answers to those questions, the most abstract questions and answers being the subject matter of minimalist inquiry.

Truth be told, MP has not really taken the world by storm. Even many syntacticians shy away from it and often denigrate the kind of research that flies under the minimalist banner. As I mentioned, this is partly due to the fact that many have failed to understand what the central minimalist question is. But many have also failed to appreciate how MH is intended to address these questions and how we might extend MH to further the program. Hopefully, this book can serve as a model of how these fit together.

And I do mean a model. As should be clear, this book more or less enshrines GB results as gospel. No agnostic grumblings from me about their adequacy. I am sure that many don't feel the same way. But that is fine. Even if you don't, hopefully this book illustrates how to take your favorite unassailable linguistic results and minimalize them. The general approach can be applied beginning from non-GB starting points. And that is fine as far as I am concerned. What Minimalism needs is some description of FL. This book has taken GB to offer one such credible description. But, should it prove inadequate, then the same minimalist questions can be asked of the more adequate formulations: Why does FL look THIS way?

This conceded, I do think GB is a pretty good theory of FL and I do think that trying to find a way of explaining why our FL has GBish properties is a very good project. But I am also pretty sure GB is not the last word on what kinds of linguistic phenomena FL regulates, and so I am pretty sure that deriving the properties of GB is not the last word in minimalist theory. What I am also pretty sure about is that just as theories of FL (like GB) need some idea of what properties individual grammars have to get off the ground, so minimalist theories need to have some conceptions of the properties of FL to get off the ground. And hopefully, dear reader, you now agree with this, if with nothing else. Thanks for your solicitude in reading all that has come before.

Bibliography

Ackerman, L., M. Frazier and M. Yoshida. 2018. Resumptive pronouns can ameliorate illicit island extractions. *Linguistic Inquiry*, 49.4: 847–59.
Aoun, J. 1986. *Generalized Binding: The Syntax and Logical Form of Wh Interrogatives*. De Gruyter Mouton.
Aoun, J., N. Hornstein, D. Lightfoot and A. Weinberg. 1987. Two types of locality. *Linguistic Inquiry*, 18.4: 537–77.
Aoun, J., L. Choueiri and N. Hornstein. 2001. Resumption, movement and derivational economy. *Linguistic Inquiry*, 32.3: 371–403.
Baltin, M. 1995. Floating quantifiers, PRO, and predication. *Linguistic Inquiry*, 26: 199–248.
Bejar, S. and D. Massam. 1999. Multiple case checking. *Syntax*, 2: 65–79.
Berwick, R. and S.D. Epstein. 1995. On the convergence of "minimalist" syntax and categorial grammar. Presented at *1st international AMSAT Workshop in Language Processing* (AMiLP) '95), University of Twente, Enschede, Netherlands, December 6–8.
Berwick, R. and A. Weinberg. 1984. *The Grammatical Basis of Linguistic Performance*. MIT Press.
Berwick, R. and A. Weinberg. 1986. *The Grammatical Basis of Linguistic Performance*. MIT Press.
Bickerton, D. 1984. The language bioprogram hypothesis. *Behavioral and Brain Sciences*, 7.2: 173–88. https://doi.org/10.1017/S0140525X00044149.
Bleam, T. and N. Hornstein. 2018. Deriving multiple "object" constructions. In A. Gallego and R. Martin (eds.), *Language Syntax, and the Natural Sciences*, pp. 9–33. Cambridge University Press.
Bobaljik, J. 2002. A-chains at the PF interface: Copies and covert movement. *Natural Language and Linguistic Theory*, 20: 197–267.
Boeckx, C. and N. Hornstein. 2007. On (non-)obligatory control. In W.D. Davis and S. Dubinsky (eds.), *New Horizons in the Analysis of Control and Raising*, pp. 251–62. Springer.
Boeckx, C., N. Hornstein and J. Nunes. 2007. Overt copies in reflexive and control structures: A movement analysis. In A. Conroy, C. Jing, C. Nakao and E. Takahashi (eds.), *University of Maryland Working Papers in Linguistics*, 15: 1–46.
Boeckx, C., N. Hornstein and J. Nunes. 2010. *Control as Movement*. Cambridge University Press.
Bowers, J. 1973. *Grammatical Relations*. Ph.D. thesis, MIT.
Branigan, P. 1992. *Subjects and Complementizers*. Ph.D. thesis, MIT.

Brody, M. 1993. θ-theory and arguments. *Linguistic Inquiry*, 24: 1–23.
Brown, R. 1973. *A First Language*. Harvard University Press.
Bruening, B. 2014. Precede-and-command revisited. *Language*, 90.2: 342–88.
Cable, S. 2007. *The Grammar of Q: Q-Particles and the Nature of Wh-Fronting, as Revealed by the Wh-Questions of Tlingit*. Ph.D. thesis, MIT.
Cartwright, N. 1999. *The Dappled World: A Study of the Boundaries of Science*. Cambridge University Press.
Chomsky, N. 1955 (printed 1975). *The Logical Structure of Linguistic Theory*. Springer.
Chomsky, N. 1964. *Current Issues in Linguistic Theory*. Mouton.
Chomsky, N. 1965. *Aspects of a Theory of Syntax*. MIT Press.
Chomsky, N. 1967. A review of B.F. Skinner's *Verbal Behavior*. In L.A. Jakobovits and M.S. Miron (eds.), *Readings in the Psychology of Language*, pp. 142–43. Prentice Hall.
Chomsky, N. 1973. Conditions on transformations. In S.R. Anderson and P. Kiparsky (eds.), *A Festschrift for Morris Halle*, pp. 232–86. Holt, Rinehart & Winston.
Chomsky, N. 1975 (1956). *Logical Structure of Linguistic Theory*. Plenum/University of Chicago Press.
Chomsky, N. 1977. On *Wh*-movement. In P. Cullicover, T. Wasow and A. Akmajian (eds.), *Formal Syntax*, pp. 71–132. Academic Press.
Chomsky, N. 1981. *Lectures on Government and Binding*. Foris Publications.
Chomsky, N. 1986a. *Knowledge of Language*. Praeger.
Chomsky, N. 1986b. *Barriers*. MIT Press.
Chomsky, N. 1993. The minimalist program. In Chomsky 1995a, pp. 167–217.
Chomsky, N. 1995a. *The Minimalist Program*. MIT Press.
Chomsky, N. 1995b. Bare phrase structure. In G. Webelhuth (ed.), *Government and Binding Theory and the Minimalist Program*, pp. 383–400. Blackwell.
Chomsky, N. 2013. Problems of projection. *Lingua*, 130: 33–49.
Chomsky, N. 2018. *What Kind of Creatures Are We?* Columbia University Press.
Chomsky, N. 2021. Minimalism: Where are we now and where can we hope to go. *Gengo Kenkyu (Journal of the Linguistic Society of Japan)*, 160: 1–41. https://doi.org/10.11435/gengo.160.0_1.
Collins, C. 2002. Eliminating labels. In S. Epstein and T.D. Seely (eds.), *Derivation and Explanation in the Minimalist Program*, pp. 43–64. Blackwell.
Collins, C. and E. Stabler. 2016. A formalization of minimalist syntax. *Syntax*, 19.1: 43–78.
Collins, J. 2007. Syntax, more or less. *Mind*, 116(464): 805–850.
Collins, J. 2020. Conjoining meanings without losing our heads. *Mind and Language*, 35: 224–36.
D'Alessandro, R. 2019. The achievements of Generative Syntax: A time chart and some reflections. *Catalan Journal of Linguistics Special Issue*: 7–26.
David, P. 1985. Clio and the economics of QWERTY. *The American Economic Review*, 75.2: 332–37.
de Marken, Carl. 1995. On the unsupervised induction of phrase structure grammars. In SIGDAT 1995. www.demarcken.org/carl/papers/sigdat.pdf.
Demirdache, H. 1991. *Resumptive Chains in Restricted Relatives, Appositives and Dislocation Structures*. Ph.D. dissertation, MIT.
Demirdache, H. and O. Percus. 2011. Resumptives, movement and interpretation. In A. Rouveret (ed.), *Resumptive Pronouns at the Interfaces*, pp. 367–94. John Benjamins.

Ding, N. L. Melloni, H. Zhang, X. Tian and D. Poeppel. 2016. Cortical tracking of hierarchical linguistic structures in connected speech. *Nature Neuroscience*, 19: 158–64.
Doliana, A. 2021. *All about Alles: The Syntax of Wh-Quantifier Float in German*. Ph.D. dissertation, University of Maryland.
Drummond, A. and D. Kush. 2015. "Reanalysis" is raising to object. *Syntax*, 18.4: 425–63.
Enc, M. 1981. *Tense Without Scope: An Analysis of Nouns as Indexicals*. Ph.D. dissertation, University of Wisconsin.
Epstein, S.D. 1999. Un-principled syntax: The derivation of syntactic relations. In Epstein and Hornstein, pp. 317–45.
Epstein, S.D. and N. Hornstein (eds.). 1999. *Working Minimalism*. MIT Press.
Epstein, S.D., E. Groat, R. Kawashima and H. Kitahara. 1998. *A Derivational Approach to Syntactic Relations*. Oxford University Press.
Epstein, S.D., H. Kitahara and T. D. Seely. 2015. *Explorations in Maximizing Syntactic Minimization*. Routledge.
Epstein, S.D., H. Kitahara and T.D. Seely. 2022. *A Minimalist Theory of Simplest Merge*. Routledge.
Evans, G. 1980. Pronouns. *Linguistic Inquiry*, 11.2: 337–62.
Ferreira, M. 2009. Null subjects and finite control in Brazilian Portuguese. In J. Nunes (ed.), *Minimalist Essays in Brazilian Portuguese Syntax*, pp. 17–49. John Benjamins.
Fujii, T. 2005. *Cycle, Linearization of Chains, and Multiple Case Checking*. Ms., University of Maryland.
Gallistel, C.R. 2018. Finding numbers in the brain. *Philosophical Transactions of the Royal Society*, B373: 20170119. http://dx.doi.org/10.1098/rstb.2017.0119.
Haddad, Y.A. and E. Potsdam. 2013. Linearizing the control relation: A typology. In T. Biberauer and I. Roberts (eds.), *Challenges to Linearization*, pp. 235–68. De Gruyter Mouton.
Haegeman, L. 1991. *Introduction to Government and Binding Theory*. Wiley-Blackwell.
Higginbotham, J. 1985. On semantics. *Linguistic Inquiry*, 16.4: 547–93.
Hornstein, N. 2001. *Move! A Minimalist Theory of Construal*. Blackwell.
Hornstein, N. 2003. On control. In R. Hendrick (ed.), *Minimalist Syntax*, pp. 6–81. Blackwell.
Hornstein, N. 2008. *A Theory of Syntax*. Cambridge University Press.
Hornstein, N. 2017. On Merge. In J. McGilvray (ed.), *The Cambridge Companion to Chomsky*, pp. 69–86. Cambridge University Press.
Hornstein, N. 2018. The minimalist program after 25 years. *Annual Review of Linguistics*, 4: 49–65.
Hornstein, N. 2019. The stupendous success of the Minimalist Program. In A. Kertész, E. Moravcsik and C. Rákosi (eds.), *Current Approaches to Syntax*, pp. 187–214. De Gruyter Mouton.
Hornstein, N. and J. Nunes. 2014. Movement and control. In A. Carnie, Y. Sato and D. Siddiqi (eds.), *The Routledge Handbook of Syntax*, pp. 239–63. Routledge.
Hornstein, N. and M. Polinsky. 2010. Control as movement across languages and constructions. In N. Hornstein and M. Polinsky (eds.), *Movement Theory of Control*, pp. 1–42. John Benjamins.
Hornstein, N., H. Lasnik and J. Uriagereka. 2003/2007. The dynamics of Islands: Speculations on the locality of movement. *Linguistic Analysis*, 33: 149–75.
Hornstein, N., J. Nunes and K. Grohmann. 2005. *Understanding Minimalism*. Cambridge University Press.

Huang, C.-T.J. 1982. Move *Wh*-in a language without *Wh*-movement. *Linguistic Review*, 1: 369–416.

Hunter, T. 2021. The Chomsky Hierarchy. In N. Allott, T. Lohndal and G. Rey (eds.), *Blackwell Companion to Chomsky*, pp. 74–95. Wiley-Blackwell

Idsardi, W. and J. Lidz. 1998. Chains and phono-logical form. In A. Dimitriadis, H. Lee, C. Moisset and A. Williams (eds.), *U. Penn Working Papers in Linguistics*, 5.1: 109–25.

Ito, Y. 2010. *Syntax and Semantics of Long-Distance Reflexives: An Overt Movement Analysis*. M.A. thesis, University of Tokyo.

Jackendoff, R. 1990. On Larson's analysis of the double object construction. *Linguistic Inquiry*, 21: 427–56.

Kayne, R. 1994. *The Antisymmetry of Syntax*. MIT Press.

Kayne, R. 2002. Pronouns and their antecedents. In S. Epstein and T.D. Seely (eds.), *Derivation and Explanation in the Minimalist Program*, pp. 133–66. Blackwell.

Keller, F. 2000. *Gradience in Grammar: Experimental and Computational Aspects of Degrees of Grammaticality*. Ph.D. thesis, University of Edinburgh.

King, J. 1986. Pronouns, descriptions and the semantics of discourse. *Philosophical Studies*, 51: 341–63.

Koopman, H. and D. Sportiche. 1991. The position of subjects. *Lingua*, 85: 211–58.

Koster, J. 1984. On binding and control. *Linguistic Inquiry*, 15: 417–59.

Kuroda, Y. 1988. Whether we agree or not: A comparative syntax of English and Japanese. *Linguisticae Investigationes*, 12: 1–47.

Landau, I. 2000. *Elements of Control*. Springer.

Landau, I. 2006. Chain resolution in Hebrew V(P) fronting. *Syntax*, 9.1: 32–66.

Landau, I. 2011. Predication vs. aboutness in copy raising. *Natural Language and Linguistic Theory*, 29: 779–813.

Larson, R. 1990. Double objects revisited: Reply to Jackendoff. *Linguistic Inquiry*, 21: 589–632.

Lasnik, H. 1986. On the necessity of binding conditions. In C.H. Lasnik, *Essays on Anaphora*, pp. 149–67. Kluwer.

Lasnik, H. 1991. On the necessity of binding conditions. In R. Freidin (ed.), *Principles and Parameters in Comparative Grammar*, pp. 7–28. MIT Press. [Reprinted in H. Lasnik, *Essays on Anaphora*, pp. 149–67, Kluwer, 1989.]

Lasnik, H. and M. Saito. 1984. On the nature of proper government. *Linguistic Inquiry*, 15: 235–89.

Lasnik, H. and M. Saito. 1991. On the subject of infinitives. In L. Dobrin et al. (eds.), *Papers from the 27th Regional Meeting of the Chicago Linguistics Society*, pp. 324–43. Chicago Linguistics Society.

Lees, R. and E. Klima. 1963. Rules for English pronominalization. *Language*, 39.1: 17–28.

Li, D., L. Grohe, P. Schulz and C. Yang. 2021. The distributional learning of recursive structures. In *Proceedings of the 45th annual Boston University Conference on Language Development*, pp. 471–85. Cascadilla Press.

Lidz, J. and A. Drummond. 2012. *Island Introducing Reflexives in Kannada*. Unpublished ms. University of Maryland.

Lu, J., C.K. Thompson and M. Yoshida. 2020. Chinese *wh-in-situ* and islands: A formal judgment study. *Linguistic Inquiry*, 51.3. 611–23.

Manzini, M.R. 1983. On control and control theory. *Linguistic Inquiry*, 14: 421–46.

Manzini, M.R. and A. Roussou. 2000. A minimalist theory of A-movement and control. *Lingua*, 110.6: 409–47.
Marantz, A. 1984. *On the Nature of Grammatical Relations*. MIT Press.
Marantz, A. 1991. Case and licensing. In G. Westphal, B. Ao and H.-R. Chae (eds.), *Proceedings of the 8th Eastern Conference on Linguistics (ESCOL 8)*, pp. 234–53. CLC Publications.
Marcus, G. 2001. *The Algebraic Mind*. MIT Press.
McCloskey, J. 1997. Subjecthood and subject positions. In L. Haegeman (ed.), *Elements of Grammar: Handbook of Generative Syntax*, pp. 197–235. Kluwer.
McCloskey, J. 2000. Quantifier float and *Wh*-movement in an Irish English. *Linguistic Inquiry*, 31.1: 57–84.
McCloskey, J. 2006. Resumption. In M. Everaert and H. van Riemskijk (eds.), *The Blackwell Companion to Syntax*, pp. 94–117. Blackwell.
Merchant, J. 2019. Roots don't select, categorial heads do: Lexical-selection of PPs may vary by category. *Linguistic Review*, 36.3: 325–41.
Moro, A. 2016. *Impossible Languages*. MIT Press.
Motomura, M. 2002. *Zibun: An analysis based on movement*. M.A. thesis, University of Maryland.
Muysken, P. 1982. *Parameterizing the notion of "head."* PDF, Radboud Repository, Nijmegen. https://repository.ubn.ru.nl/bitstream/handle/2066/14544/3884.pdf.
Nunes, J. 2001. Sidewards movement. *Linguistic Inquiry*, 32: 303–44.
Nunes, J. 2004. *Linearization of Chains and Sidewards Movement*. MIT Press.
Nunes, J. 2019. Remarks on finite control and hyper-raising in Brazilian Portuguese. *Journal of Portuguese Linguistics*, 18.1: 4.
Obata, M. and S.D. Epstein. 2011. Feature splitting, internal Merge: Improper movement, intervention and the A/A' distinction. *Syntax*, 14.2: 122–47.
Ortega-Santos, I. 2011. On relativized minimality, memory and cue-based parsing. *Iberia: International Journal of Theoretical Linguistics*, 3: 35–64.
Partee, B.H. 1971. On the requirement that transformations preserve meaning. In C.J. Fillmore and D.T. Langendoen (eds.), *Studies in Linguistic Semantics*, pp. 1–21. Holt, Rinehart & Winston.
Pesetsky, D. 1982. *Paths and Categories*. Ph.D. thesis, MIT.
Pesetsky, D. and E. Torrego. 2000. T-to-C movement: causes and consequences. In M. Kenstowicz (ed.), *Ken Hale: A Life in Language*, pp. 355–426. MIT Press.
Pietroski, P. 2018. *Conjoining Meanings: Semantics without Truth Values*. Oxford University Press.
Poeppel, D. and D. Embick 2005. Defining the relation between linguistics and neuroscience. In A. Cutler (ed.), *Twenty-First Century Psycholinguistics: Four Cornerstones*, pp. 103–18. Lawrence Erlbaum.
Polinsky, M. and E. Potsdam. 2002. Backward control. *Linguistic Inquiry*, 33: 245–82.
Polinsky, M. and E. Potsdam. 2006. Expanding the scope of control and raising. *Syntax*, 9.2: 171–92.
Polinsky, M. and E. Potsdam. 2012. Backward raising. *Syntax*, 15.1: 75–108.
Polinsky, M., L. Clemens, A. Morgan, M. Xiang and D. Heestland. 2013. Resumption in English. In J. Sprouse and N. Hornstein (eds.), *Experimental Syntax and Island Effects*, pp. 341–59. Cambridge University Press.
Potsdam, E. and J. Runner. 2001. Richard returns: Copy raising and its implications. In H.E.M. Andronis, C. Ball and S. Neuvel (eds.), *Papers from the 37th*

Regional Meeting of the Chicago Linguistics Society, pp. 453–68. Chicago Linguistics Society.

Preminger, O. 2021. *The Anaphor Agreement Effect: Further Evidence Against Binding as Agreement*. Ms., University of Maryland.

Pylyshyn, Z. 1994. Primitive mechanisms of spatial attention. *Cognition*, 50: 363–84.

Quine, W.V.O. 1982. *Methods of Logic*. Harvard University Press.

Reinhart, T. 1983. *Anaphora and Semantic Interpretation*. Croom Helm.

Reuland, E. 2011. *Anaphora and Language Design*. MIT Press.

Richards, M. 2007. On feature inheritance: An argument from the Phase Impenetrability Condition. *Linguistic Inquiry*, 38: 563–72.

Richards, M. 2012. On feature inheritance, defective phases and the movement–morphology connection. In A. Gallego (ed.), *Phases*, pp. 195–232. De Gruyter.

Rizzi, L. 1990a. On the anaphor-agreement effect. *Rivista di Linguistica*, 2: 27–42.

Rizzi, L. 1990b. *Relativized Minimality*. MIT Press.

Rizzi, L. 1997. The fine structure of the left periphery. In L. Haegeman, *Elements of Grammar: A Handbook of Generative Syntax*, pp. 281–337. Kluwer.

Rodrigues, C. 2004. *Impoverished Morphology and A Movement Out of Case Domains*. Ph.D. thesis, University of Maryland.

Ross, J. R. 1965. *Constraints on Variables in Syntax*. Ph.D. dissertation, MIT.

Schein, B. 1994. *Plurals and Events*. MIT Press.

Slobin, D. 1986. *The Crosslinguistic Acquisition of Language*, I and II. Psychology Press.

Sportiche, D. 1986. Zibun. *Linguistic Inquiry*, 17.2: 369–74.

Sportiche, D. 2005. *Division of Labor between Merge and Move: Strict Locality of Selection and Apparent Reconstruction Paradoxes*. Ms. https://ling.auf.net/lingbuzz/000163.

Sportiche, D. 2017. *Relative Clauses*. Ms. https://ling.auf.net/lingbuzz/003444.

Sprouse, J. 2007. *A Program for Experimental Syntax*. Ph.D. dissertation, University of Maryland.

Sprouse, J., M. Wagers and C. Phillips. 2013. Deriving competing predictions from grammatical approaches and reductionist approaches to island effects. In J. Sprouse and N. Hornstein (eds.), *Experimental Syntax and Island Effects*, pp. 21–41. Cambridge University Press.

Stabler, E. 2010. Computational perspectives on Minimalism. In C. Boeckx (ed.), *Oxford Handbook of Linguistic Minimalism*, pp. 616–41. Oxford University Press.

Stamp, J. 2013. Fact or fiction? The legend of the QWERTY keyboard. *The Smithsonian Magazine*. May 3, 2013.

Wilson, G. 1984. Pronouns and pronominal descriptions: A new semantic category. *Philosophical Studies*, 45: 1–30.

Woolford, E. 1999. More on the anaphor-agreement effect. *Linguistic Inquiry*, 30: 257–87.

Zwart, J.-W. 2002. Issues relating to a derivational theory of binding. In S.D. Epstein and T.D. Seely (eds.), *Derivation and Explanation in the Minimalist Program*, Generative Syntax 6, pp. 269–302. Blackwell.

Index

A'-chain. *See* chain
A'-movement. *See* movement
A'-trace. *See* trace
A-chain. *See* chain
Ackerman, L., 132
Adjunct, 30, 219, 220–23
Agree, 2, 80–85, 92, 94, 95, 98, 142, 171, 174
agreement, 93, 94, 99, 107, 125, 173, 174, 222
  feature, 198
  inverse, 95
  labeling via, 193
A-movement. *See* movement
Anaphor Agreement Effect, 120, 126
anaphor/anaphora, 6, 23–26, 32–37, 42, 45, 60, 103–6, 116, 121, 125, 139, 141–44, 147, 149, 166, 176, 177, 180, 181
  long-distance, 127, 158, 179, 182, 183
anti-locality, 26, 180
Aoun, J., 103, 132, 133, 148, 160, 162, 220, 221
A-over-A condition, 175
AP interface, 68, 99, 104, 114–16, 124, 177, 187, 191, 220, 223–27
Arabic
  Jordanian, 130, 131, 133, 160, 161
  Lebanese, 132, 133, 148, 160, 162
A-trace. *See* trace
Autonomy of Syntax Thesis, 192

Baltin, M., 114
bar level, 76
Bare Out Condition, 185, 187, 189–92, 224
Bare Phrase Structure, 77, 97, 197, 204
barrier, 45, 83, 179, 216, 217, 218, 221, 222
Basic Property, 168, 171, 185, 186, 195, 199–205, 213
Bejar, S., 107
Berwick, R., 8, 16, 216
Bickerton, D., 16
binding
  semantic, 132, 146, 147, 148, 150, 161–65
  syntactic, 132, 146, 148, 161, 164, 165

Binding Principles
  Principle A, 29, 34–38, 101–3, 104–7, 120, 138–43, 149, 176, 180, 209
  Principle B, 29, 35, 36, 82, 127, 139, 140, 141, 149, 176, 180, 209
  Principle C, 24, 25, 29, 35, 36, 39, 42, 114–17, 122, 124, 127, 134, 146–50, 163, 176, 179–83
Binding Theory, 26, 27, 33, 102, 105, 106, 138–43, 145, 147, 149, 181
Bleam, T., 229
Bobaljik, J. D., 226
Boeckx, C., x, 112, 116, 164, 180, 183
Bowers, J., 101
Branigan, P., 85
Brazilian Portuguese, 113, 118
Brody, M., 137
Brown, R., 15
Bruening, B., 68, 202

Cable, S., 94
Cartwright, N., 39
case, viii, 7, 8, 29, 30, 44, 45, 81–85, 94, 99, 102–5, 119, 142, 170–76, 179, 180, 207
Categorial Grammar, 8
c-command, 25, 39, 45, 57, 58, 60, 83, 92, 96, 104–7, 112, 113, 120, 121, 124, 145, 146, 150, 162, 169, 173, 175, 176, 180, 181, 211, 218, 229
Central Dogma of Grammar (CDG), 8
chain
  A, 75–100, 110–13, 114, 116, 118, 120–23, 126, 137, 139, 140, 149, 150, 165, 177, 178–81, 182
  A', 101–26, 135, 138, 139, 145, 149, 150, 157, 165, 177–81, 182
Chinese, 31, 221, 222
Chomsky, N., ix, 1–7, 14–18, 21, 23, 28, 31, 36, 37, 42, 46, 48, 50, 57, 58, 63, 68, 75–78, 81–85, 98, 102–10, 129–32, 137, 141, 151, 171–76, 178, 193, 197, 198, 201, 205, 208, 210, 211, 221, 226, 227, 232
Choueiri, L., 132, 133

Index

CI interface, 9, 68, 69, 98, 99, 104, 108, 134, 154, 158, 177, 184–94, 220, 224, 226
Collins, C., 64, 76, 92, 145
Collins, J., ix, 8, 76, 188, 192, 232
concatenation, 8, 70, 195, 199, 200, 205
construal, 7, 44, 102–4, 107, 116, 124, 139, 141, 142, 145, 149, 150, 176, 207, 209, 211
Control, viii, 7, 22, 29, 39, 44, 57, 64, 101, 104, 107, 112, 115, 124, 125, 144, 176
   Backwards, 113–21, 166, 183
   Non-Obligatory, 164, 176, 183, 209
   Obligatory, 101–26, 162–65, 176, 180–83, 208, 209, 212
Coordinate Structure Constraint, 40
Copy (as an operation), 55, 150
Copy Theory of Movement (CTM), 58–65, 169, 178
criterial checking, 99
crossover, 39, 133, 182, 183
   strong, 127, 131, 133, 153, 154, 160, 162, 181
   weak, 127, 131, 134, 150–54, 158, 160, 162, 181, 192
cyclicity, 39, 169, 182, 193

D'Alessandro, R., 39
Darwin's Problem, 4–7, 38, 45, 46, 54, 55, 70, 167, 182, 183
David, P., 215
Demirdache, H., 130, 131, 133, 135, 145, 158
Dependent Case Theory, 82
Ding, N., 228
Doliana, A., 130
Dresher, E., 17
Drummond, A., 146, 158, 159
D-structure, 6, 22, 29, 33, 45, 58, 62, 104, 105, 107–11, 116, 165, 177, 211
Duality of Interpretation, 47, 109, 110, 168, 210, 211

Embick, D., 227
Empty Category Principle (ECP), 12, 29, 30, 36, 40, 42, 44, 67, 103, 104–8, 169, 212, 218–25
Enc, M., 142
endocentricity, 71, 76, 90, 184, 189, 190, 194, 196, 198, 204, 232
Epstein, S., ix, x, 8, 9, 58, 76, 78, 83, 232
Equi-NP Deletion, 22, 34, 116, 144, 209
Evans, G., 181
exceptional case marking (ECM), 83, 84
exocentricity, 198
Extended Projection Principle, 126
Extension Condition, 50, 56, 65, 66, 74, 112, 168–71

feature checking, 207

Ferreira, M., 113
Fixed Subject Condition, 219
French, 89, 99
Fujii, T., 116

Gallistel, C. R., 204
government, 83
Greed, 8, 110
Grohmann, K.K., x, 107

Haddad, Y. A., 115, 116, 126
Haegeman, L., 30
Hebrew, 130, 131
Heim, I., 142
Higginbotham, J., 141, 147
Hmong, 121, 137
Hornstein, N., 26, 36, 48, 65, 68, 80–83, 85, 90, 95, 96, 98, 106, 107, 112, 114, 116–20, 122, 132, 133, 137, 138, 164, 174, 175, 179, 180, 183, 194, 212, 229
Huang, C.-T. J., 222
Hunter, T., 76

Icelandic, 120
Idsardi, W., 119
Inclusiveness Condition, 50, 56, 60–63, 74, 168, 170
is a relation, 21, 196, 199
island, 38, 39, 130–33, 148, 156, 159–65, 182, 212, 213, 216, 221, 222, 223
   adjunct, 39, 202
   strong, 39
   subject, 39
   weak, 39
   Wh-, 158, 219
Ito, Y., 156, 157

Jackendoff, R., 68, 202
Japanese, 120, 157

Kannada, 158, 159
Kayne, R., 68, 114, 119, 122, 128, 135, 136, 145
Keller, F., 132
King, J., 162
Klima, E. S., 23, 34, 36, 119, 122, 140, 141, 142, 144, 147, 165, 178
Koopman, H., 80
Koster, J., 101
Kratzer, A., 142
Kuroda, S., 80
Kush, D., 146

label, vii, viii, ix, 9, 10, 12, 57, 71, 76, 77, 78, 79, 80, 82, 86, 89, 90, 91, 92, 95, 97, 98, 99, 171, 172, 173, 174, 175, 176, 182, 184, 185, 187, 198, 206

Index

labeling (as an operation), viii, 9, 11, 12, 71, 76, 77, 78, 80, 90, 91, 98, 171, 172, 174, 175, 176, 184, 185, 186, 187, 188, 189, 190, 191, 192, 193, 194, 196, 197, 198, 199, 204, 205, 206, 207, 208, 211, 228, 232
labeling algorithm, 193, 197
Labeling Hypothesis (LH), 11, 12
Landau, I., 113, 116
languistics, 4
Larson, R., 68, 202
Lasnik, H., 85, 116, 122, 141, 173, 175, 220, 221
Lebeaux, D., 36
Lectures on Government and Binding (LGB), 3, 27–31
Lees, R. B., 23, 34, 36, 119, 122, 140, 141, 142, 144, 147, 165, 178
Lewis, R., 72
Li, D., 88, 93
Lidz, J., 119, 158, 159
Linear Correspondence Axiom, 68
Linguistic Creativity, 16, 40, 48, 49, 103, 230
Linguistic Flexibility, 15, 16, 28, 38, 230
locality, 149, 163, 175, 179, 183, 184, 190, 210–13, 216, 222
logical form (LF), 29, 30, 45, 62, 104, 107, 154, 223, 224
Lu, J., 42, 221, 223

Manzini, M.R., 81, 101
Marantz, A., 82
Marcus, G., 64, 65
Massam, D., 107
McCloskey, J., 80, 130, 146
m-command, 83
Merge
  External, viii, 54–58, 66, 109–12, 144, 151, 153, 155, 157, 168, 174, 178, 179, 182, 210, 211
  Internal, viii, 54–61, 65, 66, 75–100, 109–12, 118, 133, 136, 140, 144, 146, 152–54, 157, 163–66, 209–12
  set-, 71–74, 170
Merge over Move, 148, 150, 151, 152, 153, 154, 155, 156, 163, 177, 179, 181, 182, 183, 211, 226
Minimal Search. *See* minimality
minimality, 40, 95–97, 100, 119, 159, 172, 174–77, 179, 181, 183, 189, 190, 193, 212–15, 217
Minimality Condition, 213–16, 218
monotonicity, 32, 33, 42, 66, 73
Moro, A., 202
Motomura, M., 154, 156
Move α, 29–34, 45, 58, 61, 101, 102, 106, 108, 209, 224

movement
  A, 29, 40, 84, 100, 102–6, 110–14, 119, 120, 123, 126, 136, 149, 157, 165, 176, 178–81, 212
  A', 29, 100, 103, 106, 130, 134–38, 149, 150, 158, 178, 212, 221
  across-the-board (ATB), 130
  covert, 225
  head, 98, 175, 212
  improper, 135–39, 154, 166, 177, 178, 180, 182
  inter-arboreal. *See* sidewards
  sidewards, 65, 82, 106, 120, 146, 152, 153, 181, 229
  Wh-, viii, 94, 226
Movement Theory of Control (MTC), 112–19, 125, 180
Multiple Spell Out, 224
Muysken, P., 77

No Tampering Condition (NTC), 9, 50, 53, 56, 60–67, 78, 90, 91, 92, 94, 106, 112, 114, 120, 146, 148, 149, 152, 153, 168, 169, 172, 175, 176, 211, 225
numeration, 64, 145, 151, 152, 154–57, 179, 226
Nunes, J., x, 62, 107, 112–16, 138, 180, 229

Ortega-Santos, I., 214, 216

parasitic gap, 40, 131, 138
parsing, 214, 216
Partee, B., 145
Passive, 21, 22, 30, 31, 32, 34, 59, 84, 101, 105, 111, 123, 124, 126, 128, 136, 209, 212
Percus, O., 131, 133, 158
Periscope Property, 75, 87, 90–94, 99, 172
Pesetsky, D., 96, 220
phase, 1, 22, 151, 154–58, 178, 179, 183, 217, 218, 221, 222, 225, 226
Phase Theory, 177, 178, 179
phonological form (PF), 29, 45, 107, 115, 220, 223, 224
phrase marker, 8, 19–24, 29, 30, 51, 52, 54, 68, 69, 71, 95, 114, 186, 203
pied-piping, 98
Pietroski, P., x, 93, 145, 170, 188, 196, 198
Plato's Problem, 5, 6, 38, 41, 45, 46, 167, 182, 183
Poeppel, D., 227
Polinsky, M., x, 114–18, 119–22, 132, 142
Potsdam, E., 114–18, 120, 121, 122, 126, 137, 142
Poverty of Stimulus (POS), 26
Predicate Internal Subject Hypothesis, 173, 175

Index

Preminger, O., 120, 142
Principle of Full Interpretation. *See* Theta Criterion
Principle of Grammatical Plenitude, 164, 165, 211
Principles and Parameters, viii
PRO, 6, 27, 35, 45, 54, 111–26, 137, 142, 180
pro-drop, 40
Probe-Goal. *See* Agree
Projection Principle, 31, 32, 33, 37, 58, 62
Pronominalization, 22–25, 102, 104, 125, 127, 128, 134–42, 144–50, 160, 161, 165, 177, 180–83, 209, 212
pronoun
 bound, 6, 22–26, 35, 45, 125, 127–29, 135, 138, 139, 141, 142, 144–52, 154, 157–62, 166, 176, 181, 192
 resumptive, 127–37, 145, 146, 148, 160, 161, 166, 182, 183
Pylyshyn, Z., 64, 65

Quine, W.V.O., 162

Raising, 20–23, 31–34, 39, 59, 84, 101, 102, 105, 110–14, 118, 123, 124, 126, 128, 136–39, 209, 212, 225
 backwards, 116
 copy, 116
 to Object, 24–27
 to Subject, 32
reconstruction, 40, 47, 58, 62, 131–35, 148, 150, 168, 207
recursion, viii, 21, 22, 47–49, 51, 88, 103, 167, 185, 186, 197, 199, 204, 213
reflexive. *See* anaphor/anaphora
Reflexivization, 21–25, 32–35, 101–26, 137–42, 144, 145, 147–50, 165, 209, 212
Reinhart, T., 141, 181
relativized minimality, 42
resumption, 102, 127, 129
Reuland, E., 142
R-expression, 6, 29, 34–37, 42, 45, 117, 147, 149, 176
Richards, M., 129
Rizzi, 42, 94, 120
Rodrigues, C., 113
Rosenbaum, P.R., 117
Ross, J.R., 22, 129, 130, 132
Roussou, A., 81
rule
 lexical insertion, 19–22, 29, 54, 58
 lowering, 65, 67
 ordering, 23
 phrase structure, 18–23, 29, 38, 53, 54, 58, 110
 reconstruction, 62

transformational, 20–23, 28, 38, 45
Runner, J.T., 116, 137

Saito, M., 85, 173, 175, 220, 221
San Lucas Quiaviní Zapotec (SLQZ), 121, 137
scope, 56–59, 83, 84, 168, 173, 175, 210, 211
Select (as an operation), 72, 73, 74, 205, 206
selection, 86–93, 99, 172, 184, 187, 190, 207, 208
Skinner, B.F., 15
Slobin, D., 15
sluicing, 22
Sportiche, D., 62, 80, 154
Sprouse, J., 132, 218, 220
S-structure, 6, 29, 45, 62, 104, 107, 223
Stabler, E., 64, 69, 78, 145, 190, 207
Stamp, J., 215
Standard Theory, 23, 28–38, 59, 101, 144, 209
strong minimalist thesis (SMT), x, 78, 166, 171, 232
structure preservation, 30, 42, 61, 73, 75
Subjacency, 29, 38, 44, 45, 159, 179, 220–24
superiority effects. *See* minimality

Theta
 assignment, 7, 8, 29, 44, 58, 94
 Criterion, 40, 45, 108, 177
 marking, 79, 80, 84, 99, 172, 173, 175
 position, ix, 103, 108–11, 114, 119, 136, 178
 role, 37, 45, 57, 105, 128, 136, 155, 168, 175, 210, 211
 structure, 22
 theory, 45
third factor, 64, 65, 189, 193, 204, 215
Thornton, R., ix
Topicalization, 21, 94, 101, 209, 212
Torrego, E., 220
trace, 6, 29–34, 37, 42, 54, 58–65, 67, 105, 106, 135, 145, 169, 178, 220
 A, 35, 37, 42, 102, 105–7, 113
 A', 42, 103, 106, 130, 131, 134, 135
Transfer, 9, 68, 98, 184–91, 194, 220, 224–27
Tsez, 121, 122

Union (as an operation), 74, 205, 206
Uriagereka, J.

Weinberg, A., 16, 216
Wilson, G., 162
Woolford, E., 120

X'-theory, 29, 38, 44, 76, 80, 188

Y-model, 12, 223–27

Printed in the United States
by Baker & Taylor Publisher Services